SHAKESPEARE SURVEY

ADVISORY BOARD

SHAKESPEARE SURVEY

AN ANNUAL SURVEY OF

SHAKESPEARIAN STUDY AND PRODUCTION

38

EDITED BY

STANLEY WELLS

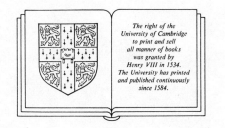

The right of the
University of Cambridge
to print and sell
all manner of books
was granted by
Henry VIII in 1534.
The University has printed
and published continuously
since 1584.

CAMBRIDGE UNIVERSITY PRESS

CAMBRIDGE

LONDON   NEW YORK   NEW ROCHELLE

MELBOURNE   SYDNEY

Published by the Press Syndicate of the University of Cambridge
The Pitt Building, Trumpington Street, Cambridge CB2 1RP
32 East 57th Street, New York, NY 10022, USA
10 Stamford Road, Oakleigh, Melbourne 3166, Australia

First published 1985

Shakespeare Survey was first published in 1948. For the first
eighteen volumes it was edited by Allardyce Nicoll.
Kenneth Muir edited volumes 19–33

Printed in Great Britain
by the University Press, Cambridge

Library of Congress catalogue card number: 49–1639

British Library Cataloguing in Publication Data
Shakespeare Survey
38
1. Shakespeare, William – Societies, periodicals, etc.
I. Wells, Stanley
ISBN 0 521 32026 7

EDITOR'S NOTE

The main theme of this volume, 'Shakespeare and History', was also the theme of the twenty-first International Conference held at the Shakespeare Institute, Stratford-upon-Avon, in August 1984, and a number of the articles originated as papers read there. Volume 39 (which will be at press by the time this volume appears) will take as its theme 'Shakespeare on Film and Television'. Volume 40 will be concerned with current approaches to Shakespeare through language, text, and theatre. Submissions should reach the Editor at 40 Walton Crescent, Oxford OX1 2JQ by 1 September 1986 at the latest. The deadline for volume 41, on 'Shakespearian Stages and Staging', will be 1 September 1987. Many articles are considered before the deadline, so those that arrive earlier stand a greater chance of acceptance. Please either enclose return postage (overseas, in International Reply Coupons) or send a non-returnable xerox. A style sheet is available on request. All articles submitted are read by the Editor and by one or more members of the Advisory Board, whose indispensable assistance the Editor gratefully acknowledges.

With this volume we extend our thanks to Lois Potter, who is retiring after reviewing work on Shakespeare's Life, Times and Stage for three years.

In attempting to survey the ever-increasing bulk of Shakespeare publications our reviewers have inevitably to exercise some selection. Review copies of books should be addressed to the Editor, as above. We are also very pleased to receive offprints of articles, which help to draw our reviewers' attention to relevant material.

S. W. W.

CONTRIBUTORS

ANNE BARTON, *Professor of English, University of Cambridge*

JONATHAN BATE, *Research Fellow in English, St Catharine's College, Cambridge*

JAMES C. BULMAN, *Professor of English, Allegheny College, Pennsylvania*

DENNIS H. BURDEN, *Vice-President and Librarian of Trinity College and Special University Lecturer in English, University of Oxford*

DEREK COHEN, *Associate Professor of English, York University, Toronto*

BRIAN GIBBONS, *Professor of English Literature, University of Zürich*

E. W. IVES, *Senior Lecturer in Modern History, University of Birmingham*

MACDONALD P. JACKSON, *Associate Professor of English, University of Auckland*

RUSSELL JACKSON, *Fellow of the Shakespeare Institute, University of Birmingham*

MARY ELLEN LAMB, *Professor of English, Southern Illinois University at Carbondale*

ALEXANDER LEGGATT, *Professor of English, University of Toronto*

GIORGIO MELCHIORI, *Professor of English, University of Rome*

MICHAEL E. MOONEY, *Professor of English, University of New Orleans*

ROBERT B. PIERCE, *Professor of English, Oberlin College*

MAURICE POPE, *Oxford*

LOIS POTTER, *Senior Lecturer in English, University of Leicester*

PIERRE SAHEL, *Professor of English, Université de Provence, Aix-en-Provence*

CATHERINE M. SHAW, *Lecturer in English, McGill University, Montreal*

NICHOLAS SHRIMPTON, *Fellow of Lady Margaret Hall and Lecturer in English, University of Oxford*

GARY TAYLOR, *Associate Editor, Shakespeare department, Oxford University Press*

CONTENTS

ILLUSTRATIONS

SHAKESPEARE'S HISTORY PLAYS: 1952–1983

DENNIS H. BURDEN

When Harold Jenkins wrote his survey of criticism of the English history plays from 1900 to 1951 for *Shakespeare Survey 6* (Cambridge, 1953) two critical approaches were dominant: firstly the reading of them in the light of the historical thesis which they were seen to present and which was particularly associated with E. M. W. Tillyard's *Shakespeare's English History Plays* (1944), and secondly close analysis of their style and imagery. It might be useful first to consider how these two modes of interpretation have developed in the period presently under review.

THE OVERALL PATTERN

The influence of Tillyard's thesis can be seen in the amount of reference to it in later work. Its attraction was that it provided the English histories with an intellectual dimension that they had previously lacked. Instead of being seen as immature and formless, perhaps the result of collaboration and revision by different hands, they were given the weight of a philosophical and political thesis. The interpretation of them in the light of the 'Tudor myth', reading English history from Richard II to Henry VIII as the working-out of a process of punishment and expiation for the deposition and murder of Richard II, God's judgement falling particularly on the house of Lancaster and more generally on the nation, provided the plays with coherence and dignity. An extract from a contemporary review of Tillyard's book illustrates in a small way how the thesis brought new significance to the plays: 'that dull old stick, Alexander Iden, becomes a steadying symbol of degree and of duty done in the allotted state of life'.[1]

The importance of the book made it perhaps more vulnerable since it was brought under such close scrutiny. It came under increasing challenge. Whereas A. S. Cairncross, editor of the new Arden *1, 2* and *3 Henry VI* (1962, 1957, 1964), accepted it, A. R. Humphreys, editor of the same series' *1* and *2 Henry IV* (1960, 1966), did not. To some perhaps it came to seem the product of the view from a Cambridge college window looking out on a world at war and nostalgic for a more stable and comprehensible historical process. Later times came to need different theses and a very different appeal was made to the 1960s by Jan Kott's very popular *Shakespeare our Contemporary* (1964). To Kott all Shakespeare's English kings faced a violent and undiscriminating historical process which exposed the hollowness of political life where the outlines of the individual face could not be discerned in the dark corridors of power. Kott's thesis is as deterministic as Tillyard's but it reflects a very different experience and ideology. To each its own, but Philip Edwards has stressed what risks of misinterpretation we run when we impose modern attitudes, for instance that social and political attitudes are necessarily alienating, upon our readings of the plays.[2]

Tillyard himself, in a later essay[3] written in answer to R. A. Law who had argued that the series showed Shakespeare moving tentatively from play

1 *Times Literary Supplement*, 6 January 1945.
2 *Person and Office in Shakespeare's Plays*, Annual Shakespeare Lecture of the British Academy (1970).
3 'Shakespeare's Historical Cycle: Organism or Compilation', *Studies in Philology*, 51 (1954), 34–9.

to play,[4] admitted that his larger plan did not exclude local opportunism in the individual play or scene. A. L. French has set his sights very effectively on particular points of rebuttal – that the political process in *Richard II* is not at all clear, that Joan's role in *1 Henry VI* is not to be a scourge of God, that there is a pervasive uncertainty about *Richard III*, that *Richard II* does not cast a long shadow on to *Richard III*, that the plays do not present a continuous picture of a moral retributive process[5] – but the objections were more often to the general outline of the thesis. Leonard F. Dean stressed the way in which Shakespeare thought his way progressively into his material, making new discoveries about it, exploiting contrasting modes, and going beyond what were coming to seem the naiveties of popular chronicle and history.[6] Michael Quinn also argued that the concept of a divine providence acting in history was much more relevant to the first than to the second tetralogy.[7] Certainly later studies in Tudor political thought established that Tillyard overestimated its orthodoxy and in particular made it too absolutist. The doctrine of obedience to the king could be based upon consent and natural law. Christopher Morris's *Political Thought in England: Tyndale to Hooker* (1953) presents a more complex picture and Morris's discussion of what the homilies actually did and did not say is very helpful. E. M. Talbert in *The Problem of Order* (Chapel Hill, 1962), by looking in particular at the thought of Sir Thomas Smith and Hooker and by going on to analyse *Richard II* in a way which emphasizes a genuine clash of political theory in the play, shows that the Elizabethan world-picture was not just a few simple ideas about order. A most important contribution is made by Henry A. Kelly's *Divine Providence and the England of Shakespeare's Histories* (Cambridge, Mass., 1970), studying the attitude of Tudor chronicles and histories to the role of divine power in history, an important part of Tillyard's thesis. Kelly establishes that there was more than one 'Tudor myth': besides the Yorkist one stressing the punishment of the house of Lancaster which Tillyard reflects, there is also the Lancastrian one which justified the overthrow of Richard II because his corrupt government did not serve the welfare of the kingdom. Furthermore Kelly shows that there was

hesitancy, inconsistency of interpretation, more off-the-cuff judgement in the sources so that the variety which literary criticism was beginning to stress in the plays could also be found in the ways in which sixteenth-century historians interpreted the same material. Kelly argues for the presence of a burlesque anti-providential myth in More's *Richard III*, a point also made by Alison Hanham in '*Richard III*' and the Early Historians (Oxford, 1975). S. Schoenbaum[8] and Gordon Ross Smith[9] have also shown that there was a variety of opinion about Richard II and Henry V in Shakespeare's time.

Of course when we look to this wider field of political and historical thought we cannot suppose that Shakespeare was necessarily familiar with it nor that he would consciously entertain some of its more radical postures if he were. He certainly reflects the age's fear of rebellion which was what helped most to keep order. The government's hand was also strengthened by its censorship of the press and stage and its exploitation of pageant and symbol (see Alice S. Venezky, *Pageantry on the Shakespearian Stage* (New York, 1951)). The most theoretical challenge to the establishment probably came from Puritan thinking but most of the Tudor rebellions were based upon specific local grievances often fanned by suspicion. In choosing Rumour to open *2 Henry IV* Shakespeare was putting his finger on one of the greatest threats to security but also at the same time unwittingly showing the threat the drama posed. Rumour, unfolding acts with his many tongues,

---

[4] 'Links between Shakespeare's History Plays', *Studies in Philology*, 50 (1953), 168–87.

[5] 'Who Deposed Richard II?', *Essays in Criticism*, 17 (1967), 411–33; 'Joan of Arc and *Henry VI*', *English Studies*, 49 (1968), 425–9; 'The World of Richard III', *Shakespeare Studies*, 4 (1968), 23–39; '*Henry VI* and The Ghost of Richard II', *English Studies*, 50 (1969), 27–43; 'The Mills of God and Shakespeare's Early History Plays', *English Studies*, 55 (1974), 313–24.

[6] '*Richard II* to *Henry V*: a Closer View', in *Studies in Honour of Dewitt T. Starnes*, ed. Thomas P. Harrison (Austin, Texas, 1967), pp. 37–52.

[7] 'Providence in Shakespeare's Yorkist Plays', *Shakespeare Quarterly*, 10 (1959), 45–52.

[8] '*Richard II* and the Realities of Power', *Shakespeare Survey*, 28 (Cambridge, 1975), 1–13.

[9] 'Shakespeare's *Henry V*: Another Part of the Critical Forest', *Journal of the History of Ideas*, 37 (1976), 3–26.

speaking of many different things, is doing what the dramatist himself had to do and it was here that the plays encountered both opportunity and risk. For in presenting, and for dramatic reasons justifying, specific cases of rebellion against established authority, exploiting traditions of oration, dispute and persuasion, the dramatist necessarily involved his drama in theory while in no way intending consciously to adumbrate it. While it might be dangerous to proffer a thesis in favour of deposition in a play, Shakespeare had to give Bolingbroke or somebody else reasons for going through with it, though in so risky a case they might get fewer and fewer and more hedged about with reservation as the crisis approached. And such a procedure might, as L. C. Knights argues, be determined by Shakespeare's own experience and imagination, his 'negative capability', not by any predetermined pattern.[10]

The majority of the critical studies during this period have been concerned with the variety of the plays, their reflection of Shakespeare's many-sided imagination, their resistance to simple interpretation, and have tended to prise the two tetralogies apart from each other and the individual plays from each other, seeing a process of growth and maturity at work. A. P. Rossiter in a set of pugnacious essays written in the early 1950s (collected in *Angel with Horns* (1961)) sees the plays as subtly undermining the 'Tudor myth' (by way of paradox, interactions of comedy and tragedy, irony and what he calls 'ambivalence'), recalcitrant to the restraints of an imposed thesis and swayed beneath their surface by a sense of obscure tragedy. Virgil Whitaker in *Shakespeare's Use of Learning* (San Marino, California, 1953) argues a progressive view of Shakespeare's intellectual development in which Shakespeare, driven by his sense of what dramatic possibilities history offered, moved from the limited intellectual range of the first tetralogy into a greater maturity of thought about the material partly deriving from a careful, more systematic use of a greater variety of sources but mostly generated from within. Robert Hapgood argues that the production of a risky flux and reflux in sympathy was a characteristic feature of Shakespeare's dramatic method. Episodes such as the deposition of Richard

II and the rejection of Falstaff deliberately engineer in us a delayed reaction leading us to reconsider them so that although we are brought to see that a certain course of action is wrong we nevertheless still keep our sympathy for a character who thought that it was right. Like Rossiter, Hapgood sees the plays as deliberately cultivating unresolved political and moral oppositions.[11] Norman Rabkin in *Shakespeare and the Common Understanding* (New York, 1967) sees the plays as consciously projecting problems and setting up 'areas of turbulence' rather than offering certain solutions. Wilbur Sanders, using Marlowe as a whipping-boy, puts forward in *The Dramatist and the Received Idea* (Cambridge, 1968), with particular reference to *Richard III* and *Richard II*, a similar view: the ability of the really great writer is to lower the threshold of orthodoxy and to let the mind play over a wide band of possibility. All these viewpoints take it as characteristic of the plays to be more interesting than any thesis that they might seem to offer and see the chafing against any particular set response or evaluation as what makes them such an impressive artistic achievement.

A most stimulating book, both from the point of view of the disintegration of the Tillyard thesis and of an intelligent assessment of the plays, is Robert Ornstein's *A Kingdom for a Stage* (Cambridge, Mass., 1972). Considered simply, the plays are, he demonstrates, about rebellion and reconciliation not legality or long-term retributions. Political orthodoxy, which Tillyard saw as such a strength, Ornstein sees very much as a limiting factor on Shakespeare's openness of mind and breadth of humanity. The discipline which the dramatist imposed is developed by the needs of art not dogma. Adjustment is the art of drama as well as of politics; and Shakespeare, like his characters, calculates, improvises, experiments, achieves dazzling success and also (and this is a very engaging part of Ornstein's book) makes mistakes. Ornstein is not afraid to be critical, seeing the plotting of *3 Henry VI* as

---

[10] *Shakespeare's Politics*, Annual Shakespeare Lecture of the British Academy (1957).
[11] 'Shakespeare's Delayed Reactions', *Essays in Criticism*, 13 (1963), 9–16.

perfunctory, *King John* as an artistic failure, the last act of *Richard II* as something of an anti-climax. His method is necessarily somewhat subjective – he values Shakespeare because he is different from and better than his contemporaries – but the measure of Ornstein's success lies in the great extent to which we concur with his readings and find them sound and persuasive.

Another approach to the plays has been to see them as presenting some pattern though not Tillyard's and to concentrate on some particular aspect or theme. Nicholas Brooke in his essay 'Marlowe as Provocative Agent in Shakespeare's Early Plays' provides a very searching account of Marlowe's influence.[12] M. M. Reese in *The Cease of Majesty* (1962), accepting the Tillyard thesis in so far as he allows that Shakespeare's approach to history was to see it as presenting events within the scheme of God's providence and so answering to the problems of the 1590s, nevertheless goes beyond that to see the plays as concerned with the wider problems of social order and partnership. From the point of view of a society's political health, if concord is to be established, then what matters is how adequately the king's nature responds to political crisis, and true kingship emerges as based upon justice, charity, kindness and a sense of community between ruler and ruled. S. C. Sen Gupta in *Shakespeare's Historical Plays* (1964) reads the series very sensibly as studies essentially of characters rather than ideas, Shakespeare's involvement being human and not political or homiletic. H. M. Richmond in *Shakespeare's Political Plays* (New York, 1967) sees the plays as providing an intelligent and evolving study of man as a political animal. Three books which are also concerned with the theme of kingship in the histories are John Bromley's *The Shakespearean Kings* (Boulder, Colorado, 1970) which attempts to show by a commentary on the plays that the kings are destroyed by the burden of their royalty and the coarseness of power, Moody E. Prior's *The Dream of Power* (Evanston, Illinois, 1973) a sensible study which sees each play as defining a different problem about kingship (the *Henry VI* plays about legitimacy for example, *Richard III* about tyranny) which can be related to contemporary thinking about politics,

and Michael Manheim's *The Weak King Dilemma in the Shakespearean Henriad* (Syracuse, 1977) which, with some twentieth-century pointing, see the plays as a series in which traditional monarchy, increasingly inadequate because of its weakness, is superseded by a more efficient but ruthless Machiavellism. Robert B. Pierce in *Shakespeare's History Plays: the Family and the State* (Columbus, 1971) also studies one aspect of the plays, in this case their presentation of the dramatic motif of the family, emblematic and personal, something which enables the audience to get close to what might else be unfamiliar experience. David Riggs in *Shakespeare's Heroical Histories* (Cambridge, Mass., 1971), attempting to break the conventional linking of the English histories with the morality plays, posits a popular tradition of heroical history – *Tamburlaine* being the key play – behind the first tetralogy which presents a deterioration of the heroic ideal, an ideal partly recovered in the second tetralogy. Two recent books are Kristian Smidt's *Unconformities in Shakespeare's History Plays* (1982) using the plays' many inconsistencies and anomalies to counter the view that they are built to a pre-arranged plan (a far cry from Tillyard), and H. R. Coursen's *The Leasing Out of England: Shakespeare's Second Henriad* (Washington, DC, 1982) which uses economic pointers (war as commerce, dislocations of the economy) as keys to the growth of the series.

Separate studies of the two tetralogies have also tended to shift the focus of the plays away from the Tillyard thesis. J. P. Brockbank's 'The Frame of Disorder' gives a cogent account of the *Henry VI* plays as the education of a tragic dramatist contemplating man's plight in a nihilistic historical and political process where virtue connives its own destruction and where retribution is ironically imposed by evil men and deeds.[13] Edward I. Berry in *Patterns of Decay: Shakespeare's Early English Histories* (Charlottesville, Virginia, 1975) studies the collapse of the values established by Henry V into the narrowing concern of the family (*1, 2* and *3 Henry VI*) and the self (*Richard III*). A. C. Hamilton (*The*

---

12 *Shakespeare Survey 14* (Cambridge, 1961), 33–44.
13 In *Early Shakespeare*, ed. John Russell Brown and Bernard Harris, Stratford-upon-Avon Studies, 3 (1961), 72–99.

Early Shakespeare (San Marino, California, 1967)), D. M. Ricks (*Emergent Form*, (Logan, Utah, 1968)), and Nicholas Brooke (*Shakespeare's Early Tragedies* (1968)) all argue for a higher evaluation of the *Henry VI* plays and their individual achievement. Emrys Jones in *The Origins of Shakespeare* (Oxford, 1977) stresses the emergence of the plays from mid-Tudor culture and humanism and from the dramatic tradition of the mysteries and insists on the conscious planning of the *Henry VI* group as a trilogy. In Jones's commentary the plays form a densely woven web of traditions and conventions and appear very convincingly not so much a start as a culmination of a tradition, topical plays embedded in older wisdoms and experience. David Frey's *The First Tetralogy: Shakespeare's Scrutiny of the Tudor Myth* (The Hague, 1976) considers the inadequacy of Tillyard's thesis. F. W. Brownlow in *Two Shakespearean Sequences* (1977) argues that the sequence *Henry VI* to *Richard II* shows the representation of motive and character as more important than historical or even moral issues.

An important book on the second tetralogy is Derek Traversi's *Shakespeare from 'Richard II' to 'Henry V'* (1957), an evolutionary account of the plays allowing for changes in direction, seeing them as a developing critique of political behaviour and tracing the various complex thematic mutations by way of close and detailed analysis. James Winny in *The Player King* (1968) concentrates on the way in which the idea of the king is developed from *Richard II* to *Henry V*, Shakespeare presenting a sequence of royal figures seeking to establish an identity which is not basically a political concept but an imaginative one that develops from play to play. Eric La Guardia,[14] Alvin Kernan[15] and Virginia Carr[16] in their different ways see the second tetralogy as concerned with lost ritual and ceremony. C. G. Thayer also argues against the plays as tracts, seeing the way in which Shakespeare presents Bolingbroke as evidence of his interest in character rather than ideology.[17]

As stated earlier it seemed convenient to base this part of this survey fairly closely upon Tillyard's book and upon the thesis which it put forward. It was in its time a most important book on the English

histories which could not be ignored. Looking back one can see how it has silted up, its timbers warped and broken, but one does not want to be ungenerous to its commitment or to its belief in Shakespeare's intellectual calibre. Certainly no book since has attempted so comprehensive a revaluation of the English histories, and most of us have cause to be grateful to it.

STYLE

The other very influential mode of criticism at the beginning of this period – one applied across the whole of Shakespeare's work – was the interpretation of the plays from within, as it were, by way of a close analysis of poetry, imagery, symbolism and theme, the plays being seen essentially as dramatic poems. Early in the period under survey R. A. Foakes argued for the adoption of a greater rigour in this approach, pointing to some logical flaws in it and to its operating on what was too narrow a definition of imagery that took the plays too far into the page and away from the theatre.[18]

Kenneth Muir in a study of the imagery noted a gradual progression in Shakespeare's use of iterative imagery, finding little in the early histories but a much more striking use later, especially in *Richard II* and *2 Henry IV*.[19] Two books devoted to a study of style are Robert Y. Turner's *Shakespeare's Apprenticeship* (Chicago, 1974) seeing, by means of a study of different types of scene and speech, the histories moving from a didactic, oratorical mode to one which more fully realized the distinctive

[14] 'Ceremony and History: the Problem of Symbol from *Richard II* to *Henry V*' in *Pacific Coast Studies in Shakespeare*, ed. W. F. McNeir and T. N. Greenfield (Eugene, Oregon, 1966), pp. 68–88.

[15] 'The Henriad: Shakespeare's Major History Plays', *Yale Review*, 59 (1969), 3–32.

[16] 'Once more into the Henriad: a Two-Eyed View', *Journal of English and Germanic Philology*, 77 (1978), 530–45.

[17] 'Shakespeare's Second Tetralogy: an Underground Report', *Ohio University Review*, 9 (1967), 5–15.

[18] 'Suggestions for a New Approach to Shakespeare's Imagery', *Shakespeare Survey 5* (Cambridge, 1952), 81–92.

[19] *Image and Symbol in Shakespeare's Histories* (Manchester, 1967).

properties of the medium, and G. R. Hibbard's *The Making of Shakespeare's Dramatic Poetry* (Toronto, 1981) positing an increasing self-consciousness on Shakespeare's part about the extravagant style of the early plays and seeing the histories as eventually developing a comprehensive and varied style which was to serve as a complete dramatic instrument for the maturer tragedies. Richard Lanhan in his chapter on the second tetralogy in *The Motives of Eloquence* (New Haven, 1976), again pressing hard on the style, saw the whole sequence as a complex structure of style and attitudes. Setting the plays within the co-ordinates of what he defines as the serious and the rhetorical he reads them as demonstrating the impossibility of imposing a rigid scheme on the material, *Richard II* dissolving a theme, Falstaff proving resistant to concepts, *Henry V* dissolving an event.

The style and manner of *Richard II* have been of especial concern. J. A. Bryant, Jr, argued that the play represented a new departure for Shakespeare: we should, as in Bushy's perspective, look at the play awry in order to see its true meaning and form, the Chronicle material being shaped into new poetic symbols and analogues.[20] Looking to the play's fascination with ceremony, T. McAlindon in his *Shakespeare and Decorum* (1973) saw it as deliberately exploiting indecorousness in order to highlight misjudgement and error, Richard's failure to adopt one consistent style marking his perverse and destructive failure to behave ceremoniously enough. Ernest B. Gilman in his chapter on *Richard II* in *The Curious Perspective: Literary and Pictorial Wit in the Seventeenth Century* (New Haven, 1978) discussed the play's shifts of perspective in relation to sixteenth-century art which often required the viewer to balance contradictory but equally valid impressions. Faced with disaster, artifice is Richard's only resource. John Baxter's *Shakespeare's Poetic Styles* (1980) is concerned mostly with *Richard II* and applies Yvor Winters's differentiation between Petrarchan and plain styles in its analysis of the play.

Two very subtle essays concerned with style are M. M. Mahood's chapter on *Richard II* in *Shakespeare's Wordplay* (1967) seeing the development within the play as being a testing of the efficacy of

the word and of the relationship between names and their bearers and at Richard's fall between words and things so that it is words that ultimately become meaningless; and Anne Barton's essay 'Shakespeare and the Limits of Language', studying the way in which *Richard II* and the following plays explore and exhaust the achievement of language setting imagination against fact, Richard II failing ultimately to dominate facts, Falstaff similarly attempting and failing to transcend reality, Henry V receding almost to colourlessness.[21]

Close to the concerns of these studies has been the development during the period under review of a study of the plays which sees concern about style as the key to the play's intention and meaning. A seminal book is Sigurd Burckhardt's *Shakespeare's Meanings* (Princeton, 1968) which in its turn owes a lot to William Empson. As a critic Burckhardt is both exciting and difficult, suggestive and baffling. His starting point can be what seems to be a minor episode or point of style which is then shown to function importantly as a clue to the play's meaning. Meaning is very much what Burckhardt thinks that the plays have, and he follows no merely aesthetic track. An important element in his criticism is his reading of the plays as self-referential, self-conscious speculations about themselves and their own nature so that the dramatist himself is involved in the action, the plays posing his own artistic problems. The treatment of Falstaff in *2 Henry IV* typifies the way in which that play retreats from solutions, consciously muffling its dramatic opportunities as *Part 1* did not. The characteristic style of *1 Henry VI* is the 'vaunt', a hyperbolic mode of writing indicative not of Shakespeare's immaturity but of his very intelligent appraisal of his material, the hyperboles being deliberately refuted in the Countess of Auvergne episode when in three lines (2.3.25–7) Talbot defines for us a new world, a different 'Tudor myth' of courtesy and understatement.

Burckhardt's book was influential, and this interest in the way in which a play can explore its own

[20] 'Linked Analogies of *Richard II*', *Sewanee Review*, 65 (1957), 420–33.
[21] *Shakespeare Survey 24* (Cambridge, 1971), 19–30.

nature, potentialities and limitations is marked in some later criticism, finding its fullest expression with James Calderwood. Calderwood works from a conception of 'metatheatre', plays that go beyond the confines of traditional drama and become a kind of anti-art form in which the boundaries between the play as a self-contained work of art and life are taken down. Calderwood's first book, *Shakespeare's Metadrama* (Minneapolis, 1971), devoted its final chapter to *Richard II* but his next, *Metadrama in Shakespeare's Henriad* (Berkeley, 1979), applied the analysis to the whole of the second tetralogy, seeing it as a self-contained metadrama in which Shakespeare was subjecting his own art to close scrutiny, the main plot being about the cyclic fortunes of drama and speech: a fall of speech with *Richard II*; a holding moment in the *Henry IV* plays; and the restoration of some sort of limited order in *Henry V*, Canterbury's speech being about order in drama as well as society, Agincourt redeeming Shakespeare as well as England, the Epilogue celebrating Shakespeare's own fugitive dramatic art. The main thesis runs the risk of drastically limiting the relevance of the plays. Language becomes a sort of substitute for religion, something in which one has faith or loses faith. Joseph A. Porter in *The Drama of Speech Acts* (Berkeley, 1979) also saw the second tetralogy as marking a shift in the way of conceiving and using language. There are familiar points in Porter's analysis – Richard II's self-consciousness, the clash between Falstaff and Hal – but they are set in a linguistic context. With *Henry V* language is seen as mastered and manageable, Hal's triumph sanctioning drama. Another study in this tradition is John W. Blanpied's *Time and the Artist in Shakespeare's English Histories* (Newark, Delaware, 1983). Here the plays are seen as an evolving process, partly one of self-education and self-realization incorporating the dramatist himself. Although Blanpied works close to some actual productions his stress falls mainly on language: the murder of Clarence becomes the destruction of the language he uses, the rebellion in *1* and *2 Henry IV* a rebellion of style. This branch of criticism offers some cogent and close readings but, as is not the case with Burckhardt, they are harnessed to what seems a very narrow aesthetic

and stylistic purpose, the critical method closing down a lot of moral and other interesting options in order to make Shakespeare's concern with the purposes and limitations of his art the central concern of the plays.

Brian Vickers in *The Artistry of Shakespeare's Prose* (1968) provides an extensive study of the prose in *1* and *2 Henry IV*, charting how it creates changes in our sympathies.

GENRE

There are obvious difficulties in defining the history play as a genre since its nature has to do with content rather than outcome or mood. F. P. Wilson in his essay 'The English History Play', working to a simple formula, saw Shakespeare as the possible inventor of the history play and certainly the first dramatist to give it any sort of coherence or dignity.[22] Studies of specific conventions that find their way into the genre are provided by Wolfgang Clemen on the set speech in tragic and historical drama[23] and by Bernard Spivack on the growth of the evil character from late medieval drama through the moralities to Shakespeare (Richard III and Falstaff), noting the increasing secularization and moral tolerance which the sixteenth century brought to the material.[24] But the most thoroughgoing study of the genre is Irving Ribner's *The English History Play* (Princeton, 1957, rev. edn. 1965) defining it as an essentially patriotic and political study of the past, establishing the relevance of the past to the present and demonstrating a rational and Christian plan in history. Ribner also allows for the presence of a certain romantic element in the genre. He covers the evolution of the history play from the late Middle Ages to 1653 and discusses the two Shakespeare tetralogies (which he sees as separate cycles) in some detail. It is clear that Shakespeare himself could not be wholly aware of some of the elements in the tradition that these various studies identify and Anne Barton in her essay 'The King

---

[22] In *Shakespearian and Other Studies*, ed. Helen Gardner (Oxford, 1969), pp. 1–53.

[23] *English Tragedy before Shakespeare* (1955).

[24] *Shakespeare and the Allegory of Evil* (New York, 1958).

Disguised: Shakespeare's *Henry V* and the Comical History' argues that what distinguishes the history play is its lack of dramatic theory, the genre essentially developing out of the contemporary theatre through a sort of dialogue among specific plays.[25] This seems a profitable way to approach them and various essays have thrown light on them from this point of view. Harold E. Toliver sees Shakespeare as facing up to some tricky problems of genre in the second tetralogy and giving the history play a new stature. The plays integrate pragmatic political concerns and timeless human impulses, Henry V learning how to counter and transcend destructive impulses and ultimately integrating them in the adjustment to history.[26]

The connection between history and tragedy and the development of Shakespeare as a tragic dramatist within the cycle have aroused much interest. R. J. Dorius argues that the role of the heroes in the histories limits their tragic potential since in history their best role is to reconcile and maintain, their virtues those of prudence and economy, whereas the truly tragic heroic role is to risk and to dare.[27] Harold F. Brooks studies the role of women and Senecan features and techniques in *Richard III*[28] and Nicholas Brooke argues that that play is ambivalent between tragedy and history, Richard by extravagantly asserting his own will being able to free himself from the mechanism of history.[29] *Richard II* is again an important play. Travis Bogard[30] and Peter Phialas[31] have both seen it as making an important step forward in Shakespeare's development towards tragedy, though, on R. F. Hill's view, it marks the limit of what one sort of tragedy – rhetorical tragedy – can achieve.[32] John R. Elliott, Jr, sees the historical concerns of the play as putting a limit to its tragic power since history demands that the play be structured as much around Bolingbroke's progress towards the crown as around the figure of Richard himself: dramatizing a political issue it contains the wider rhythms of history.[33] On the other hand Michael Quinn sees the play as a perfect blend of history and tragedy, an ethical judgement being passed upon political failings.[34]

The comic genre is also important and S. L. Bethell provides a good analysis of the different sorts of comedy found in the histories.[35] It is clearly possible to see some of the plays as accommodating happily to the comic genre. *1 Henry IV* is interpreted by Maggie Tomlinson as a unique comic success, Falstaff representing the comic spirit which brings extremes together,[36] and *Henry V* by Rose Zimbardo as a perfectly formal and balanced celebratory play.[37] The importance of pastoral in the histories has been studied by Charles R. Forker.[38]

The presence of different genres has been seen to cause some disturbing notes in the plays. C. L. Barber in *Shakespeare's Festive Comedy* (Princeton, 1959) notes the involvement of *1* and *2 Henry IV* with the comic traditions of the saturnalia (clowning and folly) and carnival, *Part 2* on his view failing since it excludes at the end the holiday sense of life. Jonas A. Barish also holds that the problems raised by the rejection of Falstaff are ultimately problems of genre, Hal's killjoy note associating him too closely with other comic killjoys (Shylock, Mal-

---

[25] In *The Triple Bond*, ed. Joseph G. Price (University Park, Pennsylvania, 1975), pp. 92–117.

[26] 'Falstaff, the Prince and the History Play', *Shakespeare Quarterly*, 16 (1965), 63–80.

[27] 'Prudence and Excess in *Richard II* and the Histories', *Shakespeare Quarterly*, 11 (1960), 13–26.

[28] '*Richard III*, Unhistorical Amplifications: the Women's Scenes and Seneca', *Modern Language Review*, 75 (1980), 721–37.

[29] Brooke, *Shakespeare's Early Tragedies*, pp. 48–79.

[30] 'Shakespeare's Second Richard', *PMLA*, 70 (1955), 192–209.

[31] '*Richard II* and Shakespeare's Tragic Mode', *Texas Studies in Literature and Language*, 3 (1961), 344–55.

[32] 'Shakespeare's Early Tragic Mode', *Shakespeare Quarterly*, 9 (1958), 455–69; 'Dramatic Techniques and Interpretation in *Richard II*', in *Early Shakespeare*, ed. John Russell Brown and Bernard Harris, Stratford-upon-Avon Studies, 3 (1961), pp. 100–21.

[33] 'History and Tragedy in *Richard II*', *Studies in English Literature, 1500–1900*, 8 (1968), 253–71.

[34] '"The King is not himself": the Personal Tragedy of *Richard II*', *Studies in Philology*, 56 (1959), 169–86.

[35] 'The Comic Element in Shakespeare's Histories', *Anglia*, 71 (1952–3), 82–101.

[36] '*Henry IV*', *The Melbourne Critical Review*, 6 (1963), 3–15.

[37] 'The Formalism of *Henry V*', in *Shakespeare: 'Henry V': a Casebook*, ed. Michael Quinn (1969), pp. 163–70.

[38] 'Shakespeare's Chronicle Plays as Historical-Pastoral', *Shakespeare Studies*, 1 (1965), 84–104.

volio) and denying him that enrichment of personality which characters traditionally enjoy at the end of comedy.[39]

Henry V has also been seen as modified comedy. Placed within a religious framework for example, the play becomes to Roy W. Battenhouse a heroic comedy of irony mocking reprobate heroism and glory;[40] to Robert Egan the comedy of a king confronting the role of conqueror, an outward prince and an inward Christian, a potentially tragic choice but one ultimately resolved, as comedy must be, by the king's discovery of his true identity.[41]

The romance is also a constituent of the histories. Thomas H. McNeal sees the Margaret of Anjou episode in *1 Henry VI* as romance material deriving from *The True Chronicle History of King Leir* and added to *Part 1* to create a link with *Part 2* which had been written earlier.[42] Paul Dean presents the *Henry VI* trilogy as creating a new genre out of Elizabethan romance dramas[43] and *Henry V* as making a sometimes disturbing mix of history and romance material,[44] a point also developed by Joanne Altieri.[45] Anne Barton in the essay mentioned earlier sees *Henry V* as providing Shakespeare with the occasion for the deliberate rejection of an outworn romantic mode.[46]

A very interesting book taking an extensive view of the genre is Herbert Lindenberger's *Historical Drama: the Relation of Literature and Reality* (Chicago, 1975). This has the excitement of the wider view, seeing the English histories in a broad context of historical fictions both English (e.g. Scott) and European (e.g. Brecht). Lindenberger takes up most of the problems that have been posed by Shakespeare's plays. On the question of sustaining the heroic illusion, for example, Lindenberger sees Talbot as Shakespeare's only uncompromised hero: the plays thereafter record a natural but progressive diminution of values, but also gain some strength from the scepticism about itself found in *Henry V*.

STRUCTURE

There have been in the period developments in the analysis of the dramatic structure of the plays. Hereward T. Price worked the plays free from classical ideas of structure and plot, the plays in his view being governed by a controlling idea best established by a careful study of individual scenes and their relationship, making his point by a detailed analysis of *1 Henry VI*.[47] Madeleine Doran in *Endeavors of Art* (Madison, 1954) has extensively discussed those elements – the literary tradition, training in rhetoric, etc. – which help to determine the structure of the plays. Richard Levin, working from Empson's discussion of double plots in *Some Versions of Pastoral* (1935), examines the various types of plot structure in *The Multiple Plot in Renaissance Drama* (Chicago, 1971). Under hierarchical and clown sub-plot categories he discusses the sub-plots of *1 and 2 Henry IV* and *Henry V* and argues that their effect is to point up the adaptability of Hal and to add dignity to the main action (not always the way they are read); he convincingly differentiates Falstaff and Hal as creatures of time. Emrys Jones's *Scenic Form in Shakespeare* (Oxford, 1971) also emphasizes the crucial nature of the scene, offering careful analysis of how individual scenes are structured. In so far as Jones is also concerned with the recurrence in the plays of certain types of scene, situation and character, the early histories are especially important since they provide some of the die-castings as it were. *Richard III* and *1 and 2 Henry IV* for example are shown to contribute to the dense

[39] 'The Turning Away of Prince Hal', *Shakespeare Studies*, 1 (1965), 9–17.

[40] '*Henry V* as Heroic Comedy', in *Essays on Shakespeare and Elizabethan Drama in Honor of Hardin Craig*, ed. Richard Hosley (1963), pp. 163–82.

[41] 'A Muse of Fire: *Henry V* in the Light of *Tamburlaine*', *Modern Language Quarterly*, 29 (1968), 15–28.

[42] 'Margaret of Anjou: Romantic Princess and Troubled Queen', *Shakespeare Quarterly*, 9 (1958), 1–10.

[43] 'Shakespeare's *Henry VI* Trilogy and Elizabethan "Romance" Histories: the Origins of a Genre', *Shakespeare Quarterly*, 33 (1982), 34–48.

[44] 'Chronicle and Romance Mode in *Henry V*', *Shakespeare Quarterly*, 32 (1981), 18–27.

[45] 'Romance in *Henry V*', *Studies in English Literature, 1500–1900*, 21, (1981), 223–40.

[46] Barton, 'The King Disguised: Shakespeare's *Henry V* and the Comical History' (see note 25).

[47] 'Construction in Shakespeare', *University of Michigan Contributions in Modern Philology*, 17 (Ann Arbor, 1951).

tragic substance of *Hamlet*. On the overall structure Jones also sees a two-part structure as more relevant than a five-act one. Mark Rose (*Shakespearean Design* (Cambridge, Mass., 1972)), and James E. Hirsch (*The Structure of Shakespearian Scenes* (New Haven, 1981)) have also concentrated upon the scene as the best key to the structural analysis of the plays. Brownell Salomon has analysed *Henry V* as a scenic play, showing how deliberate alternation between two contrary sets of values is highlighted by the play's structure.[48] Ruth Nevo in *Tragic Form in Shakespeare* (Princeton, 1973) argues that Shakespeare in the major tragedies develops the five-act division into an unfolding five-phase sequence and argues that *Richard II*, with some reservations, is already accommodating to this pattern. Larry S. Champion's *Perspective in Shakespeare's English Histories* (Athens, Georgia, 1980) studies how the plays adopt different angles of vision in order to provide effective support for their themes and is especially concerned with the development from the technique of deliberate fragmentation in the first tetralogy, through the concentration upon a single character in *Richard III* and *Richard II* to the matured perspective of the last plays in the sequence.

HISTORY

An especial feature of the history plays is the awareness of the theme of Time. The past of *Hamlet* or *Othello* is simply that of the particular play and unknown to the audience though Shakespeare might, as in the graveyard scene, wish to evoke a poignant sense of the past. But the sense of time is inherent in the histories: the characters lived in the same places as Shakespeare and his audience and hence the plays are alive with the sense both of mutability and permanence. A. R. Humphreys has discussed the importance of the geographical and temporal perspectives of the histories, the plays being significantly keyed in to space and time,[49] while Northrop Frye looks to the wider view seeing within the plays cosmic patterns of retribution and annihilation.[50] David Scott Kastan in *Shakespeare and the Shapes of Time* (1962) emphasizes how important the open-ended nature of the histories is: we share with their characters a knowledge of the

past but they do not share our knowledge of the future which is just as crucial: things will not turn out the way they hope or think or sometimes (very unprovidentially perhaps) ought. The histories catch events under pressure from the past and the future, an aspect of them discussed by Wolfgang Clemen.[51] This concern with time connects the histories especially with the Sonnets, a factor developed by L. C. Knights with reference to *Richard II* and *2 Henry IV*,[52] and by Michel Grivelet with reference to *Richard II*.[53] Longer studies concerned with this theme are Ricardo J. Quinones's *The Renaissance Discovery of Time* (Cambridge, Mass., 1972), Soji Iwasaki's *The Sword and the Word* (Tokyo, 1973), G. F. Waller's *The Strong Necessity of Time* (The Hague, 1976), and F. Wylie Sypher's *The Ethic of Time* (New York, 1976). Tom F. Driver in *The Sense of History in Greek and Shakespearean Drama* (New York, 1960) compares, with particular reference to the drama, the different historical patterns and schemes of time adopted by Greek and Christian thinking about history. John Wilders in *The Lost Garden* (1976) offers a very tragic reading of the whole sequence, seeing the individual characters as victims caught in the flux of time, reaching desperately for a lost and irrecoverable ideal, a theme often marked in *2 Henry IV* but seen by Wilders as haunting all the plays. It was part of Tillyard's thesis about *Richard II* that the play was a conscious exercise in medievalism, an elegiac salute on Shakespeare's part to a vanished world of chivalric value and ceremony. Quite apart from the assumptions about the patterns which Shakespeare saw in history here involved, the view has been challenged by Peter Phialas arguing that it is rather

---

[48] 'Thematic Contraries and the Dramaturgy of *Henry V*', *Shakespeare Quarterly*, 31 (1980), 343–56.

[49] *Shakespeare's Histories and 'The Emotions of Multitude'*, Annual Shakespeare Lecture of the British Academy (1968).

[50] 'Nature and Nothing' in *Essays on Shakespeare*, ed. Gerald W. Chapman (Princeton, 1965), pp. 35–58.

[51] *Past and Future in Shakespeare's Drama*, Annual Shakespeare Lecture of the British Academy (1966).

[52] *Some Shakespearean Themes* (1959).

[53] 'Shakespeare's "War with Time": the Sonnets and *Richard II*', *Shakespeare Survey 23* (Cambridge, 1970), 69–78.

Richard II itself that looks back to an heroic age (that of Edward III),[54] and by John R. Elliott, Jr, arguing that the play presents politics in sixteenth-century rather than medieval terms.[55]

The relevance of the histories to Shakespeare's own time is also a matter of some moment, the marker book here being perhaps Lily B. Campbell's *Shakespeare's Histories* (1947). Sigurd Burckhardt[56] and S. L. Bethell[57] in studies mentioned earlier have posited a deliberate and creative use of anachronism on Shakespeare's part intended to jolt the audience into seeing the relevance of the past to the present. The most extensive study of the plays' contemporary significance is David Bevington's *Tudor Drama and Politics* (Cambridge, Mass., 1968), which sees Shakespeare as a sensitive, moderate writer, critical without being radical. Bevington is sensible at identifying what might be the topical issues submerged beneath the plays. These topical elements are of course very important in the social realism of the plays which is contemporary and not historical. Paul Jorgensen's *Shakespeare's Military World* (Berkeley, 1956) studies the topical aspects of Shakespeare's presentation of war with reference to such matters as the conduct of battle and the organization and equipping of armies, important points in *1* and *2 Henry IV* and *Henry V*, plays which Jorgensen sees as reflecting a critical period in the defence of the realm. W. Gordon Zeeveld in *The Temper of Shakespeare's Thought* (New Haven, 1974) also attempts to relate the plays to the thought and issues of Shakespeare's time, seeing for example the concern for ceremony as being very relevant to the Puritan controversies of the 1590s.

Medieval historians from time to time deplore the way in which the popularity of Shakespeare's English histories has put into currency a misleading and over-simplified view of their period, but if Shakespeare has not always been exactly helpful to historians the contrary certainly is not true. C. L. Kingsford helped Tillyard, and modern historians of medieval and Tudor periods have provided valuable insights and provoked questions pertinent to the plays, knocking welcome holes in the walls of our own backyard. Ernst H. Kantorowicz's *The King's Two Bodies* (Princeton, 1957), differentiating the natural mortal body of the king and the spiritual

body of policy and government and tracing the development of the concept through the Middle Ages, has been influential on the criticism of *Richard II*. Studies in Renaissance historiography have also helped to draw a more helpful intellectual map of the histories of the period. Especially useful are Denys Hay's *Polydore Vergil* (Oxford, 1952); F. J. Levy's *Tudor Historical Thought* (San Marino, California, 1967); Herschel Baker's *The Race of Time* (Toronto, 1967), demonstrating the growing concern for fact shown by the historians and not shared by the creative writers of the period; and Mary McKisack's *Medieval History in the Tudor Age* (Oxford, 1971). Other helpful writers are K. B. McFarlane with his concept of 'bastard feudalism' and his fascinating essay 'At the Deathbed of Cardinal Beaufort',[58] Joel Hurstfield,[59] Maurice Keen,[60] and Malcolm Vale.[61] Two especially useful books for students are Richard Hosley's *Shakespeare's Holinshed* (New York, 1968), a selection from Holinshed presented in Holinshed's not Shakespeare's order and including some material that Shakespeare omitted, and Peter Saccio's *Shakespeare's English Kings* (1977), an account of the history of the reigns covered by the plays taking a wider and sometimes more modern view of them.

SOME PARTICULAR CRITICAL PROBLEMS

Harold Jenkins included in his survey a consideration of some particular critical problems. Most of them remain problems still. With some, for example the

---

[54] 'The Medieval in *Richard II*', *Shakespeare Quarterly*, 12 (1961), 305–10.

[55] '*Richard II* and the Medieval', *Renaissance Papers 1965*, (1966), ed. George Walton Williams and Peter Phialas, pp. 25–34.

[56] Burckhardt, *Shakespeare's Meanings* (see p. 6).

[57] Bethell, 'The Comic Element in Shakespeare's Histories' (see note 35).

[58] *The Nobility of Late Medieval England* (Oxford, 1973); *England in the Fifteenth Century* (1981).

[59] Ed., *The Tudor Age* (1973); 'The Politics of Corruption in Shakespeare's England', *Shakespeare Survey 28* (Cambridge, 1975), 15–28.

[60] *The Laws of War in the Late Middle Ages* (1965).

[61] *War and Chivalry* (1981).

order in which *1, 2* and *3 Henry VI* were written or the date of *King John*, it is possible to imagine new discoveries which would lead to their solution; with others, for example what we are to make of the rejection of Falstaff or the character of Henry V, it is not easy to see their being solved in any final demonstrable way. Most of the books discussed earlier and editions of the plays have some consideration of these various problems and they have attracted a considerable number of articles. The following brief account is merely an attempt to point to some of the more notable problems and to refer to some of the discussions of them. It cannot, naturally, be exhaustive.

(*a*) *1 Henry VI*. Leo Kirschbaum argues in the face of earlier disintegrators that *1 Henry VI* is solely Shakespeare's work.[62] As to the play's precise relationship to the other two parts Clifford Leech argues that *Parts 2* and *3* are a two-part play written by Shakespeare, that *Part 1* is a play written by another dramatist who might have known the Shakespeare two-part play, and that Shakespeare's company took this last play over, Shakespeare himself writing in some new material (for instance the Margaret–Suffolk episode) so as to graft it on to his own earlier two-play sequence.[63] On the other hand Marco Mincoff argues that *Part 1* did precede *Parts 2* and *3* and that the presence of different styles in that play indicates not other hands but firstly a growing self-confidence on Shakespeare's part as he worked his way into the play and secondly some revision of it by Shakespeare himself *c.* 1594.[64] Hanspeter Born also thinks that the three plays were written in the sequence in which the First Folio prints them and that they show increasing maturity but argues for a later date (*c.* 1592) for *Parts 2* and *3*.[65]

(*b*) *King John*. Though *King John* deals with many of the themes of the first and second tetralogies – the legality and virtues of kingship, rebellion, patriotism – yet its isolation from the other plays, in history as well as within Shakespeare's dramas, seems to point up its problems. We do not see extensively how it issued from the past nor how it stretches into the future, nor can it exploit that fascinating cross-referencing and refocusing that marks the other plays. The question of its relationship with *The*

Troublesome Reign has been given a new twist by the support of two editors (E. A. J. Honigmann in the new Arden (1954) and William H. Matchett in the Signet (New York, 1966)) for Alexander's argument that *The Troublesome Reign* derives from *John*, being in fact a bad quarto. Against this R. L. Smallwood in an appendix to the New Penguin (Harmondsworth, 1974) puts forward a very substantial case for regarding *The Troublesome Reign* as the source for *John*. Certainly to see *John* as the source play means a date for *John* before 1591 which does not suit the way many critics read the play. The problem the play poses is its organization, the puzzle of its plethora of detail and apparent rawness. Arguments for the play's unity have been made by Adrien Bonjour who sees it as being about the fall of John (hence Shakespeare's expansion of his guilt about Arthur) and the rise of the Bastard as hero;[66] by James Calderwood who interprets it as dramatizing a clash developed with some subtlety between honour and commodity, the issue being resolved by the Bastard's commitment to loyalty at the end;[67] by William H. Matchett who sees it as raising the question of who should be king, again resolved at the end by the Bastard's honourable submission to Prince Henry;[68] and by John L. Simmons who argues that it develops a thesis about the relationship between a king and his subjects, ultimately confirming the necessity for obedience.[69] On the other hand the play has been seen as treating its material with deliberate

---

[62] 'The Authorship of *1 Henry VI*', *PMLA*, 67 (1952), 809–22.

[63] 'The Two-Part Play: Marlowe and the Early Shakespeare', *Shakespeare-Jahrbuch*, 94 (1958), 90–107.

[64] 'The Composition of *Henry VI, Part 1*', *Shakespeare Quarterly*, 16 (1965), 279–87.

[65] 'The Dating of *2, 3 Henry VI*', *Shakespeare Quarterly*, 25 (1974), 323–34.

[66] 'The Road to Swinstead Abbey', *ELH*, 18 (1951), 253–74, and 'Bastinado for the Bastard?', *Supplement to 'English Studies'*, 45 (1964), 169–76.

[67] 'Commodity and Honour in *King John*', *University of Toronto Quarterly*, 29 (1959–60), 341–56.

[68] 'Richard's Divided Heritage in *King John*', *Essays in Criticism*, 12 (1962), 231–53.

[69] 'Shakespeare's *King John* and its Source: Coherence, Pattern and Vision', *Tulane Studies in English*, 17 (1969), 53–72.

ambiguity: by Jonathan R. Price who regards the 'tragedy' of John at the end as the play's only conclusive note;[70] by Eugene M. Waith who sees the play as a series of powerful emotional scenes, having no single idea but not having to commit itself to one since its concern is with things very much in the past;[71] and, a quite opposite view, by Douglas C. Wixson, who argues that the play works upon and reflects the expectations and anxieties of its contemporary audience and goes out of its way to minimize any exemplary quality it might have, the audience themselves being made to work at the dialectic of the play rather than merely responding to stereotypes.[72] Julia C. Van de Water thinks that the internal consistency and the importance of the Bastard's role have been overrated: first wit, then patriot, he is, she argues, outside the plot of the play and little more than a loyal follower.[73] *John* has also been seen as casting significant doubts at Tudor orthodoxy, something that Shakespeare might find himself inclined to do after the writing of the first tetralogy. To John R. Elliott it looks freshly at political activity, seeing it as a complex and pragmatic activity and refusing to glamorize or validate it;[74] to Eamon Grennan it is a play which makes us experience the difficult nature of history which is unsystematic and incoherent.[75]

(c) *1* and *2 Henry IV*. The debate about the relationship between the two parts has been extensive. That the two plays form a single unit with a sort of ten-act structure had been argued by Dover Wilson in his New (Cambridge) edition (1946). G. R. Hibbard comes close to this position: on his view Shakespeare started to write one play on the rebellion but, realizing that he had struck a rich vein, opened the play out into a panoramic one play in two parts, a single ten-act structure. So *Part 1* has signposts for *Part 2*. His essay is interesting for a very suggestive comparison between *1* and *2 Henry IV* and *Hamlet*.[76] Sherman Hawkins argues that Shakespeare always intended to write a two-part play about Hal's advance in the virtues crucial to good kingship though he adopted a different structure for *Part 2* and may have changed his mind about details.[77] That the two plays, though separate, run as it were in parallel and form a sort of diptych – repetition focusing attention on what is common to

both parts – is argued by G. K. Hunter[78] and supported by Sherman Hawkins revisiting the problem in a later essay.[79] That the mood of *Part 2* is more sombre has been much argued, notably by Clifford Leech,[80] L. C. Knights[81] and Harry Levin.[82] James Black also presents *Part 2* as a separate and different play from *Part 1*: though it shares a common theme – the search for a true hero (which will be fulfilled in *Henry V*) – he argues that it looks at its material in dark or mock-heroic fashion: its heroes are ironically the dead Hotspur or the gallant Feeble, its battles ironically no battles.[83] Benjamin T. Spenser sees *Part 2* as a standstill in the tetralogy as a whole, deliberately dramatizing the undramatic so as to form an effective prelude to *Henry V*.[84] J. A. B. Somerset also presents *Part 2* as a unique play, more deeply questioning than *Part 1* and closer to the estate plays of the 1580s and 1590s in its social and moral approach to its material.[85] Harold Jenkins argues that the two parts are separate in that at some

---

70 'King John and Problematic Art', *Shakespeare Quarterly*, 21 (1970), 25–8.

71 'King John and the Drama of History', *Shakespeare Quarterly*, 29 (1978), 192–211.

72 '"Calm Words Folded up in Smoke": Propaganda and Spectator Response in Shakespeare's *King John*', *Shakespeare Studies*, 14 (1981), 111–27.

73 'The Bastard in *King John*', *Shakespeare Quarterly*, 11 (1960), 137–46.

74 'Shakespeare and the Double Image of King John', *Shakespeare Studies*, 1 (1965), 64–84.

75 'Satirical History: a Reading of *King John*', *Shakespeare Studies*, 11 (1978), 21–38.

76 'Henry IV and Hamlet', *Shakespeare Survey 30* (Cambridge, 1977), 1–12.

77 'Virtue and Kingship in Shakespeare's *Henry IV*', *English Literary Renaissance*, 5 (1975), 313–43.

78 'Henry IV and the Elizabethan Two-Part Play', *Review of English Studies*, 5 (1954), 236–48.

79 'Henry IV: The Structural Problem Revisited', *Shakespeare Quarterly*, 33 (1982), 278–301.

80 'The Unity of *2 Henry IV*', *Shakespeare Survey 6* (Cambridge, 1953), 16–24.

81 *Some Shakespearean Themes* (1959).

82 'Falstaff's Encore', *Shakespeare Quarterly*, 32 (1981), 5–17.

83 'Counterfeits of Soldiership in *Henry IV*', *Shakespeare Quarterly*, 24 (1973), 372–82.

84 'The Stasis of *Henry IV, Part 2*', *Tennessee Studies in Literature*, 6 (1961), 61–9.

85 'Falstaff, the Prince, and the Pattern of *2 Henry IV*', *Shakespeare Survey 30* (Cambridge, 1977), 35–45.

point in the writing of *1 Henry IV* Shakespeare changed his mind and decided to postpone the rejection of Falstaff to a second play which, though it required some new material, was forced to repeat the reformation of Hal which had already been dealt with in *Part 1*. So, beginning as one play, it ended up as two.[86] H. E. Cain sees the two parts as totally independent of each other, *Part 2* requiring that we forget much of what has happened in *Part 1*,[87] a view shared by R. A. Law who discusses the different ways in which the source material is treated in the two parts and argues that *Part 1* is the primary source for *Part 2* which is a Falstaff vehicle, an afterthought[88] (a thesis argued in 1948 by M. A. Shaaber).[89]

(*d*) Falstaff. Various elements have been seen as contributing to the make-up of Falstaff. Joseph Allen Bryant sees him as Shakespeare's answer to the dodges of the professional clowns, Shakespeare forestalling their liberties by writing all their tricks into the part.[90] Herbert B. Rothschild studies a possible link with the picaro,[91] and D. B. Landt shows how much of the character might have been put together from different roles in *The Famous Victories*.[92] Shadowy archetypes naturally haunt so mythical a character: to Roy Battenhouse he represents a 'holy fool' figure whose piety might derive from his days as Mowbray's page;[93] to Douglas J. Stewart he has something in him of Chiron the Centaur, tutor of heroic youth.[94] R. Fiehler provides a very detailed account of the links between Oldcastle and Falstaff[95] and Alice-Lyle Scoufos in *Shakespeare's Typological Satire* (Athens, Ohio, 1979) makes large claims for the Cobham family being the subject of Shakespeare's satire. Sukanta Chaudhuri in *Infirm Glory* (Oxford, 1981) provides a study of Falstaff's scepticism, differentiating it from that of Rabelais and Montaigne. It is conceivable that the greater interest shown in the political content of the plays has tended somewhat to reduce our sympathy for Falstaff but one of our best poets and one of our liveliest critics do not concur. Both agree that Shakespeare had to keep Falstaff out of *Henry V* in order to avoid what would be a disastrous sabotaging of the serious action. On W. H. Auden's view Falstaff's exemption from a world of time and change, his energy, his happiness totally overwhelm

us[96] while Empson, on one of his marvellous critical glider-flights, soaring away, catching every puff of wind, sees Falstaff as a crucial part of the plays' dramatic ambiguities, exhilaratingly jangling our nerves and shaming the virtuous.[97]

(*e*) Prince Hal. Our responses to the rejection of Falstaff have much to do with the attitude which we take toward Prince Hal, who can be seen as the hero of either an heroic or an ironical drama. If we see Shakespeare as taking a sympathetic view of his father, as Charles Fish does, putting the responsibility for political conspiracy in *1 Henry IV* on to the rebels,[98] or, as James Black does, presenting the death of Henry IV in Jerusalem as a blessed and not ironical end to a crusade different from the one which he wished to undertake,[99] then we may think that this tactic helps Shakespeare to free the son from any moral taint of usurpation, very subtly giving Hal, as Gerald Cross argues,[100] moral as well as political right to the throne. And perhaps, as Hugh

---

[86] *The Structural Problem in Shakespeare's Henry IV* (1955).

[87] 'Further Light on the Relation of *1* and *2 Henry IV*', *Shakespeare Quarterly*, 3 (1952), 21–38.

[88] 'The Composition of Shakespeare's Lancastrian Trilogy', *Texas Studies in Literature and Language*, 3 (1961), 321–7.

[89] 'The Unity of *Henry IV*', in *Joseph Quincy Adams Memorial Studies*, ed. J. G. McManaway, Giles E. Dawson, and Edwin E. Willoughby (Washington, DC, 1948), pp. 217–27.

[90] 'Shakespeare's Falstaff and the Mantle of Dick Tarleton', *Studies in Philology*, 51 (1954), 149–62.

[91] 'Falstaff and the Picaresque Tradition', *Modern Language Review*, 68 (1973), 14–21.

[92] 'The Ancestry of Sir John Falstaff', *Shakespeare Quarterly*, 17 (1966), 69–76.

[93] 'Falstaff as Parodist and Perhaps Holy Fool', *PMLA*, 90 (1975), 32–49.

[94] 'Falstaff the Centaur', *Shakespeare Quarterly*, 28 (1977), 5–21.

[95] 'How Oldcastle Became Falstaff', *Modern Language Quarterly*, 16 (1955), 16–28.

[96] 'The Prince's Dog', in *The Dyer's Hand* (1962), pp. 182–208.

[97] 'Falstaff and Mr. Dover Wilson', *Kenyon Review*, 15 (1953), 213–62.

[98] 'Henry IV: Shakespeare and Holinshed', *Studies in Philology*, 61 (1964), 205–18.

[99] 'Henry IV's Pilgrimage', *Shakespeare Quarterly*, 34 (1983), 18–26.

[100] 'The Justification of Prince Hal', *Texas Studies in Literature and Language*, 10 (1968), 27–35.

Dickinson argues, the suppression of a feeling of guilt in the King's mind in *1 Henry IV* avoids the raising of awkward scruples in Hal himself.[101] The silence in *Henry V* about Cambridge's claim to the throne can also, as Karl P. Wentersdorf sees it, prevent Hal from having publicly to argue the rightness of his claim.[102] Hal's role as hero can be seen as more than a military one. J. P. Sisk sees him achieving the role of the full, all-round Renaissance man,[103] and to G. M. Pinciss he becomes (against Hotspur) the model of the Castiglione-type courtier.[104] Norman Sanders sees Hal as faced with the problem of finding the right role, a dissociation of identity in *1* and *2 Henry IV* being resolved by his final assumption of a public political role in *Henry V*.[105] W. Babula regards Hal's success as real but achieved only at the end of *Henry V*, a view which involves a critical account of much of that play, especially of Agincourt.[106] Some estimates of Hal, leaning hard on the Ephesians references in *1* and *2 Henry IV*, fit his character and its development into a much more religious framework, seeing him, as J. A. Bryant, Jr, does, undergoing a process of self-redemption, a process which he fails to win Falstaff to, though his hardness of heart, shown in the rejection scene, is something he needs to slough off.[107] According to Paul A. Jorgensen, he redeems the time as a Christian should;[108] on Franklin B. Newman's view he acts towards Falstaff with a very proper rigorous charity;[109] and, according to D. J. Palmer, casts off the old man in his progress towards grace.[110] Against this Keiji Aoki argues in *Shakespeare's 'Henry IV' and 'Henry V': Hal's Heroic Character and the Sun-Cloud Theme* (Kyoto, 1973) that there is no question at all of redemption or re-education in Hal's role: from the start he is presented to everyone except the audience as a master of the skilful concealment of his own ideal nature (from the English court in *1* and *2 Henry IV* and from the French court in *Henry V*) so that the recognition of it by those around him in the play comes unexpectedly. Aoki's thesis also has some bearing upon the relationship between *1* and *2 Henry IV*, Hal's defeat of Hotspur being deliberately concealed from everyone (except from Falstaff who is given good reason not to reveal it) so that the deception game can be extended into a second part. Against these

readings may be set Andrew Gurr's view that the world of *Henry V* is dominated by self-interest, that of the king and others, so that the play gives us a very low-key view of what is achievable in the world of politics.[111] Norman Rabkin puts both responses to *Henry V* together, arguing that Shakespeare in essence wrote two plays, an heroic play which is the sequel to *1 Henry IV* and a darker, more pessimistic one which is the sequel to *2 Henry IV*, inscrutably offering the audience a choice of the two and asking them to hold the two in balance.[112]

(*f*) *Henry VIII*. Standing, like *King John*, apart from the main run of the English histories, *Henry VIII* poses its own problems. Firstly the question as to whether it represents a Shakespeare–Fletcher collaboration. Of the editors, R. A. Foakes (new Arden, 1957) thinks the play wholly Shakespeare's, arguing that many of the arguments for Fletcher being Shakespeare's collaborator are either subjective or based on poor statistical grounds. On the other hand J. C. Maxwell (New Cambridge, 1962), S. Schoenbaum (Signet (New York, 1967)), and A. R. Humphreys (New Penguin (Harmondsworth, 1971)) regard the play as a Shakespeare–Fletcher collaboration. Each editor extensively presents the case. Outside the editions R. A. Law

---

[101] 'The Reformation of Prince Hal', *Shakespeare Quarterly*, 12 (1961), 33–46.

[102] 'The Conspiracy of Silence in *Henry V*', *Shakespeare Quarterly*, 27 (1976), 264–87.

[103] 'Prince Hal and the Specialists', *Shakespeare Quarterly*, 28 (1977), 520–4.

[104] 'The Old Honour and the New Courtesy', *Shakespeare Survey 31* (Cambridge, 1978), 85–91.

[105] 'The True Prince and the False Thief', *Shakespeare Survey 30* (Cambridge, 1977), 29–34.

[106] 'Whatever Happened to Prince Hal?', *Shakespeare Survey 30*, pp. 47–59.

[107] 'Prince Hal and the Ephesians', *Sewanee Review*, 67 (1959), 204–19.

[108] '"Redeeming Time" in Shakespeare's *Henry IV*', *Tennessee Studies in Literature*, 5 (1960), 101–9.

[109] 'The Rejection of Falstaff and the Rigorous Charity of the King', *Shakespeare Studies*, 2 (1966), 153–61.

[110] 'Casting Off the Old Man: History and St. Paul in *Henry IV*', *Critical Quarterly*, 12 (1970), 267–83.

[111] '*Henry V* and the Bees' Commonwealth', *Shakespeare Survey 30* (Cambridge, 1977), 61–72.

[112] 'Rabbits, Ducks and *Henry V*', *Shakespeare Quarterly*, 28 (1977), 279–96.

presents more statistical evidence for Fletcher's hand in the play,[113] while Paul Bertram in *Shakespeare and 'The Two Noble Kinsmen'* (New Brunswick, New Jersey, 1965) argues for Shakespeare's single authorship.

Secondly, there is dispute about the intention of the play. Paul Bertram in his book mentioned above sees the play as affirming the full meaning given to the office of king, Henry being at the centre of a new order and fully in command. John Wasson argues that the play perfectly fulfils the intentions of its Prologue. It is, on his view, a classic example of the history play – about historical truth, about how noblemen face up to prosperity and adversity, about pageantry – celebrating the significance of the age of Henry VIII and, what is characteristic of history as a genre, having little room for analysis of character and motive.[114] Other studies have seen the romance as an important genre in the structure of *Henry VIII*. To Howard Felperin the play is a Christian history play and its concern with suffering and regeneration and its presentation at the end of Henry and Cranmer as God's deputies brings an element of myth into history, perhaps to help along the marriage celebrations of 1613;[115] or perhaps, as Eckhard Auberlen argues, to highlight the disappointments of King James's reign by exploiting contemporary nostalgia for the days of old.[116] Ronald Berman argues that the play's world of masque and procession helps to haunt us with the vision of a political world strangely but convincingly more golden and transcendent than the one we know.[117] H. M. Richmond also sees the play as showing a world where perfection is possible.[118] Other critics have concentrated on the play's darker edges. Lee Bliss makes the point that it is not like the romances in that the redeemed characters die: its world has no room for the unambitious.[119] Frederick O. Waage, Jr, also wishes to pull the play away from the romances, arguing that the end is tacked on to the play which up to that point has been heavy with disillusion and death.[120] Frank V. Cespedes finds that the darker side to the play makes it more impressive, truer to the way things go in history, comparing it with Marvell's 'Horatian Ode'.[121] In a review of Foakes's Arden edition

Madeleine Doran contributes most helpfully to the question of collaboration and intention.[122]

The crucial issue still is what response we are meant to have to Henry and to the ethics of the political world in which he eventually triumphs, and whether the sympathy with which we come to regard certain characters who fall or are thrown by the wayside to any extent diminishes our opinion of the king to whose triumph their fall is necessary. Certainly, whatever we say about *Henry VIII* and the romances, there can be few tears in the eyes or lumps in the throat evoked by the play's titular hero.

IN THE THEATRE

A very interesting study considering the plays as theatrical performances is Michael Goldman's *Shakespeare and the Energies of Drama* (Princeton, 1972) which gives in particular an excellent account of *1* and *2 Henry IV* and of how richly they are realized in the theatre. Goldman cuts straight to the centre of the plays with cogent analysis and common sense. As he presents it *Henry V*, for example, is a drama of strenuous heroism which, for all its ironies, remains a great patriotic drama and movingly

---

[113] 'The Double Authorship of *Henry VIII*', *Studies in Philology*, 56 (1959), 471–88.

[114] 'In Defence of *King Henry VIII*', *Research Studies* (Washington State University, Pullman, Washington, 1964), 261–76.

[115] 'Shakespeare's *Henry VIII*: History as Myth', *Studies in English Literature, 1500–1900*, 6 (1966), 225–46.

[116] '*King Henry VIII*: Shakespeare's Break with the Bluff-King-Harry Tradition', *Anglia*, 98 (1980), 319–47.

[117] '*King Henry VIII*: History and Romance', *English Studies*, 48 (1967), 112–21.

[118] 'Shakespeare's *Henry VIII*: Romance Redeemed by History', *Shakespeare Studies*, 4 (1968), 334–49.

[119] 'The Wheel of Fortune and the Maiden Phoenix of Shakespeare's *King Henry the Eighth*', *English Literary History*, 42 (1975), 1–25.

[120] '*Henry VIII* and the Crisis of the English History Play', *Shakespeare Studies*, 8 (1975), 297–309.

[121] '"We are one in fortunes": the Sense of History in *King Henry VIII*', *English Literary Renaissance*, 10 (1980), 413–38.

[122] *Journal of English and Germanic Philology*, 59 (1960), 287–91.

evokes the tensions that necessarily belong to kingship. Arthur Colby Sprague's *Shakespeare's Histories: Plays for the Stage* (1964) gives a fascinating account of the history of the plays in the theatre and of the conventions that developed around them.

Annual accounts of Shakespeare productions can be found in *Shakespeare Quarterly* (world-wide) and *Shakespeare Survey*. Actual productions have provoked and indeed been indebted to critical appraisal. It is now common for directors to consult academics about the plays and the bumper programmes which present-day productions provide contrast sharply with the very brief programmes of earlier days. Those performances and their reviews still provide us with some of our best criticism. Some productions of the English histories perhaps deserve mention. In 1951–3, the Birmingham Repertory Theatre produced *1, 2* and *3 Henry VI* (director: Douglas Seale) with the conviction – not very common at the time – that they were indeed actable. The plays were presented in consecutive performances, something which had not been done since 1906. Sir Barry Jackson, the Director of the Birmingham Repertory, gives an account of the productions[123] and they are discussed by J. C. Trewin in *The Birmingham Repertory Theatre* (1953). *1, 2* and *3 Henry VI* were also produced by the Royal Shakespeare Company (director: Terry Hands) in 1977–8 and Homer D. Swander reviews these productions.[124] John Barton's *King John* for the same company in 1974 is very critically discussed by R. L. Smallwood who questions the 'thesis' of the production which, by means of some severe alteration, was directed to showing the futility of politics, Jan Kott perhaps but not Shakespeare.[125] The same director's *Richard II* for the Royal Shakespeare Company is discussed by Stanley Wells who analyses the stylization and symmetry of the production in *Royal Shakespeare* (Manchester, 1977) and by James Stredder who discusses the way in which the production, like Barton's earlier *King John*, was designed to present the characters as victims of history.[126]

In 1951 the Shakespeare Memorial Theatre at Stratford-upon-Avon devoted its whole season to productions of the four plays of the second tetralogy

in sequence (director: Anthony Quayle). The venture reflected the new status that the history plays had acquired during and since the war. The productions are discussed by J. Dover Wilson and T. C. Worsley (the scholar and dramatic critic in tandem) in *Shakespeare's Histories at Stratford, 1951* (1953) and by Richard David.[127] In 1964 the whole *Richard II* to *Richard III* sequence was produced at Stratford-upon-Avon (directors: Peter Hall, John Barton and Clifford Williams), the first tetralogy being tailored into three plays (*The Wars of the Roses: Henry VI, Edward IV* and *Richard III*). The text was published as *The Wars of the Roses* by John Barton and Peter Hall (1970). John Russell Brown gives an account of these productions in *Shakespeare's Plays in Performance* (1966). *1* and *2 Henry IV* and *Henry V* (and *The Merry Wives of Windsor*) were directed at Stratford-upon-Avon by Terry Hands in 1975 and Sally Beauman presents a full study of the *Henry V* in *The Royal Shakespeare Company's Production of 'Henry V' for the Centenary Season at the Royal Shakespeare Theatre* (Oxford, 1976) providing the playtext and including some interesting interviews with actors and others involved in the production. Richard David also discusses the John Barton *Richard II* and *King John*, and the Terry Hands *1* and *2 Henry IV, Henry V* and *Merry Wives* in his *Shakespeare in the Theatre* (Cambridge, 1978). T. F. Wharton in *Henry IV, Parts 1 and 2* (1983) discusses four productions of *1* and *2 Henry IV* (the Royal Shakespeare Company productions of 1964, 1975 and 1982, and the BBC TV production of 1979).

Perhaps it is the directors who are the University

[123] 'On Producing *Henry VI*', *Shakespeare Survey 6* (Cambridge, 1953), 49–52.

[124] 'The Rediscovery of *Henry VI*', *Shakespeare Quarterly*, 29 (1978), 146–63.

[125] 'Shakespeare Unbalanced: the Royal Shakespeare Company's *King John*, 1974–5', *Deutsche Shakespeare-Gesellschaft West Jahrbuch 1976*, 79–99.

[126] 'John Barton's Production of *Richard II* at Stratford-on-Avon 1973', *Deutsche Shakespeare-Gesellschaft West Jahrbuch 1976*, 23–42.

[127] 'Shakespeare's History Plays: Epic or Drama?', *Shakespeare Survey 6* (Cambridge, 1953), 129–39.

Wits of our day; and Daniel Seltzer[128] and Stanley Wells[129] discuss the problems of directing Shakespeare in the modern theatre. The films of the histories – Laurence Olivier's *Richard III* (1956) and Orson Welles's *Chimes at Midnight* (1966) – are discussed by Roger Manvell in *Shakespeare and the Film* (1971) and by Jack J. Jorgens in *Shakespeare on Film* (Bloomington, 1977). The latter film, a lament for Merrie England and a eulogy and an elegy for Falstaff whom Welles regards with total and moving affection is discussed by Samuel Crowl.[130]

CONCLUSION

How far have we come since Harold Jenkins wrote his survey thirty years ago? In many respects the problems are what they were. Textually there has been considerable gain in finesse and knowledge, though only perhaps in the claims made for the Quarto text of *Henry V* by Gary Taylor in his edition of the play for the Oxford Shakespeare (1982) do we find a significant change from texts which the old editions provided. There is more to be read certainly. In the matter of periodicals there are as it were more trains to catch and more passengers anxious to book a seat. Perhaps some of the critics, like Bishop Blougram, believe, say, half they speak. Perhaps the striving for novelty gets a little too desperate. But an impressive amount of work has been done and the expectation of scholarship is very high. The best work finds its way sometimes into books, certainly and most importantly into editions. And here we have God's plenty: the New Shakespeare (Cambridge), new Arden, Pelican, New Penguin, Signet and now the Oxford Shakespeare and the New Cambridge Shakespeare. And in other respects scholarship is well served. Geoffrey Bullough's eight volumes, *The Narrative and Dramatic Sources of Shakespeare* (1957–75) and Kenneth Muir's *The Sources of Shakespeare's Plays* (1977) are invaluable. Perhaps as a marker of our progress we might put to ourselves the point raised by the *TLS* reviewer of Tillyard in 1945. What would we say about the Iden episode now?

---

[128] 'Shakespeare's Text and Modern Productions', in *Reinterpretations of Elizabethan Drama*, ed. Norman Rabkin (New York, 1969), pp. 89–115.

[129] 'Directors' Shakespeare', *Deutsche Shakespeare-Gesellschaft West Jahrbuch 1976*, 64–78.

[130] 'The Long Goodbye: Welles and Falstaff', *Shakespeare Quarterly*, 31 (1980), 369–80.

SHAKESPEARE AND HISTORY: DIVERGENCIES AND AGREEMENTS

E. W. IVES

In the autumn of 1601, in the miserable atmosphere which followed the rebellion and execution of the Earl of Essex, the antiquary William Lambarde came to Greenwich to present to Elizabeth I the fruits of his long years of research in the royal archives. Turning the pages of his book, the Queen reached the reign of Richard II and said, 'I am Richard II, know ye not that?' Lambarde took her meaning at once, for earlier in the year the identification had been so commonly made by the Essex faction that the Earl's supporters had commissioned a special performance by the Lord Chamberlain's Men of Shakespeare's *Richard II*, despite the fact that it had been long out of the repertory and that the actors prophesied a poor audience.[1]

This is a well-known episode, but it does have something to say about the problems of relating the plays of William Shakespeare to the world he lived in – indeed, about the whole vexed relationship between literature and history. Insisting on the historical dimension in a book or a play is not universally welcomed by students of literature, and literature and literary evidence is certainly out of fashion among historians. They have lost the old confidence that if we want to see an Elizabethan pedlar we have only to look at Autolycus, and that we can learn everything about the Elizabethan military machine by watching Falstaff press men for Henry IV's army and march off with the diseased and feeble, and £3 in Bardolph's pocket for freeing the able-bodied. As for artistic imagination, this is feared as a distortion, not welcomed as an illumination.

The Lambarde story, however, suggests that we can explore the relationship between Shakespeare and history from an opposite direction, and this is the theme of this essay: not what Shakespeare has to tell us of his own age, but what knowledge of that age has to tell us of Shakespeare; why *Richard II* was relevant to Essex and his supporters; what we discover from the ways in which Shakespeare's stage England agreed with or diverged from England as it was outside the playhouse. It is an approach which offers more questions than answers, but at least it does attempt to treat history and literature as each having integrity and not one as the servant of the other.

This line is hardly a new one, but there is a novelty in it because of recent major changes in the understanding of life in Shakespeare's England. There are two particular areas of such change. The first arises directly from the conversation between Elizabeth and Lambarde, and is the changed way in which historians are learning to look at politics in sixteenth- and early seventeenth-century England.

I

Classic treatments of the period emphasized the importance of institutions (the Monarchy, the Parliament, the Commission of the Peace), the role of religious activists (puritans and papists), foreign dangers and overseas expansion (the Armada, Drake and the New World), with the ruler in single-handed management of it all: 'Elizabeth decided...', 'James I believed...'. Almost no attention was paid to the nature of power or the

---

[1] E. K. Chambers, *William Shakespeare*, 2 vols. (Oxford, 1930), vol. 1, pp. 353–5; vol. 2, pp. 323–7. Quotations from the plays are from the Oxford edition of W. J. Craig (1905).

origination of policy, or to the articulation of government and society. Thus Essex's rebellion was seen as a confrontation between the Earl, 'a nature not to be ruled', and Elizabeth, in whose 'old heart glowed the Tudor suspicion of a popular noble'.[2] As for the Court, this was regarded as an idle assembly of 'water-flies' and 'serviceable villains' and left to historical novelists and Hollywood.

Not any longer. Familiar as we now are with image-building in contemporary politics, it is recognized that the Tudor Court performed the conscious and important function of projecting royal majesty. To this end it mobilized art and architecture, myth and symbol, with a sophistication which has an inexhaustible fascination. We also recognize that the Court was the place of power. Elizabethan and Jacobean monarchy was 'personal monarchy' in the literal sense that the ruler's will was the essence of the state. Whatever the constitutional and intellectual value of a distinction between the king's two bodies, one politic and eternal, the other natural and mortal, in terms of power they were the same and the locale of that totality was the Court or, rather, where that totality was, the Court was.

The importance of the Court and of the individual figure of the king is something historians might not have lost sight of if they had attended the theatre more frequently. However much we may choose to explore the treatment of kingship in Shakespeare's metaphor and imagery, the brute fact over and against these discussions is that, as presented on stage, power is always personal. *Richard II* opens with the King at Court in the Presence Chamber, exercising power. *Henry IV, Part 1* starts in a similar way. When the King appears on stage for the first time in *Henry V*, his speeches pulsate with the personal pronouns of authority:

> But tell the Dauphin I will keep my state,
> Be like a king and show my sail of greatness
> When I do rouse me in my throne of France:
> For that I have laid by my majesty
> And plodded like a man for working-days,
> But I will rise there with so full a glory
> That I will dazzle all the eyes of France,
> Yea, strike the Dauphin blind to look on us.
>
> (1.2.273–80)

And if we go outside the Histories, we find not the limited monarchy of English constitutional theory but courts of instant obedience.

England was not, of course, a country where the ruler could cry 'Off with his head', like the Queen in *Alice*, but in day-to-day terms the king's will did prevail. In other words, the court ethos of Shakespeare's plays exploits what was the effective ambience of an English Court where the royal will was central. One sees this very much in the interaction between monarch and courtier. Until the arrival on the throne of that arch-snob, Charles I, relations at the English Court were remarkably unstuffy. There is the famous description by Sir John Harington of the entertainment for the King of Denmark in 1606 when James I, his guest, and a sizeable number of the English courtiers, male and female, got incapably and disgustingly drunk.[3] This was an extreme example, and such excesses would not have been tolerated by Elizabeth I, but since a major role of the courtier was to provide companionship for the monarch, a generally free atmosphere had to prevail. Stage representations of joviality between courtier and monarch are entirely in period. 'Pastime with good company', Henry VIII called it. The sentiments of his own song are highly revealing.[4]

> Pastime with good company
> I love and shall until I die.
> Grudge who list, but none deny;
> So God be pleased, thus live will I;
>   For my pastance,
>   Hunt, sing and dance;
>   My heart is set
>   All goodly sport
>   To my comfort:
>   Who shall me let?

---

[2] Francis Bacon to the Earl of Essex, quoted in J. E. Neale, *Queen Elizabeth* (1938), p. 343; J. A. Williamson, *The Tudor Age* (1979), p. 431.

[3] John Harington, *Nugae Antiquae*, ed. Thomas Park (1804), vol. 1, pp. 348–54.

[4] This song is found in a number of versions, notably in Ritson's MS [BL Add. MS 5665] and Henry VIII's MS [BL Add. MS 31922]; see J. Stevens, *Music and Poetry in the early Tudor Court* (Cambridge, 1979). I have edited and modernized the text.

Youth must have some dalliance,
Of good or ill some pastance.
Company methinks it best
All thoughts and fancies to digest.
    For idleness
    Is chief mistress
    Of vices all:
    Then who can say
    But pass-the-day
    Is best of all?

Company with honesty
Is virtue – and vice to flee;
Company is good or ill
But every man hath his free will.
    The best ensue,
    The worst eschew;
    My mind shall be
    Virtue to use,
    Vice to refuse;
    Thus shall I use me.

Relations of courtier and monarch were, in consequence, surprisingly relaxed. Or relaxed for 90 per cent of the time, since the atmosphere could change on an instant. Elizabeth I was quite prepared to box saucy ears if need be, and, on receipt of her message: 'Go, tell that witty fellow, my godson, to get home; it is no season now to fool it here', Harington took himself off, as he said, 'in good sooth I feared her Majesty more than the rebel Tyrone'.[5] Her father had thrown offending courtiers out in person and bodily. Six months before the Essex rebellion, James VI of Scotland was alone with a young courtier in a private room in Gowrie House in Perth when a quarrel blew up and the young man was stabbed by the guards, along with his brother.[6] The ultimate demand on the courtier was being challenged on his allegiance, which posed the stark choice of instant obedience or defiance of the sovereign. It was put to Essex, and his refusal was fatal; it was used by Lear against Kent, with only slightly less disastrous effect.[7] Some critics have complained that the behaviour of Leontes in *The Winter's Tale* is improbable. The dominance of the royal personality in the English Court suggests otherwise.

The position of the monarch in English affairs

meant that the paramount reality in the country was royal favour.[8] This was true of patronage, that distribution of a whole range of grants, from appointments to office, to leases, privileges and honours, which drew men to royal service like bees to honey, and presented the Crown with a major source of its political strength. It was also true of policy and executive authority. Authority was conferred by royal favour, and policy was what the king decreed after listening to those he trusted. No critic could publicly challenge this; it was the king's will. The only possible course was to attempt to gain the ear of the king, and so to oust those currently in favour. In other words, opposition on issues was the mark of disloyalty – of people like papists and sectaries – but the loyal way to fight over policies was in terms of personality. Thus, in Elizabeth's reign, the degree to which the country had a more or a less assertive attitude to Spain reflected and was expressed in the extent of the Queen's reliance on either the Earl of Leicester or Lord Burghley.

The response of the English political élite to these basic facts of life was the sophisticated organism which historians know as faction. The word had, and has, a bad connotation, but a faction was neither an ideological party nor a casual clique on the make. It

---

[5] On one notorious occasion Elizabeth hit Essex: (Neale, *Elizabeth*, p. 349; Harington, *Nugae*, vol. 1, pp. 317–18). At the time of the return of Essex from Ireland, the Queen forgave Harington, but told him to go home: 'I did not stay to be bidden twice; if all the Irish rebels had been at my heels I should not have had better speed for I did now flee from one whom I both loved and feared also': *ibid.*, vol. 1, p. 356.

[6] D. H. Willson, *James VI and I* (1956), pp. 126–30.

[7] Egerton the Lord Keeper said: 'I command you all upon your allegiance to lay down your weapons and to depart, which you ought all to do being thus commanded, if you be good subjects and owe that duty to the Queen which you profess' (*Complete Collection of State Trials*, ed. T. B. Howell, 33 vols. (1816–98), vol. 1, p. 1341); cf. *King Lear* 1.1.142–82, especially 169–70.

[8] For the following discussion of politics and faction, see E. W. Ives, *Faction in Tudor England* (1979) and the bibliography cited there, also S. Adams, 'Faction, Clientage and Party: English Politics 1550–1603', in *History Today*, 32 (December, 1982), 33–9; K. Sharpe, 'Faction at the Early Stuart Court', in *History Today*, 33 (October 1983), 39–46.

was, rather, a less or more enduring relationship which pursued royal favour. At one level it was the mechanism by which patronage operated, a hierarchy of communication topped by some leading court figure with direct access to the monarch and the rewards which came from him. The importance to Shakespeare of being taken into the Southampton clientage is well recognized, while if you were out of such a system, as Spenser discovered after offending Leicester, you were nowhere. From the point of the faction leader, of course, the flow went the other way. The clients to whom he filtered the royal goodies, directly or indirectly, were men whose adherence gave him status and gratuities – for Shakespeare's generation was not mealy-mouthed about the principle that a favour done means a reward earned. But while this made the faction leader, it also made the faction leader's reputation and wealth rest on continued success with the ruler, and if, as happened to Essex at the end, favour was lost, ruin followed.

The system of faction also had benefits and dangers for the ruler. Having a number of possible roads to favour avoided the danger of leaving powerful groups alienated from the system. It meant, also, that as faction leaders competed with each other, they had to offer a quality product, allowing the Crown a choice among the best abilities and the most cogent policies available. Faction could, furthermore, protect a ruler's independence; by balancing one group against another, the monarch could remain independent of all and above all.

The dangers, however, are equally clear. Competition could lead to violence, particularly where a faction leader had a run of ill success. It could also, given a weak or an ageing ruler, encourage attempts to monopolize royal favour which, if successful, made the sovereign not the master but the creature of faction and alienated all those outside the favoured circle. The significance in having *Richard II* performed in 1601 was not only or even primarily the identification of Elizabeth's supposed senile loss of governance with the misgovernment of Richard, nor the inference about deposition (it was never Essex's stated intention to oust the Queen although

the same may not have been true of all his followers, and the writer John Hayward was even then in the Tower for having in his *Life and Reign of Henry IV* compared Essex with Bolingbroke).[9] The main thrust was against the dominance of Richard by a corrupt faction at Court, paralleling what Essex and his supporters believed was the capitulation of Elizabeth to the Cecil interest and, in consequence, the exclusion of true-hearted Englishmen (themselves) from their rightful favour. When Bolingbroke condemned Bushy and Green, Gilly Meyrick and the rest of Essex's swordsmen saw their Earl sentencing the hated Cecil and Raleigh:

> You have misled a prince, a royal king,
> A happy gentleman in blood and lineaments,
> By you unhappied and disfigur'd clean: . . .
> Myself, a prince by fortune of my birth,
> Near to the king in blood, and near in love
> Till you did make him misinterpret me,
> Have stoop'd my neck under your injuries.
>
> (3.1.8–10, 16–19)

The message Bolingbroke sent to Richard II at Flint Castle was the message Essex would bring in person to Elizabeth at Whitehall:

> Henry Bolingbroke
> On both his knees doth kiss King Richard's hand,
> And send allegiance and true faith of heart
> To his most royal person; hither come
> Even at his feet to lay my arms and power,
> Provided that my banishment repeal'd,
> And lands restor'd again be freely granted.
>
> (3.3.35–41)

The consequence of this fresh interest by historians in the royal Court and the realities of place and patronage in Tudor and early Stuart England is the tentative beginning of a new detailed narrative

---

[9] Sir Christopher Blount admitted on the scaffold that 'although it be true, that . . . we never resolved of doing hurt to her majesty's person; . . . yet, I know, and must confess, if we had failed of our ends, we should (rather than have been disappointed) even have drawn blood from herself' (*State Trials*, vol. 1, p. 1415). In the light of this, the inclusion of the deposition scene in *Richard II*, apparently for the first time, may seem significant. For Hayward, see Chambers, *William Shakespeare*, vol. 1, p. 354.

of the policy struggles and personal manoeuvres which lay beneath the older surface story. Yet the relevance to an appreciation of the Shakespearian texts of an awareness of the working of court relationships and royal favour and of the realities of loyalty, service, dependence, reward and advancement is immediate and obvious, too obvious, indeed, to need any lengthy demonstration. Let one example suffice: the motivation of Iago's hatred of Othello which has sometimes been regarded as a weakness in the play. Certainly his final speech, answering Othello's 'Why?',

Demand me nothing: what you know, you know:
From this time forth I never will speak word.

(5.2.301–3)

is no explanation, but Iago has opened the play with what, for an Elizabethan audience, would have been a fully convincing complaint, patronage unfairly denied and given to an inferior, with disastrous financial implications:

 Three great ones of the city,
In personal suit to make me his lieutenant,
Off-capp'd to him; and, by the faith of man,
I know my price, I am worth no worse a place;
But he, as loving his own pride and purposes,
Evades them...
And, in conclusion,
Nonsuits my mediators; for 'Certes,' says he,
'I have already chose my officer.'
And what was he?
Forsooth, a great arithmetician,
One Michael Cassio...
...mere prattle, without practice,
Is all his soldiership. But he, sir, had the election;
And I – of whom his eyes had seen the proof
At Rhodes, at Cyprus, and on other grounds
Christian and heathen – must be be-lee'd and calm'd
By debitor and creditor; this counter-caster,
He, in good time, must his lieutenant be,
And I – God bless the mark! – his Moorship's
 ancient. (1.1.8–33)

And one may remark that even at the end Othello does not know 'why', does not realize that he had offended against all the canons of European lordship. The coup against Edward, Duke of Somerset, in 1549 was in part triggered off by similar blindness,

and only twelve years after Shakespeare's death, the Duke of Buckingham himself was murdered by a lieutenant to whom he had denied promotion.[10]

Thus far this paper has used the term 'Court' as a convenient generality, but it is important to realize that the Court was a large and complex organization. It was effectively divided into three parts, one comprising the stables and the outside staffs of huntsmen and the like, next the rest of the household below stairs, dealing with supplies and services, and the third and most important section, the household above stairs, or Chamber, with direct responsibility for attendance on the person of the monarch. This much has been long known, but recent research has revealed that major organizational changes within the early Tudor Chamber had significantly affected the position of the ruler. They were formally laid down under Henry VIII and completed the process of the king's withdrawal from the general Chamber to live a more private life in a suite of rooms which, from the title of the most important, was called 'the Privy Chamber', and which was staffed by a newly created élite group of gentlemen servants. To set up such a group was automatically to put men in the ideal position to influence the king, and from this point on, the Gentlemen of the Privy Chamber were in the forefront of factional alignments. Factional struggle focuses on struggle within the Privy Chamber. Apparently simple matters thereby acquired a major significance: physical access to the monarch was vital; reputation, too – what was said when you were away, which could destroy you, and against which there was no defence in the absence of allies to stand up for you at the time; keeping rivals away from the king; monopolizing the king's ear; the nice skills of picking the right time, the right place and the right person to advance or destroy a cause or an individual.

In all this the personality of the ruler was

---

[10] A. J. A. Malkiewicz, 'An eye-witness' account of the *coup d'état* of October 1549', *English Historical Review*, 70 (1955), 602–4; R. Lockyer, *Buckingham: the Life and Political Career of George Villiers, First Duke of Buckingham* (1981), pp. 458–9. John Fenton, the Duke's assassin, was also motivated by political and religious emotions.

obviously vital. Henry VIII, superficially a masterful figure, in reality was morbidly suspicious and highly vulnerable to pressure. The result was the sequence of bloody faction battles which took the lives of so many who, in Wyatt's words, were touched with 'the fire of the glory' of the Court.[11] Elizabeth, by contrast, made it clear from an early stage that she was unmoved by pressure and she had the great advantage that her ladies – most of them friends of long duration – acted as a protective screen against too great importunity. When the male courtiers grew insistent, the Queen simply walked out into her private rooms where they could not follow. Eventually faction leaders accepted the situation and settled to a limited level of competition – 'you lose some, you win some'. Only with the arrival, towards the end of the reign, of the Earl of Essex who refused to play by the rules, did the Court become deeply polarized, with Elizabeth being driven by his intolerance into the arms of his Cecil rivals. With the return of a male sovereign in 1603 all the inevitable pressures within the Privy Chamber revived, pressures which the personality of James I was quite unable to resist. As a result, a succession of Privy Chamber favourites mono-polized royal favour, with the inevitable result. Substantial sections of the political élite found themselves in the cold and it was their frustration and resentment which inspired much of the apparent political tension of James's reign. Men reduced to being ciphers at Court and on the Privy Council used Parliament in an attempt to outflank the all-powerful favourite of the day and gain the attention they felt they deserved.

The implications of this for an understanding of Shakespeare are evident. First, some minor ex-amples. What better instance can there be of the importance of access to the king than the panic of Aumerle in *Richard II* to get to Henry IV to confess his treason, something which was exactly paralleled by Bishop Stephen Gardiner in the reign of Henry VIII?[12] As for control of the king, on Edward VI's accession the future Lord Protector made a rush to Hatfield to get his hands on the new monarch.[13] In *Richard III*, Shakespeare, with no support from the sources, makes getting to the young Edward V the top priority of Gloucester and Buckingham.

> My lord, whoever journeys to the prince,
> For God's sake, let not us two stay at home.
>
> (2.2.145–6)

Rosencrantz and Guildenstern get as short shrift from critics and directors as they do from Hamlet, yet they exemplify the dilemma of courtly faction. As clients of the heir they had been nicely placed while Old Hamlet was on the throne. Called back to Denmark they are cautious in recommitting themselves to a court figure who is now falling from favour, and in the end they do what every courtier had to do, go with the king.

The court scenes in act 2 of *The Winter's Tale* are particularly revealing. The debate between Leontes and his attendants after the arrest of Hermione depends on the intimate yet distanced relationship between a king and his courtiers. Leontes's rejection of Perdita later in the act takes place in the actual Privy Chamber and begins by Paulina forcing her way in, past the gentleman usher.[14] Driven to distraction, Leontes orders his attendants to throw her out:

> On your allegiance,
> Out of the chamber with her! Were I a tyrant
> Where were her life? she durst not call me so
> If she did know me one. Away with her!
>
> (2.3.120–3)

---

[11] Thomas Wyatt, *Satire I*, ll. 14–15.

[12] John Foxe, *Acts and Monuments*, ed. S. R. Cattley, 8 vols. (1837–41), vol. 5, pp. 690–1.

[13] P. F. Tytler, *England under the Reigns of Edward VI and Mary*, 2 vols. (1839), vol. 1, pp. 15–16.

[14] *Winter's Tale*, 2.3.27–40. Control of access to the king was specially important at a number of crises in the reign of Henry VIII, and there are many other anticipations in his reign of material found in *The Winter's Tale*, for example Henry VIII's abhorrence of whispering among his courtiers, and his highly suspicious nature. The charges against Hermione (and the 'evidence' on which they were based) have definite echoes of the charges against Anne Boleyn. There are also affinities between the bastardized Elizabeth and Perdita, not least the identification of each with the Spring and the goddess Flora.

He then rounds on Antigonus, alleging first a ploy in the queen's favour and then a Privy-Chamber plot to pressure him:

> ...thou sett'st on thy wife.
> *Antigonus.*   I did not, sir:
>   These lords, my noble fellows, if they please,
>   Can clear me in't.
> *First Lord.*   We can, my royal liege,
>   He is not guilty of her coming hither.
> *Leontes.*
>   You are liars all.
> *First Lord.*
>   Beseech your highness, give us better credit:
>   We have always truly serv'd you, and beseech
>   you
>   So to esteem of us.   (2.3.141–8)

Eventually Perdita is saved from the flames as an act of patronage, in response to the united petition of the Privy Chamber staff – Shakespeare even quotes directly the standard formula in letters patent: 'for services past and to come':

> *First Lord.* ...on our knees we beg,
>   As recompense of our dear services
>   Past and to come, that you do change this
>   purpose,
>   Which being so horrible, so bloody, must
>   Lead on to some foul issue. We all kneel.
> *Leontes.*
>   I am a feather for each wind that blows.
>   (2.3.148–53)

The contention here is not that there is a slavish imitation of reality in Shakespeare's treatment of courts and princes. It is, rather, that he is able to explore a pattern of norms in political and courtly life. The most striking example of this political perceptiveness is in *Henry VIII*, which is a good deal more in accord with historical reality than has usually been allowed. Of course it makes a dog's breakfast of chronology, but we need to remember the simple point that it was impossible to write a proper history of the reign. The play might be called '*All is True*', but you simply could not tell the truth about Henry in 1613, or at least not all of it. Henry wronged either Catherine of Aragon or Anne

Boleyn or both. And if Anne, then he destroyed his own good name, for if she was not a whore, he was a murderer – a choice which their daughter Elizabeth avoided by saying nothing about it. Rowley's *When You See Me You Know Me* followed suit and ignored both Catherine and Anne, so Shakespeare can hardly be blamed for his solution which was to end with the birth of Elizabeth, a case of knowing when to quit.

That said, however, Shakespeare and/or his team produced in *Henry VIII* a series of episodes of the reign which, in detail, stick close to the sources, and are rearranged into a highly perceptive study of Tudor politics. All may not be true in the literalist sense, but how revealing a great deal of it is. Indeed, it is striking that again and again the insights are those of recent scholarship: the inconclusive opposition to Wolsey of an aristocratic faction centring on Buckingham; the effect of the Amicable Loan in undermining the Cardinal; the Cardinal's concern to manipulate courtiers with access to the King; his destruction by aristocratic pressure which utilized evidence of his own double-dealing with the Pope; Anne Boleyn's reformist opinions which echo the Cromwell–Cranmer axis; the attempt by faction to unseat Cranmer. All this, as has already been said, is taken straight from the sources. The significant point, however, is that Shakespeare should select for this near-contemporary portrayal of the Court and its politics precisely those episodes which historians are now coming to see as particularly revealing.

II

The new way in which historians are beginning to put together the interactions of politics, patronage, faction, and the Court, and which Shakespeare so remarkably anticipated, is an instance of the increasingly sophisticated and detailed scrutiny of known materials. The second area of changed knowledge which is addressed in this paper arises from a different process, from a revolution in the methodology and subject-matter of history.

The problem for the historian in handling his traditional descriptive evidence (a category which includes literature) is the obvious one of telling how characteristic of the norm that evidence is. To take again the examples of Autolycus and Falstaff. The one was a pedlar and the other a recruiting officer, but were all pedlars rogues and all musters vitiated by corruption? It does not follow that because we recognize J. R. Ewing on television as a Texas oil baron, the Dallas business community does combine the graft of the Sicilian Mafia with the lubricity of a stud farm. We ought to know how common, how typical. Historians, therefore, are being urged to turn away wherever possible from all older data of an exemplary or impressionistic kind, including literature, and to develop techniques which yield more objective material. Hamlet's, or even Shakespeare's, reflections on suicide help us little in trying to ask how common suicide was, whether its incidence fluctuated, and what its causes were. For this we are told we need hard statistical data. Against the print-out of the computer, even the time-honoured testimony of England's greatest dramatist counts for little.

Not only is literary evidence 'soft' evidence, it is minority evidence, produced by and for the educated few. By concentrating on the high culture of Elizabethan England, on its 'golden age', previous generations of scholars have, we are told, kept attention away from what really concerned most people at the time, and was significant for the country in the long term. In a recent brilliant study of English society over the century 1580 to 1680, the name 'Shakespeare' does not even appear in the index.[15]

A preoccupation with statistical evidence and a concern for the mass of the nation are two emphases of the new approach to history. There is a third: a concern with anthropological questions. We want to know about the patterns of human relationship – husband/wife, parent/child, employer/employee; about social structures and the norms of community behaviour. And we are concerned to understand the infrastructure of belief, thought-forms, and discourse patterns, and the awareness of the self in the face of the vital realities of birth, life, death and the hereafter. And lest it be thought that here, at least, is an obvious meeting ground between history

and literature, it must be stressed again that answers are sought not from the conscious literary creations of the few but the demonstrable practices of the many.

How then does Shakespeare stand in the light of this new subject-matter and methodology? Some of the most important recent work has been done on the English population. When Shakespeare was born this was about 3,100,000.[16] Already that was a third greater than when his father had been born, even though a few years before William's birth a series of disasters had killed one in twenty of the population. William, indeed, was one of a renewed boom in babies, and this boom continued for the rest of his life by which time the English nation had grown by a further 50 per cent. It was not an even growth, area by area, but the two which Shakespeare knew best, Warwickshire and London, were in the forefront; London, indeed, may have doubled in population in the years Shakespeare knew it.[17] Contemporaries were very well aware of this, and overpopulation was one of the arguments in favour of the colonization first of Ireland and then of the New World.

The rise in population was without doubt a major factor in another of the significant influences on Shakespeare's England – inflation. Money had been falling in value ever since the 1520s, but in Shakespeare's lifetime prices doubled.[18] This may not seem dramatic by modern standards, but given

---

[15] K. Wrightson, *English Society, 1580–1680* (1982).

[16] E. A. Wrigley and R. S. Schofield, *The Population History of England, 1541–1871* (1981), p. 208.

[17] V. Skipp, *Crisis and Development: an ecological case study of the Forest of Arden, 1570–1674* (Cambridge, 1978), p. 13 shows that while the population of Arden doubled overall in the period 1570–1650 (i.e. slightly below the estimated national rise of 60 per cent), there was a very sharp increase from 1575 to 1600. One calculation for London's population in 1585 suggests 108,000 to 120,000 people in 1585 and, by 1605, between 144,000 and 168,000, which, with the suburbs, reached 184,000 to 215,000: D. M. Palliser, *The Age of Elizabeth* (1983), p. 213.

[18] The widely accepted Phelps Brown and Hopkins index stands at 290 in 1565 and 562 in 1616 [base = 1451–75]: E. H. Phelps Brown and S. V. Hopkins, 'Seven Centuries of the Price of Consumables', in *The Price Revolution in Sixteenth-Century England*, ed. P. H. Ramsay (1971), pp. 39–40.

tradition and entrenched custom and the absence of any effective regulation of the economy, even that level of inflation could have serious effects. For many, including Shakespeare himself, it meant opportunity; his burgeoning theatrical business was only part of a larger boom in the hotel, catering, and entertainment industry. And the speed with which he invested his profits in more secure ventures was typical of a rising gentleman, and many an established one also. For others, inflation made life harder and harder. During Shakespeare's lifetime, the purchasing power of a craftsman's wages fell by a third.[19] Amongst those with land, from the poorest peasant to the country gentleman, there were many who were unable to profit by the new opportunities or were the victims of bad management or bad luck. At best they clung to a little prosperity but many slid inexorably downwards. An era of opportunity for Shakespeare and others to rise in the world was inevitably also an era of rapid social oblivion for others.

A growing population and serious inflation were partly responsible for a third feature of Shakespeare's society, poverty. It was not that the country could not support a larger population – the better-informed commentators were well aware that it had done so before the Black Death – but the problem was the slowness of the economy to adjust to the increasing numbers wanting work. As for inflation, this made worse the accidental disasters of bad harvests, most dramatically the four successive seasons 1594, 1595, 1596 and 1597, where near famine nationally produced actual starvation in certain areas.[20] There were other factors, too. Seasonal unemployment was a necessary feature of English agriculture which required large numbers of workers only at the hay and grain harvests, and surplus labour survived for the rest of the year on a multitude of cottage industries, most commonly the production of cloth. Wages were pitiful – in some areas these had to be paid out each day, or there would be no food on the table next morning – and workers were totally exposed to the all-too-frequent fluctuations in trade. Then we must remember the casualties of social decline. Those peasants who had only a few acres of land and could not keep pace

easily found themselves forced to sell up and join the pool of landless labour.

If we were to judge the Elizabethan poor by the literary descriptions which have come down to us, we should visualize these casualties of society abandoning their hovels and joining the marauding bands of sturdy beggars described by John Awdeley and Thomas Harman.[21] That such groups existed is beyond doubt, but they were not a new phenomenon, and it is clear that they were more formidable in rumour than in fact. A generous modern estimate is that about 20,000, say half of one per cent of the population, was on the road, and this included thousands who were genuinely seeking work.[22] The evidence suggests that they would actually have done better to stay at home where communal feeling would at least have guaranteed bare subsistence. But how bare that could be, Shakespeare knew from close acquaintance. In the Forest of Arden in the last years of the playwright's life, conditions became so bad for the poor that in 1613–14 their children began to die in dozens, in 1615 and 1616 many women ceased to ovulate and when they began to conceive again in 1617–19 found themselves all too often miscarrying.[23] It can hardly be a surprise that it was instinctive for the active poor to converge on the towns, and particularly London, in the hope of casual work and a more generous relief provision. The Elizabethan poor should, therefore, be seen not on the road but infesting the urban slums. In the year of Shakespeare's marriage, paupers in the county town of

---

[19] *Ibid.*, pp. 39–40. It is, however, important to note (i) that what is being measured is the *rates* of wages, not wages *paid*, and (ii) that relatively few persons were wholly dependent on money wages.

[20] During Shakespeare's fifty-two years, harvests 25 per cent below average or worse occurred eight times, and 10 to 25 per cent below, twice; harvests 10 to 25 per cent above average occurred twenty-one times, but bumper harvests only three times: W. G. Hoskins, *The Age of Plunder* (1976), p. 87.

[21] John Awdeley, *Fraternitye of Vacabondes* (1565); Thomas Harman, *A Caueat or Warening for Commen Cursetors* (1567).

[22] A. M. Everitt, in *Agrarian History of England and Wales, iv, 1540–1640*, ed. Joan Thirsk (Cambridge, 1967), p. 406.

[23] Skipp, *Crisis and Development*, pp. 33–5.

Warwick made up 30 per cent of the population.[24] In Stratford itself, perhaps half the town was in receipt of poor relief in 1601.[25] There are no figures for London, but most of the immigrants who raised the population by 2,000 to 4,000 a year came to swell the ranks of the poor; and this is a net figure – many of the newcomers arrived to find an early grave.

A rising population, long-term inflation and short-term crises, social mobility, poverty, slums – these were some of the formative experiences of Shakespeare's England. Were they formative for Shakespeare? It seems to the non-specialist that the probable response should be: 'not very'. It is possible to show by a study of language and imagery that Shakespeare was aware of much of this, but it gave him few explicit themes. One must allow, perhaps, a good deal of interest in social mobility, while the concern in the plays with wealth, and particularly credit, certainly does chime with contemporary emphases in the world at large. Yet to the historian, the remarkable thing – and a contrast to Shakespeare's sensitivity to the realities of politics and the Court – is the distance there seems to be between his plays and the socio-economic realities of Elizabeth and Jacobean England. *Coriolanus*, for example, is a major treatment of the lower classes which was performed against the background of the perennial concern of the City of London for the feeding and control of the city's poor. But the play takes very much an establishment point of view, and it stands alone.

It might be expected that there would be less divergence between the writings of Shakespeare and the real world when it comes to that other interest of historians in recent years – interest in the family and human relationships. That expectation, however, is not always borne out. We may remind ourselves here of one divergence which has received some notice, the quite remarkable treatment of the age of marriage in *Romeo and Juliet*. Juliet is presented in the play as a girl of almost fourteen, a lower age than in sources Shakespeare used, and one which he deliberately emphasizes in two scenes even to the point of dating her birthday exactly as 31 July.[26] He backs this up by the specific assertion by Juliet's mother that she and other ladies of Verona were married and pregnant when only twelve or thir-

teen.[27] Elizabethan women, however, did not marry young; the average age was twenty-two or twenty-three. Juliet, of course, was an aristocrat, and they did tend to marry somewhat younger, but even then the age was nineteen or twenty. What is more, increasing knowledge of the history of human physiology makes it difficult to believe the claims of Lady Capulet that she and other aristocratic ladies had borne children at so young an age. In sixteenth-century Europe, girls, on average, reached the menarche about sixteen, and the youngest recorded aristocratic mother of Shakespeare's day was the $14\frac{1}{2}$-year-old Countess of Exeter in 1589.[28]

As this last example shows, there were young brides and mothers in Elizabethan England, but the point is that they were very much the exception. Marriage normally became a concern of the aristocratic English girl in her late teens. In this respect, the flowering of the sixteen-year-old Miranda's interest in men in *The Tempest* was very much on cue. The majority of so-called child marriages were actually instances of espousals or betrothals which could be voided up to the age of consent – twelve for girls, fourteen for boys – and still needed a church wedding and physical consummation before they became final.[29] In other words, by putting Juliet, a child of thirteen, on the marriage market and later taking her from espousals to marriage and

---

[24] Palliser, *Age of Elizabeth*, p. 122.

[25] S. Schoenbaum, *William Shakespeare, A Documentary Life* (Oxford, 1975), p. 39.

[26] *Romeo and Juliet*, 1.2 and 1.3; cf. 1.3.17; ed. Brian Gibbons (1980), p. 39.

[27] Although the exchange clearly indicates that Lady Capulet is aged twenty-seven or twenty-eight, stage directions in the quarto text describe her as 'Old Lady': *ibid.*, p. 103.

[28] For the above, see P. Laslett, *The World We Have Lost, Further Explored* (1983), pp. 81–90.

[29] Many of the examples cited of aristocratic early-teenage pregnancy (e.g. that Henry VII's mother, Lady Margaret Beaufort, was under fourteen when the future king was born in 1457) are highly anachronistic in the context of the reigns of Elizabeth and James I. There is some (but not unanimous) evidence that such marriages were more common in medieval times, but to bring in examples such as Lady Margaret is equivalent to citing evidence from the time of the Crimean War in a discussion of social habits today. For the age of consent, see Lawrence Stone, *Crisis of the Aristocracy* (Oxford, 1965), p. 652.

consummation in one day, Shakespeare was deliberately creating a situation unfamiliar to his audience.

The matter becomes more mysterious because many of his audience would have disapproved. General opinion, including that of persons as diverse as the Common Councillors of London, Henry Percy the 'Wizard Earl' of Northumberland, and the Puritan moralist Philip Stubbes held that young marriages were improvident – as they well might be, since convention dictated that a newly-married couple must leave the family home – as well as being potentially unstable and physically debilitating.[30] Adolescent sex was bad for you. As always, Lord Burghley was the typical Elizabethan, refusing an earl for a son-in-law with the remark that his daughter 'should not, with my liking, be married before she were near eighteen or twenty'.[31] Mr Peter Laslett, whose research is summarized here, notes an illuminating comment by the clerk of a London parish in 1623 who, when registering the marriage of a seventeen-year-old threadmaker to a girl of fourteen, added the note 'a worthy ancient couple of young fools'.[32] There can be no doubt about it. In the minds of many of the audience, Juliet's deliberately plotted sexual precocity must have appeared shocking.

It is not the purpose of this paper to offer a critical interpretation of what this may mean for the understanding of Shakespeare. Is *Romeo and Juliet* an extravagant piece of popular escapism – Peter Pan and Wendy? Or a fantasy of love and marriage among girls and boys – the idealization of juvenile passion? Or a warning of the tragic fate which awaits those who snatch at the forbidden fruits of adult sexuality (the moral drawn by the source which Shakespeare used)?[33] Or was Shakespeare writing about the breakdown of proprieties – proprieties between neighbours and proprieties between immaturity and experience, the destructive self-indulgence of Romeo and Juliet paralleling the self-indulgent destructiveness of Montague and Capulet? Perhaps. But what is clear is that to create an equivalent shock in the changed circumstances of today, producers should cast Juliet as a child of ten.

Romeo and Juliet is an interesting play to students of the Elizabethan family for other reasons too. It is one of the few Shakespeare wrote which presents what today would still be regarded as the 'normal' family unit of husband, wife and child. Far more usually the plays present a single father and child, or children – Prospero and Miranda, Shylock and Jessica, Leonato and Hero, Egeus and Hermia, Titus with his children, Lear with his daughters, Gloucester and Edgar and so on. When, in *The Winter's Tale* and *Cymbeline*, surrogate fathers appear, each is a widower. There are a number of widows with children too. Even more common, perhaps, than the one-parent family is the young adult with both parents dead, as in *As You Like It*, *All's Well that Ends Well*, *Twelfth Night* and *Measure for Measure*.

This is not evidence of what Lady Bracknell would call carelessness or confirmation of Dr Johnson's views on the improbability of some Shakespearian plots. It agrees rather with what seems to have been the reality in Shakespeare's England. In the first place, the country was a country of young people. An estimated one person in three was under the age of fifteen, and over half were less than twenty-five.[34] This does not mean that Shakespeare diverges from reality when he also presents the old or the very old. At an age of thirty, life expectancy in a healthy district was about sixty, and 7 per cent or 8 per cent of the population at any one time would be even older.[35] On the other hand, life expectancy is an average and there were many who died much younger, notably married women who all too often failed to survive the rigours of childbirth.[36] Shakespeare's own thirty-three years of

---

[30] *Ibid.*, pp. 656–7; Lawrence Stone, *Family, Sex and Marriage* (1977), pp. 50–1; Wrightson, *Society*, p. 124; Laslett, *World We Have Lost*, p. 99.

[31] Palliser, *Age of Elizabeth*, p. 41.

[32] Laslett, *World We Have Lost*, p. 86.

[33] *Narrative and Dramatic Sources of Shakespeare*, 8 vols. (1957–75), ed. G. Bullough, vol. I (1957), pp. 271, 284–5.

[34] Wrigley and Schofield, *Population*, p. 528.

[35] *Ibid.*, pp. 250, 528.

[36] In three out of four cases where marriages ended in ten years or less, the reason was the death of the wife; there was a 30 per cent chance of a marriage being ended by death within fifteen years: Stone, *Family*, pp. 55, 80; see also P. Laslett, *Family Life and Illicit Love* (Cambridge, 1977), pp. 168–90.

marriage was unusual, and bettered by only one couple in five.[37]

It was, thus, very common for young people in Elizabethan and Jacobean England to have lost one parent – many had lost both – and often at an early age. Among the aristocracy and gentry, one child in three had lost one parent by the age of fourteen, and at the age of marriage perhaps fewer than one person in two still had a father alive.[38] There is no divergence between life and the stage here. Bereaved families were commonplace. Remarriage was also commonplace – about a quarter of all spouses married more than once – and, for men, this was often remarriage with a widow who could take on immediately the task of running the home, offer mature companionship and, in particular, see to the completion of the upbringing of his children.[39] A good number of the audience for *Hamlet* and *Cymbeline* would have known at first hand about the problems of step-relationships.

The broken nature of so much of Elizabethan and Jacobean family life which is thus found reflected in Shakespeare raises the question of the quality of family relations at the time, a matter of current historical controversy. The historical issue can be simply put. Did the brevity of human relationships affect their intensity? Not only were marriages often tragically brief, but children were frighteningly vulnerable to infection. Whereas today, out of every forty people who die in England, nineteen will be over eighty years of age and only one under ten, in Shakespeare's time there would have been two or three octogenarians and thirteen or fourteen children.[40] With odds like this, any deep emotional commitment to spouse or offspring would seem a guarantee of misery, and probably sooner rather than later. As a consequence, or so it has been powerfully argued by Lawrence Stone and others, family relationships in Elizabethan and Stuart England were characterized by distance – formality between husband and wife, patriarchal authority and filial deference.[41] On this argument, romantic attachment of the kind we find so commonly in Shakespeare and other writers was a divergence from reality, a fantasy for the élite minority which played the old game of courtly love and rapidly

came down to earth when marriage became a serious possibility. Concern to make deep personal commitments of the kind now expected in the family, what has rather unhappily been called 'affective individualism', begins its slow emergence after the Restoration – or so it is said.

The evidence assembled in support of this proposition is considerable. To take husbands and wives first. William Perkins, the influential Puritan, defined a husband as 'he that hath authority over the wife' and a wife only as 'the other married person, who being subject to her husband yieldeth obedience to him'.[42] Convention dictated that the wife had publicly to defer to her husband. Marriage gave control of a woman's property to her spouse who could order affairs as though his wife were a chattel. English law even allowed the husband to beat the wife, provided he did not exceed the limits of 'moderate correction'.

Dramatic stories of the subjugation of wives to husbands lose nothing in the telling, but as has been noticed earlier, examples may mislead. What is more – and this applies to the whole thesis about harshness in the family – much of the evidence is by nature suspect. Horror stories come mainly from cases where family breakdown has become an issue of open recrimination, and it is simply not safe to generalize from the pathological and contentious to what was normal.[43] Substantial evidence does in fact

---

[37] This figure is calculated from the peerage, and so may be above average (Stone, *Aristocracy*, pp. 590, 787).

[38] Stone, *Family*, p. 58.

[39] *Ibid.*, p. 56.

[40] Wrightson, *Society*, p. 105. 25 per cent of all children failed to reach the age of ten.

[41] Stone, *Family*, passim.

[42] Wrightson, *Society*, p. 90.

[43] It must be emphasized also that conventional patterns of expectation condition individuals as to what is normal. For instance, the skimmington which in Shakespeare's time expressed disapproval of over-assertive wives had, by the nineteenth century, come to focus on wife-beating: M. Ingram, 'Ridings, rough music and "the reform of popular culture" in early modern England', in *Past and Present*, 105 (1984), 86–90; cf. attitudes to what made a 'good' marriage, below at n. 58.

exist to show that extreme disregard for human relations was increasingly an eccentricity. The conventional public submission of the wife was often accompanied by a strong private emphasis on co-operation and companionship. The wives of all but the wealthiest were actively involved in running a household, a large economic unit if the wife of a gentleman or yeoman, and, if humbler, then augmented by responsibilities for work on the land or at the loom. With anyone who travelled, and there were many, from pedlars to merchants, lawyers, and gentlemen involved in public affairs, the time this took meant that at home it was the wife who was in charge for long periods. And respect and affection were there too; wives were not merely brood animals and housekeepers.[44] This is Sir Thomas Barrington in 1629, at the delicate task of excusing his wife to his formidable mother for not having written to her: 'And now my wife tenders her lame leg for an excuse that her hand presents you not with her duty. Truly she is not yet well, but amending, and so I pray God we may all.'[45] Sir Thomas Hoby, who was two years younger than Shakespeare, wore his wife's picture in a bracelet on his arm until the day he died.[46]

Evidence, therefore, is by no means conclusive in support of the view that relations in an Elizabethan marriage were normally distant and severe, though in exceptional instances they well may have been.[47] What is seen in Shakespeare, it can be suggested, is the exploitation of this variety to present a whole range of marital responses. The autocratic paternal model is reflected in Capulet and his wife, and in Leontes. *The Taming of the Shrew* sees the triumph of moralist theory – the totally obedient wife subsumed in the personality of a loving lord and master. Between Macbeth and Lady Macbeth and Cornwall and Regan we have more the marriage of equals in initiative and villainy. The rights of the woman in marriage are specifically debated in *The Comedy of Errors*, while *Hamlet* gives a taste of the greater independence and opportunity to satisfy desire which was enjoyed by widows like Gertrude. Finally, *The Merry Wives of Windsor* gets nearest of all to a picture of mundane companionate marriage concealed under a guise of male authority.

The debate about the quality of relationships within the family is concerned not only with husbands and wives but with the place of children in Elizabethan and Stuart England. Some contemporary commentators, indeed, equated wives with children, and the latter were certainly also supposed to be indoctrinated from infancy with the need to obey.[48] The horrific lengths to which this could lead need no elaboration. The custom of wet-nursing, it is also argued, destroyed the possibility of bonding between mother and baby, while the almost universal practice of sending children away from home in the early teens hardly seems a recipe for close parent–child relations.

On the other hand, does this interpretation stand up to scrutiny? Parents can be shown to have expended enormous efforts to bring up their children well, and to settle them in adult life, with little calculation of any repayment in an old age they would probably not live to see. Nor was this cold-blooded duty or pride in blood. There is plenty of evidence to show close ties with children, and it is, one may suggest, legitimate to draw a conclusion from the evidently sympathetic response which Shakespeare expects when he portrays children on stage. The sending of offspring away in the early teens was precisely to give opportunities which could not be provided at home. The idea that because infant and child mortality was so high, parents and fathers in particular were inured to losing their offspring is simply untrue. This is

---

44 The letters of Sir Gilbert Gerrard to his mother-in-law, Lady Joan Barrington of Hatfield Broad Oak in Essex, from April to July 1631, show a very personal anxiety for his wife's comfort and progress during pregnancy: *Barrington Family Letters, 1628–1632*, ed. A. Searle, Camden Society 4th series, 28 (1983), nos. 178, 181, 184, 188, 191; cf. no. 125.

45 Sir Thomas Barrington to Lady Joan Barrington, 14 Oct. 1629: *ibid.*, no. 72.

46 Wrightson, *Society*, p. 101.

47 For recent judicious summaries see *ibid.*, pp. 89–104, and R. A. Houlbrooke, *The English Family, 1450–1700* (1984), pp. 96–119.

48 William Perkins defined parents as 'they which have power and authority over children'; cf. above at note 42.

another Essex gentleman this time reporting the loss of an unborn child to his mother-in-law.[49] He writes:

to let you know some ill of my wife, who was young with child and has miscarried this day. It is the greater grief to us, having been long without; I pray God sanctify this affliction to us,...It is his mercy that he hath given us any children [they already had two or three] and that he hath continued them unto us with his blessing upon them. We know not the cause of this...she was very well. [And he then gives the latest news as he seals the letter] My wife is now somewhat better than she was.

As for wet-nursing, two points must be made. First, given the high incidence of death in childbed, most babies were wet-nursed perforce, and not from fashion. Second, there is good evidence that where there was a choice, some of the pressure to employ a wet-nurse was precisely to avoid pain should the child die, and was firmly rejected nevertheless by well-born women who took pride in their role as successful mothers – Lady Macbeth was in good company.[50] And at least some husbands showed a considerable interest and pride in their wife's performance: 'She hath brought me a very fine fat girl; she never was so good a nurse to any as to this.'[51]

The most sensitive point in parent–child relations was, without doubt, the finding of a marriage partner for the child. Older commentators assumed that arranged marriage was typical in Tudor times – and Stone finds powerful support in this for the authoritarian, distant interpretation of the family.[52] Recent research, however, again suggests a more complex situation.[53] With the exception of royal children – for example, Princess Elizabeth and the Elector Palatine, or Prince Charles and the Spanish Infanta – arranged marriage in the strict sense was foreign to English custom. According to theory parents were supposed to take a responsibility for the marriage of their offspring, but we should think of this as responsibility to guide and assist the choice of the best partner, and not as something akin to arranged marriage in Eastern communities. To compel a child to marry against its will was recognized as bad.

We need to remember, in any case, that many young people were in no position to consult parents.

This was true not merely of orphans, but of the many who had left home to enter service of some kind. Even though for the most part this was short-distance migration, it was very common, and separation from home by only a few miles would confer effective independence. Admittedly such young people were expected to take advice from their elders, but there can be no doubt that they found it comparatively easy to pursue their own fancies if they wanted to. Indeed, this is only what might be expected, given the considerable freedom of association enjoyed by English young people at the time, at all levels of society.[54]

On the other hand, it was accepted that there was more to marriage than four legs in a bed, and it is clear that young people did not expect to indulge romantic fancies, or knew themselves to be fools if they did. They shared with their elders a sober and realistic attitude to what made a good marriage. It was all a matter of setting up a new and independent family unit within the close-knit and highly personalized relationships in which Shakespeare and his contemporaries lived their lives, and in addition to compatibility, this involved an appropriate investment both of funds and personal capacities and, just as important, acceptance by the community.

It is the particular importance of such broader considerations for the aristocracy and gentry which has given rise to the myth about arranged marriages, where nothing but property and status mattered, and a man like Sir Edward Coke could flog his daughter into accepting an uncongenial husband.[55] In fact arbitrary disregard of the interests of marriage

---

[49] Sir William Masham to Lady Joan Barrington, 26 Nov. 1631: *Barrington Letters*, no. 218.

[50] Vivienne Larminie, 'The Lifestyle and Attitudes of the Seventeenth-Century Gentleman...the Newdigates of Arbury Hall' (unpublished Ph.D. thesis, University of Birmingham, 1980), pp. 224–5.

[51] Sir Richard Everard to Lady Joan Barrington, 28 May 1630: *Barrington Letters*, no. 144.

[52] Stone, *Family*, pp. 180–91.

[53] Wrightson, *Society*, pp. 71–4; Houlbrooke, *Family*, pp. 68–88.

[54] Stone, *Family*, pp. 104–5; Wrightson, *Society*, p. 72.

[55] Stone, *Family*, p. 182; Stone, *Aristocracy*, p. 596.

partners was also increasingly out of fashion among the upper orders of society. Coke is only alleged to have used force, which his daughter herself denied.[56] One must remember the universal acceptance and approval of paternalism, and even where parents do seem to have taken all the initiative in making or vetoing a marriage, it was almost always for what was believed to be, and perhaps was, the true good of the son or daughter concerned. Thus when, as has been seen, aristocratic parents resisted premature marriage, this was despite the clear advantage of protecting a family's property against the danger of interference from the royal Court of Wards. Health took preference over money. Even in the few cases in which youthful brides and bridegrooms were pressed beyond espousals (which they could later break) to undertake apparent consummation, the night spent together could be token and platonic and the couple could separate afterwards. One fate for the young aristocratic bridegroom was being packed off the next day on the Grand Tour, a totally effective way to delay marital cohabitation at home and the wiles of scheming matchmakers abroad.[57]

There is, of course, no doubt that young people could be put under pressure: threats of disinheritance, family ostracism, nagging – even, in the case of Coke's daughter, the wishes of the king. There is no doubt either that some parents expressed their opinion in a highly peremptory manner, although this might be as attributable to anxiety as to insensitivity. But without doubt the principal reason why parental initiative played such a part among the propertied élite was that the prospective brides and bridegrooms from that background agreed that property and family prestige was important to marital success. Consider, for example, the reception of Oliver St John, the future Parliamentarian leader and an exact contemporary of Shakespeare's godson, William Sadler, when he went wooing in 1629.[58] He was at least the eighth prospective husband proposed for Joan, the heiress of Sir James Altham of Mark Hall, Essex, a girl who on occasion could appear remarkably choosy and cold-blooded.[59] Her mother wrote of an earlier proposal that she should marry the son of Sir Robert Bevell of Chesterton in Huntingdonshire:[60]

Jugg [i.e. Joan] is desirous to keep her own land, though she have less jointure, and I think her own inheritance will be better for her preferment in a second match, if God should take away her husband without issue, than her jointure [would be].

We see another side of matchmaking, however, in the letter in which her step-father defended himself against the accusation that his awkwardness had killed that proposal:[61]

And whereas you lay the breach upon that of not selling the land, I conceive otherwise, that if her affections had stood right at first, this could not have directed them, considering that this point was yielded to...But there is more in it than you know: my brother Knightly told us now at last that he [the suitor] hath been to see another gentlewoman, who it may be likes [i.e. suits] better, not approving our [puritan] way, which he may hold too strict. God is the great marriage maker, and therefore we must submit to his will in all these proceedings, who overrules all for the best good of his children.

When St John appeared, highly personable and very much of the right puritan complexion, the mother still wrote of the need to get a good financial deal:[62]

I confess the man, moveth me much to approve of it, but I know God commands me to have a care in the second place of the outward conveniences. Though I desire to accept of much less with such a man, yet I shall be much taxed of her friends if I look not for a competency of outward estate.

Jugg too was taken with St John, but kept her feet firmly on the ground:[63]

Jugg hath a good affection to the gentleman, yet is very desirous of some good inheritance for her posterity, and hath herself expressed as much to him.

[56] C. D. Bowen, *The Lion and the Throne* (1957), pp. 343–52.

[57] For the above, see Stone, *Aristocracy*, pp. 657–9.

[58] The progress of the suit can be followed in *Barrington Letters*, pp. 116, 119–21, 123, 125, 131–2, 136–7, 147, 149.

[59] For these earlier negotiations, see *ibid.*, pp. 84, 92, 103–7.

[60] Lady Elizabeth Masham to Lady Joan Barrington, [?] Nov. 1629: *Barrington Letters*, no. 80.

[61] Sir William Masham to the same, 30 Nov. 1629: *ibid.*, no. 84.

[62] Lady Elizabeth Masham to the same, [?18] Jan. 1630: *ibid.*, no. 99.

[63] The same to the same, 1 Mar. 1630: *ibid.*, no. 118.

There can be little doubt that most of the children of the élite would have wanted their parents to take exactly the same attitude.

All in all, it is impossible to speak of any standard pattern of English matchmaking in the age of Shakespeare. Certainly the evidence does not suggest the dominance of arbitrary marriage imposed by a distant, autocratic father. Each alliance was the outcome of a unique combination of family circumstances, personality, and calculation. And such is the picture which we get from Shakespeare. We have Old Capulet, like Lord Burghley, anxious to resist early marriage for Juliet and insisting that his daughter's preference among the list of the eligible is what counts, only to revert under pressure to an outdated heavy-handedness.

Capulet.
 My child is yet a stranger in the world,
 She hath not seen the change of fourteen years;
 Let two more summers wither in their pride
 Ere we may think her ripe to be a bride.
Paris.
 Younger than she are happy mothers made.
Capulet.
 And too soon marr'd are those so early made....
 But woo her, gentle Paris, get her heart,
 My will to her consent is but a part;
 An she agree, within her scope of choice
 Lies my consent and fair according voice.
(1.2.8–19)

Capulet.
 God's bread! it makes me mad.
 Day, night, hour, tide, time, work, play,
 Alone, in company, still my care hath been
 To have her match'd; and having now provided
 A gentleman of noble parentage,
 Of fair demesnes, youthful, and nobly train'd,
 Stuff'd, as they say, with honourable parts,
 Proportion'd as one's thought would wish a
  man;
 And then to have a wretched puling fool,
 A whining mammet, in her fortune's tender,
 To answer 'I'll not wed,' 'I cannot love,'
 'I am too young,' 'I pray you, pardon me;'
 But, an you will not wed, I'll pardon you:
 Graze where you will, you shall not house with
  me.   (3.5.177–90)

Only a few of the original audience would have experienced the like Turkish treatment, and fewer still would have approved. On the other hand, Juliet also exercises her allowed initiative quite improperly, marrying to betray not only her family, but all right-thinking propriety. Again, few would have approved.

In *A Midsummer Night's Dream* the approach is different. Here, three of the lovers are entirely free of parental authority, and Egeus' command to Hermia to marry Demetrius, disguised as an ancient privilege of Athenian fathers, is little more than a stage device to set the imbroglio in motion – and with a token gesture to Egeus, the lovers get their way in the end. In *As You Like It*, it is a case of virtual free choice, but always observing the social equations and shading the freedom nicely according to rank. In *The Merry Wives of Windsor* youthful initiative triumphs in the end but, interestingly, only after parental opposition aroused initially by the emphasis on property rather than affection.

Fenton.
 I see I cannot get thy father's love;
 Therefore no more turn me to him, sweet Nan.
Anne.
 Alas! how then?
Fenton.   Why, thou must be thyself.
 He doth object, I am too great of birth,
 And that my state being gall'd with my expense,
 I seek to heal it only by his wealth...
 And tells me 'tis a thing impossible
 I should love thee but as a property. (3.4.1–10)

Most striking of all, perhaps, is the way in which the binding legality of betrothal is exploited in a number of plays to enforce the personal choice of the parties, for example, *Titus Andronicus* and *Measure for Measure*, although in *Romeo and Juliet* that same course is specifically repudiated. Perhaps one may indulge a speculation here about Shakespeare's own marriage! In *All's Well* and, apparently, *Othello* and *The Merchant of Venice*, the device is powerful enough to allow love to force a way across even social, racial and religious divides.

New developments, therefore, in the understanding of the family, society, and the economy, to set alongside that other new development in historical study, the investigation of the Royal Court and politics. Yet the title of this paper is 'Divergencies and Agreements', and it remains to attempt to strike a balance. Divergencies there certainly are between the world which Shakespeare puts on stage and the world the historian uncovers by his research. This is particularly so in the absence of emphasis on what scholars now see as the central social and economic stress of the Elizabethan and Jacobean years. If we wished, we could explain this in terms of Shakespeare's narrowed vision; divergence becomes agreement when we reach the world of the Court and high culture where Shakespeare belonged. On the other hand, we ought also to explain this in part by reference to ourselves. Perhaps the questions we ask say more about our contemporary values and the potential of our methodology than about Shakespeare's age in its own terms. Perhaps our aim is too exclusive a depiction of the past from a modern perspective.

As for the agreements, there is much more to be said for Shakespeare's picture of his own world than some scholars, swayed by a modern sociological model, have been prepared to allow. We must not, however, go to the other extreme and reinstate literature as a direct source of historical evidence, imagining that Shakespeare will give us all we know, and all we need to know, about Elizabethan and Jacobean times. The historian must not only insist that literature cannot be appreciated out of context, he must also continue to insist that literature is not reported data. The conclusion is not that the world Shakespeare shows us is a contact print of the world of reality, but that in selecting from reality in the cause of artistic composition, Shakespeare becomes a guide to contemporary significances. Put bluntly, the reaction against literary evidence in history has gone too far. In the dark tunnel where the historian labours, all light should be welcomed, even illumination via a prism.

SHAKESPEARE'S GEORGIC HISTORIES

JAMES C. BULMAN

Source studies of Shakespeare's history plays usually focus on matters of direct influence. Most attempt to define Shakespeare's dependence on those works that presumably inspired his own, the chronicles of Hall and Holinshed – to assess how much he borrowed from each and whether that borrowing confirms or contradicts a providential view of English history. Other studies discuss sources for his dramatic structures, such as hybrid political–morality plays, or for his rhetorical configurations. Seldom do such studies account for indirect or 'deep' sources – works that may have influenced Shakespeare's conception of history more suggestively because less consciously recalled.[1] In this essay I shall propose a deep source for the agricultural references in the history plays. These references are often dismissed as conventional for the time, stock metaphors for good and bad government, probably scriptural in origin, and of limited suggestive power. A closer examination of them and their origins, however, may reveal Shakespeare's darker purpose.

Caroline Spurgeon noted fifty years ago that Shakespeare conceived of the Wars of the Roses in terms of agriculture: the 'decay and destruction' of England's garden 'brought about by ignorance and carelessness on the part of the gardener, as shown by untended weeds, pests, lack of pruning and manuring, or on the other hand by the rash and untimely cutting or lopping of fine trees'.[2] Yet Spurgeon may limit agricultural activity unnecessarily to gardening. Shakespeare in fact had a more self-sufficient farm in mind. He alluded often to bee-keeping and animal husbandry as well – to raising cows, chickens, sheep, and oxen. The English, after all, were not exclusively vegetarian.

A brief look at *2 Henry VI* will demonstrate how Shakespeare employed such references to delineate rivalries between the houses of Lancaster and York. One of the play's chief concerns is whether Gloucester is husbanding the land and tending the King as a good lord protector should, or selfishly gathering a harvest for himself alone. Under the weight of suspicion, he 'droops...like overripen'd corn, / Hanging the head at Ceres' plenteous load' (1.2.1–2);[3] and well he might, for his enemies, aspirant farmers themselves, wish to pluck him down.

Chief among those enemies is the Queen, who poisons her husband's mind against Gloucester with a metaphor identifying weeds as ambitious men that Tilley shows had already become proverbial:[4]

Now 'tis the spring, and weeds are shallow-rooted;
Suffer them now, and they'll o'ergrow the garden
And choke the herbs for want of husbandry.

(3.1.31–3)

Shakespeare first employed this metaphor in the Temple Garden scene of *1 Henry VI*, where he

---

[1] For the ensuing argument I adopt the method of Robert S. Miola who, in his study of how Shakespeare's conception of Rome evolved, 'seeks not to discover direct sources...but to penetrate into the deep sources lying below the surface of the text'. Sources here may thus be 'broadly defined as possible influences and analogs'. See *Shakespeare's Rome* (Cambridge, 1983), pp. 15–16.

[2] Caroline F. E. Spurgeon, *Shakespeare's Imagery and What It Tells Us* (Cambridge, 1935; New York, 1936), p. 216.

[3] All references are to *The Complete Works of Shakespeare*, ed. David Bevington, 3rd edn. (Glenview, Ill., 1980).

[4] M. P. Tilley, *A Dictionary of the Proverbs in England in the Sixteenth and Seventeenth Centuries* (Ann Arbor, 1950), W242.

played on the political connotations of roses and thorns, rooting and plucking, ripening and withering; and he gave it fullest expression in the garden scene of *Richard II*. Its function in the histories is different from the reference to an unweeded garden in, say, *Hamlet*, for Queen Margaret is didactic. Her emphasis on how, why, and when to uproot the weeds is instructive rather than merely descriptive. Gloucester's other opponents, Suffolk and York, prefer to define him in different terms. For them, he constitutes some kind of pest who has pre-empted the role of the farmer. He is 'an empty eagle...set / To guard the chicken from a hungry kite' (ll. 248–9); he is 'the fox' become 'surveyor of the fold' (l. 253); and they vow, like good husbandmen, to catch him 'by gins, by snares, by subtlety' (l. 262). When they succeed in doing so, Henry likens Gloucester to a calf borne away to be butchered and himself to its dam that 'runs lowing up and down, / Looking the way her harmless young one went' (ll. 210–15). In this rapid metamorphosis of agrarian images, Shakespeare envisages England as a farm threatened by disputes in governance. Crops and livestock alike are mismanaged.

Warwick reports Gloucester's death in a welter of such images. He has found 'the heifer dead and bleeding fresh'; next to it, 'a butcher with an axe' (3.2.188–9). In another reference to crops, he reports that Gloucester's beard was 'made rough and rugged, / Like to the summer's corn by tempest lodg'd' (ll. 175–6). He links evidence of foul play with agricultural mayhem in a way that anticipates Richard II's lament that his sighs and tears together 'shall lodge the summer corn, / And make a dearth in this revolting land' (3.3.161–3). Of one thing Warwick is certain: Gloucester's murder will rouse the commons to a mutiny that he, like Mark Antony in a later play, will hold in check only 'Until they hear the order of his death':

> The commons, like an angry hive of bees
> That want their leader, scatter up and down
> And care not who they sting in his revenge.
> (3.2.125–9)

This reference anticipates Canterbury's praise of the orderly kingdom of bees in *Henry V*; but here the hive is disordered, it has no king. It becomes a metaphor for civil chaos. When statesmen act unnaturally, Shakespeare implies, nature herself rebels.

The patterns of tilling the soil, sowing and reaping, husbanding animals and keeping bees that gather around the drama of Gloucester invoke ideas of order and stability, moral as well as agricultural, that imaginatively oppose the turbulence of political events. Those events subvert the farmer's best efforts, however: order yields to disorder, predators seize the sheep, livestock are slaughtered too young, bees sting for revenge, crops lie in ruin.

In subsequent plays of the first tetralogy, Shakespeare conceives of intestine strife largely in terms of trees – the planting and grafting of saplings, the hewing and lopping of limbs. Even in *2 Henry VI*, Suffolk attacks Warwick as one in whom 'noble stock / Was graft with crab-tree slip – whose fruit thou art' (3.2.213–14); and in the next play, Warwick is cut off by the sons of York, who use a more aggressive arboreal imagery. Rather than nourish and protect, they lop and hew. Queen Margaret they disdain as a 'usurping root', and so they set an axe to her to make their own garden flourish:

> We'll never leave till we have hewn thee down
> Or bath'd thy growing with our heated bloods.
> (*3 Henry VI*, 2.2.168–9)

Richard, who wields the axe more skilfully than his brothers, likewise has no mercy for Clifford,

> Who, not contented that he lopp'd the branch
> In hewing Rutland when his leaves put forth,
> But set his murd'ring knife unto the root
> From whence that tender spray did sweetly spring.
> (2.6.47–50)

Lines such as these have a grotesque effect, for in them agricultural imagery, usually suggestive that good husbandry leads to fruition, instead disguises unnatural acts of revenge and destruction.

This tension between agricultural process and its violation grows even stronger in *Richard III*, where Richard derisively uses verbs such as ripen and graft, reap and harvest to advance his own political ends. Only the Earl of Richmond can resolve the tension.

He vows to rid England of the 'wretched, bloody, and usurping boar, / That spoil'd your summer fields and fruitful vines' and to 'reap the harvest of perpetual peace / By this one bloody trial of sharp war' (5.2.7–8, 15–16). For once war will be, not an enemy to agrarian order, but a means to reachieve it. Unlike those earlier battles that devastated the land, Richmond's 'one bloody trial' will return the land to productivity. He will husband the land anew; he will redeem the vocabulary of farming as surely as he will make the summer fields teem with plenty. He ends the play, in fact, by declaring a kind of Augustan peace. 'England hath long been mad, and scarr'd herself,' he explains; but in the fertility of their marriage, he and Elizabeth will

Enrich the time to come with smooth-fac'd peace,
With smiling plenty, and fair prosperous days!

(5.5.23, 33–4)

After years of deprivation, the English will once again 'taste this land's increase' (l. 38). In Richmond's promise, historical reality yields to pastoral myth.

Charles Forker has amply demonstrated that pastoral mythology threads its way throughout the histories as a counter to the realities of dynastic struggle. Pastoral 'suggests the possibility of an ordered and harmonious cosmos in Hooker's terms – a great universal garden created, tended, and brought to ultimate fruition by a supreme and loving Gardener'.[5] By doing so, it would seem to endorse the Tudor, or providential, conception of English history. Yet it is crucial to understand the differences between pastoral passages, such as the one in which Henry VI contemplates the virtues of a shepherd's life, and those passages which deal with farming. Farming differs from pastoral activity through *work*. If pastoral recalls an unfallen world, farmers acknowledge and try to atone for the fall. By working the land, they strive to bring order out of chaos; but, like sinning statesmen, they often destroy what is given them to tend. If pastoral provides an idyllic retreat from war, agricultural processes in many ways mirror those of war. Shakespeare's repeated association of bloodshed with husbandry makes that clear. Agriculture in the

histories is devoid of idealism: farmers, like politicians, dig in dirt. And if Richmond's pastoral vision puts a period to decades of dynastic struggle, it does not erase from our memories all the devastation that led him to Bosworth Field. Pastoral remains mythic – it is never given dramatic substance – whereas agricultural imagery expresses the plays' most insistent reality: the savagery of civil war.

The question of why Shakespeare found such imagery suitable to convey his understanding of English history, or whence he derived it, is difficult to answer. Shakespeare grew up in a market town, and a firsthand knowledge of farming may account for the abundance of agrarian references in the histories. But it cannot, I think, fully disguise their literary nature and provenance. One has only to look at various editions of the plays to discover how many possible sources and analogues exist. Many of the references are said to be scriptural: in so far as they *are* scriptural, they may indicate that Shakespeare embraced a providential view of history. Comparisons of the social order of a kingdom to the order of a garden, for example, were popular among medieval preachers, who derived them from the parable in Matthew 20 about the labourers in the vineyard. Likewise, the parable of the seed and the tares in Matthew 13 may underlie the metaphor of weeds' sucking the soil's fertility from wholesome plants; but as Peter Ure argues, Shakespeare could have found the metaphor's implications developed elsewhere, especially in sixteenth-century political satires.[6] H. J. Leon shows that the metaphor of cutting off the heads of too fast-growing sprays may owe a debt to an anecdote in Livy's *History*, repeated in Ovid's *Fasti*.[7] Ovid is probably the source of other

---

[5] Charles R. Forker, 'Shakespeare's Chronicle Plays as Historical–Pastoral', *Shakespeare Studies*, I (1965), 85–104; p. 101. Forker also discusses in some detail the way in which Shakespeare links blood with growth and vegetation in both tetralogies as a violation of the pastoral theme (pp. 94–5).

[6] Peter Ure discusses many possible sources for garden imagery in his Arden edition of *Richard II* (1961), pp. lii–liv.

[7] H. J. Leon, 'Classical Sources for the Garden Scene in "Richard II"', *Philological Quarterly*, 29 (1950), 65–70.

isolated images too, as are Pliny, Elyot, and Lyly. Those few history plays thought to precede or be contemporary with the *Henry VI* plays make very little use of such imagery; the chroniclers, even less.[8] In any case, editors tend to dismiss these possible sources and analogues as localized phenomena, of use to illuminate a phrase, a line, at most a scene – no more. And there is good reason for this. None of the works identified offers the wide range of agricultural reference that Shakespeare does; none uses the imagery so coherently to communicate a vision of history. One seldom-mentioned work, however, does these things; and I wish to suggest that in Virgil's *Georgics*, we find a deep source for Shakespeare's conception of history as agricultural process.

The four books of the *Georgics* deal, respectively, with tilling, planting, animal husbandry, and bee-keeping. Each affirms the virtue of agrarian order; and together, they promise that with hard work, *labor*, Italy may once again, after years of civil war, teem with plenty: 'Meanwhile the husbandman has been cleaving the soil with crooked plough.... No respite is there, but the season teems either with fruits, or with increase of the herds, or with the sheaves of Ceres' corn, loading the furrows with its yield and bursting the barns' (2.513–18).[9] When such labour reaps bounteous rewards, Virgil invokes memories of the Golden Age, as if it were once again within grasp: 'such was the life golden Saturn lived on earth, while yet none had heard the clarion blare, none the swordblades ring' (ll. 538–40). The Golden Age, however, cannot be restored: Italy *had* heard the swordblades ring, had suffered too much in the Age of Iron to make such a return possible. By working, however, farmers could at least redeem the land that years of war laid waste. In farming, Virgil celebrates how an enlightened ruler, Octavius, may return his country to a fruitful peace with good governance. In their glorification of the social stability and moral regeneration inherent in such husbandry, the *Georgics* anticipate the *Pax Augusta*.

Yet if Virgil celebrates peace, he is also deeply concerned with the wars that for years devastated the land. He wrote the *Georgics* between 37 and 30 BC: in them, he responds to the political situation of Rome in the turbulent period between the assas-

sination of Julius Caesar and the Battle of Actium, which made Octavius sole sir of the world.[10] The poems are rife with memories of cruelty, of bitter struggles among the triumvirs, of civil wars that took farmers from their farms and wrought havoc on the countryside; and of war's aftermath – of Octavius' uprooting countless peasants from their farms so that he could settle 100,000 veterans on the land after Philippi. Maecenas (so the story goes) urged Virgil to write the *Georgics* to instruct these veterans how to farm – that would account for their didacticism – and also to awaken the interest of the Roman aristocracy in agricultural renewal as a basis for prosperity. But beneath every promise of bounty lurks a memory of devastation. 'A time shall come when in those lands, as the farmer toils at the soil with crooked plough, he shall find javelins eaten up with rusty mold, or with his heavy hoes shall strike on empty helms' (1.493–7). Soldiers may turn their swords to ploughshares, but not without Virgil's reminding us of the horrors of Philippi or of Emathia and the broad plains of Haemus that 'twice batten[ed] on our blood' (ll. 491–2). Even as the happy husbandman reaps his plentiful crops and tends his faithful herds, others, Virgil tells us, still are suffering the iron laws, the Forum's madness, dashing upon the sword, pressing into courts and the portals of kings, wreaking ruin on cities and their hapless homes, gleefully steeping themselves in their brothers' blood (2.500–10). Against the turbulence

---

8 Plays such as *The Troublesome Raigne of King John* and Peele's *Edward I* make scant use of agricultural metaphor to illustrate political themes. *The True Tragedy of Richard III*, which uses such metaphor more extensively than other non-Shakespearian history plays, and once was thought to be a source for Shakespeare's *Richard III*, is now widely regarded as a memorial reconstruction of it: its agrarian references may thus echo, and not anticipate, Shakespeare's.

9 All quotations are from the Loeb edition of *Virgil: Eclogues, Georgics, Aeneid, 1–6*, trans. H. R. Fairclough (1916; repr. Cambridge, Mass., 1967).

10 The political background of the *Georgics* is discussed by L. P. Wilkinson, *The Georgics of Virgil: A Critical Survey* (Cambridge, 1969), pp. 49–55; and by John Chalker, *The English Georgic: A Study in the Development of a Form* (Baltimore, 1969), pp. 1–15.

and transitoriness of political life, as John Chalker notes, Virgil balances the enduring patterns of agriculture, the seasonal activities of ploughing, sowing, and reaping.[11] The tensions created thereby complicate a poem customarily regarded, especially by the English Augustans, as politically optimistic.

Virgil does not view history as a progressive movement toward enlightenment or fruition. Rather, he views it as a constant struggle against the forces of darkness that only hard work, and often not even hard work, can win. Much of the *Georgics* is concerned with the agony of toil itself, with the frustration and futility of trying to tame nature. Virgil's instructions are edged with pessimism: it is the nature of things, he argues, to work *against* man. *Sic omnia fatis / in peius ruere ac retro sublapsa referri*: 'Thus by the law of fate all things speed towards the worst, and slipping away fall back' (1.199–200). Nature herself becomes the enemy, and against her man's efforts sometimes are not enough. *Georgics* 3, which details so hopefully how to breed, tame, and tend to cattle, oxen, and sheep, ends not with a promise of increase, but with a description of a plague that kills all the livestock and leaves the farmer destitute. *Georgics* 1, in the midst of advising the farmer when to harvest his rich crops, describes an epic storm that ruins those crops and belittles the labours of oxen:

> Often, as the farmer was bringing the reaper into his yellow fields...my own eyes have seen all the winds clash in battle, tearing up the heavy crop far and wide from its deepest roots and tossing it on high; then with its black whirlwind the storm would sweep off the light stalk and flying stubble. (1.316–21)

Such storms, in Virgil's eyes, take on more than natural qualities. They appear as a kind of divine retribution: rivers flood, Jove hurls his thunderbolt, the earth shivers. Though Virgil does not invoke them as a metaphor for political turmoil, he does ally them with war and bloodshed as anti-georgic forces that defeat the farmers' efforts to tame the land. Caesar's assassination, in fact, is portended in terms of agricultural destruction; and it is worth noting that the most significant allusion to the *Georgics* in Shakespeare's Roman plays occurs in the portents of

Caesar's death in *Julius Caesar* (2.2.13–24).[12] Shakespeare thus apparently understood Virgil's poem to be at least in part a political statement about regicide and its consequences. The assassination of Caesar was the source of the tumult to come. It brought a curse on Rome that years of bloodshed had to expiate. To farmers, it brought a curse on the land; and in Virgil's imagination, the storms and plagues that impeded farming were yoked to that curse.

The *Georgics* were a staple in the Elizabethan grammar school curriculum. They were among the first poems read in the upper school and, together with the *Eclogues*, were studied for their 'moral weight', usually with commentaries by Servius, Willichius, and others.[13] Furthermore, A. Fleming

---

[11] Chalker, *The English Georgic*, pp. 8–10.

[12] Kenneth Muir, in *The Sources of Shakespeare's Plays* (London, 1977; New Haven, 1978), p. 124, quotes the passage from *Georgics* 1 (467–88), which includes an eclipse of the sun, an earthquake, ghosts, wolves howling in towns, thunder and lightning, and comets. 'Shakespeare's thunder and lightning may have been suggested by this passage', writes Muir; 'and his lion may have derived partly from Virgil's wolves.' But Muir cites other possible sources for the portents of Caesar's death (pp. 122–5): Plutarch's *Life of Caesar*, Ovid's *Metamorphoses* 15, and Lucan's *Pharsalia* most prominently. In general, the Roman plays seem to have been little influenced by the *Georgics*, though, as two scholars have recently demonstrated, the *Aeneid* figures quite prominently in them: see John W. Velz, 'Cracking Strong Curbs Asunder: Roman Destiny and the Roman Hero in "Coriolanus",' *English Literary Renaissance*, 13 (1983), 58–69, and Robert S. Miola, *Shakespeare's Rome, passim*. Velz argues (p. 60) that 'like Vergil, Shakespeare had a strongly teleological view of history: to both writers the destiny to be fulfilled is the whole meaning of history'. It is significant, I think, that the *Georgics*, composed before Augustus had proven himself an emperor of peace, are far less confident of Roman destiny than the *Aeneid* is; and by echoing them rather than the *Aeneid* in his English histories, Shakespeare re-creates some of the tentativeness and ambivalence that Virgil apparently felt in the aftermath of Caesar's assassination and the civil wars that followed.

[13] T. W. Baldwin, in *William Shakspere's Small Latine & Lesse Greeke*, 2 vols. (Urbana, 1944), vol. 2, pp. 456 ff., discusses how Virgil was taught in the upper-school curriculum. Chances are fair, writes Baldwin, that Shakespeare's Virgil was the text edited by Paulus Manutius, first prepared for the Aldine Press in 1558; subsequent and revised editions followed. Most school texts included the

made a popular translation of the *Georgics* in 1589, perhaps the very year in which Shakespeare began work on the first tetralogy.[14] It would be remarkable for Shakespeare to have studied the *Georgics* in school, perhaps returned to them later on, and to have missed Virgil's conception of history as an agricultural process. The *Georgics* would have been particularly pertinent to the era Shakespeare dramatized in his histories, wherein the murder of Richard II, like Caesar's, was regarded by some chroniclers, notably Holinshed, as a primal curse from which Henry Tudor rose like Octavius to offer a lasting peace. I shall not press a case for the *Georgics* as a direct source for the histories; deep sources may be the more potent for being less immediate. I want only to suggest that Shakespeare conceived of history with a Virgilian sensibility and used patterns of agriculture to delineate the complex political forces at work in fourteenth- and fifteenth-century England.

A few passages indicate that Shakespeare may have recalled the *Georgics* when writing his early histories. Andrew Cairncross identifies one or two possible references to them. When, for example, the Duchess asks Gloucester why he hangs his head 'at Ceres' plenteous load', she may allude to the opening of *Georgics* 1, which sings the praises of *alma Ceres*, bounteous goddess of crops. When Warwick, moralizing his own death, calls himself a cedar 'Whose top-branch overpeer'd Jove's spreading tree' and protected bird and shrub alike, he may allude to Jove's mighty oak in *Georgics* 3, *magna Iovis...quercus* (l. 332), which stretches out its branches to shelter flocks of sheep and goats.[15] To these, one could add that most Virgilian image of 'summer's corn by tempest lodg'd', which seems to echo the storm in *Georgics* 1 that tears up the heavy corn by its roots, then sweeps off the light stalk and flying stubble.

Even Alexander Iden, the one good farmer in England's ruined garden, may owe something to Virgil's description of the *fortunatus agricola*. A Kentish farmer, Iden declares his affinity with many a classical gentleman in retirement:

Lord, who would live turmoiled in the court,
And may enjoy such quiet walks as these?
This small inheritance my father left me
Contenteth me, and worth a monarchy.

(*2 Henry VI*, 4.10.16–19)

One may compare Virgil's paean to the 'happy husbandmen...for whom, far from the clash of arms, most righteous Earth, unbidden, pours forth from her soil an easy sustenance' (*Georgics* 2.458–60). Other writers such as Horace, Martial, and especially Cicero in *De Senectute* extol the virtues of a life of repose; but there is no reason why Shakespeare may not have had Virgil in mind as well. After all, Jack Cade explicitly identifies Iden as a farmer – 'the lord of the soil come to seize me for a stray' (ll. 24–5); and by killing Cade, Iden rids England's garden of the 'thief' who would 'rob' it (l. 33) and returns it, though bloodied, to peace.

If Shakespeare recalled the *Georgics* when he was writing his history plays, one would expect to find stronger evidence in *Richard II*, the play that deals with the slaughter of a prince and the curse it brings upon the land. And indeed, *Richard II* is rich in

---

notes and commentaries of Servius, Ascensius, and Willichius. 'It would seem clear that Shakespeare's ultimate Virgil was of this type', Baldwin suggests (p. 478), though Shakespeare would not have been likely to use such a text for reading Virgil *after* grammar school.

I. A. Shapiro kindly loaned me his copy of the *Illustrium Poetarum Flores* (1582) to examine for passages from the *Georgics*; and indeed, some of the more famous passages are included, though without commentary. The *Aeneid* is far better represented. In any case, such collections of *Flores* are long (this one is over seven hundred pages); and though they may have been convenient references for writers to have, just as *Bartlett's Familiar Quotations* may be for modern writers, it is illogical to think that Shakespeare would have derived classical material from them rather than from the original sources, most of which were included in the school curriculum.

[14] *The Georgiks of Publius Virgilius Maro: Otherwise called his Italian Husbandrie*, trans. A. Fleming (1589). The British Library copy bears the signature of Ben Jonson.

[15] See Andrew S. Cairncross's Arden editions of *The Second Part of King Henry VI* (1957; repr. 1962), p. 16, n. 2; and *The Third Part of King Henry VI* (1964), p. 124, n. 14.

correspondences: its configurations of agricultural and military metaphor are provocatively Virgilian. When, for example, Richard says that his 'eyes do hate the dire aspect / Of civil wounds plough'd up with neighbors' sword' (1.3.127–8), one may be reminded of those ploughs in Virgil that turn up remnants of civil war at Philippi. When Richard warns that 'our kingdom's earth should not be soil'd / With that dear blood which it hath fostered' (ll. 125–6), and when Carlisle later prophesies that if Bolingbroke is crowned 'The blood of English shall manure the ground' (4.1.38), one may recall those broad plains of Haemus that twice battened on Roman blood. Such passages reveal an unnatural union of bloodshed and husbandry similar to that in the first tetralogy: blood, the spilling of which connotes political upheaval and moral disorder, here functions as manure, the rich *fimum* with which Virgil's farmer fertilizes the land. The substitution of blood for dung perverts natural process; yet only by spilling such blood will the English, like the Romans in their civil wars, be able to expiate the curse which, in Carlisle's view, will be brought on their nation by the deposition of its rightful monarch. Only by fertilizing the soil with blood will they be able to make the land flourish anew. Such a process would seem to validate a providential view of history.

The famous garden scene, too, may owe a small debt to Virgil. True, the metaphors that govern the scene – tilling the fat soil, eradicating weeds, and executing fast-growing sprays – were, as I have said, traditional, and Shakespeare may have gleaned them from many sources. But none of the supposed sources deals with these activities so didactically as Virgil does in *Georgics* 3. When Shakespeare's gardener instructs his man how to plant and prune trees, or tells him that

> We at time of year
> Do wound the bark, the skin of our fruit-trees,
> Lest, being over-proud in sap and blood,
> With too much riches it confound itself
>
> (3.4.57–60)

we of course understand that he is referring to the proper tending of the kingdom. Virgil is not so

overtly metaphorical. Yet at times his voice sounds remarkably like that of Shakespeare's Gardener:

> Some trees await the arches of the bent layer, and slips set while yet quick in their own soil; others need no root, and the pruner fears not to take the topmost spray and again entrust it to the earth....Up! therefore, ye husbandmen, learn the culture proper to each after its kind; your wild fruits tame by tillage, and let not your soil lie idle. (ll. 26–37)

Such are the voices of practical wisdom and common sense. Their home-spun didacticism is a quality lacking in other sources and analogues.

These correspondences, of course, do not persuade us that Shakespeare had immediate recourse to the *Georgics* while writing his history plays. Deep sources may work like subterranean springs, nourishing and enriching the soil but unobserved, only occasionally bubbling to the surface to make their presence known. Much of the imagery I have cited is too commonplace to allow us to assume in good faith that Shakespeare was conscious of his source. Yet other evidence may make that assumption more tenable, and one finds it in *Henry V*.

In an exhaustive study, T. W. Baldwin has shown that Canterbury's analogy between the kingdom of men and the kingdom of bees was drawn from the *Georgics* and commentary by Willichius.[16] Canterbury's diction and sentiment are, like Virgil's, didactic. His emphasis on the division of labour, on the various elements of society working in harmony for the common good and in obedience to a monarch, distils the essence of *Georgics* 4, where Virgil's bees, too, are emblematic of hard-working citizens who labour co-operatively in the service of a king who is 'the guardian of their toils', *ille operum custos* (l. 125). Some scholars think that Shakespeare may have been indebted for the analogy to Pliny's *Natural History* 11 or to Plato's *Republic* 8, probably by way of Lyly's *Euphues* or Elyot's *Governour*. Baldwin proves otherwise. Shakespeare, like Willichius alone, begins his passage by defining the

---

[16] See Baldwin, *Small Latine & Lesse Greeke*, vol. 2, pp. 472–9.

function of rulers in an ideal city – 'They have a king, and officers of sorts' (1.2.190) – following which he differentiates the bees who stay at home from those who work abroad much as Virgil does:

> some, like magistrates, correct at home;
> Others, like merchants, venture trade abroad;
> Others, like soldiers, armed in their stings,
> Make boot upon the summer's velvet buds...
>
> (ll. 191–4)

Shakespeare then returns to Willichius to classify his bees, though he takes many of his verbal details from Virgil: the emperor surveys his masons (masons is a word one finds only in Virgil); civil citizens knead up honey; mechanic porters crowd in their heavy burdens at his narrow gate; the sad-eyed justice delivers up the lazy drone to execution. In the end, Shakespeare reshapes both the classification and the details 'in accordance with his own fundamental concept of the English commonwealth';[17] but there is no better evidence than this speech that his reading of Virgil was guided by a humanist commentary that encouraged him to relate agriculture to broader moral and historical concerns.

Canterbury's speech crowns the references to bees found in earlier plays. We may recall that as early as *2 Henry VI*, Warwick imagined that Gloucester's murder would spark the citizens to mutiny like bees without their king. Henry IV, too, used a bee analogy to distinguish the order of his own reign from the disorder he fears will threaten Hal's. Henry begins his diatribe proverbially: 'Most subject is the fattest soil to weeds,' he says of Hal; 'And he, the noble image of my youth, / Is overspread with them' (*2 Henry IV*, 4.4.54–6).[18] To press the point, he forsakes garden imagery for apian. He borrows Virgil's description of bees engendered in the molten flesh of slaughtered oxen (*Georgics* 4.281 ff.) and turns it into a metaphor for Hal's unwillingness to give up his riotous companions: ''Tis seldom when the bee doth leave her comb / In the dead carrion' (ll. 79–80).[19] Henry looks back upon his own kingship, in contrast, as a period of georgic productivity. When he awakens to find his crown missing and thinks that Hal, in his zeal to supplant him, has stolen it, Henry comments on the contrast.

As king, Henry claims, he, 'like the bee', sucked 'from every flower / The virtuous sweets'; and, his 'thighs pack'd with wax', his mouth 'with honey', he brought it 'to the hive'. But his boast yields to lament when he notes that in payment for his industry, he, 'like the bees', is 'murd'red for [his] pains' (4.5.74–8). Such activity may occur within nature; but it leaves Henry, who thinks Hal wishes him dead, with a 'bitter taste'. Canterbury's assurance that Hal has restored a Hyblaean order to the kingdom, therefore, merely puts such fears to rest and brings the bee imagery full circle.

Hal's reign is dramatized in imaginative opposition to Richard's. Richard farmed the realm badly: he neglected to prune superfluous branches, his garden swarmed with caterpillars, and his vanity yielded a dismal harvest of disobedience. Hal's 'vanities', on the other hand, merely disguised his

> discretion with a coat of folly,
> As gardeners do with ordure hide those roots
> That shall first spring and be most delicate.
>
> (*Henry V*, 2.4.38–40)

Throughout the second tetralogy Shakespeare insists that prudence and economy are the cornerstones of good government, as they are of farming; and for the most part, he uses agrarian imagery to illustrate the extremes of excess and neglect of which Richard, Henry, and, of course, Falstaff are guilty.[20] Only Hal

---

17 Baldwin, *Small Latine & Lesse Greeke*, vol. 2, p. 477.

18 Compare Tilley, *A Dictionary of the Proverbs*, W241: 'Weeds come forth on the fattest soil if it is untilled.' Lyly uses the proverb in *Euphues* as well.

19 In his Arden edition of *The Second Part of King Henry IV* (1966), p. 143, A. R. Humphreys suggests that this image may echo Judges 14: 8: 'he [Samson] turned out of the way to see the carkeise of the Lion: and beholde, there was a swarme of Bees and hony in the carkeise of the Lion.' Shakespeare's allusion may be biblical; but the Virgilian analogue, dealing as it does with the order of a kingdom and the myth of goodness springing from decay, would seem to have more suggestive power.

20 R. J. Dorius, in 'A Little More than a Little', *Shakespeare Quarterly*, 11 (1960), 13–26, argues convincingly that through agrarian imagery in the histories, Shakespeare meditates on the virtues of prudence and economy. His reading focuses largely on the garden scene in *Richard II* and on Falstaff as an emblem of imprudent growth and excess.

achieves the Aristotelian mean. As Falstaff puts it, the cold blood Hal inherited from his father 'he hath, like lean, sterile, and bare land, manur'd, husbanded and till'd with excellent endeavor of drinking good and good store of fertile sherris' (2 Henry IV, 4.3.116–20); and allowing for Falstaff's humorous identification of cause, we recognize in these lines a truth. Hal's good husbandry *does* cleanse England of the blood that for too long manured the ground and sprinkled his guilty father to make him grow.

Ironically, Hal husbands England best by making wars on France. There, he attempts to forge an alliance between military and agricultural terminology much as Virgil does. He rallies the confidence of his soldiers by telling them he is proud of their roots:

> And you, good yeomen,
> Whose limbs were made in England, show us here
> The mettle of your pasture.
> (*Henry V*, 3.1.25–7)[21]

The true hero, as is implied in the pun on mettle, is he who willingly gives up the ploughshare for the sword; and the Chorus approves the exchange when 'honor's thought / Reigns solely in the breast of every man', and 'They sell the pasture...to buy the horse' (2. Chorus. 3–5). In times of national crisis, such a sale is worthy of the farmer; and though he may exchange one occupation for another, the idea of labour remains constant. Farmers become 'warriors for the working day' who toil 'in the painful field' (4.3.109, 111).

Hal's victory over France is marked by a strikingly Virgilian speech by the Duke of Burgundy. He describes France as a place of political and moral decay – the 'best garden of the world', he calls her, from whom 'mangled Peace' has 'too long been chas'd':

And all her husbandry doth lie on heaps,
Corrupting in it own fertility.
Her vine, the merry cheerer of the heart,
Unpruned dies; her hedges even-pleach'd,
Like prisoners wildly overgrown with hair,
Put forth disorder'd twigs; her fallow leas
The darnel, hemlock, and rank fumitory
Doth root upon, while that the coulter rusts

That should deracinate such savagery.
The even mead, that erst brought sweetly forth
The freckled cowslip, burnet, and green clover,
Wanting the scythe, all uncorrected, rank,
Conceives by idleness, and nothing teems
But hateful docks, rough thistles, kecksies, burrs,
Losing both beauty and utility.
And all our vineyards, fallows, meads, and hedges,
Defective in their natures, grow to wildness.

(5.2.39–55)

As John H. Betts observes, Burgundy's fourfold division of husbandry into 'vineyards, fallows, meads, and hedges' may owe something to Virgil's division of the *Georgics* into 'viticulture, crops, pasture, and bee-keeping'.[22] More persuasively, Betts notes that Shakespeare uses a catalogue of noxious weeds – 'darnel, hemlock, and rank fumitory' that invade the cornfield, and 'hateful docks, rough thistles, kecksies, burrs', the pasture – remarkably similar to a catalogue in *Georgics* 1:[23] 'Soon, too, on the corn fell trouble, the baneful mildew feeding on the stems, and the lazy thistle bristling in the fields; the crops die, and instead springs up a prickly growth, burs and caltrops, and

---

21 Compare, for example, Virgil's testimony that Italy's soil has produced a vigorous breed of men, hardy warriors: *Georgics* 2.167–70.

22 John H. Betts, 'Classical Allusions in Shakespeare's *Henry V* with Special Reference to Virgil', *Greece and Rome*, 15 (1968), 147–63; pp. 156–7. Betts also discusses the debt Shakespeare owed to Virgil for Canterbury's speech on the kingdom of bees (pp. 152–5), though for the most part he simply repeats Baldwin's findings.

23 Fleming's translation of this passage (*Georgiks* 1, p. 7) is perhaps closer in tone to Burgundy's speech than Fairclough's translation, is though there are not enough verbal parallels, in this passage or in others, to suggest that Shakespeare had recourse to the Fleming translation:

And by and by mishap was sent [and casualtie] to corne
[Namely] that blasting mischeefous should eat the stems and stalks,
And idle [frutelesse] thistles should grow stiffe and rough in fields;
The corne decaies and dies, great store of sharpe and pricking weeds,
As burs and brambles come in place, and naughtie darnell with
The barren otes beare sway among the goodly plowed lands.

amid the smiling corn the luckless darnel and barren oats hold sway' (ll. 150–4). But most persuasively, I think, in this speech a factual account of agricultural devastation becomes, as it does in Virgil, a mirror of the moral sickness that war inflicts on a nation. Burgundy's speech is reminiscent of the famous passage in which Virgil bids Octavius to get back to the business of peace. 'Gods of my country,' he prays, 'stay not this young prince from aiding a world uptorn!': 'For here are right and wrong inverted; so many wars overrun the world, so many are the shapes of sin; the plough meets not its honor due; our lands, robbed of the tillers, lie waste, and the crooked pruning-hooks are forged into stiff swords' (1.498–508). In his fine edition of *Henry V*, Gary Taylor marks the similarity between Virgil's *aratrum* (l. 506) – plough or coulter – that lies idle while war rages, and Shakespeare's 'coulter' that 'rusts' while farmers, turned soldiers, 'do but meditate on blood' (l. 60).[24]

In a sense, when Burgundy pleads for 'gentle Peace' to 'bless us with her former qualities' (ll. 65, 67), he makes the same plea that Virgil makes to Octavius. Hal, of course, has already brought a *Pax Henriciana* to England; and here, he is asked merely to spread the *pax* to France. Burgundy's speech thus holds the promise of stability. But the promise goes unfulfilled. History does not move inexorably toward a final fruition. As the Epilogue reminds us, war will return to France, blood will once again manure the English soil, and only after another tetralogy will the boar who ravages the land be slain by a shadowy character named Henry Tudor who, in dramatic terms, is far less substantial than those characters who turn the land to dust.

The Virgilian source that I contend underlies these plays ought further to suggest that Shakespeare was far from endorsing a simple, schematic, providential view of English history – what Tillyard called the Tudor myth.[25] The first tetralogy, true, ends with the promise of a Tudor peace; but the agrarian imagery in those plays points clearly to a conception of history that is less secure, in which labour does not guarantee a good harvest, and in which it is the nature of things to speed towards the worst. Something in his direct sources, Hall and Holinshed, must

have inspired Shakespeare to imagine the period of English dynastic struggle as an unresolved tension between farming and politics, natural and unnatural behaviour, progress and relapse – a period wherein tilling the soil and spilling blood, no matter how opposed in spirit, were metaphorically linked.[26] Yet he would have found this tension only implicit in the chronicles: in so far as they adopted a Tudor bias, Hall and Holinshed reconciled such oppositions in one purposive design. Virgil, however, by yoking agricultural processes to civil war in the *Georgics*, made the tension explicit; and by doing so, he provided a source compatible with Shakespeare's less orthodox understanding of English history.

---

[24] See Gary Taylor's edition of *Henry V* for The Oxford Shakespeare (Oxford, 1982), p. 267, n. 46. Fleming translates *aratrum* as both 'plough' and 'coulter': though 'plough' is now the preferred translation, 'coulter' evidently was acceptable and common in Elizabethan England.

[25] The most cogent refutation of Tillyard is Robert Ornstein's *A Kingdom for a Stage: The Achievement of Shakespeare's History Plays* (Cambridge, Mass., 1972), which demonstrates that few chroniclers espoused what Tillyard regards as the Tudor myth, a Yorkist interpretation of the usurpation of Richard II's throne. Hall, though he glorifies the Tudor accession, does so largely by casting aspersions on Richard III and his family, not by subscribing to their reading of the curse brought about by a Lancastrian sin against God's anointed. Among Shakespeare's known sources, argues Ornstein, Holinshed alone subscribes to that version of history. Yet Holinshed, one ought to keep in mind, was one of Shakespeare's *chief* sources, particularly for the second tetralogy.

[26] It is curious that Shakespeare does not employ agrarian imagery to define historical patterns in any history plays other than the two tetralogies. *King John* is devoid of such imagery, and so are the Roman histories where, by Virgilian example, one might most expect to find it. Apart from the possible allusion in the portents of Caesar's death, Shakespeare ignores the *Georgics* even in *Julius Caesar*, which was written within a year of *Henry V*, the play in which agricultural reference is most abundant. One answer for the disparity may lie in Shakespeare's response to his direct sources. The English chronicles – full of intricate political manoeuvres, actions repeated and frustrated, patterns of behaviour – may have suggested to Shakespeare the cyclical nature of agricultural process, while Plutarch, who was less interested in patterns than in the individual achievements of noble men, may not.

Occasionally in the history plays we are offered a glimpse of an ideal state. Perhaps Shakespeare believed that patterns of agriculture, long disrupted by war, might again prevail if kings, like good farmers, laboured to master the land. But he also knew, like Virgil, that such mastery might be a fleeting thing. As John Wilders argues in *The Lost Garden*, Shakespeare 'was too conscious of the precariousness of peace and the destructiveness of human nature to entertain any ideas of progress'.[27] Thus reference to agriculture, nourished by his reading of the *Georgics*, became a vehicle by which he tested and subverted any such notion of progress fostered by the chroniclers.

---

[27] John Wilders, *The Lost Garden: A View of Shakespeare's English and Roman History Plays* (London, Basingstoke and Totowa, Nj, 1978), p. 18.

THE NATURE OF TOPICALITY IN 'LOVE'S LABOUR'S LOST'

MARY ELLEN LAMB

Love's Labour's Lost remains something of an anomaly among Shakespeare's plays. Of all his comedies, this one is still often perceived as narrowly aristocratic, an obscure piece of coterie drama never truly intended to appeal to a general audience. This view has been formed by the massive commentary on the play's references to the Harvey–Nashe controversy, Raleigh's supposed 'School of Night', and other 'topical puzzles' still referred to, often in passing or in footnotes, by even the best and most recent scholarship.[1] A re-examination of existing evidence about the probable original audience for *Love's Labour's Lost* casts grave suspicions on the kind of topicality understood only by Renaissance courtiers. Yet topicality itself cannot be altogether dismissed in a play for which the major male characters – the King of Navarre, Boyet, Marcade, Armado, Moth, Berowne, Longaville, and Dumain – were all named after military leaders then waging a civil war in France.[2] In this essay, I argue that *Love's*

Studies, 10 (1977), 17–41) mentions contemporary allusions to John Florio, Gabriel Harvey, Thomas Harriot (p. 40, n. 14); R. S. White, 'Oaths and the Anticomic Spirit in *Love's Labour's Lost*', in *Shakespeare and His Contemporaries*, ed. Alan Brissenden (Adelaide, 1976), admits the possibility of obscure topicality with the clause, 'whether this play is a satire on a particular group of Englishmen (the "School of Night") or not', before going on to other matters (p. 13); older but influential are Ronald Berman, *A Reader's Guide to Shakespeare's Plays* (Glenview, Illinois, 1973), p. 34, which cites Bradbrook's *School of Night* as 'of great interest'; the most recent Arden edition's introduction by Richard David (1951, repr. 1968), which describes the play as 'a battle in a private war between court factions', p. xliii; Geoffrey Bullough, in *Narrative and Dramatic Sources of Shakespeare*, 8 vols. (1957–75), mentions the topical references to the School of Night and others briefly, to describe the play as 'an intellectual fantasy, the nearest to a play of ideas that Shakespeare ever wrote, except perhaps *Troilus and Cressida*' (vol. 1, p. 427). A notable exception is John Kerrigan's edition of *Love's Labour's Lost* (Harmondsworth, 1982), pp. 7–13, which defends the play as a crowd-pleaser and discourages the topical approach.

[2] I am adopting the standard 1593–5 date for *Love's Labour's Lost*; later revisions would not have altered the basic concept of the play. Other critics who have noted this topicality are discussed below. Navarre's name 'Ferdinand' in the dramatis personae and some speech headings is puzzling, but since no one in the play calls him Ferdinand, the audience would not have been bothered: see John Dover Wilson, ed., *Love's Labour's Lost* (Cambridge, 1923; 2nd edn. 1962), p. 138n. Longaville was the Duc de Longueville, probably Henri d'Orléans who died in 1595 rather than Leonor; Henri was with Navarre and his English allies at the siege of Rouen: see Sir Thomas Coningsby, *Journal of the Siege of Rouen, 1591*, ed. John G. Nichols for *Camden Miscellany*, 1 (1847), 17, 67n. Berowne referred either to Armand de Gontant, Marshal Biron, Navarre's principal general who died in 1595, or to his son Charles who replaced his father in that post. Boyet was probably the Boyset who led Huguenot

---

[1] Typical is Marion Trousdale's excellent study, *Shakespeare and the Rhetoricians* (Chapel Hill, North Carolina, 1982), pp. 95–113; among the 'topical puzzles' she accepts are allusions to Gabriel Harvey, Raleigh, Chapman, and the School of Night, before she goes on to more interesting material with the admission 'it is a game difficult for all but source hunters to play' (p. 96); while discounting its importance, the presence of 'a good deal of topical satire' of the kind described by M. C. Bradbrook and Frances Yates is acknowledged in Kenneth Muir, *The Sources of Shakespeare's Plays* (1977), p. 78; Louis A. Montrose's brilliant article, '"Sport by sport o'erthrown": *Love's Labour's Lost* and the Politics of Play' (*Texas Studies in Literature and Language*, 18 (1976–7), 528–52) mentions briefly the 'infamous School of Night' as one of two foci of topical hypotheses (p. 550, n. 14); R. Chris Hassel, 'Love Versus Charity in *Love's Labor's Lost*' (*Shakespeare*

Labour's Lost was no more or less 'aristocratic' in appeal than Shakespeare's other earlier plays, that what topicality it possesses was available to a wide audience, and that, finally, we need to revise our way of looking at topicality at least in *Love's Labour's Lost* and perhaps in other plays, as well.

The power of this narrow perception of the play as purely aristocratic extends beyond criticism to productions, as demonstrated by the descriptions of recent reviewers: it is Shakespeare's 'most artificial comedy', 'learned', a 'comedy of language'.[3] The implication is clear: *Love's Labour's Lost* is unsuited to modern audiences, often composed at least in part of common folk bored by such arcane matters. But this perception of the play ignores its very real success on stage, at least from the time of Peter Brook's 1946 production at Stratford-upon-Avon and Hugh Hunt's 1949 production at the Old Vic.[4] More recently, John Barton's 1978 Royal Shakespeare Company production has been judged the 'most successful of the four productions presented on the main stage' that season, while Michael Langham's Stratford, Ontario production was so popular in its 1983 Third Stage performances that it was moved to the Main Stage for the summer of 1984.[5] This stage success of a supposedly unactable play indicates that it is time for a reassessment.

As with any convincing distortion, the old perception of *Love's Labour's Lost* is not entirely without grounds. The play is concerned with language – what Shakespeare play is not? The language of its lovers is at times mannered – but is not the language of the early Romeo and the lovers in *A Midsummer Night's Dream* equally artificial in places? The bright thrusts of verbal wit exchanged, for example, between Rosaline and Boyet (4.1) are not more sophisticated than the exchange between Romeo and Mercutio (2.4).[6] Its lovers are aristocratic, but so are the lovers in most of Shakespeare's comedies. In short, the sophistication present in *Love's Labour's Lost* does not make it qualitatively different from his other early plays. It appears that the concept of the play as 'aristocratic' has encouraged an emphasis on its less 'popular' elements generally unappreciated by modern audiences.

To focus on the 'mannered' quality of *Love's*

Labour's Lost, as many critics have done, is to miss its truly broad and sometimes gross humour, not beyond the reach of most twelve-year-olds, Renaissance or modern. The male lovers spying on each other reading love sonnets, each unaware that he himself is spied upon in return; the disastrous Masque of the Muscovites in which the young lords are so thoroughly put down ('they have measur'd many a mile / To tread a measure with you on this grass.' Reply: 'Ask them how many inches / Is in

---

forces: see Antony Colynet, *The True History of the Civill Warres of France...1585–1591* (1591), LL1. Dumain was the powerful Charles de Lorraine, Duc de Mayenne, the League's most prominent general and Navarre's most formidable enemy. Marcade, Philippe Emmanuel de Lorraine, Duc de Mercoeur, 'Duke Mercury' in English reports, also fought for the League, especially in Britanny, where he was governor: Sir John Norreys, *The True Report of the Service in Britanie* (1591), A2ᵛ–A3. For Moth and Armado, see discussion below. Further background information, somewhat different from mine, is included in Hugh M. Richmond, 'Shakespeare's Navarre', *Huntington Library Quarterly*, 42 (1979), 193–216.

3 Jean Fuzier, review of Royal Shakespeare Company *Love's Labour's Lost*, *Cahiers Élisabéthains*, 14 (1978), 123–4; Anthony Curtis, review of RSC *Love's Labour's Lost*, *Drama*, 133 (1979), 52; Carol Rosen, review of *Love's Labour's Lost* in New York, *Shakespeare Quarterly*, 31 (1980), 198.

4 T. C. Kemp and J. C. Trewin, *The Stratford Festival* (Birmingham, 1953), p. 216; 'Stratford', *Drama*, Summer, 1946, p. 33, 'Old Vic Opens Season with Shakespeare Play', *New York Times*, 24 Oct. 1949, p. 18; J. C. Trewin, 'The World of the Theatre', *Illustrated London News*, 5 Nov. 1949, p. 712; R. D. Smith, 'Arts and Entertainment: The Old Vic Made New', *The New Statesman and Nation*, 29 Oct. 1949, p. 483. Possibly influential in the Hunt production was Harley Granville-Barker, *Prefaces to Shakespeare*, 2 vols. (Princeton, 1946–7), vol. 2, pp. 413–49 (first published 1930), which presents concrete ideas for productions although his general tone is pessimistic about the possibility of success.

5 Fuzier, p. 123. Many other recent productions are listed together with their reviews in the *Shakespeare Quarterly* bibliography (1979–82), which lists nineteen separate performances in the past few years in England, the United States, France, Greece, Bulgaria, and Italy. Available reviews are generally favourable.

6 All citations from *Love's Labour's Lost* are from Richard David's Arden edition (1951, repr. 1968); citations from other plays are from *The Riverside Shakespeare* (Boston, 1974).

one mile', 5.2.186–9); the naive incompetence of the Masque of the Nine Worthies ('If your ladyship would say, "Thanks, Pompey," I had done', 5.2.551): the humour of these pivotal points is not subtle. Other broad strokes are scattered through the play: Armado's verbal pretensions which slide helplessly to impossible obscenities ('It is the king's most sweet pleasure and affection to congratulate the princess at her pavilion in the posteriors of this day', 5.1.79–81); Costard's denial of Jaquenetta's virginity to avoid imprisonment ('I deny her virginity: I was taken with a maid', 1.1.287); Holofernes's pedantic conceit ('This is a gift that I have, simple, simple; a foolish extravagant spirit, full of forms, figures, shapes, objects, ideas, apprehensions, motions, revolutions . . . I am thankful for it', 4.2.64–70). The occasional obscurity of language that does exist in, for example, the exchange between Moth and Costard (5.1) can be better explicated by reference to Ellis's book on *Shakespeare's Lusty Punning in 'Love's Labor's Lost'* than to Yates's book on the School of Night and the Harvey–Nashe controversy in *A Study of 'Love's Labour's Lost'*.[7] In fact, it was for the vulgar passages 'which ought not to have been exhibited, as we are told they were, to a maiden queen',[8] that Samuel Johnson criticized the play, not for its élitism.

Despite claims to the contrary, the play's early stage history does not suggest 'a peculiar connection with the court'.[9] According to the title-page of the First Quarto, it was performed for the Queen in 1597 or 1598, but court performances were not unusual for Shakespeare's plays. According to the title-page of the Second Quarto, it was acted at the Globe as well as at Blackfriars. While the audience at the Globe was apparently better-heeled than has been previously assumed, neither audience contained large numbers of nobles high enough in rank to be familiar with the court gossip imagined as the primary subject of this 'coterie' drama. Another performance for James's queen in 1604 or 1605 at Southampton's house does not reflect any special respect for the play as aristocratic entertainment. According to the letter which records this performance, Sir Walter Cope had been searching unsuccessfully for 'players, jugglers, and such kind of creatures' when Burbage approached him with the revival of an old play named 'Love's Labour Lost' [*sic*] which he recommended for its 'wit and mirth', since there was 'no new play that the Queen has not seen'.[10]

Neither Cope nor Burbage conveyed the impression that *Love's Labour's Lost* was a particularly aristocratic play – quite the reverse, in fact. Cope classed 'players' with 'jugglers and such kind of creatures', while Burbage praised *Love's Labour's Lost* as filled with 'mirth' as well as 'wit', suitable because the Queen had not yet seen it. Surely Queen Anne, new to the throne of England, could not have been expected to follow the ins and outs of supposed topical allusions, several years out of date by then, with any real pleasure. Burbage apparently expected her to enjoy the play for its humour, not for its references. This transaction between Cope and Burbage also lends strength to Harbage's discounting of the claim that *Love's Labour's Lost* was originally intended for performance at court or in some noble's private house.[11] Often, nobles would simply hire an old play already in a company's repertory, as Cope apparently hired *Love's Labour's Lost* from Burbage. Thus, there is no evidence in the play's stage history that this was more or less 'aristocratic' than Shakespeare's other plays.

---

[7] Herbert Ellis, *Shakespeare's Lusty Punning in 'Love's Labor's Lost'*, Studies in English Literature, 81 (The Hague, 1973); Frances Yates, *A Study of 'Love's Labour's Lost'* (Cambridge, 1936).

[8] Samuel Johnson, 'Johnson on Shakespeare', *The Works of Samuel Johnson*, ed. Arthur Sherbo (New Haven, 1968), vol. 7, p. 287. It is the meaning of the obscenities, more than topical allusions, that has been lost over time: Granville-Barker pronounces the highly spirited sexual innuendoes between Rosaline and Boyet in 4.1 as 'gibberish', elsewhere exclaiming 'how few of Shakespeare's love scenes now or later need it embarrass anyone to overhear!' (pp. 435, 444).

[9] David, p. xliii. I cite David extensively because of the influence of his edition.

[10] Letter from Sir Walter Cope to Viscount Cranborne, *HMC Report on the Calendar of MSS of the Marquess of Salisbury* (1933), vol 16, p. 415.

[11] Alfred Harbage, '*Love's Labor's Lost* and the Early Shakespeare' (*Philological Quarterly*, 41 (1962), 18–36) p. 19, citing Kittredge and also similar claims by E. K. Chambers, Dover Wilson, and Richard David.

Similarly, two contemporary notices of *Love's Labour's Lost* do not reflect any particularly élite concept of the play. There are no grounds for suspecting that Francis Meres, a learned schoolmaster soon to become a lowly rector, moved in elevated circles. Yet he, like another viewer Robert Tofte, a 'gentleman' without high rank or courtly status, saw the play and appeared to approve it. Meres made no distinction between *Love's Labour's Lost* and *The Merchant of Venice* in his comparison of Shakespeare and Plautus (a very funny and not especially aristocratic playwright) as 'best for Comedy'.[12] Tofte's description reflects his perception of the play as a love comedy, not a 'coterie' drama. Drawn to see the play by his 'froward Dame', he suffered love pangs for his companion throughout the performance while she 'did sit as skorning of my woes the while'. While the play was 'Tragick' to him as it played out the grief of 'those entrapt in *Cupids* snare', he recognized that 'to euery one (save me) twas *Comicall*'.[13] Like Burbage, Tofte perceived *Love's Labour's Lost* as a *funny* play (at least to one not suffering the pain of love).

How then did this view of *Love's Labour's Lost* as 'coterie' drama get started? The answer lies in the play's topicality. The history of how critics have dealt with the play's topicality, in fact, forms an important record of the kinds of assumptions made about allusions in this play and others. This history falls basically into three phases. The first, exemplified by Sidney Lee's excellent study of 1880, was to identify any obvious similarities between characters and the historical counterparts they were named after; he examined similarities between the character Berowne and Marshal Biron, prominent leader of Navarre's forces, to find them both brave, intelligent, well-loved, but with a fondness for extravagant language. Lee also looked for similarities between events in the play and those in French history. He found as a model for the meeting between Navarre and the Princess of France a conference between Catherine de Medici and Navarre at Saint-Bris in 1586; in each case the Princess was attended by an 'escadron volant' of beautiful ladies.[14] Other critics, following Abel Lefranc, endorsed a meeting between Marguérite de

Valois and Navarre at Nérac in 1578; and, for various reasons, this latter conference became recognized as the general source for the events of the play.[15] A source for the 'academe' in Shakespeare's play was also located in an academy composed of four young lords described in Pierre de la Primaudaye's *French Academie*.[16]

This first phase of criticism was generally marked by impressive historical knowledge and balanced good sense. It recognized the strong impact of these names in England, for the outcome of the French civil wars directly affected the safety of England itself: a victorious French Catholic League, aided by England's old enemy Spain, would pose a direct military threat to England. Moreover, Englishmen, led by the dashing Earl of Essex, were actually fighting and dying beside Navarre's troops; those who survived returned to London to tell their tale. There was little talk of 'coterie' drama or 'in-jokes' with this criticism. Interest in the French civil wars was assumed to be widespread and intense among general audiences. Unfortunately, it was the very meticulousness of this historical method that marked the downfall of this phase: critics using this method looked for consistencies in character and event, and *Love's Labour's Lost* is marked by inconsistencies, notably the inclusion of the Catholic Dumain among three Protestant lords. At that time, the four historical counterparts could not have interacted so amicably and so, Lee suggested, Shakespeare had made a mistake, one natural enough since de Mayenne's name 'was so frequently mentioned in popular accounts of French affairs'.[17] This same search for consistency led to intricate discussions of dating, for the play could not have been written,

---

[12] 'Treatise on Poetry', in *Palladis Tamia* (1598), ed. Don Cameron Allen (Urbana, Illinois, 1933), p. 76.

[13] Robert Tofte, *Alba* (1598), G5.

[14] Sidney Lee, 'A New Study of *Love's Labour's Lost*', *Gentleman's Magazine*, Oct. 1880, pp. 450–1; a recent continuation of Lee's approach is Richmond.

[15] Abel Lefranc, *Sous le Masque de William Shakespeare* (Paris, 1918); accepted by David, p. xxix and Geoffrey Bullough, vol. 1, p. 430.

[16] David, p. xxix; Bullough, vol. 1, p. 427.

[17] Lee, p. 448.

critics claimed, after 1593 when Navarre converted to Catholicism. Assuming the necessity for consistency of tone, Harbage even claimed that the play could not have been written after 1589, when Navarre began his struggles with the League: the play is too light for such a serious subject.[18]

But even discounted, this criticism had its effect on the perception of *Love's Labour's Lost*. It was now established as a topical play, and now critics merely looked elsewhere for less obvious and more consistent allusions. They found them. Holofernes was George Chapman, Gabriel Harvey, and any number of other Elizabethan pedants. According to Fleay, Moth was Nashe and his interactions with Holofernes were a clue to the play's part in the Harvey–Nashe controversy. According to Acheson, the play was an assault on Raleigh's supposed 'School of Night' (born of a phrase in the play) composed of Marlowe, Chapman, Harriot, and others. Yates put both theories together and came up with a concept of the play as a defence of Essex against Raleigh's group, drawing in other Elizabethan figures like Vives and John Eliot, the Duke of Northumberland and Giordano Bruno, into the mixture. The arguments were labyrinthine and endless, making of the play a kind of competitive game, a cross between a crossword puzzle and a tennis match, performed for the diversion of bejewelled courtiers exchanging amused glances as they recognized the references in the play to their acquaintances.[19]

Like the previous phase, this phase assumed biographical counterparts for the characters in the play. For this second group of critics, however, the counterparts were no longer recognizable to a general audience. Dumain was no longer the French de Mayenne: he was Someone Else. The primary meaning of the play lay, in fact, in the recognition of the 'true' identities of the characters. According to an edition as recent and as influential as Richard David's Arden, *Love's Labour's Lost* was 'a battle in a private war between court factions'.[20] Clearly, the only audience for this war of wit was the court itself, a small coterie of Elizabethan nobles. Perhaps just as small a coterie of twentieth-century scholars could, with hard work, be let in on the secret. The rewards were considerable. According to David, the

'solution of the puzzle' of *Love's Labour's Lost* would 'illuminate Shakespeare's own early life'.[21] Like the earlier phase, this phase too fell under its own weight: the arguments became too intricate; the identities became too numerous. It is not so much that the theories were entirely disproved (who could prove that Holofernes was *not* Gabriel Harvey?).[22] Instead, scholars began turning their attention elsewhere, to more literary matters. But, just as the first phase left in its wake the assumption that the characters had consistent, biographical counterparts, so this second phase left the vague but lingering impression that *Love's Labour's Lost* appealed to an élite coterie who alone could properly 'understand' it.

Scholars of the play's topicality are now entering a third phase, in which strict consistency between character and counterpart is no longer assumed. This looser approach may well have been influenced by studies of history plays, for example David Bevington's work on Tudor plays, political 'in terms of ideas and platforms rather than personalities'.[23] Thus, for R. Chris Hassel, including a Catholic among three Protestant lords no longer creates incongruity; instead, it points to 'a central doctrinal debate' between Catholic and Protestant beliefs.[24] Similarly, Albert Tricomi sees the presence of these French lords as forwarding some positive purpose. For him, they are 'part of a deliberate contratopicality' which makes of the play 'an

---

18 Harbage, pp. 24–6.

19 Arthur Acheson, *Shakespeare and the Rival Poet* (1903); supported by M. C. Bradbrook, *The School of Night: A Study in the Literary Relationships of Sir Walter Raleigh* (Cambridge, 1936); Yates, *passim*; summarized in David, pp. xxxiv–xlii.

20 David, p. xliii; Bullough, p. 433 claims the play best suited to 'the intellectuals in the Essex circle and the Inns of Court'.

21 David, p. xvi.

22 The School of Night theory was convincingly put down by Ernest A. Strathmann, *Sir Walter Raleigh: A Study in Elizabethan Skepticism* (New York, 1951), pp. 262–70.

23 David Bevington, *Tudor Drama and Politics: A Critical Approach to Topical Meaning* (Cambridge, Mass., 1968), p. 25. This insight is not, however, applied to *Love's Labour's Lost*.

24 R. Chris Hassel, pp. 11–42.

appealing piece of Arcadian escapism and fantasy'.[25] This broader focus seems promising, although there are perhaps still problems in these particular studies. The intensity of English interest in the civil wars was based most strongly on their potential threat against English safety; furthermore, the characters were named after military leaders, not theologians. In this context, the French names suggest the play's concern with political problems more than with doctrinal matters. Tricomi's 'contratopicality' seems a partial truth. The contemporary associations with the names no doubt made Love's Labour's Lost seem all the more removed from the grim problems of the real world, set as it is in a removed garden of a country estate. But works of 'Arcadian escapism' in that day were notoriously bound up in the problems of the civilized world. Whether in works by Sidney, Spenser, or lesser authors, simple shepherds piping on a hill usually pointed, in one way or another, to the situation at court or in urban society. In the same way, the apparent frivolity of the 'escapist' Love's Labour's Lost in no way precludes a concern with deeper matters.

While some problems and differences of opinion remain in recent topical criticism of this play, these studies are successfully struggling against negative attitudes towards this form of criticism. These attitudes proceed in part from the excesses of the second stage, which acted upon otherwise reputable scholars 'as catnip acts upon perfectly sane cats'.[26] But there is another more deep-seated concern as well, expressed by George K. Hunter in his review of Hugh M. Richmond's *Puritans and Libertines: Anglo-French Literary Relations in the Reformation*:

His account of the actual play of *Love's Labor's Lost* is fatally weakened...by his tendency to explain what appears in the play as if it were a mirror of what happened at Nérac in 1578. The internal economy of the play, that by which it is either good or not good, is lost sight of; and better reasons why things are as they are seem to be ignored in favor of dubious historical speculations.[27]

Hunter's criticism points out the tendency of studies in topicality to locate the primary 'meaning' or focus of the play outside the play in the historical

counterparts themselves, thereby diverting the critic from more central concerns, such as the play's quality.

Hunter's criticism of Richmond's study cannot be overlooked by scholars of topicality. We must invest the play, not the sources, with meaning. Perhaps the problem lies in treating topical sources too differently from literary ones.[28] We seldom fall into the same error with literary sources. We do not locate the meaning of *The Winter's Tale*, for example, in its similarities or differences from *Pandosto*. We do not expect its audience to smile in bemused delight when Leontes does not commit suicide as did his literary counterpart. We do not expect its audience to mentally tick off the differences between *The Winter's Tale* and *Pandosto* and to discuss them with animation after the performance. Similarly, identifying the topical sources underlying *Love's Labour's Lost* is not necessary to an understanding of the play for the average theatre-goer. An audience does not need to chuckle at obscure references to the goings-on at Nérac to appreciate the broad humour of the lords' bumbling attempts to woo their ladies. Such an expectation would make the play inaccessible to all but a few Renaissance courtiers and modern historians of sixteenth-century France.

However, just like literary sources, topical sources can provide a valuable critical tool. It is useful, for example, to consider how *Pandosto* and the Greek

---

25 Albert Tricomi, 'The Witty Idealization of the French Court in *Love's Labor's Lost*', *Shakespeare Studies*, 12 (1979), 25–33; Louis A. Montrose, pp. 528–52, recognizes political implications in this play but concludes that the characters were named to recall the French wars because Shakespeare was contriving to point up the wavering interest of some of his characters (p. 544); Kerrigan states that 'where the play uses history, it uses it as something to escape from' (p. 11).

26 Harbage, p. 23.

27 George K. Hunter, 'Recent Studies in the Renaissance', *Studies in English Literature, 1500–1900*, 23 (1983), 145–76; pp. 158–9.

28 An interesting treatment of *Love's Labour's Lost*, Stanley Wells's title 'Shakespeare without Sources' shows how far topical sources are considered to be 'real' sources: in *Shakespearian Comedy*, ed. Malcolm Bradbury and David Palmer, Stratford-upon-Avon Studies, 14 (1972), pp. 58–74.

romances it draws on fit into the ideas and problems explored in *The Winter's Tale*. One result of this study is to give prominence to the powerlessness of man over his own destiny, an important issue present in both works. Similarly, the real-life events underlying *Love's Labour's Lost* show striking consonance with a theme emerging from purely literary studies of the play: oath-breaking.[29] Historically oriented critics have glanced at Navarre's bad record in keeping promises in his romantic liaisons and his religious affiliation.[30] However, a fresh examination of topical sources for *Love's Labour's Lost* suggests that they reflect on oath-breaking even more than has previously been suspected.

It is with some trepidation that I offer this re-examination of the sources underlying *Love's Labour's Lost*. Especially when I suggest a new historical model for Moth, I feel vulnerable to the charge of engaging in 'dubious historical speculations'. Let me say two things in my defence. First, topical source-hunting, as with literary source-hunting, involves a certain amount of fishing. One can hardly ever 'know' absolutely which source Shakespeare used. Perhaps the best test, after its availability is determined, is its usefulness, the extent to which it illuminates a problem or issue in a play. In this respect topical sources face the same problems as literary sources, and the standards for accepting or rejecting them should be no more or less rigorous. The topical sources I suggest below are possible and useful; I do not claim more for them. Secondly, the topical sources examined below must not be invested with more meaning than a literary source. If Moth and Armado are indeed drawn from a military context, as I claim, their presence does not make of the play some abstruse political allegory. Their 'meaning' is in the play itself, in their interactions, in their jokes, in their interpretations, just as if they had been drawn from a sixteenth-century poem of romance instead. It is this insistence that the locus of meaning lies in the play itself, not in the play's relationship to its topical sources, that separates this study from many others before it. The topical sources underlying *Love's Labour's Lost* focus on the theme of oath-breaking already in the play. Knowledge of them is no more necessary for an understanding or appreciation of this play than the knowledge of literary sources underlying other plays, although, like literary sources, they provide a useful critical tool, nothing more. With these disclaimers, then, let me proceed.

As critics have often pointed out, much of the plot and even much of the humour of *Love's Labour's Lost* turns on the forswearing of vows. In their ignorance of their own natures, the lords in the play swear impossible oaths: to study for three years, in which time they will not see a woman, or eat more than one meal in a day, or sleep more than three hours in a night. This resolved, with some objections from Berowne, they immediately fall in love with the Princess of France and her three ladies who have come to their court to negotiate her father's business. Rationalizing their breach of honour with many arguments, the lords disguise themselves as Muscovites to court their ladies. The ladies, warned of their disguise, don masks and exchange favours so that each lord woos the wrong woman and is again forsworn. After Marcade's sudden entrance with news of the King's death, the ladies agree to accept their lords' marriage proposals only if they perform certain penances for a year to prove the strength of their vows.

Oath-breaking is even more of an issue in the topical sources for the play than has been previously assumed by critics. Much has been written of the real Navarre's notorious sexual infidelities and how they relate at some level to the necessary testing of the character Navarre's vow of love for the Princess of France at the end of *Love's Labour's Lost*. But his open adultery, and its consequences leading to war, during the oft-cited embassy of his wife Marguérite de Valois, his mother Catherine de Medici, and the 'escadron volant' of beautiful ladies to his estate at Nérac in 1578 have not been related to the theme of

---

29 James L. Calderwood, '*Love's Labor's Lost*: A Wantoning with Words', *Studies in English Literature, 1500–1900*, 5 (1965), 317–32; pp. 324–5; R. S. White, 'Oaths and the Anticomic Spirit in *Love's Labor's Lost*', in *Shakespeare and His Contemporaries*, ed. Alan Brissenden (Adelaide, 1976), pp. 11–29.

30 Bullough, p. 430; Hassel, p. 26; Richmond, pp. 119–200; Tricomi, p. 30.

the play.[31] From the beginning, those assembled at Nérac, ostensibly to celebrate the reunion of Navarre and his wife, paid scant respect to marital vows. Instead of courting his wife, Navarre immediately fell in love with Victoria d'Ayola Dayolle, one of the ladies-in-waiting. The subsequent residence of Navarre and his Queen at Nérac was characterized by such a quantity of adulterous love-making on both sides that an outbreak of Catholic–Protestant hostilities in 1580, called 'La Guerre des Amoureux' after them, was said to be caused by the scandal their goings-on created at court.[32] This scandal was as open as it was bitter.

What use can we make of this congruence? Clearly, *Love's Labour's Lost* does not 'mirror' the events at Nérac. The fictional lords' escapades are tame by comparison with the real ones. It is only the lowly Jaquenetta, not a lady-in-waiting, who gets pregnant; and the sexual offender is the foolish knight Armado, not the King of Navarre. *Love's Labour's Lost* does not present its leading characters as sexually untrustworthy in any truly sinister sense. Responding to performances of the play, I, at least, believe in the sincerity of the lords' vows at the end of the play, while at the same time I recognize the prudence of the ladies' testing of the lords' intentions through time. The real-life events underlying the play demonstrate the fragility of vows even more than does the play itself. They perhaps explain various unsettling tonalities, such as Berowne's exceedingly ungallant imputation about the ladies' virtue at the end of act 4, Moth's precocious jokes about horns, and the song of the cuckoo, placed so prominently at the end of the action, reverberating its threat: 'Cuckoo, cuckoo, O word of fear, / Unpleasing to a married ear!' (5.2.902–3). These allusions to the ugly side of sexuality perhaps derive as much from the scandal at Nérac and the spectacular failure of Navarre's marriage in general as from the events of the play itself. The fine points of this observation may be of interest to scholars of the play, those who study what Shakespeare did with his sources. To the general public, knowledge of this source only confirms the serious interest in

this light play with keeping one's word in affairs of the heart. But it is in no way necessary for a 'true understanding' of the play.

The play's use of the names of the French generals provides a broader topical context for *Love's Labour's Lost*, and with this source, as well, the theme of oath-breaking emerges more strongly than has been recognized. Not only did Navarre break a religious oath when he converted to the Church of Rome in 1593, but contemporaries perceived the violation of oaths as a contributing cause of the French wars. Often cited as the source for the lords' 'academe', La Primaudaye's *French Academie*, written in 1577 and translated and widely distributed in England by 1589, points to breach of faith as a primary reason for the wars:[33]

| The cause of the present miseries of France | But what need we search in antiquitie for testimonies of the fruits which commonly proceed from breach of faith, seeing ex- |

amples are daily before our eyes to our cost?...The distrust that one hath of another, which is so great amongst us, that it hath been one principall cause of kindling the fire of division so often in this desolate kingdom.

La Primaudaye's perception was not unique. Another contemporary Frenchman points to oath-breaking as a central cause of the French wars in an anonymous pamphlet translated into English as *The*

---

[31] Hugh M. Richmond, *Puritans and Libertines: Anglo-French Literary Relations in the Reformation* (Berkeley and Los Angeles, 1981), pp. 309–11, comes the closest to recognizing the importance of adultery at Nérac, but he relates it to English views of the French as 'libertines'.

[32] Desmond Seward, *The First Bourbon: Henri IV, King of France and Navarre* (1971), pp. 53–8; Lord Russell of Liverpool, *Henry of Navarre, Henry IV of France* (1969), pp. 56–65.

[33] Peter de la Primaudaye, *The French Academie*, trans. T.B. (1589), Dd5ᵛ; for its possible use as source see Bullough, vol. 1, p. 427; Frances Yates, *The French Academies of the Sixteenth Century* (1947; repr. Nedeln, Liechtenstein, 1968), pp. 123–4, traces connections between ideas of Primaudaye's Academy and Navarre's, and cites the popularity of Primaudaye's work in England; Muir mentions it as a possible source (p. 77).

Restorer of the French Estate Discovering the true cause of these warres in France and other countries and delivering the right course of restoring peace and quiet to all Christendome (1589). According to this observer, swearing 'in jest' had become a major problem in the French civil wars in general. Besides those untrustworthy leaders who made concessions when their position was weak only to overturn them when they gained strength, honest Frenchmen of both sides believed that God intended them to achieve victory by whatever means possible. They broke vows for their religion's sake, for to them promises made to 'heretics' had no validity. Since neither side could trust the other, broken treaties littered the civil wars and peace became increasingly impossible. This writer warns his readers, 'If ye be resolute to practise this doctrine, ye shall make all our warres endlesse and immortall' (C1).

This background may have influenced statements like Berowne's 'It is religion to be thus forsworn' (4.3.359) and 'By yea and nay, sir, then I swore in jest' (1.1.54), or Longaville's 'Vows are but breath, and breath a vapour is' (4.3.65). Navarre's argument that the Princess and her ladies must lodge with them 'on mere necessity' (1.1.147) may have echoed his explanation to Queen Elizabeth when he converted to the Church of Rome: 'For when the King, my Predecessor, was dead, I was under a kind of necessity to govern myself by the same Council and Ministry.'[34] Perhaps even more convincing is the predominant imagery of *Love's Labour's Lost*. Filled with cannonballs, rapiers, standards, corporals, treasons, military encounters, forfeit states, and leaden swords, the imagery in *Love's Labour's Lost* depicts the major interactions of its characters in terms of war.[35]

The Moth–Armado sub-plot also draws from this martial context. The very presence of a Spanish soldier among these particular French lords reflects distressing historical fact, for Philip II was pouring Spanish troops into France to fight for the Catholic League, apparently in the hope of becoming the next king of France.[36] Armado's poverty, literally exposed at the end of the play by his lack of a shirt, perhaps reflects the terrible poverty of the Spanish

soldiers and of Spain itself at the end of the century. In 1589 and 1590, thousands of Spanish soldiers mutinied for lack of salary and even food; many were cashiered in the Netherlands with only a dollar to find their way home.[37]

But it is the pairing of the Spanish Armado with Moth that resonates with the theme of oath-breaking. Valentine Pardieu, variously called la Motte, La Mote, and la Mothe in English reports, was governor of Gravelines in 1578, when Flanders was resisting Spanish domination; and he sold out his troops and the city of Gravelines itself to the Spanish for a relatively small fee. Other Flemish nobility followed his lead and Spain's subsequent control of Flanders prepared the way for the Armada.[38] La Motte did not change his untrustworthy ways. The pairing of Moth and Armado (the Spanish Armada was also spelled Armado in papers of the time) perhaps derives in part from his disloyalty to the Spanish during the attempted invasion by the Spanish Armada, for the Duke of Parma had him briefly imprisoned for the feebleness of his efforts to rescue Spanish ships in the disastrous Battle of

---

34 William Camden, *The History of the Annals of England during the whole life and Reign of Elizabeth* in *A Complete History of England* (1706), p. 573; see also Richmond, p. 200.

35 Caroline F. E. Spurgeon, *Shakespeare's Imagery and What It Tells Us* (Cambridge, 1935; repr. 1968), pp. 271–3.

36 Camden, p. 562.

37 *List and Analysis of State Papers, Foreign, Elizabeth, 1* (*1589–1590*), p. 346; Geoffrey Parker, *The Army of Flanders and the Spanish Road, 1567–1659* (Cambridge, 1972), pp. 158–64; Jaime Vincens Vives, *An Economic History of Spain* (Princeton, 1969), pp. 330–42.

38 Charles Wilson, *Queen Elizabeth and the Revolt of the Netherlands* (Berkeley and Los Angeles, 1970), pp. 73, 134; see also Thomas Churchyard, *A Description of the Warres in Flaunders* (1578), I2–I2ᵛ, for a contemporary description of the atmosphere around la Motte at that time: 'A notable souldier called Monsieur de la Moet, governour of *Graveling*, went from the states at this time (as hee sayd) to keepe the town, for the king...the world was so sorrowful, or so suttle, that a man might not scarcely at that season laugh with his friend, nor trust his owne brother. For cunning and craft, had put constancie out of countenaunce, and finnesse, with ficklenesse, were matched togither in one corner of Flaunders or another.'

Gravelines at that time.[39] Yet Parma's trust in la Motte was somehow reinstated, and la Motte's presence as Parma's general marshal, commanding the rearguard of his troops as they invaded France in 1590, locates him in the same place and time as the French generals whose names are used for the leading male characters in *Love's Labour's Lost*.[40]

This military background may have affected the military imagery of perhaps the most memorable exchange between Moth and Armado. When Moth promises to deliver Armado's message 'As swift as lead', Armado extends his metaphor: 'He reputes me a cannon, and the bullet, that's he – / I shoot thee at the swain' (3.1.54, 61–2). More particularly, la Motte's relationship with the Spanish in general possibly provides the model for the relationship between Moth and Armado, a relationship lacking in the loyalty and trustworthiness hoped for between master and servant. Like la Motte, Moth is two-faced to his Spanish master. While Armado's position of power over him readily secures his apparent submission when he dares too much, Moth expresses his constant and profound contempt for Armado to the audience:

Armado. I do say thou art quick in answers: thou heat'st my blood.
Moth. I am answered, sir.
Armado. I love not to be crossed.
Moth. He speaks the mere contrary: crosses love not him.   (1.2.29–32)

Moth humours or challenges Armado's elaborate fantasies as the whim and his own self-interest strike him, and the pleasure he enjoys from the exercise of his own wit at Armado's expense distances him from real attachment from his master. Like la Motte and the Walloon nobility in general, Moth is an ultimately unreliable servant, for he owes his only real loyalty to himself. Like the Duke of Parma and the Spanish in general, Armado seems sublimely unaware of the tenuousness of his hold on his servant.

The Moth–Armado sub-plot, like the main plot, shows the flexibility possible to Shakespeare's method. The topical sources are manipulated and changed around with the same freedom shown with literary sources. Shakespeare apparently thought nothing of changing the age or even the sex of characters in his literary sources; similarly, the 'tender juvenal' Moth shows little resemblance to the leathery warrior la Motte. There seems to be no pressure towards consistency, either, for Armado seems to have been named after an event rather than a person; his relationship with Moth seems to have been modelled upon something more abstract and nationalistic than a relationship between an actual person and an actual servant. Perhaps for Armado, no biographical counterpart came to mind as a source for his name. Similar discrepancies occur between the fictional lords and their real counterparts: there were radical differences in age between the lords, and Dumain was not only Catholic, he was fat as well.[41]

These differences would pose little difficulty to scholars of literary sources. In fact, the presence of the Catholic lord among the Protestants could be a point of interesting complexity. The play needed a fourth lord from somewhere. Why not a Catholic? Catholics were as guilty of breaking oaths as Protestants. This freedom with historical material can come as no surprise to students of the history plays. In the Renaissance, apparently, there was not the reverence for 'facts' presumed today, and Shakespeare, like other Renaissance writers, freely manipulated the material even of history to produce a character like, for example, Richard III, or a grown-up queen for Richard II, instead of the eleven-year-old that was the actual Queen Isabella. Within limits, even historical sources were treated with some of the freedoms allowed literary sources, so it is not surprising that Shakespeare's 'topical' play is not historically accurate in details of age and religion. Quite obviously, *Love's Labour's Lost* examines

---

39 *Calendar of State Papers, Foreign, Elizabeth*, 22 (1588), pp. 36, 122, 158; John Lothrop Motley, *History of the United Netherlands* (New York and London, 4 vols. (1860–7), vol. 2, pp. 499–500; *List and Analysis of State Papers, Foreign, Elizabeth*, 1 (1589–1590), p. 345.

40 Motley, vol. 4, pp. 75–6; see also Colynet, G1ᵛ–G2 for la Motte's betrayal of Huguenots through pretended friendship.

41 Tricomi, pp. 27–8.

issues, not personalities; and these differences from its topical sources are easily subsumed, as they would be for other kinds of sources, into the general aim of the play: to create a light comedy with oath-breaking as a theme.

These speculations about Shakespeare's treatment of the topical sources underlying *Love's Labour's Lost* conform to concerns of traditional scholarship of sources: what is a possible source, and how is it changed in the play? Perhaps the most interesting question, as Tricomi rightly pointed out, is the discrepancy in tone between source and play. The broken oaths of the fictional lords make us laugh. The historical Armado was a grim reality; Don Armado is foolish and harmless, 'fashion's own knight' (1.1.178). *Love's Labour's Lost* centres on the foibles of youth in love; its underlying context is a long and bloody civil war. The presence of so many broken oaths in these topical sources makes 'contra-topicality' too easy an answer, it seems to me. Instead, as the broken vows in the sources emphasize the broken vows in the play, they show a pre-occupation with genre that continued throughout Shakespeare's entire career. The gravity of the real-life sources for *Love's Labour's Lost* shows Shakespeare's early struggle, increasingly marked in his last plays, to transcend the limitations of genre, to stretch the boundaries of comedy to imply a darker reality hovering at its edges. This technique is consonant with other experimental decisions in the play, especially its unconventional ending with the announcement of the death of the King of France.

To what extent would Shakespeare have expected his audience to share his preoccupation? How much of the underlying context would they have been expected to 'get'? Would the names in this play have made them suspect a graver 'point' somewhere, or would they have made the play even funnier? (One thinks of the song 'Springtime for Hitler' in the movie *The Producers*, which creates hilarity from the use of a horror-ridden name in a frivolous context.) Did most of the audience scratch their heads in puzzlement, shrug, and then merely enjoy the lords' antics for their own sake? Undoubtedly, different members of the audience would have reacted in different ways, and we will probably never be able

to recreate their responses. But it seems clear that *Love's Labour's Lost* does not depend upon an audience's recognition of the gravity of its sources for any 'meaning'. Nowhere else in his entire canon does Shakespeare depend on an audience's recognition of even commonly known sources in order to understand his play. For *Love's Labour's Lost*, as for his other plays, the 'meaning' is in the play itself, not in its relationship with its sources.

For modern audiences, the topicality of *Love's Labour's Lost* is dead. Their responses to the names in *Love's Labour's Lost* pose no problem at all; for it is in the nature of topical allusions to be ephemeral, and any associations with the French civil wars have long since been lost. *Love's Labour's Lost* does not need them. It stands on its own, as recent directors and audiences have discovered. *Love's Labour's Lost* is a play which appealed, then as well as now, to a popular audience, not just to courtiers in certain élite circles. While we do not need to have the Princess of France peeling carrots,[42] experimentation with fresh presentations, freed from the concept of the play as 'learned' and 'aristocratic', are in order.

But while I hope to help in the rescue of *Love's Labour's Lost* from its image as coterie drama, I am not disparaging topicality as a valid field of inquiry. The names of characters drawn from real-life contemporaries in other plays tease us with possibilities: Orsino in *Twelfth Night*, Don John in *Much Ado About Nothing*, Dumaine in *All's Well that Ends Well*. What do these names imply about underlying topical sources? We already know that Shakespeare often drew on a social as well as a literary milieu, from *Measure for Measure* and *Macbeth*, both of which nod or even bow to James I, to *The Tempest*, which draws on contemporary news of exploration. I suspect that Shakespeare's plays are even more topical, more grounded in the social concerns of the day, than is now believed. A more even-handed approach to topical sources, in which they are treated with the restraint accorded literary sources, may well provide us with an interpretative tool of value for several plays besides *Love's Labour's Lost*.

---

[42] RSC production, see Fuzier, p. 123.

THE TRAGIC SUBSTRUCTURE OF THE 'HENRY IV' PLAYS

CATHERINE M. SHAW

In reporting Queen Elizabeth's conversation with William Lambarde, the Keeper of the Records in the Tower of London, about the staging of *Richard II* on Saturday, 6 February 1601, most scholars emphasize the Queen's words, 'I am Richard II, know ye not that?' Less often repeated but of much greater significance to the play which gave rise to the exchange and those that followed it, are the Queen's next words which, in referring to Essex, make significant comment on the dramatic role into which she cast the treacherous earl. 'He that will forget God,' she said, 'will also forget his benefactors...'[1] And Francis Bacon, who was one of the crown prosecutors at the trial which followed the unsuccessful insurrection, left no question as to the ultimate condemnation of any who would defy divine authority. In speaking of Sir Gilly Meyrick, one of Essex's supporters, Bacon said, 'So earnest hee was to satisfie his eyes with the sight of that tragedie which hee thought soone after his lord should bring from the stage to the state, but that God turned it upon their owne heads.'[2] Both of these speakers seem less concerned with Shakespeare's hero than they are with the nature of Elizabeth's antagonist and with divine providence. 'That tragedie' which was to have been brought from 'the stage to the state' would seem to refer as much to the usurpation of Richard's throne as to his downfall and death, perhaps more. Their words, however, in addition to suggesting a tacit acceptance of Richard's fate, imply an impending dramatic aftermath ripe with potential for further tragic enactment – as if somehow, the play of *Richard II* is not yet over – and they are right. Shakespeare's *Richard II* ends in scenes which only partially fulfil the play's dramatic obligations;

scenes which promise that the full tragic resolution will come only in the plays which follow – those titled with the name of the usurper king.

It is true that the tragedy of Richard II himself is, to all intents and purposes, over at the end of act 5, scene 5. Aumerle, Richard's last noble ally, has taken to his knees before the new king, and the playwright can now turn full dramatic attention to the death of Richard of Bordeaux. To use the metaphors of the play itself, Richard, having abused that divinely ordained time within which he should have been the caring gardener of the realm, must, in a kind of continuation of that strong morality theme dominant in the first tetralogy, pay for his errors against the state; for what Holinshed calls, 'wrongfull doings'.[3] And pay he does; one king falls and another takes his place.

As well as King Richard's private tragedy, these happenings also take care of the on-going narrative of the history plays; what A. P. Rossiter has referred to as the 'story-matter' gleaned from 'historical records to show that the course of events has been guided by a simple process of divine justice, dispensing rewards and punishments'.[4] We also know, however, from these records and the dramatization of them in the *Henry VI* plays and *Richard III*, that national tragedy has not yet run its course. And that is not all. Although divine ordination may have

---

[1] E. K. Chambers, *William Shakespeare*, 2 vols. (Oxford, 1930), vol. 2, pp. 326–7.
[2] Chambers, vol. 2, p. 326.
[3] Geoffrey Bullough, *Narrative and Dramatic Sources of Shakespeare*, 8 vols. (1957–75), vol. 3 (1960), p. 388.
[4] *Angel with Horns* (1961), pp. 1–2.

shortened Richard's days as king, *human* ordination shortened his physical life, and for this the wicked may not thrive. It is a deed, says Exton, 'chronicled in hell' (*Richard II*, 5.5.116).[5] Regardless, then, of what Shakespeare might owe to his audience in terms of a continuing historical narrative with all its political implications, he also must complete the artistic and moral obligations which tragedy demands. And Shakespeare pays these obligations in the *Henry IV* plays which, in many ways, are a rerun of the dramatic concerns of *Richard II* – only the actors who play the central parts are different. The roles played by protagonist and antagonist in *Richard II* are in the *Henry IV* plays reassigned to a larger cast of principals who, against a suitably expanded setting, continue the saga of misrule and insurrection. I am not referring here to the replaying of banishments and rebellion and the like; although scholars have long noted that Shakespeare emphasizes the parallel historical events in each reign. I mean that the potential for tragedy spills over from the last scenes of *Richard II* in which all four of the major figures of the next play are assembled, if not in person then in the conditioned mind of the audience, and operates subliminally in the *Henry IV* plays.

The 'unthrifty son' of the new King, however, the 'young wanton' Prince of Wales, already holds a special place in English hearts and indulgent smiles are the only reactions to references in act 5, scene 3 of *Richard II* to the undisciplined boy and his 'unrestrained loose companions' (5.3.7). Nothing disastrous can happen to England's favourite prodigal son who will one day wear the crown in victory at Agincourt. On the other hand, reason dictates that his lewd companions and, in particular, one fat knight, will be by then a youthful though sad memory. It is also fitting that young Harry Percy, the prince's rival in honour, be the person who responds to the King's question about his profligate son's reaction to summons to court. The prince's answer, repeated by the valiant Hotspur, was that

> he would unto the stews,
> And from the common'st creature pluck a glove,

And wear it as a favour; and with that
He would unhorse the lustiest challenger.

> (*Richard II*, 5.3.16–19)

Although Hal's response is couched in appropriate gutter language (taking 'unhorse' as a pun on 'un whores') the words, heavy with irony, so prophesy Hal's strategy in *1 Henry IV* that one suspects the playwright went back and inserted them after the initial and overall planning of the second tetralogy had progressed well along into actuality. Be that as it may, it is Hal who redeems the nation from the moral bankruptcy which faces it at the end of *Richard II* and movement towards this redemption which has its climax under God's hand at Agincourt is the 'story matter' of the *Henry IV* plays. Besides that, if historical familiarity has not separated Hal from the others, then the dramatic Hal does it for himself in the soliloquy at the end of act 1, scene 2 of *1 Henry IV*. Unlike the others, Hal is made the conscious actor who creates a role which he will play until he 'please[s] again to be himself' (*1 Henry IV*, 1.2.195).[6]

Setting the future king aside then, as already having been given his role by history and by the playwright who was dramatizing it, we have at the end of *Richard II* his 'lustiest challenger', young Harry Percy, his 'unrestrained' companions later personified in Sir John Falstaff, and his father, the solemn guilt-ridden Henry IV; the three characters, I might add, who are in turn left behind when Hal moves on into his own play – prisoners of history within plays in which at the same time as they act and interact within the historical process, each pursues his own line of dramatic action. It is these new players who act out the subliminal substructure for the *Henry IV* plays and which effect the necessary purgation, national and dramatic, before Henry V's reign of unexampled triumph can proceed.

Of these characters, Hotspur displays most clearly

---

[5] William Shakespeare, *Richard II*, The Arden Shakespeare, ed. Peter Ure (1956). All references to *Richard II* are from this edition.

[6] William Shakespeare, *1 Henry IV*, The Arden Shakespeare, ed. A. R. Humphreys (1960). All references to *1 Henry IV* are from this edition.

the potential for tragedy in the traditional sense of that word. Although introduced early in *Richard II* as 'tender, raw, and young', by the end of that play Harry Percy has already moved into a very firm position at Bolingbroke's side; almost, one might say, in the position of a son. Certainly Henry would wish that relationship, seeing in Hotspur valiant and princely traits in the opening scenes of *1 Henry IV* and later as a mirror image of himself when he arrived at Ravenspurgh. Hotspur is, however, more like the King than Henry might care to admit. Richard's words of Bolingbroke, that he is 'High stomach'd' and 'full of ire, / In rage, deaf as the sea, hasty as fire' (*Richard II*, 1.2.18–19), characterize that angry nobleman in the same way as do Northumberland's to his son, 'wasp-stung and impatient fool... / Tying thine ear to no tongue but thine own!' (*1 Henry IV*, 1.3.233–5). There is little doubt that both Henry and Hotspur say and do foolish things in anger. Once he is King, Henry does try very hard to control his temper and most times he succeeds, as when he defers judgement when prisoners are refused him after Holmedon. 'For more is to be said and to be done', he says at that point, 'Than out of anger can be uttered' (*1 Henry IV*, 1.1.105–6). When he does not, however, he makes provoking statements and commits rash actions just as Hotspur later does. Indeed, that very 'ire' coupled with conviction of personal injury and family dishonour is what leads Hotspur to rebellion and attempted usurpation just as surely as it had previously led Henry.

Henry, however, won and Hotspur does not. Why? For Henry it is because history wills it so; for Hotspur it is because Shakespeare wills it so. It is true, Holinshed records that 'the lord Percie' did die at Shrewsbury[7] but the Hotspur in *1 Henry IV* is almost totally of Shakespeare's creation and Shakespeare's Hotspur dies because his 'high stomach' and his 'ill-weaved ambition', characteristics which he holds in common with his king as surely as he holds bravery and valour and courage, lead him to rebel against that king and to his own disaster. And in this, Hotspur is acting out a tragedy in which the hero might just as well have been Henry Bolingbroke; their crimes are, after all, the same.

Hotspur's tragedy, however, is also personalized and his wilfulness is made the cause of peevish as well as dangerous actions. His uncle Worcester's exasperated words emphasize the flaws in the young man's nature:

> You must needs learn, lord, to amend this fault.
> Though sometimes it show greatness, courage, blood,
> – And that's the dearest grace it renders you –
> Yet oftentimes it doth present harsh rage,
> Defect of manners, want of government,
> Pride, haughtiness, opinion, and disdain,
> The least of which haunting a nobleman
> Loseth men's hearts and leaves behind a stain
> Upon the beauty of all parts besides,
> Beguiling them of commendation.
>
> (*1 Henry IV*, 3.1.174–83)

And after his death, it is not only Hal who acknowledges the tragic fall of a noble gentleman, but one of his own associates in the rebel cause, Lord Bardolph, confirms that for all his greatness, Hotspur

> with great imagination
> Proper to madmen, led his powers to death,
> And winking leap'd into destruction.
>
> (*2 Henry IV*, 1.3.31–3)[8]

The fact remains, however, that the origins of rebellion, attempted usurpation, and national disorder lie in *Richard II*. As Herschel Baker has pointed out, in addition to *Richard II* recording 'the deposition of a king who showed himself unfit to rule', the play also dramatizes '*with indignation* the course and outcome of insurrection'.[9] Warning after warning has occurred in *Richard II* of what will be the inevitable outcome of 'gross rebellion and detested treason'. Someone must pay for these crimes as Richard paid for his errors and misgovernment and if history disallows Henry Bolingbroke from the role then someone else must be his understudy: that understudy is Harry Hotspur. Thus, Hotspur is part

---

7 Bullough, vol. 4, p. 191.

8 William Shakespeare, *2 Henry IV*, The Arden Shakespeare, ed. A. R. Humphreys (1966). All references to *2 Henry IV* are from this edition.

9 Introduction to *Richard II*, *The Riverside Shakespeare*, ed. G. Blakemore Evans (Boston, 1974), p. 801.

of the tragic substructure of this play on two levels. At the same time as his personal tragedy is independently significant, Hotspur's fall acts out within the historic scheme of things in *1 Henry IV* what could and perhaps *should* have happened to Bolingbroke had history not willed otherwise.

Sir John Falstaff is also a major actor in this tragic subtext of the *Henry IV* plays and his roles are without doubt the most complex of the play. In the opening scene of *1 Henry IV*, the new king may speak of the peace which, he says, has united 'acquaintance, kindred, and allies' (1.1.16), but the words are no sooner out of his mouth than the issues which are to become the dramatic conflicts of both *Henry IV* plays take the stage. These are not, however, new issues but a continuation of old ones. The realm is, in fact, no better off for Richard's overthrow and murder. Rather, to that national disharmony for which Henry must now share the fault with Richard has been added dynastic disordering for which he is alone guilty. As Richard Plantagenet is dead, the responsibilities for national chaos and for the disorder of familial descent should fall on Henry Bolingbroke. History, however, let me repeat, has placed Henry as head of state and thus, within the drama, he may intone with great gravity that royal 'we' which symbolizes the union of rightful king and nation. That dual role which personifies both national and dynastic disordering now passes to Sir John Falstaff. Both men, as James Winny has seen, have 'the semblance and manner of a king without the stamp of divine authority' and 'the farcical and disrespectful posture by Falstaff [in the play-within-a-play scene] gives visible form to the moral reality of Bolingbroke's kingship'.[10]

As Hotspur is the dramatic heir to that 'harsh rage', that 'want of government' in Henry's private nature that led him to challenge the King and embroil the nation in civil war, so Falstaff and Eastcheap are the visual representations of the public results of such actions. Falstaff's realm may be Eastcheap and his castle the Boar's Head Inn but the fat knight lords it both in misrule and in familial disruption. His very credo is lawlessness and he has at his side as devotedly a wished-for heir in Hal as ever Hotspur is for Henry.

That such a realm has any permanence, however, is denied from the moment it is presented on stage. Like those of its king, the chief of 'Diana's foresters', its fortunes, although at the flood at the beginning of *1 Henry IV*, will also 'ebb' as Hal prophesies for the 'gentlemen of the shade', being 'governed as the sea is, by the moon' (1.2.26–33). The world of the stews represents in miniature the nation which Henry brought to further disorder by violating fealty and primogeniture. Lawlessness breeds lawlessness and history, at least Shakespeare's version of it, demands the reassertion of natural and familial unity. And, although Falstaff is a creation of the Shakespearian imagination, his fate in the role of king of Eastcheap is determined by the same historical factors as control the King for whom he provides a dramatic substructural counterpart.

Within this larger and historic scheme of things, Falstaff's fall outlines as clearly as does any Shakespearian tragedy how the abuse of power and position can lead to personal and national disaster and that only by repudiation of the perpetrator can the ordered state be re-established. As for the concerns of lineal disordering, Falstaff's pseudo-parental authority too must go. At the end of *2 Henry IV*, Hal chooses a new father in the Lord Chief Justice – Falstaff's *and Bolingbroke's* antithesis – the man who represents the time-honoured traditions of order and loyalty and justice. The new king expresses the dual transformation which has taken place both in himself and in the nation by picking up the earlier metaphor:

> The tide of blood in me
> Hath proudly flow'd in vanity till now.
> Now doth it turn, and ebb back to the sea,
> Where it shall mingle with the state of floods,
> And flow henceforth in formal majesty.
>
> (*2 Henry IV*, 5.2.129–33)

As does Hotspur, however, Falstaff also acts out his own personal tragedy and his part within the subliminal tragic enactment of the *Henry IV* plays also has a multiple complexity. History may will that the nation must suffer and then be purged of

---

[10] *The Player King* (1968), pp. 100, 107.

treason, of chaos, and of dynastic discord, but Shakespeare wills that Falstaff's fall, like Hotspur's, be motivated by characteristics inherent within the very nature of his creation. And as Hotspur's weaknesses mirror those of Henry Bolingbroke, ironically, Falstaff's mirror those of Richard of Bordeaux who, like Falstaff, tries to perpetuate a mode of existence which is in direct conflict with the historical process of which he is a dramatic part. I say ironically because Richard's 'skipping' qualities (*1 Henry IV*, 3.2.60) which Henry lays to his son are in truth Falstaff's and not the Prince's. It is Falstaff's 'fattest soil' (*2 Henry IV*, 4.4.54) that, like Richard's, nurtures weeds. Both live *off* their realms, not *for* them. Both are egocentric. Both charm others and themselves with words. Both appear to move toward their dramatic expulsions refusing to see the danger signals so obviously there. Richard acknowledges the 'high pitch' to which Bolingbroke's 'resolution soars' (*Richard II*, 1.1.109) but proceeds not only to ignore it but also to add momentum to it. And who except Falstaff could ignore Hal's 'I do, I will' (*1 Henry IV*, 2.4.475) after the eloquent plea not to banish fat Jack from the Prince's world and then proceed to behave even more outrageously? And look to their endings. Richard has with him an unidentified groom to recall a regal past; not one of his noble subjects is left. Indeed, Richard's personal tragedy is, as many of Shakespeare's tragic heroes' are, one of progressive isolation. And so is Falstaff's. Isolated as he is already from his former world, Sir John has with him Shallow and Silence, lean-witted remnants of a past glory with whom he has been able to establish briefly another king–subject relationship. Pistol is there, and Bardolph who has escaped the purging of Eastcheap only because he hurried out of the city toward Gloucestershire. But they, like Aumerle, the last of Richard's royal associates, finally also become followers of a new king.

Both Richard and Falstaff also come to public humiliation and private self-recognition. These confrontations for Richard, however, come separately. Richard is first rendered defenceless against the new political world of Bolingbroke; then in the prison scene, stripped of previous misconceptions, he gains a majesty of self of magnificent proportion. For Falstaff, the exposures of public and private self come at the same time and the sudden abutting of the historical and the comic worlds is such that the personal tragic moment can be and indeed is most often overlooked.

The words which Falstaff calls out to Hal as he passes in the coronation procession are progressively more intimate: 'King Hal, my royal Hal!', 'my sweet boy!' and then 'my heart!' and they encourage the expectation of confrontation on a personal level. There is nothing intimate, however, in the King's response. Even the overture of an instinctive comic gesture is cut short by the King's abrupt 'Reply not to me with a foolborn jest' (*2 Henry IV*, 5.5.41–5). Intellectually, of course, ample preparation has been made for this moment. And visually, in the scene itself, the strewing of rushes in the street, the coronation procession which passes over the stage, all the grandeur of the royal regalia insist upon the public and ritualistic nature of the event. Historic reality not only breaks through the comic world as it has done on numerous occasions before in these plays, but this time it stays in full view. For the first time, says Robert M. Torrance in his study of the development of the type, 'a comic hero has met irrevocable defeat.... Death Falstaff could outwit, but from the righteous judgement of a Christian king there is no reprieve; he stands defenseless, as no pagan or heretic comic hero ever stood, against his anointed antagonist's monopoly of moral authority.'[11] All this is true, but surely there is more. Intellectual moral justification for the expulsion of Falstaff can be accepted as can the historical actuality, but the disquietude which greets the end of *2 Henry IV* is not intellectual; it is emotional.

As Falstaff stands staring after the departing King and his rag-tag band begin to shuffle their feet in the rushes, there is something quietly heart-rending in the way the fallen knight tries to gather about himself the shreds of his shattered dignity. To say that Falstaff really believes that Hal will call for him once out of the public eye is to misread every confrontation between the two in both plays. In a

---

[11] *The Comic Hero* (Cambridge, Mass., 1978), p. 142.

brief moment and in his own strange way, there is a splendid simplicity in Falstaff's attempt to assert a positive sense of self. The old man's words, 'I will be the man yet that shall make you great', have about them the same sense of desperate majesty as Lear's 'I will do such things; – / What they are, yet I know not' (*King Lear*, 2.4.283–4). Words, however, the weapons which served him so well in the past, are not enough to save him now any more than Richard's defence was able to ward off historic inevitability. Symbolically, Falstaff dies at this instant. No prison scene in Fleet allows further exploration of the tragic moment. All that is left is a sense of emptiness as the great girth moves from the stage. Torrance explains this emptiness and links it to a previous fallen knight. 'A kingdom', he says, 'that has lost first Hotspur, then Falstaff, along with all that they embodied, has been irreparably diminished, even though the excision be a condition for its survival.'[12]

King of Eastcheap – King of England: the parallels between these two are so obvious that it seems only fitting that on the national level Henry Bolingbroke should share with Falstaff the roles of Richard II. Each king faces similar political crises, as I suggested earlier, but there is more to being a king than merely acting out historical events. In his own plays, however, Henry is no longer the author of these events but their victim and, as such, he is forced into Richard's role. In addition, not only is the role of victim Henry's, so is the language. In act 4, scene 1 of *Richard II*, Richard hands over his crown to Henry; then in act 5, scene 1, he prophesies the cares and insecurities that will come with it. Once Henry's role changes from perpetrator to threatened victim and confidence in loyal allies 'converts to fear' (*Richard II*, 5.1.66), those very insecurities lead Bolingbroke to the same verbalizing of despair that Richard was prone to:

Let all the tears that should bedew my hearse
Be drops of balm to sanctify thy head,
Only compound me with forgotten dust.
Give that which gave thee life unto the worms;
Pluck down my officers; break my decrees;
For now a time has come to mock at form –
. . . Up, vanity!
Down, royal state!   (*2 Henry IV*, 4.5.113–20)

The voice here is Henry's but the words might well be Richard's.

Shakespeare, however, denies to Henry Richard's heroic ending. The sense of loss at the death of Richard II is not felt when Henry dies. For one thing, unlike Richard's, and indeed unlike Hotspur's and Falstaff's, Henry's departure from the dramatic and historic world is underplayed. Warwick's news that the King has 'walk'd the way of nature' (*2 Henry IV*, 5.2.4) quickly turns to concern for the future of the Lord Chief Justice. M. M. Reese would add to this that 'long before the end the proud and confident Bolingbroke has shrunk into a sleepless neurotic'.[13] I'm not sure that this is true but if it is, the description refers to the private Henry; the Henry that has been for so long the source of sickness in the realm; the Henry that has hidden throughout his plays behind the role granted him by history while others act out what should have been his parts. At this Henry has been remarkably successful. Even at Shrewsbury he had 'many marching in his coats' (*1 Henry IV*, 5.3.25).

From the time he landed at Ravenspurgh, the public Henry is a winner. He achieves a crown and, although he gains little honour from either, his forces continue to be triumphant at Shrewsbury and Gaultree Forest. It is true that privately he is plagued by guilt but he is eventually able to dispel any fears he may have had of his son's capabilities to rule, to blame his sleeplessness on the heavy duties of wearing a crown, and to convince himself that he had committed treason because 'necessity so bow'd the state'. Warwick is also by to soothe him with platitudes when his mind runs to Richard's prophecy of a time when 'foul sin, gathering head, / Shall break into corruption' (*2 Henry IV*, 3.1.73, 76–7). Finally, although he admits to the 'by-paths and indirect crook'd ways' that took him to the crown, he also assures Hal that 'the soil of the achievement' will go with him into the earth (4.5.184–90).

Dramatically, however, the soil of the achievement has passed to surrogates – Hotspur and Falstaff – and their demises, real or symbolic, are the prices paid for Henry's crimes against the state. But

---

[12] *Ibid.*
[13] *The Cease of Majesty* (New York, 1961), p. 312.

there remains 'one most heinous crime' for which Henry must pay his own piper – the murder of Richard Plantagenet. By Exton's use of direct quotation when he reiterates the king's words, 'Have I no friend will rid me of this living fear?' (5.4.2), Shakespeare gives to Henry a scene in which he commits the grave error of allowing political expediency to hold sway over moral judgement. In other words, a quality which in all other regards has stood Henry in good stead and as a quality of kingship can be admired in him all the more because Richard so clearly lacks it, becomes in this instant a 'mole of nature'. I mean here that quality of knowing when to seize the moment, of knowing exactly when and how to motivate men and events to pursue his own ends. It is the dominant characteristic of Henry IV the political realist that emerges from the *Chronicles*. The Bolingbroke within the hollow crown in the *Henry IV* plays, however, is the playwright's artistic creation and Henry's decision not to abide Richard Plantagenet alive, whether made as the result of policy or in a fit of pique is, in Shakespeare's play, a tragic mistake in judgement.

The facts of history only deny Henry a Crusader's death but for this grave error Shakespeare's dramatic metaphor suggests another punishment. Although it is to the instrument of murder that Henry directs his biblical intonations at the end of *Richard II*:

With Cain go wander thorough shades of night,
And never show thy head by day nor light,

(5.6.43–4)

Exton completely disappears from the dramatic progression. Shakespeare refuses to pass this crime on to a surrogate. Rather, Henry himself must bear the mark of Cain and live and ultimately die with the blood of Richard on his hands. Henry's plea, 'How came I by the crown, O God forgive' (*2 Henry IV*, 4.5.218), involves his treason and his violation of dynastic succession; Richard's death is parricide, linked by the Cain metaphor to the 'eldest primal

sin,' and for this he is denied the true Jerusalem. This is the tragedy of Henry Bolingbroke.

Of Henry's former adversaries, Richard II had died weapon in hand, prophesying, 'Mount, mount, my soul! thy seat is up on high' (*Richard II*, 5.5.111); Hal's words over the fallen Hotspur at Shrewsbury indicate that the Prince's praise will go 'to heaven' with the fallen warrior (*1 Henry IV*, 5.4.98); and Falstaff 'went away an it had been any christom child' (*Henry V*, 2.3.11–12). Even the loyal knight, banished Thomas Mowbray, after valiant years 'in glorious Christian field', gave up 'his pure soul unto his captain Christ, / Under whose colours he had fought so long' (*Richard II*, 4.1.93–100). But not so for Henry Bolingbroke. 'Then said the king,' reports Holinshed, 'Lauds be given to the father of heaven for now I know that I shall die heere in this chamber, according to the prophesie of me declared, that I should depart this life in Jerusalem.'[14] The words which Shakespeare gives to Henry carry no such tone of thanksgiving; no such surety of destiny. Rather, they are heavy with irony and the recognition of God's judgement and his own vanity:

Laud be to God! Even there my life must end.
It hath been prophesied to me, many years,
I should not die but in Jerusalem,
Which vainly I suppos'd the Holy Land.
But bear me to that chamber; there I'll lie;
In that Jerusalem shall Harry die.

(*2 Henry IV*, 4.5.235–40)

Thus, by the end of *2 Henry IV*, the crimes unpunished in the action of *Richard II* have all been accounted for in the tragic substructure of the *Henry IV* plays. It is true that in 'small time' civil war will again pitch Englishman against Englishman in the Wars of the Roses, but for the dramatic present, debts are paid and 'civil swords and native fire' (*2 Henry IV*, 5.5.106) may turn toward France and Agincourt.

---

[14] Bullough, vol. 4, p. 278.

HAL AND THE REGENT

JONATHAN BATE

It is a cliché that the English get their history from
Shakespeare and their theology from Milton. As a
result of Shakespeare's rewriting of history for the
purposes of drama, Henry V is a national hero and
Richard III a national villain. The influence of the
history plays on subsequent perceptions of pre-
Elizabethan history is widely recognized; their
influence on later English history is less well
documented. In this article I shall show how certain
public, polemical, and parodic perceptions of the
future George IV, up to and during the Regency
years, were mediated through Shakespeare.

The most socially and politically influential art of
the late eighteenth and early nineteenth centuries
was caricature. In the 1790s James Gillray developed
a reputation as one of the foremost artists of his age;
his works 'were bought up with unparalleled
eagerness, and circulated not only throughout
England, but all over Europe'.[1] Nathaniel Wraxall
wrote of the famous 'Carlo Khan' prints in which
James Sayers attacked C. J. Fox, 'It is difficult to
conceive the moral operation and wide diffusion of
these caricatures through every part of the
country.'[2] Furthermore, according to Lord Eldon,
'Fox said, that *Sayers's caricatures* had done him more
mischief than the debates in Parliament or the works
of the press.... These and many others of these
publications, had certainly a vast effect upon the
public mind.'[3]

Although satirical engravings could damage
reputations and careers in this way, the butts of the
caricaturists often viewed attacks with considerable
indulgence; according to one commentator, 'the
King was frequently incensed, sometimes gratified,
and generally inclined to be amused by the sallies of

Gillray'.[4] The Prince of Wales and many other
leading figures in high society had accounts at the
most famous print-shop in London, that of Mrs
Humphrey. She received regular visits from men
such as Fox, especially after she entered into her
liaison, both commercial and personal, with Gillray.
The encounter between the Prince and Fox, Gillray
and his fellows, and Shakespeare's Hal and Falstaff
held a generation in thrall but is now neglected by
historians and literary critics.

Satirists frequently appropriated Shakespeare for
political purposes. The young Henry Brougham
advised that 'different people should at their spare
hours be reading Shakespeare and Swift with a view
to selecting passages suitable to the time, as, descriptions of base courtiers, particular characters of bad
ministers, hits at bishops (if safe) etc.'.[5] One extraordinary thing about the period is the way that
history and, more particularly, the heir-apparent,
played into the hands of caricaturists who knew that
their audiences would particularly appreciate a
Shakespearian frame of reference for their satire. In
1780, when he was eighteen years old, Prince George

---

[1] 'Life of Gillray', in Thomas Wright and R. H. Evans,
*Historical and Descriptive Account of the Caricatures of James
Gillray* (1851), p. xi.

[2] Wraxall, *Historical and Posthumous Memoirs, 1772–1784*,
edited by H. B. Wheatley, 5 vols. (1884), vol. 3, p. 254,
quoted by M. Dorothy George, *English Political Caricature*, 2 vols. (Oxford, 1959), vol. 1, p. 169.

[3] Horace Twiss, *Life of Lord Eldon*, 3 vols. (1844), vol. 1, p.
162, quoted in *English Political Caricature*, vol. 1, p. 169.

[4] J. Grego, *The Works of James Gillray, the Caricaturist*,
edited by T. Wright (1873), p. 13.

[5] Quoted by John Wardroper in *Kings, Lords, and Wicked
Libellers: Satire and Protest 1760–1837* (1973), p. 187.

1   William Dent, *A Shaksperean Scene*

was much struck by Mrs Robinson, the actress who played Perdita in Garrick's adaptation of *The Winter's Tale* at Drury Lane. Since she was known as 'Perdita Robinson', because of her success in the role, the Prince signed his admiring letters 'Florizel'. When she became his mistress, the 'low-born lass' and the Prince proved irresistible to satirists; there was a string of 'Florizel and Perdita' caricatures,[6] not to mention such pamphlets as a *Poetical Epistle from Florizel to Perdita: with Perdita's Answer. And a Preliminary Discourse upon the Education of Princes.* The Prince soon moved into a new circle of acquaintance,[7] and interest shifted to Shakespeare's fullest exploration of 'the Education of Princes'.

From the mid-1780s onwards, George spent a great deal of time with the Opposition group who were consistently criticized for their dissolute life-style – heavy-drinking C. J. Fox, theatrical R. B.

Sheridan, and adventurer Colonel Hanger. Gillray was especially well placed to watch their activities, for his lodging at Mrs Humphrey's in St James's was just down the street from Brooks's, the Club where the group most frequently met. Fox was over-weight, Sheridan had a red nose, Hanger was a swaggerer: enter Falstaff, Bardolph, and Pistol to lead the Prince astray. Horace Walpole wrote in his

[6] Numbers 5767, 5865, 6117, 6266, 6318, 6655, 6811 in *Catalogue of Political and Personal Satires Preserved in the Department of Prints and Drawings in the British Museum,* 11 vols. (1870–1954), edited by F. G. Stephens (vols. 1–4) and M. Dorothy George (5–11). Vols. 6–9 cover 1784–1819, the period on which I shall concentrate; all subsequent references to prints are followed in my text by their catalogue number.

[7] Mary Robinson continued her career as a poetess and, like so many others, wrote a neo-Shakespearian blank verse drama – *The Sicilian Lover. A Tragedy* (1796).

journal in March 1783, 'The Prince of Wales had of late thrown himself into the arms of Charles Fox, and this in the most indecent and undisguised manner.... Fox's followers... were strangely licentious in their conversations about the King. At Brookes's they proposed wagers on the duration of his reign.'[8] They almost seem to be self-consciously mimicking the behaviour of Falstaff and his followers at the Boar's Head.

Thus in May 1783 John Boyne published *Falstaff & his Prince* (6231), with an Elizabethan Fox and a fashionably dressed Prince. Next came the identification of the whole group as the cast of *Henry IV. A Shaksperean Scene* (6974, Aug. 1786, fig. 1) by William Dent, an amateur caricaturist active throughout the 1780s, shows the Prince's friends rejoicing at the rumour that the King had been killed (Margaret Nicholson, a madwoman, had attempted to stab him to death on 2 August 1786).

Dent's dramatis personae include not only the major figures, and Mrs Fitzherbert as Doll Tearsheet, but also several lesser luminaries: Shallow is the Duke of Portland, Silence is Devonshire, the page Lord John Cavendish, and serving-man Davy, Louis Weltje, the Prince's cook and favoured servant. Dent, using a technique at which Hogarth had excelled, reinforces his argument by means of objects on the wall: the placard points to *2 Henry IV*, the crucifix to the fact that not the least disturbing aspect of the Prince's liaison with Mrs Fitzherbert was her Catholicism. Hanger's lines are those of Pistol as he enters with the news that Henry IV is dead, culminating in 'Sir John, thy tender lambkin now is King'; the Prince's, on the other hand, are from Hal's fulsome speech of filial repentance in 4.5:

> Thy due, from me,
> Is tears, and heavy sorrows of the blood,
> Which nature, love and filial tenderness,
> Shall, O dear Father, pay thee plenteously.

Dent's allusion openly asserts that George owes his father a similar humble apology. But there was no reconciliation, despite Fox's attempts to bring one about. The latter was aware of the dangers of a split between the King and the prince, but the public did not perceive this to be his position and partisan

caricaturists would take every opportunity to make him seem more self-interested than he was.

The political aspirations of the Foxites were given a fillip by the Whig success in the Westminster by-election of July 1788. It was a highly controversial campaign. One allegation, that the Whig candidate Townshend had tried to seduce the Duchess of Rutland, gave Boyne the opportunity to combine an image of Fox as Falstaff with the quasi-Shakespearian intonation, 'I am thy injured Husband's Ghost. Beware of the foul Deeds done in the Flesh while I was on earth' (*Falstaff & the Merry Wives of Westminster, Canvassing for their Favourite Member Ld T——d*, 7343). The following day, J. Atkins published another print that branded Fox as Townshend's procurer. *Falstaf & the Merry Wives of Westminster Returning from Canvassing for Ld T——* (7345) shows him wearing the antlers of the final act of *Merry Wives* and escorting two ladies who look as if they are of questionable morals.

Four months later, the King fell into his first serious, incapacitating bout of insanity. (The precise nature of the King's illness is still being debated, but at the time it was perceived as insanity.) Once again, Hanger could say 'thy tender lambkin now is King'. He does so in Gillray's *King Henry IVth The Last Scene* (7380), where Falstaff–Fox is given the lines 'The Laws of England are at my commandment. Happy are they which have been my friends; & woe to my Lord Chancr.' The change from 'woe to my Lord Chief Justice' (*2 Henry IV*, 5.3.138) hints at Fox's opposition to the secret negotiations between the Prince and Thurlow, the Chancellor, on their possible co-operation in the event of the King's death or permanent incapacity.

The influence of Gillray's print – or perhaps the force of the Shakespearian parallel *per se* – was such that in the Parliamentary Debate of 19 December 1788, James Martin said that Fox's behaviour

brought to memory a scene in Shakespeare's play of Henry 4, where Falstaff reckoned upon what would be done for him and his associates, when the Prince

---

8 *The Last Journals of Horace Walpole*, edited by A. F. Steuart, 2 vols. (1910), vol. 2, p. 496, quoted in *Catalogue* no. 6237.

2   Isaac Cruikshank, *False Liberty Rejected*

should come to the crown, which was then daily expected, and was assigning places of dignity and character to the most deserving of his friends.[9]

Once Dent and Gillray had established the frame of reference, comparisons with *Henry IV* became common. In May 1792 the Prince of Wales made his first speech in the House of Lords, on the occasion of the debate on the King's Proclamation against Seditious Writings, a response to Paine's *Rights of Man*; he spoke vigorously in defence of the Proclamation, and from that point on broke – at least for a time – with the Foxites. Thus in March 1793 Fores published Isaac Cruikshank's *False Liberty Rejected or Fraternizing & Equalizing Principles Discarded* (8311, fig. 2). The Prince is given a version of Hal's rejection of Falstaff, quoted in prose and slightly altered: 'I know you not, Vain Proffligates. fall to your prayers; how ill White hairs become a fool & jester; I have long Dream'd of such kind of Men, so surfeit swelld. Seditious and Profane; but

being awake, I do despise my dream...the Tutors & the Feeders of my Riots.' This is a good example of Shakespearian quotation being particularly effective because the context is especially resonant and very few words are changed. Since the alterations are slight – 'Vain Proffligates' for 'old man'; 'man', 'tutor', and 'feeder' made plural; above all, the substitution of 'Seditious' for 'old' – they are emphatic. Cruikshank's public would have alighted on 'Vain Proffligates' and 'Seditious' because these are novel intrusions into an otherwise highly familiar text.

False Liberty Rejected is among Cruikshank's most allusive prints. Contained within the title are the three principles of the French Revolution, *liberté*, *égalité*, *fraternité*; this association is picked up in the engraving itself, for Sheridan and Fox are dressed as

---

[9] Hansard, *The Parliamentary History of England*, 36 vols. (1806–20), vol. 27, p. 793, cited in *Catalogue*.

72

sansculottes. A second comparison is invoked for the Prince's relationship with the King. George III's reference to the fatted calf and the Prince's 'I will return to my Father & say unto him...' make the print biblical as well as Shakespearian (the *Prodigal Son* parallel had first been used in a print of January 1787, no. 7129).

A year after *False Liberty Rejected*, Sayers's *Citizen Bardolph Refused Admittance at Prince Hal's* (8441) was published by Hannah Humphrey. It shows Sheridan being turned away from Carlton House and, like Dent's *Shaksperean Scene*, reinforces its point with a play-bill on the wall. Dent's bill had been a double thrust, since it had included both *2 Henry IV* and an after-piece entitled *The Mistake*; Sayers's is a triple one, listing Shakespeare's play, George Colman's *The Manager in Distress*, a cut at Sheridan's dual life as politician and manager of Drury Lane, and Otway's *Venice Preserved*, with its ominous subtitle 'a Plot discovered'. The identification of Sheridan with Bardolph remained popular (see 7528, 7837, 7920). In September 1806, another Westminster by-election was caused by Fox's death; Sheridan was going to stand, but withdrew and was replaced by Lord Percy. This afforded Williams a marvellous opportunity to play with *Henry IV* in his *The School for Scandal* (the title is another telling allusion to Sheridan's theatrical life): 'Gallant Hotspur——Let me uphold my drooping Fame, / By tacking Bardolphs unto Hotspurs name' (10106: Hotspur was, of course, a Percy).

Gillray made another contribution to the field in 1796. *Hint to Modern Sculptors, as an Ornament to a Future Square* (8800) shows the future George IV, albeit rather portly, splendidly attired on horseback; the inscription is from Vernon's speech on Hal's transformation, 'I saw young Harry with his beaver on...' (*1 Henry IV*, 4.1.104). Gillray changes 'young Harry' to 'him', so that his 'readers' will think 'to whom did this originally refer?' On remembering that it was Hal, they would hope that George was on the way to becoming another Henry V – or, more likely, despair at the contrast between the fat prince and his forebear who was 'like feather'd Mercury'.

A Morning Ride (10230, Feb. 1804) also makes a

comparison between the Prince and Henry V, but at one remove from Shakespeare. Gillray's inscription is Burns's 'Yet aft a ragged Cowte's been known / To mak a noble Aiver; / So, Ye may doucely fill a Throne', a stanza that goes on to take as an example of this dictum the progress of Hal from friend of Falstaff to hero of Agincourt.[10]

Two further examples of the convention that has Fox as Falstaff and Sheridan as Bardolph should be mentioned. Gillray's *Homer Singing His Verses to the Greeks* (9023) is aimed at their drinking habits; Fox is given Falstaff's 'come, sing me a bawdy song, make me merry' (*1 Henry IV*, 3.3.13) with 'bawdy' changed to '*Boosey*'. Rowlandson's *Falstaff and his Followers Vindicating the Property Tax* (10557) attacks their increase of income tax in the budget of 1806 after the formation of the so-called 'Ministry of All the Talents'.

But by this time the Prince was being given other roles. His corpulence led to a variation whereby he became Falstaff. As early as 1794 he had been given some of Falstaff's words in Isaac Cruikshank's *John Bull's Hint for a Profitable Alliance* (8487), but the first time he is actually represented as Sir John is Williams's print on his infatuation with Lady Hertford, *All for Love* (10625, Dec. 1806). Curiously enough, despite his allusion to *Merry Wives*, Williams fails to make any overt capital out of the possible pun in 'heart-Ford'. The parallel with Falstaff endured after George had taken the throne. Heath's *Falstaff and his Ragged Crew* (13766, July 1820) is a satire on the disreputable witnesses he obtained to support his allegations against Queen Caroline. In 1827, Heath again used *King Henry IV* (15411) in a satire on the King's sexual affairs; this time, Lady Conyngham plays the part of Doll Tearsheet, her husband, Mistress Quickly. A hanging on the wall depicts the Prodigal Son, an allusion back to that earlier image of George.

Since he was both overweight and a lover of women, the Prince of Wales was also caricatured as Henry VIII. In 1802 there was a masquerade at the Union Club to celebrate the Treaty of Amiens; the

---

[10] Burns, *Poems and Songs*, edited by James Kinsley (1969), no. 113, 'A Dream', stanza XI.

Prince seems to have gone as Henry VIII, though some accounts say he was a Sicilian noble.[11] In Williams's *The Union Club Masquerade* (9871) he is cast as Henry, with Mrs Fitzherbert as Anne Boleyn. Ten years later, in *He Has Put his Foot in it* (11887), Williams makes the identification again. The engraving is a satire on the Prince's desire to get rid of Lady Hertford, whose political influence was proving embarrassing. There are two portraits on the wall; one is labelled 'Henry Fifth' and the other, immediately above the Prince, 'Henry Eighth'. The head of each portrait is cut off by the top of the print; that of Henry V is badly torn. We may read them as follows: were the heads visible, they would both be the Prince; 'Henry V' is torn because hopes that George would follow Hal in outgrowing his misspent youth were in tatters; he is instead in the shadow of Henry VIII, a monarch well known for his tendency to dispose of women when they were no longer of any use to him (and – remembering Mrs Fitzherbert's Catholicism – to be led by marriage into religious controversy).

The most effective prints of George as Henry VIII are those that also cast Caroline as Queen Katherine. The first investigation into the conduct of the prince's wife, a stratagem to see if there were sufficient grounds for divorce proceedings to be initiated, took place in 1813. One of Williams's engravings on the subject has Caroline quoting Katherine's plea, 'Sir I desire you do me right and Justice...'.[12] The same speech is used in a print entitled *King Henry VIII. Act. II, Scene iv* (13829) on the occasion of the 1820 Bill of Pains and Penalties to deprive the Queen of her rights and title. Here George plays Henry again and Castlereagh is Wolsey.

There are other caricatures of George as Henry VIII which do not allude to Shakespeare (12041, 12056, 13664, 14118), just as Byron's squib 'Windsor Poetics' accuses the Regent of being 'Henry to his Wife', but does not refer to Shakespeare. Nevertheless, chiefly because of the opportunity it provided for spectacle, *Henry VIII* was highly popular on the early nineteenth-century stage, so he would have been another monarch who was always seen through a Shakespearian lens.

But it was the parallel between the youth of the Regent and that of Prince Hal that was used most frequently and most powerfully. It was not restricted to the world of the caricaturist. During the session of the Court of Common Council on 8 January 1811, Alderman Birch spoke on the subject of whether to give absolute power to the Regent.

He then quoted from the play of Henry IV.

> 'Are you in such haste
> 'To count my sleep as death? This speech of thine
> 'Will add to my distemper.'
>
> (*The Courier*, 9 January 1811)

After the Regency Act was passed the following month, advice to Prince George came swiftly off the presses. *The Satirist* of that month carried the first of a series of 'Letters to his Royal Highness the Prince of Wales'. Some passages are worth quoting at length because, as Alderman Birch did, they make explicit the parallel with Shakespeare's Hal.

Shew the world that if you once practised some of *Harry Monmouth*'s indiscretions, you also possess the kingly virtues of *Henry the Fifth*: tell those who would basely influence you to sacrifice your duty to your father, your king, and your country, for the gratification of their own avarice or ambition, in the words of this illustrious monarch:

> 'Presume not that I am the thing I was,
> For Heaven doth know, so shall the world perceive
> That I have turn'd away my former self
> So will I those that kept me company.'
>
> (*The Satirist*, 8 (1811), p. 105)

'In the words of this illustrious monarch' suggests that Shakespeare's history plays determined popular conceptions of English kings; the words of Shakespeare's Henry V are treated as if they were those of the monarch himself.

---

[11] According to *Catalogue*, no. 9871, the *Annual Register* said that he was Henry, the *London Chronicle*, the Sicilian. I have checked *The Observer*, 6 June 1802, and *The European Magazine*, 41 (1802), p. 499, which both say that he went as Henry VIII – but *The Times*, 2 June, plumps for the Sicilian.

[12] *State Mysteries* (12028), quoting *Henry VIII*, 2.4.13 ff. Another of Williams's engravings on the allegations against the Queen, *A Key to the Investigation or Iago Distanced by Odds* (12031), has as epigraph the lines from *Othello*, 3.3, on filching of 'good name'.

The writer goes on to condemn the opposition members who seemed to be sorry that the King's health was improving slightly. They are described as base characters whose enthusiasm in the future King's favour has brought about a change in their political creed which

might induce a man, unacquainted with the virtues of your [the Regent's] heart, to believe that you had exclaimed in the language of Shakespeare:

'All your sage counsellors hence!
And to the English court assemble now
From every region, imps of idleness...'

The quotation continues for another seven lines, describing the ruffians, revellers, robbers, and murderers who, says Bolingbroke, will be given 'office, honour, might' under 'the fifth Harry' (2 Henry IV, 4.5.119–29). The Shakespeare parallel is the linchpin of the rhetoric here. It works on two levels. First, there is the power of the language itself; it is a vision of corruption so telling that the Prince is, one senses, being forced to come out and say that of course he will no longer move in bad company. The quotation, along with the phrase 'unacquainted with the virtues of your heart', corners the Prince: he must prove that he has those virtues by showing that the quotation is not applicable. At a deeper level, but one altogether comprehensible in the context of the tradition associating George with Hal, there is the fact that the Prince's reply has already been written for him; he must re-enact Hal's 'O pardon me, my liege...' and follow his forebear in committing himself to his duty as a future king.

The parallel is clinched just before the end of the 'Letter' by an allusion to the Lord Chief Justice's speech in 5.2:

On the assumption of the royal power, I conjure your Royal Highness to exercise your own understanding, be guided by the genuine impulse of your own excellent heart:

'Question your royal thoughts, make the case yours,
Be now the father and propose a son.'

In this way, the Regent is exhorted to do as Harry does in this scene and affirm that he will follow the dictates of Justice and a King's innate nobility, not be swayed by his sometime followers.

The frontispiece to the following month's *Satirist* provides a visual 'reply' to the Letter. Entitled *The Cats Let Out of the Bag or the Rats in Dismay* (*Catalogue*, no. 11714), it portrays Sheridan and other reformers as rats, while the Prince is given a fine bearing and says the crucial lines from the 'rejection' speech in *2 Henry IV* that had been quoted in the Letter.

In this context, for the distinguished legal historian Alexander Luders to publish in 1813 an essay entitled *The Character of Henry V when Prince of Wales* was a political as well as a scholarly act. Luders uses historical sources to vindicate Hal from the wantonness and irresponsibility that Shakespeare had thrust upon him; in doing so, he implicitly challenges the current Prince to follow his historical rather than his Shakespearian precursor.

When the Regent eventually took the throne and became George IV, as Hal had become Henry V before him, Shakespeare's political influence spilled over from graphic satire and polemical prose on to the stage. *2 Henry IV* had not been played in London since 1804; in the summer of 1821 it was revived at Covent Garden with strong emphasis on the spectacular ending: according to the playbill '4 additional scenes will be introduced displaying the grand Coronation'. The run began on 25 June; on 19 July, 'This being the day of the Coronation, the King commanded the theatre to be opened gratuitously to the public – Henry 4th pt. 2d – with the Coronation'. The play's success may be judged from the fact that on 7 August, the last night of its run, 'some of the Performers' benefits were bought up – an additional pit door was opened, and orders [complimentary admissions] of every description were refused'.[13] We know from the fact that *King Lear* was not performed during the years of the old King's madness that Shakespeare's plays were conceived of in contemporary political terms. The free performance of *2 Henry IV*, in which Hal was seen to reject Falstaff and his ragged crew, to be crowned in splendour, to become Henry V of glorious memory, was George IV's final rejoinder to the satirists.

---

[13] John Genest, *Some Account of the English Stage*, 10 vols. (Bath, 1832), vol. 9, pp. 113–14.

THE RITE OF VIOLENCE IN '1 HENRY IV'

DEREK COHEN

Hotspur is a character whose career runs the gamut of dramatic expression. Commencing on a note of furious, even farcical, comedy, it concludes on a note of tragic grief so poignantly realized as to have inspired Northrop Frye's perception that his dying remark, 'thoughts, the slaves of life', comes out of the heart of the tragic vision.[1] Hotspur's brave death is placed squarely and deliberately before the audience and provides the final means by which they can comprehend the nature and meaning of his life. Gradually the character has been moulded and determined by forces and events that culminate in the great encounter between himself and Prince Hal. The forces, both those seen by and those hidden from Hotspur, are the means by which the audience and reader are able to apprehend the development of a character whose existence has been bent into the shape of tragic suffering shown by that last speech:

O Harry, thou hast robb'd me of my youth!
I better brook the loss of brittle life
Than those proud titles thou hast won of me;
They wound my thoughts worse than thy sword
    my flesh:
But thoughts, the slaves of life, and life, time's fool,
And time, that takes survey of all the world,
Must have a stop. O, I could prophesy,
But that the earthy and cold hand of death
Lies on my tongue: no, Percy, thou art dust,
And food for —   (*1 Henry IV*, 5.4.76–85)

This speech, to which I shall return, is the apotheosis of Hotspur. By virtue of the transmogrifications wrought in drama through deliberately vivid depictions of dying moments, Hotspur becomes, during this quiet, nearly still, moment in the play, hero, god, and sacrificial creature of society.[2] The fallen hero speaking and looking upwards at his conqueror commands the world he has lost just as he leaves it; and he does so in a manner and with a completeness that have been denied him up to now. It is the concentration of the audience's, the reader's, the prince's passive energy upon the spectacle of the dying soldier that emphasizes his role as the sacrificial victim of his and our world – a transcendence which involves us with his conqueror and his society in a silent collusion in the sacrifice. The production and reproduction of this play over the centuries testifies to a persisting pleasure (aesthetic and moral) in what is arguably the central emotional event of the drama.

Hotspur's death, a palpable and carefully prepared ritual, is directly referable to Prince Hal's vow of fealty to the King, his father.

Do not think so, you shall not find it so;
And God forgive them that so much have sway'd
Your Majesty's good thoughts away from me!
I will redeem all this on Percy's head,
And in the closing of some glorious day
Be bold to tell you that I am your son,

---

[1] Northrop Frye, *Fools of Time* (Toronto, 1967), p. 4. References to *1 Henry IV* are taken from the new Arden, ed. A. R. Humphreys (1960).

[2] In *The Scapegoat* (1913), p. 227, James Frazer discusses the role and function of that human being upon whom the evils and sorrows of the society are concentrated and through the death of whom the society is released from its suffering. The process of Hotspur's death suggests that he is Hal's and the nation's scapegoat. Frazer remarks the many ceremonies in primitive and ancient societies whereby regeneration and purification were possible only after the killing of a human scapegoat or the death of a god.

When I will wear a garment all of blood,
And stain my favours in a bloody mask,
Which, wash'd away, shall scour my shame with it;
And that shall be the day, whene'er it lights,
That this same child of honour and renown,
The gallant Hotspur, this all-praised knight,
And your unthought-of Harry chance to meet.
For every honour sitting on his helm,
Would they were multitudes, and on my head
My shames redoubled! For the time will come
That I shall make this northern youth exchange
His glorious deeds for my indignities.
Percy is but my factor, good my lord,
To engross up glorious deeds on my behalf,
And I will call him to so strict account
That he shall render every glory up,
Yea, even the slightest worship of his time,
Or I will tear the reckoning from his heart.
This in the name of God I promise here,
The which, if He be pleas'd I shall perform,
I do beseech your Majesty may salve
The long-grown wounds of my intemperance:
If not, the end of life cancels all bands,
And I will die a hundred thousand deaths
Ere break the smallest parcel of this vow.

(3.2.129–59)

The power of the speech derives not only from the solemnity of the vow and its invocation of the imagery of blood sacrifice, but also from the variegation of mood within it. The telling first line contains a note of beseeching which hovers on the verge of the imperative. It takes strength from its repeated negatives and urgent exhortation. 'Do not think so; you shall not find it so' – the first 'so' neatly dividing the line and balancing with the second in a parison of rhythm and harmony of logic. The monosyllables of the line, coming as they do immediately after King Henry's Latinate, almost otiose, 'degenerate', emphasize the contrast between the speakers.

Hal's speech is the climax of the play in the sense that here the death of Hotspur is given substance and form as an inevitable consequence of what is occurring between the King and the prince.[3] Thus is the destruction of Hotspur by Hal transformed from a shadowy probability into a central fact of the play. It is the fact by which Hotspur becomes the ritual object of a revenger's quest. Resolution through death, as Lawrence Danson argues, 'is necessary to assure the sort of enduring memorial [the hero] and his creator seek, and is an integral part of the play's expressive form'.[4] This shift in emphasis from the probable to the actual takes force less from the known historical details on which the play is based than from the nature of the sacred vow, taken in private and hedged with such images of bloodshed as are traditionally identified with ancient, pre-Christian rites of purification.

As the willing captive of drama's most private moments and thus the willing possessor of the secret thoughts and desires of characters in a play, the audience becomes, perforce, a collaborator in the action. That is, the mere fact of silent observation of a ceremony (social, religious, theatrical) compels one into a posture of collusion. That the audience is forced to collude in Hal's oath-taking is a consequence of the natural, but nonetheless dramatically contrived, fact of Hotspur's absence which further separates the warrior from the ethical circle of 'right' action to which the audience is willy-nilly a party. The confrontation of father and son, with its ramifying features of paternal accusation leading directly to the solemn blood oath, is a re-enactment of a mythical encounter, a direct step towards purification in a blood ritual through which society itself will be saved. The blood images of this speech are unlike almost all the other blood images in the play. Where those elsewhere are emotionally and morally neutral, in Hal's vow the images of the bloody mask and the garment all of blood harness the full force of traditional, even archetypal, mythic sanctity. Hal's promise to redeem himself by shedding Percy's blood is the moment to which the play has logically tended from his first soliloquy – 'I

---

[3] In describing dramatic climax, Fredson Bowers emphasizes the conscious ethical decision of that moment in the drama which determines the inevitability of its outcome. He argues that 'the rising complications of the action culminate in a crucial decision by the protagonist, the nature of which constitutes the turning point of the play and will dictate the…catastrophe' ('The Structure of King Lear', Shakespeare Quarterly, 31 (1980), 7–20; p. 8).

[4] Lawrence Danson, Tragic Alphabet (New Haven and London, 1974), pp. 20–1.

know you all...' – where he promised to reveal his hidden and greater self to the world. In this later private scene, the playwright significantly extends the circle of confidence by one; to the theatre audience is added King Henry himself.[5] In staking his life upon his honour, Hal adds potency to his promises by reference to a set of quasi-magical acts and symbols which help to conjure up dire images of fulfilment through the enactment in blood of timeless rites. Such primitive ceremonies inform the conventional concepts of honour and loyalty with new depth and so diverge from the mainstream of acts and images of the drama as to reinforce the idea of Hal's separateness and superiority. Virginia Carr has noted the violations of the ceremonies of kingship in the Henriad, commencing with Richard II's part in the murder of Thomas Duke of Gloucester and reaching their extreme form with the murder of Richard himself in which 'we see the ultimate violation of the sanctity of kingship'.[6] If we accept this view of the causes and manifestations of the destruction of ceremony, we might recognize in Hal's highly ritualized oath and performance of his vow a gradual, but concrete, reintroduction of the substances and linked ceremonies of kingship into the state.[7]

It is in distinguishing between beneficial and harmful violence that this drama advances through mime and illusion an age-old practice of blood ritual. Ritual, René Girard reminds us, 'is nothing more than the regular exercise of "good" violence'.[8] He adds: 'If sacrificial violence is to be effective it must resemble the nonsacrificial as closely as possible.' Hal's is a promise to commit a deed of 'good' violence, and the elements of ceremony with which he intends to inform the deed only add to its ritualized nature. To Hal, his blood-covered features and the garment of blood are the necessary stage of pollution precedent to the promised regeneration. In these images, Hal imagines himself stained with Hotspur's blood and presenting himself to his father as the conqueror of his father's – and of 'right' society's – enemy, and thus the saviour of the nation. The bloody mask is a token or a symbol of his effort on behalf of established order and will publicly proclaim him as hero.

And yet it is a mask. As such, it can possess the power to disguise the wearer. Hal imagines himself not precisely bloody or blood-smeared, but as wearing bloody robes. To *wear* a garment of blood is different from bloodying one's own garments: it can mean to wear outward dress or covering which is stained with blood or to be so covered in blood as to seem to be wearing such a robe. It is likely that both meanings are intended. The latter is used as an assurance of heroic behaviour, as a part of the ritual of purification being described and, furthermore, the latter use accords more literally and immediately with the notion, two lines later, of washing away the accumulated gore on garment and face. The idea of the garment, however, as a separate robe and of the mask as an adopted guise enforces an impression of Hal as separate from the bloody object. In part, the self-imagined picture of the prince clad in his garment and mask has the effect of portraying Hal as priest or ritual slaughterer. As such, the image helps make concrete the early notion, gleaned from Hal's first soliloquy, that Prince Hal is in control of

---

[5] If the status of Hal as hero is acknowledged, we must recognize that it is owed in large measure to the sheer stage power of the soliloquy. Hal's presumption in addressing us directly has the effect of placing him uppermost: he goes beyond the audible reflection of, say, Falstaff on honour, to the point of taking us into his confidence, promising *us* a happy surprise, and then, here, realizing that promise.

[6] Virginia M. Carr, 'Once More into the Henriad: A "Two-Eyed" View', *Journal of English and Germanic Philology*, 77 (1978), 530–45; p. 535.

[7] Carr's reference to the gradualism of the reintroduction of ceremonies which integrate their primitive substances is consistent with the prince's so-called 'lysis' conversion, described by Sherman Hawkins as one which 'may include more than one crisis experience separated by periods of steady advance' ('The Structural Problem of Henry IV', *Shakespeare Quarterly*, 33 (1982), 278–301; p. 296). I am suggesting that Hal's use of ritual in this scene is more significant than a single stage of development or an advance to his next strength: he is demonstrating, by this use of the language of ritual, his own actual control of a situation which by rights belongs to the monarch. King Henry's subjection to this control is signalized by the conviction of his acceptance of the vow.

[8] René Girard, *Violence and the Sacred* (Baltimore, 1979), p. 37.

the events of this drama. Seeing himself in this functionary role, Hal is enforcing upon our attention his confident knowledge of himself as director of events. The idea of the garment is more usually associated with the softness of the priest's robes than with steely armour. The mask, too, is a part of the garb of the priest of the common imagination and known tradition who participates in the ritual.

If this is convincing – if Hal's perception of his killing of Hotspur can be accepted as an act of cleansing ('Which washed away shall scour my shame with it') – then we might also accept that Shakespeare has identified yet another crucial, if not *the* crucial difference between the hero and his heroic antagonist. The image of their encounter is variously imagined by Hal and Hotspur, and in this very variety of imagination lies the key to their essential characters. Hal shows his own control of his emotions and of his imagination. As Hotspur can be driven beyond the bounds of patience by imagination of huge exploits, Hal remains firmly anchored within his own sensible sphere. He is the most entirely self-controlled character in the play, perhaps in the canon. In identifying the difference between Hal and Hotspur, James Calderwood notes that 'as a future king Hal knows very well that his business is to shape history, not to be shaped by it. To Hotspur history is a fixed and final reality to which he is irrevocably committed. He has given his word, as it were; he cannot alter his role. To Hal on the other hand history is a series of roles and staged events.'[9]

Hal decidedly lacks what Maynard Mark once characterized as the first quality of the tragic hero: the driving impulse to overstatement,[10] which is possessed in such impressive abundance by Hotspur. For many, Hal seems to have an overdeveloped sense of right and wrong. Equally, and equally unlike Hotspur, part of Hal's amazing political success in the play has to do with his ability to move familiarly through a variety of speech styles, each apparently selected with a view to the occasion. We have noted in the speech quoted above the impressive opening line – its straightforwardness, its rhythm, its explicit contrast with the words to which it is a response. Immediately thereafter follow seventeen lines in which Hal commits himself to the fulfilment of a mission. These seventeen lines form a unit which is separate from that dramatic, assertive first line whose loneliness in the speech lends it an air of authenticity of emotion separable from the carefully contrived rhetoric of all that follows it. Within the following lines lies deep the notion of vengeance sanitized by reference to the cleansing ritual described. The idea of revenge is concentrated in the imagined destruction of an even greater Hotspur than exists – 'For every honour sitting on his helm, / Would they were multitudes, and on my head / My shames redoubled!' – and is given an even sensual texture by the use and placing of the two key Latinate words in the sentence, 'multitudes' and 'redoubled'. The contrast of these words and this entire section of the speech with the blunt monosyllables of line 1, of the large and conventionally noble concepts of this part of the speech with the sound of outrage and grief conveyed by that first line, lends the speech the tinge of self-consciousness. What follows these seventeen lines seems to me, even more obviously, to point to a kind of cleverness in Hal that diminishes the felt rage he is trying to express: for he overlays it with metaphors too mundane to be able to carry with them the burden of moral distress by which he is ostensibly moved. I refer to the mercantile terminology by which Hal concludes his plea: 'factor', 'engross up', 'strict account', 'render every glory up', 'tear the reckoning from his heart', 'cancels all bands', 'smallest parcel', establish in the oath-taking a tone of marketplace transaction which tends to dull the burnishing imagery of ritual and heroism with which he begins. He introduces here a new mode of speech that contrasts with the heroically extravagant promise of the culminating lines of the preceding part –

> For the time will come
> That I shall make this northern youth exchange
> His glorious deeds for my indignities.

Norman Council observes that the speech demonstrates the pragmatic side of the prince who deter-

---

9 James L. Calderwood, '*1 Henry IV*: Art's Gilded Lie', *English Literary Renaissance*, 3 (1973), 131–44; p. 137.

10 Maynard Mack, 'The Jacobean Shakespeare', in *Jacobean Theatre*, ed. John Russell Brown and Bernard Harris, Stratford-upon-Avon Studies, 1 (1960), pp. 11–41; p. 13.

mines here 'to use Hotspur's reputation for his own gain...Hotspur's honourable reputation is useful to Hal and he means to acquire it.'[11] The speech as a whole speaks of the sheer, even miraculous, *competence* of the speaker. The manipulation of styles and the variegation of tones and metaphors all denote a virtuosity which, while commendable in itself, is somewhat vitiated when compared to the different kind of virtuosity of Hotspur's speeches. Finally we must note that the rhetoric of Hal's speech, in all its variety, accomplishes its end of gaining the King's good opinion. In this sense, of course, the speech is bound to be suspect, since the whole is motivated by a desire or need of the prince to persuade the King, his powerful father, of his loyalty. And there must be satisfaction for Hal and his partisans in Henry's clear change of heart, conveyed by his confident assertion, 'A hundred thousand rebels die in this'.

All theatre audiences are accustomed to seeing people temporarily transformed into other people for the duration of the play. Audiences and participants in rituals, however, see the process and function of ritual as a means to permanent transformation of a person into, essentially, another person – a boy becomes a man, a girl a woman, a man a priest. Most Shakespeare critics have been united in recognizing the transformation of Hal from wayward boyhood to manhood after this speech. Harold Jenkins, for example, sees this exchange between father and son as the 'nodal point' of the play.[12] One may go further, I believe, in recognizing the transformation of Hal as being the transformation of the protagonist of the play into a hero – and one may identify the moment of transformation as the first line of this speech. To recognize the transformation as made permanent by virtue of a ritualized oathtaking has the effect of strengthening and universalizing the nature and extent of the change and, hence, of adumbrating with certainty the triumph of this hero in a drama which seems to depend frequently upon the formal modes of myth.

I say 'this hero' because the uniqueness of *1 Henry IV* resides very largely in the fact that this is a play with two heroes, each of whom stands at the centre of a world which has been conceived in opposition to that of the other. Those worlds are separately defined units of place and ideology which cannot coexist; for their separate existences are partially defined by the pledge of each to destroy the other. The ideologies for which the two heroes stand are at bottom the same – those of power and control.

The encounter between them is the occasion of the play's greatest emotional intensity. The moment has been predicted, vaunted, hoped for by participants and heroes alike. The privacy of the confrontation – interrupted briefly by Douglas and Falstaff – does not in any sense diminish the timeless ritual with which it is informed. We note the common expressions of recognition and identification, whose tone of defiance maintains the note of hostility necessary to such life-and-death meetings as these. And we note the nearly compulsive need of each hero to articulate to the other his sense of the meaning of the moment. The form of the expression of each is remarkable: Hal's chivalry and Hotspur's haste are appropriate symbolic denotions of each as he is given the opportunity to express his sense of the significance of the moment, demonstrating that he knows, as his opposite knows, that for one of them it is a last encounter. It is this awareness of finality that endues the moment with solemnity and the ritual with its form – that of a last accounting, in the dazzling light of a certain death to follow.

The encounter, when it finally comes, is preceded by a provocative ritual of boasting in which each of the combatants – almost as if to rediscover the basis of his hatred of the other – recalls the very spirit of his own animosity. In Hal's recollection of the Ptolemaic principle that 'Two stars keep not their motion in one sphere', he falls back upon the natural law, resistance to whose principles he has begun to abandon since his vow to the King. And indeed it is in obedience to the laws of nature that Hal has ritually dedicated himself. Hotspur's overweening vanity makes him hark back, compulsively almost, to the lust for greatness that dooms him. But it is when Hal, oddly and mockingly, borrows Hotspur's

[11] Norman Council, 'Prince Hal: Mirror of Success', *Shakespeare Studies*, 7 (1974), 125–46; pp. 142–3.

[12] Harold Jenkins, *The Structural Problem in Shakespeare's Henry the Fourth* (1956), p. 9.

own demotic language and metaphors of violent action, that the Northern youth is finally left without images and must act:

Prince.

    I'll make it greater ere I part from thee,
    And all the budding honours on thy crest
    I'll crop to make a garland for my head.

Hotspur.

    I can no longer brook thy vanities.   (5.4.70–3)

Hal's words, his image of Hotspur's 'budding' honours, suggest to his adversary that those honours are not yet full-grown, not really the honours of an adult hero. His threat to 'crop' them from his crest contains an insulting contempt: to crop, according to the *OED*, is 'to poll or to lop off'. The term, in other words, carries all the easy arrogance of a simple, almost casual, single deadly blow. In Hal's brilliantly infuriating image we and, more important, Hotspur are presented with the image of Hotspur as an unresisting plant and the prince as a carefree courtier in search of 'a garland for [his] head'. Hotspur's single line of reply is, thus, reasonably one of powerful anger: his only possible reply to Hal's vanities is the testing action of combat.

Of the dying Hotspur, George Hibbard has written that he 'eventually becomes capable of seeing all human endeavour, including his own, in relation to the great abstract ideas of time and eternity, and voices this vision of things in the moving lines he utters at his end'.[13] This observation in part explains the tragic element of this character in the coalescence of his comic and tragic selves into mutually supporting images of comedy and tragedy whose very extremism lends intensity to the character. There is tragedy, too, in the dying man's sheer magnificent truth to himself, to what he is and has ever been;

    I better brook the loss of brittle life
    Than those proud titles thou hast won of me

comes not from the large heart of the tragic vision but from the authentic, single, separate self of Harry Hotspur, uniquely and eternally apart. That difference from his fellows, from all other heroes, is gloriously captured in the penultimate realization that the instrument by which he has lived, by which his life and character have been defined, has been

stilled – 'the cold hand of death / Lies on my tongue'. Hotspur, whose eloquence has elevated him, is unimaginable in a silent state, and Shakespeare, knowing the absolute truth of this for the character and the audience, rivets all attention upon the death of his hero's speech. Thus does silence become synonymous with tragedy.

The prolonged antagonism of Hal and Hotspur has no obviously alternative outcome to this final violent conflict. And in the conflict itself we can discern the fact that the physical closeness of the antagonists is a metaphor for a larger issue evident in the spectacle: that, as the two have been driven gradually closer through the play, so have they become with the subtle aid of ritual more and more alike until, in the moments of, and those immediately after, the fatal fight, they are almost images of each other. During the violent encounter differences between combatants tend to evanesce: the violence itself is the correlative by which individuals are connected as their whole selves are absorbed by physical contention. Hal and Hotspur do not speak during their fight and thus are transformed by their attempts to kill each other into a single unit of dramatic action – the differences between them disappear; their personalities meld. And, indeed, it would seem that in killing Hotspur, and through the combat itself, Hal has absorbed something of his opponent's vital essence. There is an indication, in his tribute to the fallen hero, of love and something, too, of the generosity of soul which is Hotspur's hallmark.

Prince.

    For worms, brave Percy. Fare thee well, great
       heart!
    Ill-weav'd ambition, how much art thou shrunk!
    When that this body did contain a spirit,
    A kingdom for it was too small a bound;
    But now two paces of the vilest earth
    Is room enough. This earth that bears thee dead
    Bears not alive so stout a gentleman.
    If thou wert sensible of courtesy
    I should not make so dear a show of zeal;
    But let my favours hide thy mangled face,
    And even in thy behalf I'll thank myself

---

13 George Hibbard, *The Making of Shakespeare's Dramatic Poetry* (Toronto, 1981), p. 180.

For doing these rites of tenderness.
Adieu, and take thy praise with thee to heaven!
Thy ignomiy sleep with thee in the grave,
But not remember'd in thy epitaph!

(5.4.86–100)

The ritualistic element of the speech takes the form of a loving tribute to the fallen hero and an action of passing symbolic import. Hal, Herbert Hartmann has convincingly argued, disengages his own royal plumes from his helmet to shroud the face of his dead rival.[14] These plumes are equivalent to Hotspur's 'budding honours' and thus Hal's act of placing them upon the face of the beloved enemy is a gesture of weight. In the purest sense of the phrase, Hal *identifies with* Hotspur, and that identification is given a poignant depth by the ritualistic means through which it is achieved. In addition, by concluding Hotspur's dying speech Hal has appropriated to himself something of the power of his rival's speech; he has almost literally absorbed his last breath. Despite the obviousness of the tendency of Hotspur's last words, Hal's mere capacity to utter them cements the identification.

Ten lines later, concomitantly with his 'rites of tenderness', Prince Hal bends over the body of Hotspur to lay his favours on the soldier's face. In so doing he closes once again – and for only the second time in the drama – the physical space between them as he touches his erstwhile adversary. Hal thus bathes his own favours in the blood of Harry Hotspur. And thus, ironically, does Hotspur acquire a mask soaked in his own blood *and* the blood of the prince. For, as Hal performs his act of homage, we are powerfully reminded of his solemn oath to the King to 'stain my favours in a bloody mask'. In the mingling of the blood of Prince Hal and Harry Hotspur is the fusion of their two souls symbolically extended. The words by which Hal accompanies his gesture complete the connection: 'And even in thy behalf I'll thank myself...'. The pronouns of that line, by their self-conscious interplay, bind their subjects ever more firmly to each other. As well, history furnished Shakespeare with one additional means by which the two characters are made to merge; that is, of course, the unforgettable fact that they have the same Christian name.

The degradation of honour and courage which

Falstaff's presence offers the scene has often been discussed. One is reminded of Falstaff's capacity for sheer bestiality as he defiles the body lying near him; a capacity made more real, perhaps, by the use to which he subsequently puts the newly mangled corpse. As an ironic travesty, the gesture has an axiomatic dramatic function in keeping with the structure of parody running through the drama. However, less obvious – aside from the action's merely narrative purpose – is the reason for the action in relation, not to the scheme or structure of the drama but, precisely, to the Prince's killing of Hotspur.

A nation in a state of civil war is one in which law has failed to create or maintain order. And so it is beyond the law that the state must seek the means of stability. The means are often those of repression, which always carries the threat of resistance. Thus do the two opposing forces of tyranny and resistance to tyranny promise the fruition of actual conflict. Societies suffering repression can explode in violence which is artistically expressed as an image of the artist's political prejudice. As the violent riots of *Henry VI* are devoid of the seeds of social order, in *1 Henry IV* the conflict and its hero are presented so as to emphasize a socially beneficial outcome. Here, the blood that is shed fulfils the requirements of blood rituals. It is, one might say, 'clean' blood resulting from what René Girard has called 'good' acts of violence.[15] That is, it is blood which has been shed for the larger advantage of national welfare. And as we look back at the blood imagery related to the Hal/Hotspur conflict, it becomes clear that Hotspur's blood has been represented as that of the sacrificial creature whose death will redeem his world, and into whose life and person are concentrated the rage, anxiety, and fear of a threatened nation. His death, then, sometimes regarded as tragic, is also utterly necessary for the continuation of the nation. Dover Wilson regards it as a favourable feature of Hal's character that his 'epitaph on Hotspur contains not a word of triumph',[16] and

---

[14] Herbert Hartmann, 'Prince Hal's "Shewe of Zeale"', *PMLA*, 46 (1931), 720–3; p. 720.

[15] Girard, p. 37.

[16] J. Dover Wilson, *The Fortunes of Falstaff* (Cambridge, 1964), p. 67.

perhaps he is right. But for Shakespeare and his audience, more significant, perhaps, is the fact that Hotspur's greatness was very nearly sufficient unto his purposes: the world was almost overturned, and with it the reign of the regicide Henry IV. Hal's presence here naturally palliates the thought, since Hal is the successor to the throne of the tyrant and, just as surely, the golden hero of the drama.

At his death and because of it, Hotspur is transformed into a hero of tragic magnitude. Thus, when Falstaff rises and hacks at his corpse, he commits a direct assault upon the sanctity of the ritual that has just been performed. His act suddenly infuses the scene with uncleanness by an almost casual reversal of ritual that has just passed. The return to life of Falstaff is no miracle, but a rather sour joke, made somewhat sourer by the attitude of shallow boasting which accompanies it. The return to prose, to a disordered, unrhythmic speech which breathes selfish relief and opportunism is a wicked riposte to Hal. But the physical attack on Hotspur's corpse is a *crime* against the ethos of heroism to which the prince and, in a dramatic sense, the nation have been committed. Falstaff's act is a negation and a degradation of the cleansing by blood. And yet the repeated exposure to violence can inure us to it. While we are indeed shocked by the callous treatment of Hotspur's corpse, the very brutality of that treatment and its very extensiveness gradually accustom us to the initially shocking fact that a slain hero is being dragged around like a side of beef. The corpse of Hotspur gradually becomes the focus not merely of Falstaff's opportunism, but of a grotesque, huge, successful joke – 'one of the best jokes in the whole drama'[17] – upon whose point is balanced the question of ritual purification. Yet Falstaff's imitative act of violence rebounds upon himself: any doubts as to his locus in the moral scheme of the play are vividly resolved by his disruption of the cycle of the ritual. The emphatic terminus implied by Hal's parting words is crassly mocked by Falstaff rising up. The act of cutting Percy's thigh is represented as antithetical to Hal's death-fight with Percy: as the fight was a lucid example of the purifying violence seen only in drama and ritual, so the attack on the corpse affirmed the value of the rite by its implied but debased re-enactment of the encounter.

Hal, Hotspur, and Falstaff are, then, related through ritual, both in itself and as depicted through the dark glass of parody and travesty. Furthermore, it is through ritual that they are connected to their world in the play's intensest moments. To call Falstaff's impersonation of Hal's father in the tavern scene a parody is to diminish the force of a scene in which a youth enacts one of the deepest universal desires of man as he overthrows his tyrannical father. The scene of oath-taking, discussed earlier, is a conscious, deliberate, and calculated retraction of the desires enacted in the tavern. As such, it is either utterly false or it is the heroic conquest of reason and responsibility – i.e. social pressure and expectation – over the urging of the unconscious mind – i.e. individual nature. It is thus profitable to see the tavern ritual and its climactic, if soft-spoken, conclusion ('I do, I will') as a ritual of exorcism by which Prince Hal, through the contrived dramatization of his innermost promptings, rids himself of the demons of his deepest desires. As J. I. M. Stewart has argued with reference to the rejection of Falstaff: Hal, 'by a displacement common enough in the evolution of a ritual, kills Falstaff instead of killing the king, his father'.[18]

Hotspur, on the other hand, does not grow or change. From first to last his purpose is to gain glory and renown. Even at his death, it is to his honours that he refers as having been more dearly won of him than his life. His sheer consistency makes him an apt victim in the cruel drama of ritual sacrifice. A Hotspur who can go to his death proclaiming the value of a moral system which is by its nature exclusive of the vast world from which it derives, cannot be the hero who heals the world. His presence nearly always provides discordancy – charming and witty though it may be. He is the heart of the whirlwind that rages through the nation, and it is this heart that must be stilled for the sake of peace. In short, as with other tragic characters, it is Hotspur's death alone that can heal the world.

---

17 *Ibid.*, p. 89.
18 J. I. M. Stewart, *Character and Motive in Shakespeare* (1965), p. 138.

THE FORTUNES OF OLDCASTLE

GARY TAYLOR

All Shakespeare's plays were subjected to political censorship. Every play had to be licensed before it could be performed or published; even after that, it could get its author or actors into trouble, if objection was subsequently taken to its performance.[1] Editors recognize these facts, and can sometimes retrospectively save a writer from the censor. When a play survives in an early quarto, set from Shakespeare's own draft, we can sometimes restore material excised in the First Folio. When a Jacobean text of an Elizabethan play shows little or no sign of authorial revision, but does omit an insulting reference to the Scots, it seems reasonable enough to infer that the change was made because the sensibility of William Shakespeare had in this instance to bow to that of James Stuart.[2] We infer that the text has been censored, and we act on that inference. But in one play we can do more than 'infer' that political interference has occurred. In one case we possess abundant contemporary evidence that the text was changed, we know what Shakespeare originally wrote, what his company originally performed, and that political pressure was applied in order to force him to alter his text. Nevertheless, no editor has ever restored the original reading – despite the fact that in this case the censor's intervention makes more difference to the meaning of the play than in any other known or suspected instance.

We all know that the character called 'Falstaff' in every modern edition of *Henry IV, Part 1* was originally called 'Oldcastle'. The formidable textual and historical evidence for this fact is ably marshalled in S. B. Hemingway's New Variorum edition, and in A. R. Humphreys's new Arden one.[3]

The text itself punningly alludes to 'My old lad of the castle' (*Part 1*, 1.2.41); the only verse line in which the character's surname appears would be metrical if a three-syllable name had originally stood in place of the two-syllable 'Falstaff';[4] a speech-prefix identifies Sir John as 'Old.' (*Part 2*, 1.2.138). The Epilogue to *Part 2* goes out of its way explicitly to deny that 'Falstaffe' is 'Olde-castle' (ll. 31–2) – a denial surely unnecessary unless the previous play had given audiences good reason to make just that identification. This 'internal evidence' is confirmed by extensive external evidence. Thomas Middleton (1604), Nathan Field (*c.* 1611), the anonymous author of *Wandering-Jew, Telling Fortunes to Englishmen* (*c.* 1628), George Daniel (1647), Thomas

---

[1] See G. E. Bentley, *The Profession of Dramatist in Shakespeare's Time, 1590–1642* (Princeton, 1971), pp. 145–96; and, for a more thorough survey, Janet Clare, 'Art made tongue-tied by authority: a study of the relationship between Elizabethan and Jacobean drama and authority and the effect of censorship on the plays of the period' (unpublished Ph.D. thesis, University of Birmingham, 1981).

[2] See *The Merchant of Venice*, 1.2.77, where 'the Scottish Lorde' in the Quarto (B1^v) becomes 'the other lord' in the Folio (TLN 267).

[3] Hemingway (Philadelphia, 1936), pp. 447–57; Humphreys (1960), pp. xv–xviii. Line references follow Humphreys's text.

[4] *Part 1*, 2.2.103: 'away good Ned, Falstalffe sweates to death' (C4^v; the Quarto sets the whole speech as prose, but it is clearly verse). At 2.4.521, Peto's speech would be metrical if the name were altered ('Falstallfe: fast asleepe behind the Arras'), but the passage as a whole is less certainly verse. In both passages – as throughout Q – the substituted name is spelled with an 'l' in the second syllable.

Randolph (1651), and Thomas Fuller (1655, 1662) all testify to the character's original designation as 'Oldcastle'.[5]

The most explicit deposition comes from Dr Richard James (1592–1638), friend of Ben Jonson and librarian to Sir Robert Cotton, in an autograph epistle addressed 'To my Noble friend S^r henry Bourchier', and prefixed to James's own manuscript edition of Hoccleve's 'The legend and defence of ye Noble knight and Martyr Sir Jhon Oldcastel' (Bodleian Library, James MS 34; also British Library, Add. MS 33785).[6] Halliwell-Phillipps, who first printed this epistle, dated it '*c.* 1625'; it cannot be earlier than 1625, and more probably dates from *c.* 1634.[7] In it, James refers to *Henry IV, Part 1* as 'Shakespeares first shewe of Harrie ye fift':[8]

A young Gentle Ladie of your acquaintance having read ye works of Shakespeare, made me this question. How Sir Jhon Falstaffe, ⌐or Fastollf as he is written in ye statute book of Maudlin Colledge in Oxford where everye daye y^t societie were bound to make memorie of his soule¬ could be dead in ~~y^e~~ Harrie ye fifts time and againe liue in ye time of Harrie ye sixt to be banisht for cowardize. Whereto I made answeare that this was one of those humours and mistakes for which Plato banisht all poets out of his commonwealth.

After a thumbnail biography of the historical Sir John Fastolfe, James continues

That in Shakespeares first shewe of Harrie ye fift, ye person with which he vndertook to playe a buffone was not Falstaffe, but Sr Jhon Oldcastle, and that offence beinge worthily taken by personages descended from his ⌐title,¬ as peradventure by manie others allso whoe ought to haue him in honourable memorie, the poet was putt to make an ignorant shifte of abusing Sr Jhon ~~Falstaffe or~~ Fastolphe, a man not inferior ⌐of¬ Vertue though not so famous in pietie as the other, whoe gaue witnefse vnto the truth of our reformation with a constant and resolute martyrdom, vnto which he was pursued by the Priests, Bishops, Moncks, and Friers of those dayes.

Dr James not only confirms that the change was made: he tells us why, and testifies that the poet was 'putt to...an ignorant shifte'. James's literary and court connections make his evidence impossible to dismiss. The 'personages descended from [Old-

castle's] title' can be readily identified as Sir William Brooke, Lord Cobham, Lord Chamberlain from August 1596 to March 1597, and his son, Sir Henry Brooke; one of Sir William's daughters was married to Sir Robert Cecil. The Lord Chamberlain was of course the master of the Master of the Revels, who licensed plays; moreover, *Part 1* was almost certainly written in 1596 or early 1597, when Lord Cobham was Lord Chamberlain. Thus, the character's name was changed as the result of the intervention of a peer of the realm, member of the Privy Council, intimate friend of Lord Burghley, and father-in-law of Sir Robert Cecil.[9] These his-

---

[5] Hemingway, pp. 447–57; Humphreys, pp. xv–xvii. Humphreys attributes the anonymous *Meeting of Gallants at an Ordinarie* (1604) to Dekker, but Middleton now seems more likely to have written it (unless they both did); see David J. Lake, *The Canon of Thomas Middleton's Plays* (Cambridge, 1975), pp. 270–3. Neither Hemingway nor Humphreys mentions the allusion in Randolph's *Hey for Honesty*, p. 28; this is quoted and discussed by Alice-Lyle Scoufos, *Shakespeare's Typological Satire: A Study of the Falstaff-Oldcastle Problem* (Athens, Ohio, 1979), p. 38, as part of her full survey of the allusions (pp. 32–43).

[6] This dedication was first noted and transcribed by J. O. Halliwell[-Phillipps] in *On the Character of Sir John Falstaff, as originally exhibited by Shakespeare in the two parts of King Henry IV* (1841), pp. 18–20; the entire manuscript was transcribed in *The Poems Etc., of Richard James, B.D.*, ed. A. B. Grosart (1880), where the dedication occurs on pp. 137–8. Grosart's introduction provides the fullest account of James's life and work, though it is updated and corrected in a few respects by C. L. Kingsford's entry for *The Dictionary of National Biography*.

[7] The evidence for dating the manuscript is re-examined in my 'William Shakespeare, Richard James, and the House of Cobham' (forthcoming in *The Review of English Studies*), which also discusses the probable date and circumstances of the Brookes' interference with *Part 1* and *Merry Wives*; I argue there that the change to Falstaff occurred before much if anything of *Part 2* was written.

[8] My transcript is based on the Bodleian manuscript; interlinear insertions are signalled by half brackets. The British Library manuscript seems to be a later copy.

[9] The most thorough account of the Elizabethan Cobhams is the late David McKeen's unpublished doctoral dissertation, '"A Memory of Honour": A study of the House of Cobham of Kent in the Reign of Elizabeth I' (University of Birmingham, 1966). McKeen was an historian, whose account of the Cobhams is much more reliable and level-headed than all others.

torical facts have long been appreciated; Nicholas Rowe, Shakespeare's first editor, knew of the change, and provides independent confirmation that the Cobhams were responsible for it.[10] As Humphreys bluntly says, 'Falstaff was certainly once Oldcastle'. No one now disputes this conclusion. But no one has acted upon it either. No one has restored the name Shakespeare intended for the character, before he was forced to change it. Why not?

Editors might be inhibited by the fact that in changing 'Falstaff' back to 'Oldcastle' in *Part 1* they would 'create' an inconsistency in the canon: Prince Hal's companion, identified as 'Oldcastle' in *Part 1*, must have been firmly identified as 'Falstaff' by the time Shakespeare wrote *Henry V* and *Merry Wives* – not to mention *Part 2*. But in fact editors are also left with inconsistencies if they retain 'Falstaff'. The 'young Gentle Ladie' who accosted Dr James was bewildered by one such inconsistency, 350 years ago: the reappearance, in *Henry VI*, of the character who apparently died in *Henry V*.[11] Everyone recognizes that the Sir John of the *Merry Wives* differs from his counterpart in other plays; the character in *Henry V* does not fulfil the role promised by the Epilogue to *Part 2*; almost all critics since A. C. Bradley have accepted that there are substantial differences in the character even between the two parts of *Henry IV*.[12] Such inconsistencies bother us less if we respond to *Henry IV, Part 1* and its successors not as fragments of a 'tetralogy' but as whole, individual plays, written over the course of several years and never in Shakespeare's lifetime performed – so far as we know – as a cycle.

As for the fictive unity of the character himself, the old reprobate who appears in three different plays, that can be recognized by using the designation 'Sir John' for all his speech-prefixes in *Part 1*, *Part 2*, and *Merry Wives*. In fact, 'Sir John' is how the dialogue most often identifies him: the linked title and Christian name occur on their own 120 times in the four plays, whereas the surname on its own is used only 57 times, and never in any single play more often than 'Sir John'. The character could remain, in speech-prefixes and hence in critical discussion, 'Sir John with all Europe' – thus retaining a single designation which neither falsifies Shakespeare's intentions nor robs the character of what unity he does possess; but in the dialogue and in stage directions he would be either 'Sir John Oldcastle' (in *Part 1*) or 'Sir John Falstaff' (elsewhere) – thereby restoring Shakespeare's original intention and recognizing the disparity between *Part 1* and the later plays.

The inconsistency 'created' by an editor's reversion to 'Oldcastle' in *Part 1* is created not by the modern editor, but by the sixteenth-century censor. Shakespeare wrote and produced *Part 1* using the surname 'Oldcastle'; he wrote – or at least finished – *Merry Wives*, *Henry V*, and (I believe) *Part 2* after he had been forced to change the surname to 'Falstaff'. An editor who restored the original surname would thus be preserving inconsistencies in Shakespeare's own writing – just as we preserve inconsistencies of time, place, and action. In 1.3 and 2.1 of *Merry Wives* Shakespeare confuses the characters of Ford and Brooke in ways no editor can untangle; in *Henry V* Pistol begins married to Nell (2.1), but apparently ends married to Doll (5.1); in *The Two Gentlemen of Verona* Silvia's father is both a duke and an emperor, living simultaneously in both Milan and Verona. If Shakespeare was so careless of elementary consistency even within a single play, we can hardly presume that he would have been offended by an inconsistency *between* plays. Sophocles' three plays on the myth of Oedipus, though often spoken of as a 'trilogy' (with

---

[10] '[T]his Part of *Falstaff* is said to have been written originally under the name of *Oldcastle*; some of that Family being then remaining, the Queen was pleas'd to command him to alter it' (vol. 1, p. ix). Rowe can hardly have seen James's manuscript dedication, and in any case he adds the detail of the Queen's role.

[11] George Walton Williams argues – in 'Fastolf or Falstaff', *English Literary Renaissance*, 5 (1975), 308–12, and 'Second Thoughts on Falstaff's Name', *Shakespeare Quarterly*, 30 (1979), 82–4 – that 'Falstaff' in *Henry VI, Part 1* is a sophistication, and that the original name 'Fastolf' has in the Folio been contaminated, under the influence of his more famous counterpart. If Williams is right, then someone else had confused the two characters, even before Dr James's young lady.

[12] 'The Rejection of Falstaff', in *Oxford Lectures on Poetry* (1909), pp. 247–75.

no less and no more justice than Shakespeare's histories are grouped into 'tetralogies'), are on many points mutually incompatible in their account of events. Consistency of this kind worries editors more than it does artists. In the matter of Sir John's surname, history produced an inconsistency, which we have no right to tidy up. The change of name was forced upon Shakespeare after he had completed *Part 1*, and had it performed; we can therefore restore *Part 1* to the form it took in Shakespeare's original conception. The other plays cannot be 'restored', because by the time he finished them Shakespeare had been forced to change his conception of the role.

It might be objected that, even in *Part 1*, Shakespeare's original conception is beyond recall. What if the change of name was accompanied by other, more substantial changes of dialogue, character, or structure? Dover Wilson believed – for this play as for most others – that the extant text represents a wholesale revision of an earlier lost Shakespearian original, written entirely in verse. No one now takes this speculation seriously. But Wilson's elaborate hypothesis has had the unfortunate effect of making even those editors who reject it continue to talk about the problem of Sir John's surname as a question of 'revision'. Wilson, following A. E. Morgann, supposed that Shakespeare had extensively revised his whole play;[13] for this conjecture there is no external evidence and no credible internal evidence. The historical record and the internal evidence instead testify that, because of complaints in high places, Shakespeare was compelled to change at least one character's name.[14] The change of name is not an instance of revision but of censorship. But what if the censor also objected to other aspects of the original? If he did so, then those other features are lost beyond recovery. But we have no evidence that such additional changes were ever made. None of the many extant witnesses refers to lost episodes or actions – though we do know of lost material in less famous plays, like *Tamburlaine* and *Pericles* and *The Merry Devil of Edmonton* and *The Conspiracy and Tragedy of Charles, Duke of Byron*.[15] The fact that the extant texts of *Part 1* do not even remove the pun on Oldcastle's name, or attempt to smooth the metre

of the only verse line in which the new name was substituted, or change his Christian name, or change his social rank, or take out of the character's mouth the many religious allusions so hypocritically appropriate to his original identity, do not suggest that the 'revision' was overly painstaking. Shakespeare seems – like many another writer in this situation – to have done the bare minimum demanded by his masters. Those who took offence at the portrayal of Oldcastle could insist either that the portrait of his character be reformed, or that the unreformed character not be identified with Oldcastle. Obviously, the easier of these two options was elected. Once the name was changed, there would be no need to alter the character. There is no reason to believe that the play has suffered more than a reformation of nomenclature; the censorship seems to have been literally 'nominal'. But even if we could be absolutely positive that the censor did enforce other changes, which we cannot now identify or undo, that impotence would not relieve us of the responsibility to undo those depredations which we can identify. Not all textual corruption is detectable; editors nevertheless correct whatever corruption they can detect. In the case of Sir John's surname, there can be absolutely no doubt that interference has occurred, and no doubt either about what should be restored.

In fact, such considerations have probably not

---

13 A. E. Morgann, *Some Problems of Shakespeare's 'Henry IV'* (1924), and Wilson, 'The Origins and Development of Shakespeare's *Henry IV*', *The Library*, IV, 26 (1945), 2–16.

14 The names of two of Oldcastle's companions – Rossill and Harvey – seem also to have been changed, presumably for similar reasons. For a full reconsideration of these names, see John Jowett's 'The Thieves in *1 Henry IV*' (forthcoming).

15 The omissions from *Tamburlaine* are alluded to in the printer's preface to the first edition; for *Byron*, see E. K. Chambers, *The Elizabethan Stage*, 4 vols. (Oxford, 1923), vol. 3, pp. 257–8. For *Pericles* and *Merry Devil*, prose pamphlets clearly influenced by the play suggest that some material has been omitted: see *Pericles Prince of Tyre*, ed. Philip Edwards (Harmondsworth, 1976), pp. 21–6, and *The Merry Devil of Edmonton*, ed. W. A. Abrams (Durham, North Carolina, 1942), pp. 257–8. (For this last reference I am indebted to G. R. Proudfoot.)

influenced editors at all. Humphreys, for instance, does not raise them. So far as the printed text of his edition accurately reflects the progress of his textual decision-making, he seems never even to have considered the possibility of reverting to the original name. Partly, perhaps, this silence results from the fact that in this case rectification of censorship does not require the time-honoured practice of editorial conflation, but calls instead for something which radically departs from time-honoured practice. Falstaff vies with Hamlet as Shakespeare's most famous character. How can an editor *possibly* change his name, in the very play which first made him famous? Editors have not simply recoiled in horror from this thought; they have, apparently, failed even to think it. The idea is unthinkable – one might say, heretical. It may be worth remembering that Sir John Oldcastle was himself burned as a heretic. In some sense the Protestant Reformation may be characterized as an exceptionally acrimonious dispute between textual critics. The works of Shakespeare are now treated with some of the veneration usually reserved for Holy Writ, and – as in all idolatries – believers vociferously object to any tampering with the particular text of Holy Writ to which they are accustomed. Indeed, the priesthood of an idolatry – those persons entrusted with the institutional authority to teach and interpret it – is the group most likely to be most offended by any change to the received text. In Shakespearian terms, a proposal to change Falstaff's name back to Oldcastle is as heretical as Oldcastle's own opinion that the Eucharist was not literally transformed into the body and blood of Jesus Christ Our Lord.

Of course, what I am proposing is not really a heresy, but simply a single emendation, based on unimpeachable historical evidence. So far as I can see, the chief, indeed the only objection to restoring the original reading (Oldcastle) is that the substituted reading (Falstaff) has become famous: an entire tradition of criticism and performance has been based upon it. In response to this objection I can only reply, 'So much the worse for tradition; it is time the tradition was abandoned.' After all, in forty or at most fifty years every current critic and teacher of Shakespeare will be retired or dead; for a whole

new generation of readers 'Oldcastle' could become as familiar as 'Falstaff' is now to us. What shocks us will not shock them. If I may quote Sir Walter Greg:[16]

RULE I

The aim of a critical edition should be to present the text, so far as the available evidence permits, in the form in which we may suppose that it would have stood in a fair copy, made by the author himself, of the work as *he* finally intended it.

When Shakespeare finished *Part 1*, when it was performed by his own company, the name of his fat knight was undoubtedly Oldcastle.

But is Greg right? In the 'final' version of *Part 1*, the version being performed for most of Shakespeare's career, the character's name was 'Falstaff', and an editor might decide that the *reasons* for a particular change of nomenclature are none of our business: Shakespeare acquiesced in the alteration, and so should we. This is an intellectually respectable editorial position, much favoured by modern German textual scholarship;[17] but I think it is wrong in theory, and in Shakespeare's case deeply undesirable in practice. If a colleague suggests changes to a play, Shakespeare is at liberty to accept or reject those suggestions, and since he determines which changes to incorporate he becomes intentionally and voluntarily responsible for the final result. By contrast, if the Master of the Revels or the Lord Chamberlain says, 'Change this character's name', Shakespeare cannot ignore that advice – or, if he does so, he accepts that the play can no longer be performed, or ever printed. Theoretically, even this liberty might be denied him: the authorities might

---

[16] *The Editorial Problem in Shakespeare: A Survey of the Foundations of the Text*, 3rd edn. (Oxford, 1954), p. x (emphasis mine).

[17] See Hans Zeller, 'A New Approach to the Critical Constitution of Literary Texts', *Studies in Bibliography*, 28 (1975), pp. 245–9. Where political interference is uncertain, and in any case inextricably entangled with a thoroughgoing revision, editorial restoration is of course much more questionable: see my 'Monopolies, Show Trials, Disaster, and Invasion: *King Lear* and Censorship', in *The Division of the Kingdoms: Shakespeare's Two Versions of 'King Lear'*, ed. Gary Taylor and Michael Warren (Oxford, 1983), pp. 75–119.

insist that the play be publicly performed or printed with the new name, in order to demonstrate to everyone the change of identity – just as heretics were forced to recant publicly.[18] In such cases, an author 'acquiesces' in alterations only to the extent that he wishes to avoid imprisonment or imposed silence, and as a result the author effectively ceases to be responsible for such changes, which might be made without even consulting him. If an editor nevertheless chose to accept the change of name as an alteration Shakespeare passively endorsed, then the same policy must be applied to such changes throughout the canon: all the Folio's excisions of politically sensitive or profane material must also be accepted, since they can be justified on exactly the same grounds as the change to 'Falstaff'. Of course, two of the plays most seriously misrepresented by such a policy would be the two parts of *Henry IV*, which suffered considerable pruning in the Folio. An editor can hardly reject those politically imposed changes while accepting the politically imposed change to Sir John's surname.

Nor is it clear that Shakespeare or his company did entirely acquiesce in the change. In the absence of a private diary or letter, or a report of his conversation, we simply do not know (and never will) what Shakespeare's 'final' thoughts were. We do know what Shakespeare originally intended, and why that intention was abandoned; what we know is more important than what we imagine or speculate about thought processes never committed to paper. Moreover, since only *Part 1* was composed with 'Oldcastle' in mind, the later intentions of Shakespeare and his company only matter in relation to a single question: would he (or they) have restored 'Oldcastle' to *Part 1*, if given the chance, even after *Part 2*, *Henry V*, and *Merry Wives* were written? Of course, Shakespeare and his colleagues might have harboured such a wish, even if they could never translate it into reality. But as it happens, considerable evidence exists that the play was, even after 1597, sometimes privately performed with the original designation intact.

On 6 March 1600 Rowland Whyte referred to a private performance of 'Sir Iohn Old Castell' by the Chamberlain's Men for their patron the Lord

Chamberlain, before the visiting Austrian ambassador Verreiken, in England to negotiate peace with Spain;[19] on 6 January 1631 the same company (by then the King's Men) performed 'Old Castle' at court 'At the Cock-pitt';[20] on 29 May 1639 they again performed 'ould Castel' at court, on 'the princes berthnyght'.[21] The first of these cannot be a reference to Henslowe's *Oldcastle* play, which stayed in his possession from October 1599 until at least September 1602, and could hardly have been performed by a rival company at that time;[22] nor is it probable that Shakespeare's company would wish to perform a play which so clearly represents an attack on one of their own; they would, on the contrary, probably be asked to perform one of their own most successful plays, and that they did so is suggested by the ambassador's 'great Contentment' with what he saw. Moreover, since *Part 1* was sometimes referred to as 'Falstaff', it could evidently be identified by means of its chief comic character;[23] so it should not

---

[18] Since Chambers made the suggestion – *William Shakespeare: A Study of Facts and Problems*, 2 vols. (Oxford, 1930), vol. 1, p. 382 – it has been generally assumed that *Part 1*'s publication early in 1598 was required, in order to publicize the change of names: the company would normally have resisted publication of so recent and popular a play.

[19] Arthur Collins, *Letters and Memorials of State*, 2 vols. (1746), vol. 2, p. 175; abstracted in *HMC De L'Isle and Dudley Papers*, vol. 2, p. 443. On Verreiken, see *Calendar of State Papers, Venetian, 1592–1603*, p. 397. Cobham was at the time incapacitated by a leg injury (McKeen, pp. 1004–5); we do not know whether he knew or would have objected to the performance of the play at all, or to the restoration of Sir John's surname, on an occasion specifically designed to demonstrate the compatibility of English and Spanish points of view.

[20] James G. McManaway, 'A New Shakespeare Document', *Shakespeare Quarterly*, 2 (1951), 119–22.

[21] Chambers, *William Shakespeare*, vol. 1, p. 382; vol. 2, p. 353.

[22] *Henslowe's Diary*, ed. R. A. Foakes and R. T. Rickert (Cambridge, 1961), pp. 125, 126, 129, 132, 213, 214, 216.

[23] Hemingway, p. 477. This alternative title was especially favoured in court records: it occurs in relation to performances of 20 May 1613 (Chambers, *Elizabethan Stage*, vol. 4, p. 180) and 1 January 1625, and in a manuscript note by Sir George Buc *c.* 1619–20. See G. E. Bentley, *The Jacobean and Caroline Stage*, 7 vols. (1941–68), vol. 1, p. 95. '*Henry IV*' never appears in court records, so that

surprise us if the uncensored version were identified as 'Oldcastle'. Finally, since the Lord Chamberlain was the chief censor, and since in 1600 the Lord Chamberlain was no longer a Cobham but instead the patron of Shakespeare's company, he was obviously in a position to allow a private performance of the original version. It therefore seems probable that Shakespeare was able to change the name back to 'Oldcastle' at least once after 1597 – and that he did so, despite the fact that *Part 2*, *Merry Wives*, and *Henry V*, which identify the character as 'Falstaff', had by 1600 all been written. This apparent reversion to the original surname constitutes fairly reliable external evidence that (as we would expect) Shakespeare was not happy with the enforced change and was willing to have the character in *Part 1* identified as 'Oldcastle' even after the alternative designation 'Falstaff' had become current in other plays.

It seems intrinsically likely that the later court performances of 'Oldcastle' also involve Shakespeare's play. The fact that one of these took place on the birth-night of the Prince of Wales makes this particularly probable: Henslowe's play has no noticeable pertinence to such an occasion, but *Part 1* would be remarkably appropriate fare for the young prince. Moreover, Queen Henrietta Maria – notorious for her interest in the theatre – was an avowed and fervent Catholic; Charles I himself was often suspected of Catholic inclinations. The list noting the 1630 performance may well be, according to McManaway, in the hand of the actor John Lowin. The well-informed and generally reliable James Wright, writing in 1699, claimed that Lowin (1576–1653) actually played '*Falstaffe*'; he was certainly, on the basis of a variety of much earlier, reliable evidence, a huge, overweight man who regularly played gruff soldiers, either as comedians or villains.[24] The fact that this actor apparently identified the play – and hence the character – as 'Olde Castle' is therefore especially intriguing. But even if these Caroline court performances did not restore the original name, the two documents do suggest that, even in the 1630s, some people continued to identify Sir John as Oldcastle. Knowledgeable spectators restored Shakespeare's

intention mentally, even if it could not be restored in print or on stage. And it may even have been restored in the theatre on more occasions than the one documented in 1600. Thomas Fuller's 1655 allusion to the play claims that Falstaff's name 'of late is substituted' for Oldcastle – an explicit statement difficult to reconcile with the assumption that all performances after 1597 accepted the change of name.[25]

In addition to such evidence that 'Oldcastle' was sometimes restored in performance, modern bibliographical analysis of the sequence of printing of the First Folio suggests that Heminges and Condell may have attempted to restore the original name. Henry Brooke, Lord Cobham, was arrested in July 1603, convicted of treason in November, and spent the rest of his life in the Tower, where he died in 1619; the title lapsed until 1645, when it was conferred on Henry's second cousin. (See *The Dictionary of National Biography*.) Hence, from 1619 to 1645 the Cobham barony was vacant, and in no position to exert the political pressure it could have brought to bear in 1596–7. As a result, after 1619 Shakespeare's fellow-actors, who were also the editors of the First Folio, may have hoped that a restoration of the original surname was possible. Certainly, during the setting of *Richard II* there was an unexplained change in the sequence of composition, skipping over both *Henry IV* plays, so that *Henry V* and most of the three parts of *Henry VI* were set into type before the compositors returned to *Henry IV*. It has usually been assumed that difficulty in securing copyright caused this delay; that difficulty may then have been

---

the two references to 'Oldcastle' fit a consistent court pattern of identifying the play by the name of its chief comic character. (The only exception is 'the Hotspur', alternatively used of the 1613 performance.) The currency of the name 'Oldcastle' for Shakespeare's play may well explain why William Jaggard and Thomas Pavier included the Henslowe play in their 1619 collection of reprinted Shakespeare quartos: see E. E. Willoughby, *A Printer of Shakespeare: the books and times of William Jaggard* (1934), pp. 128–9.

24 Wright, *Historia Histrionica*, p. 4; Chambers, *Elizabethan Stage*, vol. 2, pp. 328–9; Bentley, vol. 2, pp. 499–506.

25 *The Church-History of Britain: From the Birth of Jesus Christ, until the year 1648*, Book 4, p. 168.

overcome by acquisition of a new manuscript, enabling the Folio editors to supply variant readings, and hence to claim that they were publishing a new or different version of the play, not covered by the existing copyright.[26] But this conjecture is speculative: we do not *know* that there was any difficulty over the copyright to *Part 1*. On the other hand we *do* know that there had been difficulty over the name of an important character in *Part 1*, and that a key figure in that controversy had recently died, without a successor. The delay in printing Folio *Henry IV* could easily have arisen because of an attempt to secure permission from the new Master of the Revels (who by then also licensed the publication of plays) to restore the original surname. Indeed, this explanation could easily coexist with the other, for the change of Sir John's surname would surely circumvent copyright as effectively as the introduction of a few score of insignificant verbal variants. If Heminges and Condell did attempt to restore 'Oldcastle', they obviously failed, presumably because religious objections to the name remained, even after the family objections of the Cobhams had lost their force: publication of the play with 'Oldcastle' restored, especially in an impressive folio volume 'printed in the best Crowne paper, far better than most Bibles', would have looked like an official public endorsement of its scurrilous portrayal of a 'martyr'.[27] The failure of their attempt would then have forced Heminges and Condell either to come to some arrangement with the copyright holder, or to provide the publishers with a variant manuscript. Such complications could easily account for the postponement of printing.

My reconstruction remains speculative too, of course, but at least it uses known events to account for known events, and illustrates the folly of assuming too readily that Heminges and Condell, as Shakespeare's literary executors, were happy enough to perpetuate 'Falstaff' in *Part 1*. It is possible that Heminges and Condell tried unsuccessfully to restore 'Oldcastle' in print in 1623; it is probable that the name was, as Fuller implies, actually used in some private performances in the 1630s. If so, then the players – as well as the playwright – demonstrated their dissatisfaction with the imposed change

of name, when they could. Final acquiescence was only secured when Puritans ruled England and theatres were closed. The editorial concept of 'final intention' can have little value in a case like this, where social restraints only successfully finalized their domination of the author's meaning decades after his death.

Some readers may be willing to concede that, in principle, Oldcastle should be restored, and yet still protest that the change is impracticable: 'however right it may be, it would cause too much trouble'. Such arguments have also been heard recently in relation to *King Lear*, and they expose a fundamental contradiction in critical attitudes toward textual scholarship.[28] Critics do not object when an edition like *The Riverside Shakespeare* departs from its predecessors in hundreds of individual readings, because such scholarly labours increase one's confidence in the text, while at the same time making no difference to its interpretation. But when the

---

26 See Charlton Hinman, *The Printing and Proof-Reading of the First Folio of Shakespeare*, 2 vols. (Oxford, 1963), vol. 1, pp. 27–8 (on copyright), 159–60; vol. 2, pp. 14–106, 489–503 (on the sequence of setting). For further discussion of the possible influence of copyright on the editorial treatment of certain Folio texts (including *Part 1*), see John Jowett and Gary Taylor, 'Sprinklings of Authority: The Folio Text of *Richard II*', *Studies in Bibliography*, 38 (1985), 151–200. The copyright to *Part 2* was owned by a member of the syndicate which published the Folio.

27 William Prynne, *Histrio-Mastix. The Players Scourge or Actors Tragædie* (1633), 'To the Christian Reader', fol. I[V]. Similar antipathy is expressed in *Mercurius Britannicus* for 2 September 1644 (E. 8. (3), p. 386), where '*Shakespeares Workes*' are included among 'such Prelaticall trash as your Clergy men spend their Canonical houres on'; the works it is there linked with – 'some Lady Psalters, and *Cosins* Devotions, and *Pocklingtons* Altar, and *Shelfords* Sermons' – were especially hated by the Puritans for what was thought to be their 'Popish' influence. See Ernest Sirluck, 'Shakespeare and Jonson among the Pamphleteers of the First Civil War: Some Unreported Seventeenth-Century Allusions', *Modern Philology*, 53 (1955), p. 94.

28 Andrew Gurr, 'The Once and Future *King Lears*', *Bulletin of the Society for Renaissance Studies*, 2 (1984), 7–19; similar objections were raised in the Textual Seminar of the Shakespeare Association of America conference at Cambridge, Massachusetts, 1984.

same labours lead an editor to propose restoring both early versions of *King Lear*, or the original name of Shakespeare's most famous comic character, then some critics will object that the changes are impractical simply because they make so much difference. This attitude creates a situation in which the results of textual scholarship are always trivial, because if the results are *not* trivial they will be disregarded. It also creates the paradox that minor authors will always be better edited than major ones – because the perceived imperative of 'practicality' exists only in so far as an author is already widely read and interpreted. Hence, Shakespeare's editors continue to produce texts which, in one way or another, they do not believe in; each succumbs to the weight of tradition, and thereby adds to the weight on any subsequent editor. At some point this vicious cycle must be broken, and Shakespeare edited with as much care as Robert Sidney or Edward Fairfax.

Even if it made no difference whatever to the play's meaning, the restoration of the character's original name would be, editorially, the proper thing to do. But reverting to Oldcastle does more than restore the tag by which Shakespeare identified a role: it restores the meaning and the shape which that identification gave to the character and the play. Oldcastle really was a soldier, who had fought for Henry IV in France and Wales: 'this valiant Knight', John Foxe called him; 'that thrice valiant Capitaine', in John Weever's words; 'a meetely good man of war', wrote John Stow; 'a valiaunt capitain and an hardy gentleman', according to Edward Hall.[29] The title-page of John Bale's influential, popular apologia actually portrays Oldcastle, described as a 'moste valyaunt warryour', with sword and shield.[30] Sir John's appearance at the King's side, in the council before the battle of Shrewsbury (5.1), would therefore not have seemed as incongruous with 'Oldcastle' as it does with 'Falstaff'. All the chroniclers agree that Oldcastle was 'well liked' by and 'highly in the...fauor' of Henry V, before his disgrace.[31] Aside from his appropriate presence at Shrewsbury, Shakespeare's Sir John takes no part in the major political events of the play; nor would this surprise anyone familiar with Foxe's description of

him as 'but a priuate subiect, and a poore Knight'.[32] Oldcastle was also hanged on the gallows, before being burned – an unusual form of execution gruesomely illustrated by a large woodcut in Foxe's influential 'Book of Martyrs'.[33] *Part 1* alludes half a dozen times to Sir John's anticipated death on the gallows. Shakespeare's Oldcastle also has affinities with the character of that name in the anonymous *Famous Victories of Henry the Fifth*, which Shakespeare undoubtedly knew: he participates in a robbery, swears profusely, and looks forward to being a hangman when Hal is king.[34] Shakespeare's Sir John recognizably reflects features of the earlier historical and dramatic portrayals of Oldcastle.

But the historical Oldcastle was also the subject of one of the sixteenth century's running religious controversies: 'whether this foresayd sir Iohn Oldcastle', as Foxe put it, 'is rather to be comm̄eded for a Martyr, or to be reproued for a traytor'.[35] In these relatively ecumenical times it may seem unlikely that Shakespeare intended Sir John to represent a man incinerated for his religious convictions. But the polemicists of the sixteenth century were not inhibited by such tender decorums. Foxe, for instance, describes the portrait of

---

[29] Foxe, *Actes and Monuments of Martyrs, Newly revised and inlarged by the Author* (1583), p. 643b; Weever, *The Mirror of Martyrs, or The life and death of that thrice valiant Capitaine, and most godly Martyre* Sir Iohn Old-castle knight, *Lord Cobham* (1601); Stow, *The Annales of England* (1592), pp. 550–1; Hall, *The Union of the Two Noble and Illustre Families of Lancastre and Yorke* (1548), a.iiᵛ (of 'The Victorious actes of kyng Henry the V').

[30] *A brefe Chronycle concernynge the Examinacyon and death of the blessed Martyr of Christ Syr Iohan Oldecastell the lorde Cobham* (1544; repr. 1545? 1548?). The title-page is reproduced in Scoufos, p. 68.

[31] Hall, a.iiᵛ; Foxe, pp. 566a, 568b; Raphael Holinshed, *The Third Volume of Chronicles* (1587), p. 544a.

[32] Foxe, p. 573b; see also 'beyng but a poore Knight by his degree' (p. 573a).

[33] Foxe, p. 643; reproduced in Scoufos, p. 57.

[34] The text of *Famous Victories* is reprinted in *Narrative and Dramatic Sources of Shakespeare*, ed. Geoffrey Bullough, 8 vols. (London and New York), vol. 4 (1962), pp. 299–343. In Bullough's text Oldcastle speaks or is referred to in ll. 15–38, 447–58, and 701–56; he is not the chief of Hal's companions, and speaks only 28 lines.

[35] Foxe, p. 568b.

Oldcastle drawn by the 'English Chroniclers' – Fabian, Hall, Polydore Vergil, Cooper, Grafton – as 'malicious railing, virulent slanders, manifest vntruths, opprobrious contumelies, & stinking blasphemies, able almost to corrupt & infect ye aire'. Matthew Sutcliffe called Walsingham 'a lying Monke' and claimed that 'Stow hath the most part of his lyes concerning the Lord Cobham out of Walsingham, which notwithstanding he vnderstood not being Latine, and he a meere English Taylor'.[36]

The historical tradition which so irritated these divines was first documented by Wilhelm Baeske in 1905 and, more thoroughly, by Alice-Lyle Scoufos in 1979; it characterizes Oldcastle as a robber, traitor, heretic and hypocrite.[37] Even Bale admitted that 'his youthe was full of wanton wildenesse'; Tyndale, Bale, and Foxe all quoted Oldcastle's confession, during his trial, that 'in my frayle youth I offended thee (Lord) most greuously in pride, wrath, and gluttony: in couetousnes, and in lechery. Many men haue I hurt in mine anger, and done many other horrible sinnes.'[38] Hall introduces his discussion of Oldcastle and other Lollards with a reference to 'certayne persones callyng themselfes spirituall fathers, but in deede carnall coueteous and gredy glottons'. Foxe devotes twenty folio pages of his revised edition to 'A defence of the Lord Cobham, agaynst Nich. Harpsfield'.[39] Shakespeare need not have read Harpsfield, or Walsingham, or the fifteenth-century histories, because their version of Oldcastle is expounded in considerable detail by Foxe himself – as well as Hall, Holinshed, and Stow, all readily available and clearly consulted by Shakespeare when writing his history plays.[40]

According to these authors, Oldcastle's 'intent was to destroy his soueraigne Lord the king' and 'to destroy Gods law' and 'to destroy all maner of policie, & finally the lawes of ye land'.[41] Shakespeare's character, in outline and detail, has a good deal in common with this archetypal champion of moral chaos, and the presence of Oldcastle emphasizes the play's religious themes. The first speech in Part 1 is devoted – irrelevantly, so far as the traditional text is concerned – to Henry IV's intended crusade to Jerusalem:

> those holy fields,
> Ouer whose acres walkt those blessed feet,
> Which 1400. yeares ago were naild
> For our aduantage on the bitter crosse.

(1.1.24–7)

Sir John's moralizing, swearing, threats of repentance, and mimicry of Puritan idiom would have been especially delicious, and satirical, in the mouth of Oldcastle. At Gad's Hill Oldcastle and his companions plan to rob, of all people, 'pilgrims going to Canturburie' (1.2.121–2). Bale and Foxe – and later Matthew Sutcliffe, and Dr Richard James himself – contrasted Oldcastle with Thomas à Becket, to Becket's disadvantage.[42] When Hal at

---

36 Foxe, p. 576b; Sutcliffe, A Threefold Answer vnto the third part of a certain triobolar treatise (1606), p. 24.

37 Baeske, Oldcastle-Falstaff in der englischen Literatur bis zu Shakespeare, Palaestra, 50 (Berlin, 1905); Baeske is summarized by Hemingway, pp. 453–5. Most of Scoufos's book is devoted to dubious parallels between Shakespeare's plays and the lives of the Elizabethan Cobhams; her discussion of Sir John's links with the historical Oldcastle occur on pp. 44–78. See also L. M. Oliver, 'Sir John Oldcastle: Legend or Literature?', The Library, V, 1 (1946–7), 179–83, and R. Fiehler, 'How Oldcastle Became Falstaff', Modern Language Quarterly, 16 (1955), 16–28.

38 Foxe, p. 561a; Bale, pp. 26–26^v. For Tyndale see The examinacion of master William Thorpe... The examinacion of Syr J. Oldcastell (Antwerp, 1530; STC 24045). This book was proscribed, and long thought to be lost; it does not figure in the discussions by Baeske or Scoufos.

39 Hall, a.ii^v; Foxe, pp. 568–88. Nicholas Harpsfield was the author of Dialogi Sex contra Summi Pontificatus...et Pseudomartyres (Antwerp, 1566, repr. 1573; under the pseudonym Alanus Copus).

40 Shakespeare's use of Holinshed and Hall was habitual. Foxe probably influenced 2 Henry VI, King John, and Henry VIII, and was of course enormously influential more generally. The clearest case of the influence of Stow is in fact Part 1 itself: see Bullough, vol. 4, pp. 177–9. Bullough reprints Stow's 1580 text, but as there is no evidence that Shakespeare used Stow before 1596 he might just as well have referred to the 1592 edition, which considerably expanded the account of Oldcastle. See also Humphreys, pp. xxxi–xxxii.

41 Foxe, pp. 572b, 573a, 573b. To these charges Foxe sarcastically adds, 'And why doth not he adde moreouer, to set also all London on fire, and to turne all England into a fishe poole' (p. 573a).

42 Bale, pp. 52–55^v; Foxe, p. 579b. For James's views on

first declines to accompany them, Oldcastle swears, 'By the Lord, ile be a traitor then, when thou art king' (1.2.140–1). The historical Oldcastle did become a traitor when Hal became king. In what is perhaps his most famous speech, Oldcastle claims that he was 'a cowarde on instinct'; as he asks, 'was it for me to kill the heire apparent? should I turne vpon the true prince?' (2.4.264–5). The historical Oldcastle did indeed allegedly turn upon the true prince, joining in a plot to kill him. Historically, Henry V made a considerable personal effort to persuade his friend to renounce his heresies; Oldcastle would not relent. Shakespeare's Sir John declares, 'ile be damnd for neuer a kings sonne in Christendom' (1.2.94–5); as Hal says, 'Sir Iohn stands to his word, the diuell shall haue his bargain, for...he will giue the diuell his due' (1.2.113–15).

The two contrasted portraits of Hal's companion given in the play scene – as 'a vertuous man' with 'vertue in his lookes' (2.4.413, 421–2), or as 'a diuell...in the likenesse of an olde fat man...that reuerent vice, the gray iniquity...That villanous abhominable misleader of youth' (2.4.44–56) – correspond to the two opposing conceptions of Oldcastle current in the sixteenth century. Hal even envisages Oldcastle as 'a rosted Manningtre Oxe' (2.4.446–7): the many members of the audience familiar with Oldcastle's historical fate must have considered this one of Hal's – and Shakespeare's – most unsavoury similes. At Shrewsbury, Shakespeare's fat knight rises, apparently, from the dead; Oldcastle allegedly said, just before his execution, that he would 'rise from death to life again, the third day'.[43] And in his final speech Sir John, looking forward to the reward he expects for having 'killed' Hotspur, promises 'If I do growe great, ile growe lesse, for ile purge and leaue Sacke, and liue cleanlie as a noble man should do' (5.4.162–4). This is not a speech many of us remember, or credit with much importance. But the historical Oldcastle did undergo a religious conversion, abandoning what Bale had conceded to be a certain wantonness 'in his youth': in the last years of Henry IV's reign, he did – according to the Protestants – both 'growe great... and liue cleanlie'. For many of the original audience to Part 1, these words would have clearly hinted –

even if only parodically – at Oldcastle's subsequent career. But in the mouth of a fictional character called Falstaff, the words lose their historicity and ambiguity. To some extent, this is what happens to the whole character. The name 'Falstaff' fictionalizes, depoliticizes, secularizes, and in the process trivializes the play's most memorable character. It robs the play of that tension created by the distance between two available interpretations of one of its central figures.

The change of name affects the interpretation of other characters, too. Many of the original audience of Part 1 would have known that the historical Oldcastle was eventually executed on the orders of the historical Henry V. The outcome of the relationship between Hal and his pal was never in doubt; the death of 'Falstaff' in Henry V was not an artistic accident, as some have claimed, an unfortunate change of plan forced upon Shakespeare by the departure of Will Kemp from the company, but part of his conception of Henry's character from the beginning.[44] But Oldcastle was indicted for heresy soon after Henry V was crowned; Henry intervened in order to save his old friend from the ecclesiastical authorities, delayed his trial and punishment, and personally attempted to save his soul. Oldcastle, unconvinced, escaped from the Tower, and was implicated in an uprising and a conspiracy to assassinate Henry. In the sequel that Shakespeare eventually wrote (under the eye of the censor), the sequel we all know, Hal rejects Sir John only because his old friend has become a political embarrassment: Henry's sense of his own destiny, his responsibility as monarch, demands their separation. The motivation lies entirely within Henry. But when he wrote Part 1, Shakespeare was anticipating a sequel with a

---

Becket, see his voluminous 'Decanonizatio Thomæ Cantuariensis et Suorum' (Bodleian Library, James MS 1).

43 Stow, Annales, p. 572 (noted by Scoufos, p. 109). Stow's account is taken from Walsingham.

44 For claims that Falstaff's demise was fortuitous, see Wilson, 'The Origins...Henry IV', and J. H. Walter, 'With Sir John in it', Modern Language Review, 41 (1946), 237–45. I have challenged these views, for other reasons, in my Oxford Shakespeare edition of Henry V (1982), pp. 19–20, 290–2.

different 'Sir John in it' – a sequel in which Henry's rejection of his old friend might easily have been based, in part at least, on that friend's own treachery (like Scrope's). The change of Oldcastle's name may have changed Prince Hal's role in both *Part 2* and *Henry V*.

Moreover, all the other plays in which Sir John appears allude to his change of name: slyly and ironically, Shakespeare reminds audiences of Sir John's previous identity, and of 'how [he has] been transformed' (*Merry Wives*, 4.5.95). The Epilogue to *Part 2* explicitly resurrects that old self, by denying it; but other passages make the same point implicitly.

Master Ford. Where had you this pretty weather-cock?
Mistress Page. I cannot tell what the dickens his name is my husband had him of. – What do you call your knight's name, sirrah?
Robin. Sir John Falstaff.
Master Ford. Sir John Falstaff?
Mistress Page. He, he. I can never hit on's name.

(3.2.15–21)

Mistress Page's lapse of memory, in what was probably the first play Shakespeare finished after Sir John's surname had been censored, has no dramatic point beyond its comic allusion to the confusion created by the change in name of an already famous character. An almost identical oblivion, equally pointless, overtakes Fluellen in *Henry V*:

As Alexander killed his friend Cleitus, being in his ales and his cups, so also Harry Monmouth, being in his right wits and his good judgements, turned away the fat knight with the great-belly doublet – he was full of jests and gipes and knaveries and mocks – I have forgot his name.
Gower. Sir John Falstaff.
Fluellen. That is he.

(4.7.40–7)

Part 2 itself also plays upon the change of name. Consider Sir John's rebuke by the Lord Chief Justice, in the first scene in which either appears: 'Do you set down *your name* in the scroll of youth, that are *written down* 'old' with all the characters of age?' (1.3.177–9; my italics). Or the opening of Sir John's letter to Prince Hal, with the satirical comment it

evokes: '"John Falstaff, Knight" – every man must know that, as oft as he has occasion to name himself' (2.2.103–5). Just as passages of *Part 1* lose some of their significance if Sir John is not called 'Oldcastle', so passages in three other plays lose some of their significance if 'Falstaff' is not a new, and potentially confusing, surname.

Even in *Part 1*, of course, Shakespeare's Sir John is much more than a dramatic amalgamation of certain elements in sixteenth-century attitudes toward a fourteenth-century Lollard. He is a comic character of genius, who owes as much to the Vice of morality drama as to the chronicles of Henry IV's reign. But Shakespeare's decision to conflate the historical Oldcastle with the theatrical Vice was itself a daring and provocative inspiration – moreover, an inspiration obscured for centuries by the imposed change of name. Because of Falstaff's false association with the allegedly cowardly soldier Fastolf, most critics before John Dover Wilson believed that Sir John's key literary antecedent was the *miles gloriosus* of Roman comedy; not until 1943 did any critic elaborate on his much more important similarities to the allegorical Vice.[45] Bad texts do not encourage good criticism.

Many of the parallels between the dramatic and the historical Sir John have been noticed before, but they have never been discussed in terms of the editorial issue they raise. Such details are not important as 'proof' that Falstaff was once Old-castle; we already *know* that. Instead, the parallels demonstrate that the name of the character, his historical identity, forms a part of the meaning of the extant text. They confirm that little if anything of the nature of the original character has been altered: 'only the names have been changed, to protect the innocent'. And in this case the parallels cannot be dismissed as a bizarre growth nurtured in the hothouse of a twentieth-century imagination in search of tenure. Undeniably, many of Shakespeare's

---

[45] Wilson, *The Fortunes of Falstaff* (Cambridge, 1943), pp. 17–35. This had been anticipated only by a brief discussion in Katherine H. Gatch, 'Shakespeare's Allusions to the Older Drama', *Philological Quarterly*, 7 (1928), 27–44.

contemporaries took Shakespeare's character as a portrayal of and comment upon the historical Oldcastle. It is not surprising that the Jesuit Robert Parsons alluded to Shakespeare's play in his own attack, in 1604, upon Oldcastle as 'a Ruffian-knight...commonly brought in by comedians in their stages: he was put to death for robberyes and rebellion'.[46] But John Speed, in 1611, replying to Parsons, also assumed that the 'poet' and the 'stage-plaiers' meant to calumniate the martyr.[47] The team of playwrights who in 1599 produced Henslowe's derivative potboiler, 'The first part of the true and honorable historie, of the life of Sir *Iohn Old-castle, the good* Lord Cobham', specifically contrasted their play, which presents 'faire Truth', with the 'forg'de inuention' of Shakespeare's – just as Foxe had contrasted his pietistic interpretation with that of earlier chroniclers.[48] John Weever, in 1601, in a verse hagiography of Oldcastle demonstrably indebted to Shakespeare, claims to reveal 'of [his] life and death the veritie', in contrast to what 'thousands flocke to heare'.[49] This cannot be a complaint about Henslowe's play, which presented an entirely favourable picture of Oldcastle, comparable to Weever's own; moreover, the stanza in which it occurs is immediately followed by one in which all scholars recognize an allusion to Shakespeare's *Julius Caesar*.[50] Weever complains,

O times vntaught, men scorners of sound teaching,
Louers of playes, and loathers of good preaching.

(D2)

Oldcastle's ghost goes out of his way to deny charges of 'cowardize' and of having fraternized with 'meane *Cumrades*' and 'base associates' (A6). Neither of these accusations is brought against Oldcastle by sixteenth-century historians, even the hostile ones; yet they have an obvious pertinence to Shakespeare's *Part 1*.

Most explicitly of all, of course, the very suppression of the name 'Oldcastle' from Shakespeare's play testifies to the influential and offended reactions of 'personages descended from his title' – and 'manie others allso whoe ought to have him in honorable memorie'. Right-minded Protestants can hardly have been pleased by the fact that Shake-

speare's 'buffone' bore the name – and some of the alleged characteristics – of a revered Lollard martyr. James testifies explicitly to the hostility of such people, and Shakespeare himself implicitly recognizes it in the Epilogue to *Part 2*, promising that his next play will dramatize Henry V's adventures in France – 'where (for any thing I knowe) Falstaffe shall die of a sweat, vnlesse already a be killd with your harde opinions; for Olde-Castle died Martyre, and this is not the man'. No one seems to have remarked upon the syntactical role of 'for' in this unusual sentence, perhaps because its implication is obvious. In worrying that Falstaff might already be 'killd with your harde opinions', Shakespeare may merely be allowing, humbly and conventionally, for the possibility that his new play has failed to please its audience; but the immediate change of subject, and the assertion of a causal link between the two statements, makes it seem to me probable that Shakespeare here alluded to the displeasure of *some* spectators at the original identification of the character as Oldcastle.

The traditional modern assumption is that the Cobhams, James, Weever, Parsons, Speed, Munday,

---

[46] N.D. (= Nicholas Dolman, pseudonym of Robert Parsons), *Examen of the Calender or Catalogue of Protestant Saints: The last six months* (1604) p. 31.

[47] *The Theatre of the Empire of Great Britaine*, 2 vols. (1611), vol. 2, p. 637a.

[48] The most helpful edition is in Michael Drayton, *Works*, ed. J. William Hebel, 4 vols. (rev. edn. Oxford, 1961), vol. 1, pp. 393–468, with Notes and Introductions in volume 5, ed. Kathleen Tillotson and Bernard H. Newdigate, pp. 44–52.

[49] *Mirror of Martyrs*, A3[v]. As Shakespeare unhistorically did Falstaff (*Part 2*, 3.2.24–5), Weever describes Oldcastle as a former page to Thomas Mowbray, Duke of Norfolk – a connection first noted by Isaac Reed in 1813. Weever's indebtedness to *Part 2* suggests either that Oldcastle originally appeared in it, too, or – more probably – that some people continued to associate the character with Oldcastle, despite the change of name.

[50] Halliwell-Phillipps first spotted the reference to *Caesar*: see his edition of Shakespeare's *Works*, 16 vols. (1853–65), vol. 13 (1865), p. 365. But this adjacent allusion has never been related to the question of whether Weever refers to *Henry IV*: the allusion books overlook any such connection, and even Scoufos is unaccountably vague about it (p. 35).

Drayton *et al.* were all wrong; that Shakespeare's contemporaries woefully misunderstood, glibly assuming that 'Oldcastle' meant 'Oldcastle'; that we alone, centuries later, can see that there was – as Hamlet assures Claudius – 'no offence i'th' world' intended by these apparent parallels between the play and the past. Geoffrey Bullough sums up this view when he claims that Shakespeare used the name Oldcastle 'without *arrière pensée* and without linking his Sir John with the martyr'.[51] Not surprisingly, this hypothesis of innocent inadvertence was first advanced by an Anglican bishop, who also happened to be an editor of Shakespeare, the Right Reverend William Warburton: 'I believe there was no malice in the matter. *Shakespear* wanted a droll name to his character, and never considered whom it belonged to.'[52]

Warburton's faith-saving fantasy has been perpetuated partly because of a confusion between two kinds of inadvertence. Shakespeare might not have expected or intended to offend the Cobham family. David McKeen, who knew more about the Cobhams than any modern scholar, found no reason to believe that Shakespeare set out to insult or caricature Oldcastle's living descendants, and much reason to doubt any such intention;[53] it seems to me intrinsically improbable that any dramatist would deliberately satirize the Lord Chamberlain, the one official who could do a theatrical company most good or harm. Noticeably, neither *Famous Victories* nor *Part 1* ever identifies Oldcastle by his alternative title, Lord Cobham, though all the chroniclers and divines habitually mix the titles; equally important, neither play gives him a wife. The absence of the name from the extant texts might of course be due to censorship, but there seem to be no puns on or allusions to the title either. Moreover, since Oldcastle acquired his title by marriage, and since the Elizabethan Cobhams descended not from Oldcastle himself but from his wife, the absence of Lady Cobham from both plays – and her corresponding presence in Henslowe's hagiographic rejoinder, and Weever's poem – is probably significant. Shakespeare, like the author of *Famous Victories*, might naturally have assumed that it was safe to bring Oldcastle on to the stage so long as he was never connected with the Cobhams or their ancestress. But Shakespeare's innocence of any intentional libel on the living Cobhams by no means exonerates him from responsibility for a deliberate and brilliant caricature of the dead Oldcastle. You do not call a hypocrite 'Sir John Oldcastle' without giving any thought to the fact that a 'Sir John Oldcastle' – who lived in the period in which your play is set – was famous as, depending on your taste, a martyr or a heretic. Moreover, Shakespeare clearly did 'link' his character and the historical one.

The controversy over whether Shakespeare intended to satirize the Cobhams has obscured the much more important fact that he portrayed a Protestant martyr as a jolly hypocrite. That is the inconvenient truth Warburton wishes to ignore. Warburton's reasoning was articulated much more openly, five years later, by a certain 'P.T.', who may have been Warburton himself, and who was certainly indebted to Warburton's arguments: 'What, I say, could *Shakespeare* make a pampered glutton, a debauched monster, of a noble personage, who stood foremost on the list of *English* reformers and Protestant martyrs...? 'Tis absurd to suppose, 'tis impossible for any man to imagine.'[54] England's national poet could not be guilty of such treasonable

---

51 Bullough, vol. 4, p. 171. In the same vein Bullough denies that there is 'any real evidence' that the Cobhams were responsible for the change of name (vol. 4, pp. 155–6). He gives no explanation for this parenthetical dismissal of the testimony of both James and Rowe.

52 *The Works of Shakespear*, 8 vols. (1747), vol. 4, p. 103. Warburton ignores the long, learned, intelligent note by Lewis Theobald on this matter: see *The Works of Shakespeare*, 8 vols. (1733), vol. 3, pp. 348–9. Scoufos misrepresents Theobald, saying that he believed Shakespeare used the name 'unwittingly of course' (p. 28); Theobald neither says nor implies any such thing.

53 McKeen devoted an appendix to the relations between the Cobhams and Shakespeare's plays (pp. 961–1024); this usefully, and one hopes definitively, disposes of the notion that Sir William Brooke was a theatre-hating Puritan, on whom Shakespeare and his company were seeking revenge. McKeen also demonstrates that the notion of an Essex–Southampton alliance against the Brookes in 1596 cannot be sustained.

54 'Observations on Shakespeare's Falstaff', *Gentleman's Magazine*, 22 (1752), 459–61; noted and discussed by Fiehler, pp. 18–19.

heresy. And there the matter rested for almost a century: not until 1841, when Halliwell printed Dr James's epistle, did anyone dare again maintain that Shakespeare had ever called his character 'Oldcastle'.

Editors must of course disabuse themselves of any devotion other than allegiance to their author. Shakespeare might in this instance be usefully contrasted with Thomas Middleton. In the second-most-famous instance of censorship in English Renaissance drama, Middleton got into trouble for his caricature of prominent Roman Catholics; Shakespeare, by contrast, got into trouble for his caricature of a famous proto-Protestant. John Speed (in 1611) and Richard Davies (c. 1660) both alleged or assumed that Shakespeare was a 'papist'. There is documentary evidence that both Shakespeare's father and one of his daughters may have been popishly inclined.[55] In *Hamlet* Shakespeare exploited the Catholic belief in Purgatory; in *Richard III* he exploited Catholic beliefs about All Souls' Eve;[56] in both *Twelfth Night* and *Measure for Measure* he mocked the hypocrisy of Puritans. In 1609–10 both *Pericles* and *King Lear* were performed by a band of English recusant players with – in other respects – an obviously papist repertoire.[57] *Pericles* was also included in a continental Jesuit book-list of 1619, and twice performed before visiting Catholic ambassadors (in 1607–8 and 1619).[58] *King Lear*, as is well known, draws upon passages in Samuel Harsnet's *Declaration of Egregious Popish Impostures* (1603); what is perhaps not so well known is that Harsnet's book quotes extensively from a Catholic manuscript account of the same events, 'The Booke of Miracles'.[59] Virtually everything which Shakespeare allegedly took from Harsnet could have been taken, instead, from the lost manuscript; at the very least, Shakespeare's interest in Harsnet's pamphlet may have been stimulated by the fact that it made available, in print, excerpts from a proscribed account. What Shakespeare's treatment ignores entirely is Harsnet's own contribution: his ceaseless mockery of the whole idea of demonic possession. Edgar's performance as Poor Tom – whatever else it may be – does not seem designed to provoke cynical laughter; although he announces an intention to disguise himself as a bedlam beggar, he does not specifically promise to be possessed by devils; nor does his professed intention 'to put an antic disposition on' allow us to infer, in his case any more than in Hamlet's, that the resulting mental disequilibrium is entirely feigned. In 3.4 especially, where he never steps out of his 'role', Edgar's tortured hallucinations can be, in performance, triumphantly and disturbingly real. *King Lear* exploits dramatically a series of incidents in recent English recusant history, just as clearly as *Hamlet* and *Richard III* exploit elements of Catholic belief. And in *King John* – as in *Part 1* – Shakespeare tells the story of an early proto-Protestant 'martyr', whose life had been celebrated earlier in the century by both Bale and Foxe; but again, as in *Part 1*, Shakespeare's account of this figure is not very flattering.[60] Such evidence does not prove that Shakespeare was a secret Catholic, but it does demonstrate, at the very least, his willingness to exploit a point of view which many of his contemporaries would have regarded as 'papist'. In such circumstances, the possibility that Shakespeare deliberately lampooned Oldcastle can hardly be denied.

---

[55] See S. Schoenbaum, *Shakespeare: A Compact Documentary Life* (Oxford, 1977), pp. 45–62. When the alleged John Shakespeare testament was found, neither Speed's nor Davies's reference to Shakespeare was known to scholars, and there was hence no obvious motive for manufacturing 'evidence' of his Catholic upbringing.

[56] Emrys Jones, *The Origins of Shakespeare* (Oxford, 1977), pp. 227–9.

[57] C. J. Sisson, 'Shakespeare's Quartos as Prompt-copies', *Review of English Studies*, 18 (1942), 129–43; a much fuller account is now available in John L. Murphy, *Darkness and Devils: Exorcism and 'King Lear'* (Athens, Ohio, 1984), pp. 93–118.

[58] Willem Schrickx, '*Pericles* in a Book-List of 1619 from the English Jesuit Mission and Some of the Play's Special Problems', *Shakespeare Survey 29* (Cambridge, 1976), 21–32.

[59] Harsnet's use of 'The Booke of Miracles' is noted by Murphy, pp. 7, 22–3, 36, 205; he does not discuss the critical implications of this dependence.

[60] *King John* has things in it of which continental Catholics would not have approved; but most English Catholics in and after 1588 were genuinely torn between a desire for restoration of the old religion and a patriotic resistance to the prospect of foreign invasion.

I do not know whether Shakespeare meant to satirize the Cobhams, though I rather doubt it. I do not know whether Shakespeare was ever 'a papist', though I rather suspect it.[61] But I do know that Oldcastle is what Shakespeare wrote; that Oldcastle is what Shakespeare meant; and that Oldcastle is what his contemporaries understood. If editors nevertheless refuse to restore Shakespeare's name for the character, then they might as well confess that they care more about an artificial *post hoc* consistency than they do about the integrity of the individual work of art; that they care more about the preservation and intellectual authority of a cultural tradition than about the recovery and restoration of the original authoritative *logos*. In other words, they must join defenders of the corrupt and derivative Vulgate, against the reforms of Erasmus. We all know who won that argument.

---

[61] Since this essay was written E. A. J. Honigmann, in *Shakespeare: The Lost Years* (Manchester, 1985), has provided new evidence of Shakespeare's early links with recusants in Lancashire.

HAND D IN 'SIR THOMAS MORE': AN ESSAY IN MISINTERPRETATION

GIORGIO MELCHIORI

The literary and dramatic qualities of the addition in Hand D to the manuscript of *The Booke of Sir Thomas Moore* are outside of my brief here. I am not concerned with its artistic value *per se*, or with the identification of Hand D with Shakespeare or any other Elizabethan playwright. What is disturbing, I feel, is that those three pages have been from the beginning and are still beset, even at a merely textual approach, by a number of misunderstandings and misinterpretations. No doubt this is largely due to the state of the manuscript, with all the deletions, corrections, interlineations and additions in two separate hands which, following Greg's critical edition of 1911 for the Malone Society, we are accustomed to call D and C. There have been since a number of more and more sophisticated and annotated diplomatic transcriptions of the text, beginning with Greg himself in the appendix to the collective volume *Shakespeare's Hand in the Play of 'Sir Thomas More'* (Cambridge, 1923), reprinted in Peter Alexander's Tudor Shakespeare (1951), Thomas Clayton (*The 'Shakespearean' Addition to The Booke of Sir Thomas Moore*, Shakespeare Studies Monographs, 1, Dubuque, Iowa, 1969), and finally G. Blakemore Evans (*Riverside Shakespeare*, Boston, 1974); but in spite of the fact that they provide in visual terms clear representations of the actual state of the manuscript, the necessary inclusion in them of all the alterations it originally underwent obscures to a certain extent a precise understanding of the intentions of D when he first drafted it. It must be assumed that, whoever D might have been, he was asked for some reason to reshape part of a scene of *Sir Thomas More* originally written (or at least transcribed) by Anthony

Munday; therefore, when he set about his task, D must have had under his eye Munday's original text of the scene, now irretrievably lost. I propose to re-examine the two successive layers of corrections and alterations to the manuscript (first by D himself, then by C) in order to reconstruct D's original first draft; I hope in this way (*a*) to ascertain which alterations were made by D himself, and why; (*b*) to assess how far C's interventions in the text are correct and justified; (*c*) to see whether and to what extent it is possible to reconstruct from what we have the contents of Munday's lost original.

Line references in this paper are to Greg's 1911 edition, which remains the most clearly set-out reproduction of the whole play, with the revisions and integrations provided by Harold Jenkins (the Malone Society's *Collections*, vol. 6, Oxford, 1961) and, for this passage, by Greg himself in his already cited 1923 transcript. I have taken into account also the further readjustments in the transcripts I mentioned earlier, especially Evans's, and Peter Blayney's numerous new readings and unpublished notes which he generously communicated to me privately. Suggestions have been received from the modernized-spelling editions of the whole play by John Shirley (Canterbury, [1939]), Harold Jenkins (*The Complete Works of Shakespeare*, ed. C. J. Sisson, 1953), and Vittorio Gabrieli and G. Melchiori (Bari, 1981).

The three pages are known as fols. 8a, 8b and 9a of the manuscript (there is also the speech heading *all* and a single letter, variously interpreted by Blayney and Evans,[1] at the top of 9b, but I shall not

---

[1] First noticed in P. M. W. Blayney, '*The Booke of Sir Thomas Moore* Re-examined' *Studies in Philology*, 69

be concerned with it). In Greg they are Addition II, lines 123–270. The entrance stage direction to the scene, in Hand C, is found at the bottom of the previous page, 7b (for Greg, Add. II. 121–2).

THE FIRST LAYER: ALTERATIONS IN HAND D

The alterations introduced by D himself into his draft of the scene can be grouped under three headings:

1. Deletions and corrections made *currente calamo*, when the author realized that there was something wrong with what he was writing, crossed it out, and continued on the same line with the correct form.

2. Corrections of single words made by the author upon rereading the manuscript.

3. Additions by the author himself to the original text.

The first group is the most numerous (twenty-one alterations) and the least relevant. It includes corrections of slips of the pen or misspellings,[2] changes of mind on how to continue the sentence or the speech,[3] and, in three cases, changes of words for stylistic improvement. This last kind of amendment occurs at lines 131, where *a watrie* is corrected to *a sorry* [parsnip]; 194, where *advauntage* replaces *helpe*; and 236, where, realizing that he had already used the word *warrs* in the preceding line, the author replaces it with *hurly*; this last substitution is worth keeping in mind since it occurs in a passage which C completely misunderstood and deleted. It will be discussed later.

The five belated alterations under my second heading do not differ in nature from those in the first group: *n* interlined above *mutyes* (l. 238) corrects a misspelling, *yo*^r interlined for a deleted *their* (l. 260) makes good a previous slip; stylistic improvement accounts for *w*^t interlined above a deleted *and* at l. 198 and for *&* written over and replacing *his* at l. 226; *he* inserted at the beginning of line 225 to replace a deleted *god* was probably not motivated by the fear of giving offence but by the fact that the name of God is mentioned no less than five times between lines 218 and 229. There is also a cancelled correction: Blayney has recognized as *those* the

smudged-out word interlined above the undeleted *your* in line 233: the author probably intended to modify the sentence, but thought better of it even before crossing out the word that *those* should have replaced.

The third group of authorial alterations – four in number – is far more significant for an understanding of D's method of composition and of his feeling for dramatic effect. These are not just stylistic improvements but additions to the original text affecting the substance of the speeches which they modify. It is surprising that modern editors have nearly always misunderstood or disregarded these additions and their relevance to the text. Each of them deserves a separate discussion.

LINE 144: HOW SAY YOU NOW

After the Sergeant-at-arms's impatient remark, 'yo^u ar the simplest things that eu^r stood in such a question', D had given Lincoln a brief and violent retort: 'prentisses symple downe wth him' (no punctuation in the manuscript; see fig. 3). On second thoughts he squeezed in between the speech heading 'Lin' and the beginning of the speech the words 'how say yo^u' and, interlined just above the last part

---

(1972), 167–91. Evans identifies the single letter (*Riverside Shakespeare*, p. 1694) as 'c', but Blayney rejoins (private communication, May 1983): 'The most that can be said is that it resembles an unfinished 'a', that it has been smudged, and that it is impossible to know whether or not it was intentional.'

[2] They occur at lines 150 ('sh' corrected to 'Ch[arge]'), 157 ('ar' corrected to 'or'), 174 ('mv' corrected to 'nv[mber]'), 193 ('D' in stage direction for 'Doll', corrected to 'Bett'), 195 ('y', repeating previous word 'yor'), 202 ('yo', repeating previous word 'yor'), 225 ('le', anticipating next word but one, 'lent'), 230 ('ar' corrected to 'as'), 248 ('c' smudged out at the beginning of the line; identified by Blayney while previous editors indent the line taking the smudge for a fault in the paper), 251 ('to' suppressed for metrical reasons), 264 ('vs' suppressed because included in preceding 'letts').

[3] These occur at lines 159 ('But' at beginning of speech, replaced by 'what'), 190 ('theise' replaced by 'the state'), 218 ('in' replaced by 'no'), 234 ('that' – change of sentence structure), 239 ('th' – probably for 'thee' – replaced by 'a traytor'), 245 ('sayeng' replaced by 'say'), 252 ('why yo^u' – change of sentence structure).

3. The manuscript of *Sir Thomas More*, fol. 8a, lines 141–5

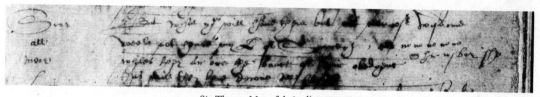

4 *Sir Thomas More*, fol. 8a, lines 159–63

of the addition, 'now prenty'. In view of the reaction produced by Lincoln's speech, D had decided to give it more weight by introducing a sentence questioning the Sergeant's words before attacking him directly; 'how say you now' echoes somewhat ironically the Sergeant's earlier question: 'What say yo^u to the mercy of the king[?]' The interlined word 'prenty' has been considered an abbreviated form of 'prentysses', like 'Shr' for 'Shrewsbury' at line 161 below. The speech has therefore been taken by all recent editors as addressed to the crowd and modernized (with only slight variants in punctuation) as 'How say you now, prentices? Prentices simple! Down with him!' Only Shirley leaves a margin of ambiguity rendering it with: 'How say you? Now, prentices, prentices simple!', etc.[4] Nobody has thought of taking 'prenty' not as an abbreviation of a separate word but as a cue-word representing the beginning of the original speech, 'prentisses'. In this case the additional sentence 'how say you now' would be addressed directly to the Sergeant, implying: 'A moment ago you pretended to speak fair, offering the King's pardon, but see how you speak now: you insult the prentices calling them simple.' Only after this Lincoln turns to the prentices calling out in turn: 'Down with him!' This double form of address, first to the offender, then to the offended, gives greater dramatic impact to the central insulting words,

'prentices simple'. This elementary demagogic device of interpreting another speaker's innocent words as insults to the populace has a close parallel in one of the riot scenes of *2 Henry VI*, where the same verbal formula is applied. Lord Say, captured by Jack Cade's followers, tries to address them (4.7.52–5; Folio version, sig. o1):

Say. You men of Kent.
Dic[k]. What say you of Kent.
Say. Nothing but this: 'Tis *bona terra, mala gens*.
Cade. Away with him, away with him, he speaks Latine.

I suggest that, in *Sir Thomas More*, the intention of D in adding to his own text at this stage, could be best rendered by modernizing Lincoln's speech as:

Lincoln. How say you now: prentices simple? Down with him!

LINES 160–1: NO, NO, NO, NO, NO, SHREWSBURY, SHREWSBURY!

Another afterthought of D, with, this time, an interlineation *below* the line, flush to and partly in the right margin (Greg numbers it as a separate line), has

---

4 In the already mentioned edition, 1939, p. 18; Shirley takes the interlined words as the beginning of a new sentence, and in fact his reading cannot be dismissed offhand.

also been partly misunderstood, first by C, and then by modern editors (see fig. 4). The line originally read:

all   weel not heare my L of Surrey

D added later, leaving much more than the usual space after the last word, 'all no no no no no' and, under the last additional words and in the margin: 'Shrewsbury shr'. C crossed out *all*, considering it merely a repetitive speech heading, so as to give the impression that the speech continued uninterrupted except by a comma. All recent editors follow suit and modernize the line (with some variants in punctuation) as:

All. We'll not hear my Lord of Surrey, no, no, no, no, no! Shrewsbury! Shrewsbury!

In fact the added words were not meant by D as a continuation of the speech, but, as the new prefix *all* makes clear, a separate speech by a different group of rioters. A few lines later D had envisaged the same situation, with two consecutive speeches both prefixed by the heading *all* (lines 171–2):

all   Surrey Sury
all   moor moor

which most modern editors correctly render with: '*Some*. Surrey, Surrey! / *Others*. More, More!' The confusion in line 160 arises from the fact that, having thought of adding the second speech only after completing the page, D was prevented from interlining it by the presence of the dividing rule between the existing speech and the next, so he added it as a marginal insertion in the only available space. Obviously it should be modernized as:

All [or *Some*].   We'll not hear my lord of Surrey!
All [or *Others*].   No, no, no, no, no, Shrewsbury, Shrewsbury!

LINE 236: IN, IN TO YOUR OBEDIENCE!

My concern is with the words 'in in to yor obedienc' interlined above line 236, but in this case the confusion is much more serious because D's addition occurs in a passage (lines 234–7) that, as all recent

editors recognize, C had so badly misunderstood that he crossed out entirely lines 235 and 236 (including the interlineation), and the first part of line 237, which is a full line of verse in itself, replacing them with the four words in his own hand 'tell me but this' (see fig. 5). C's muddle was due in turn to D's extremely sparing use of punctuation, marking the end of a sentence in the middle of a line simply by leaving a wider space between its last word and the first word of the next sentence.[5] Confronted with line 234, 'make them your feet   to kneele to be forgyven', C took the last five words to be the conclusion of the sentence begun several lines earlier, instead of the beginning of a new one, and, unable to make sense of the following passage, crossed it out. Greg in 1923[6] and Shirley in 1939 followed suit, omitting the deleted lines, but Jenkins (1953) and the more recent editors restore the passage (omitting of course the word 'warrs' in line 236 which, as I had occasion to remark before, was deleted *currente calamo* by D himself), and modernize lines 234–7 as follows:

234   Make them your feet. To kneel to be forgiven
235   Is safer wars than ever you can make
236   Whose discipline is riot. Why, even your hurly
237a   Cannot proceed but by obedience.

None of them, though, finds room for the words 'in in to yor obedienc' interlined above 'why euen yor hurly' in line 236, though Greg (1923, p. 243) conjectures that they 'should be inserted between *ryot;* and *why*', but hastens to add: 'the whole passage is clumsy'. Evans, substantially accepting Greg's conjecture, proposes a peculiar new line division:

Modernized, the whole passage would then read: 'To kneel to be forgiven / Is safer wars than ever you can

---

[5] This seems to be Shakespeare's practice, from the evidence of texts set from his foul papers. It is the case for instance of the 1600 Quarto of *2 Henry IV*, Induction, 15: 'And no such matter   Rumour is a pipe', where 'Rumour' is the first word of a new sentence; Folio reads: 'And no such matter? *Rumour*, is a pipe'.

[6] In his edition of the 'ill May Day scenes' appended to *Shakespeare's Hand in the Play of 'Sir Thomas More'*, p. 213.

5   *Sir Thomas More*, fol. 9a, lines 233–9

6   *Sir Thomas More*, fol. 9a, lines 244–7

make / Whose discipline is riot. In, in to your obedience! / Why, even your hurly cannot proceed / But by obedience.'

It is difficult to see why a regular iambic pentameter ('cannot proceed but by obedience') is divided to contribute to two irregular lines.

What modern editors have not realized is that 'warrs' is not the only word that D (*not* C!) crossed out in line 236, before the radical intervention of C. An examination of the manuscript shows that while the groups of words 'whose discipline is ryot' and 'euen yor [warrs] hurly' are cancelled, obviously by C, each with a continuous thick stroke of the pen (covering the previous cancellation of 'warrs'), the word 'why' is crossed out separately with a lighter stroke, leaving an uncrossed semicolon before and a clear space after it. I submit that 'why' was not crossed out by C, but earlier by D, when he decided to insert at this point, and in its place, the new interlined sentence; 'in in to yor obedienc' was meant as the first part of a new line, to be completed with 'euen yor hurly' ('even' being considered a monosyllable). A modernized version of the passage should therefore run as follows (I am including also part of the immediately preceding and following passages, with the punctuation now generally accepted):

233	...and your[7] unreverent knees
234	Make them your feet. To kneel to be forgiven
235	Is safer wars, than ever you can make
236a	Whose discipline is riot.
236b	In, in to your obedience: even your hurly
237a	Cannot proceed but by obedience.
237b	What rebel captain,
238	As mutinies are incident...

This is by no means clumsy, as Greg put it. Line 236a is left metrically short for dramatic emphasis at the conclusion of a strong argument (the same rhetorical device is used at the end of More's two previous speeches, line 210 and the last part of line 218: 'yo^u wer in armes gainst g⟨od⟩').[8] The introduction of a new imperative sentence transforms aphorism into firm injunction; lines 236b and 237a – with all the weight of the repeated quadrisyllable 'obedience' – become the central mandatory statement of the whole speech. After it, More begins a new and more elaborate argument with

---

[7] See the discussion above of the cancelled correction of this word to 'those'.

[8] Dyce conjectured the words 'your sovereign' instead of 'god' in order to complete the line, but Greg is surely right in suggesting that 'god' (of which only the first letter is readable) is the concluding word, since there is no space on the page for more.

another short line – an arresting oratorical device which he had already employed at the very beginning of this long speech, line 220. The misunderstanding of D's addition, of its placing and function, has marred the central point of a masterly exercise in the rhetoric of persuasion.

LINE 245: ALAS! ALAS!

The last addition by D is of the same nature. In line 245, 'to slipp him lyke a hound; [sayeng] say nowe the king', D had cancelled *currente calamo* the word 'sayeng' probably because he considered it more effective to begin a new sentence rather than add a dependent clause to an already lengthy passage (see fig. 6). Upon rereading his manuscript, the sight of the mid-line deletion may well have suggested to him the idea of employing here as well the rhetorical device that we have noted in the previous instance: beginning a new section of the speech with a short line, as in the case of line 237b, 'What rebel captain'. D introduced therefore the exclamation 'alas alas' to complete the first part of line 245, envisaging a metrical arrangement that in modern spelling should be rendered as:

244 And lead the majesty of law in lyam
245a To slip him like a hound. Alas, alas!
245b Say now the king,
246 As he is clement if th'offender mourn...

The editors' failure to see D's reasons for adding here 'alas alas' is justifiable, since it is hard to say whether their later deletion is another unwarranted interference by C or represents D's own decision to revert to his original text.

THE SECOND LAYER OF ALTERATIONS: HAND C

It is generally accepted that Hand C (responsible for the second layer of alterations in the three pages) is that of a scribe, or more precisely a company bookkeeper who was in charge of transcribing those additional passages in different hands to the text of *Sir Thomas More* which were not sufficiently legible, and to assemble the 'book', adding all the necessary directions in order to make it usable as a prompt-book

for stage performance. It is to be presumed that he was given for this purpose the additional leaves (or at least their rough copies) and those parts of the original which were to be preserved, but not the sheets eliminated because reworked by other hands. In the specific case of these three pages, we can say then that, while D had seen Munday's original manuscript, C did not know it, and had to fit the pages into the text and prepare them for the stage not on the basis of Munday's original version of them, but of the surviving parts of the text before and after the rewritten pages. The entrance stage direction and all C's additional speech headings and other corrections, therefore, were neither suggested by D nor based on C's knowledge of the original version of the same scene; they were merely C's own conjectures.

Here is a list of C's interventions in this passage (folio and line numbers as in Greg):

7b. 121–2: Entrance stage direction: 'Enter Lincoln · Doll · Clown · Georg betts williamson others / And A sergaunt at armes'

8a. 126: speech heading: 'Geo bett', replacing D's 'other'

129: speech heading: 'betts clow', replacing D's 'other'

132: speech heading: 'willian', replacing D's 'oth'

138: speech heading: 'Clown · betts', replacing D's 'o' (for 'other')

139: C adds 'Enter', interlining it above and to the left of D's speech heading 'Seriant'

148: speech heading: 'Maior', replacing D's 'Sher'

152: speech heading: 'williamson' written over D's 'Sher'

153: speech heading: C inserts 'Ge' before D's 'bettes' to indicate that the speaker is George Betts and not his brother the Clown (he considers it unnecessary to repeat the insertion in the similar speech headings at lines 155 and 193; but cf. line 212)

160: C crosses out D's 'all' in the middle of the line (a point already discussed in connection with D's additions)

8b. 212: speech heading: 'lincoln', replacing (unnecessarily) D's 'Bettes'

9a. 235–7: C crosses out these two and a half lines, inserting the words 'tell me but this' – discussed above.

245: C may have crossed out the words 'alas alas' interlined by D: see above the discussion of the last of D's additions

265: speech heading: 'Linco', replacing D's 'all'.

The last correction is fully justified: D, who probably followed the common practice[9] of adding speech headings only after completion of the text, seems to have become particularly careless towards the end of his contribution to the play; he misplaced by one line (263 instead of 264) the previous heading, and in this case assigned to the crowd a speech which was surely meant for only one speaker. I feel, though, that C would have done better to give the speech to Doll rather than to Lincoln. What is totally unjustified instead is C's transfer to Lincoln, at line 212, of a speech that D had rightly meant for George Betts: probably C was thinking in terms of Betts the Clown instead of his brother George the shopkeeper.

C intervened in the text itself of the speeches only once or possibly twice (lines 235–7 and 245), and these two cases have already been discussed. For the rest, his concern was with speech headings and stage directions, and his interventions are concentrated in the first page of the Addition, since the other two pages are largely occupied with More's long speeches and contain very few other headings.

In order to see how the bookkeeper C set about his job, I propose to disencumber the first thirty-five lines or so of the scene from C's corrections and additions. The state of the manuscript when it came into C's hands is shown in fig. 7. At first sight, the most striking features of the passage are:

1. The casual treatment of speech headings: in four cases D had written merely 'other', that is to say he had left it for the bookkeeper to decide the name of the actual speaker; the only names of London citizens indicated by D in the whole of his Addition are Lincoln, Betts (never used in the

previous part of the original as a speech heading – he is designated with his first name, George – but mentioned in stage directions and in speeches), and Doll (lines 165, 181 and 211), apart from an abundant sprinkling of the even vaguer 'all'. Besides, there are the two instances of the intriguing 'Sher' (lines 148 and 152) which deserve a separate discussion.

2. The absence of an entrance stage direction at the beginning, while the entrance of three more characters at lines 146–7 is centred and placed in clear evidence.

The absence of an opening direction induced Blayney[10] to think that this was not the beginning of a scene, and he postulated the existence of a now lost 'folio Z', also in Hand D, which preceded fol. 8a. It is true that – as it stands now – the scene begins *in medias res*, but this is far from rare in plays, and Blayney himself is now inclined to reject his previous suggestion.[11] The abruptness of the beginning, more marked here than in most plays of the time, may be due to D's preoccupation with compressing into a relatively small number of lines what must have been a much more extended treatment of the first part of this scene in the original, in order to make room for *his* much ampler development of More's crucial speeches shortly afterwards. As for the missing entrance direction, it is worth noticing that the same is true of the first part of Addition II of the play, in Hand B: apparently the revisers in supplying substitute scenes relied on the bookkeeper to provide such directions by copying them out from the discarded parts of the original. Unfortunately in this particular case the relevant page of the original seems to have disappeared before the bookkeeper had the opportunity of seeing it. The entrance stage direction added by C at the bottom of fol. 7b is probably mere guesswork on his part. His uncertainty is shown also by his insertion of

---

9 There is evidence of this practice in Addition VI in Hand B of *Sir Thomas More*, fol. 16a, 21–35, where several speeches, marked for omission because completely refashioned immediately after, are left without speech headings.

10 In the paper mentioned in note 1.

11 Private communication.

123	Lincolne	Peace heare me, he that will not see a red hearing at a harry
124		grote,butter at a levenpence a pounde meale at nyne shillinge a
125		Bushell and Beeff at fower nobles a stone lyst to me
126	other	yt will Come to that passe yf straingers be sufferd mark him
127	Linco	our Countrie is a great eating Country,argo they eate more in
128		our Countrey then they do in their owne
129	other	by a half penny loff a day troy waight
130	Linc	they bring in straing rootes, which is meerly to the vndoing of poor
131		prentizes, for whate ~~a watrie~~ a sorry psnyp to a good hart
132	oth	trash trash, :they breed sore eyes and tis enough to infect the
133		Cytty w^t the palsey
134	Lin	nay yt has infected yt w^t the palsey,for theise basterde of dung
135		as you knowe they growe in Dvng haue infected vs,and yt is our
136		infeccion will make the Cytty shake which ptly Coms through
137		the eating of psnyps
138	o	trewe and pumpions togeather
139	Seriant	what say yo^u to the mercy of the king do yo^u refuse yt
140	Lin	yo^u woold haue vs vppon thipp woold yo^u no marry do we not,we
141		accept of the kinge mercy but wee will showe no mercy vppõ
142		the straingers
143	seriaunt	yo^u ar the simplest thinge that eu�À stood in such a question
144	Lin how say	yo^u $\wedge$ now prenty prentisses symple downe wth him
145	all	prentisses symple prentisses symple
146		Enter the L. maier Surrey
147		Shrewsbury
148	Sher	hold in the kinge name hold
149	Surrey	frende masters Countrymen
150	mayer	peace how peace I ~~sh~~ Charg yo^u keep the peace
151	Shro·	my masters Countrymen
152	Sher	The noble Earle of Shrowsbury lette hear him
153	bette	weele heare the earle of Surrey
154	Linc	the earle of Shrowsbury
155	bette	weele heare both
156	all	both both both both
157	Linc	Peace I say peace ar yo^u men of Wisdome ~~ar~~ or
158		what ar yo^u
159	Surr	~~But~~ what yo^u will haue them but not men of Wisdome
160	all	weele not heare my L of Surrey , all no no no no no
161		Shrewsbury shr

7 *Sir Thomas More*: the opening of Hand D's portion as originally written

'Enter' before the speech heading of the Sergeant-at-arms at line 139 – when he had already added 'And A sergaunt at armes' to his own opening direction (7b, 122) – and by his overlooking the fact that the all-important entrance of More is marked at no point of the scene, and neither is that of Palmer and Cholmley, present in the surviving part of the original version of the scene (see lines *493 and *496). The omission in D's text of More's (and possibly Palmer's and Cholmley's) entrance with the rest at lines 146–7, and of that of the Sergeant before line 139, suggests that for D – who relied on the entrance direction in the now missing original – these characters were all present from the beginning. This is confirmed by the first speeches assigned by D to the Sergeant and to More: 'what say yo^u to the mercy of the king   do yo^u refuse yt' do not sound like the words of somebody who is just arriving on the scene of trouble, but rather like those of a person who has already spoken to the crowd and then has been patiently watching the antics of a tribune while waiting for a reply; the scene begins *in medias res* and, as is true of all such scenes, what is being said now reveals what had been going on before. In the same way, it is significant that More's first words (lines 162–3: 'whiles they ar ore the banck of their obedyenc / thus will they bere downe all things') are not addressed to the crowd but to the newcomers, Surrey, Shrewsbury and the Lord Mayor, who have taken it upon themselves to speak to the rioters; they are the words of a man who has been watching for some time the behaviour of the people before the arrival of the authorities, and now informs the latter that their way of tackling the situation is unproductive.

Before attempting to reach a conclusion about the sort of entrance stage direction that D envisaged for this scene on the basis of what he had read in Munday's original, let us look at the other peculiarity of the passage – the question of speech headings. Peter Croft has remarked[12] that while Munday in the rest of the play presented the leaders of the rebellion as fairly substantial citizens, for D they seem to be thoughtless apprentices, one and all, an indiscriminate mass led by a trouble-maker. There was no Clown in Munday's original text: the role

was introduced in the additions by Hand B. In his turn D, ignorant of this 'improvement', had no thought of devising the part for a clown, since for him all the members of the populace were clownish in their behaviour – their leader most of all, just like Jack Cade and his followers. C's later efforts to individuate different characters in the scene (the clown, Williamson) among the 'others' are simply pathetic, though necessary in the preparation of a prompt-book. He must have been particularly baffled by D's two identical speech headings 'Sher' at lines 148 and 152, prefixed to speeches which must belong to characters on different sides of the dispute: the one speaking 'in the king's name' at l. 148 was obviously on the side of authority, so that C plumped for the Lord Mayor, while the speaker of l. 152, who addresses the crowd with 'let's hear' the Earl of Shrewsbury, identifies himself with the citizens, being obviously a moderate among them. Rather carelessly, C gave him the name of the resentful Williamson, while the citizen characterized in the previous scenes as the most recalcitrant to join the insurrection was the goldsmith Sherwin, in spite of the effrontery of De Bard who had taken away his wife and sent him to prison (see lines 50–60 and especially 429–30, when he objects to the firing of the aliens' houses). There is no doubt in my mind that in writing 'Sher' at this point D was thinking of Sherwin (and there might well have been a similar line assigned to him in Munday's lost original). As for the first 'Sher' at line 148, D must have meant 'Sheriff' – not More himself but the 'other Sherife' who appears in scene 2 (see l. 105) and more prominently in scene 7 (*566–*701), and should have accompanied More as his partner from the beginning of the action; alternately, 'Sher' could be a slip of the pen for 'Ser', i.e. the 'Seriant' (line 139) who, being mobbed by the crowd, shouts his injunction at the sight of the rescuers, the Mayor and the other Lords. The implication in either case is that D envisaged the presence on the stage of More, the Sergeant-at-arms and other representatives of law and authority confronting the rioters from the very beginning of the scene. A further corollary to this is

---

[12] Private communication, August 1983.

that the same must have been true also of the now lost original version of the scene in Munday's hand. Taking as a model the entrance stage directions devised by Munday for other scenes in the play (notably scenes 1, ll. 1–3, and 4, ll. 410–11),[13] I suggest that his entrance direction to scene 6 must have run more or less thus: 'Enter at one end Lincoln, Bettses, Doll, Williamson, Sherwin and others armed; at the other end More with the other Sheriff, Palmer, Cholmley and Downes, a sergeant-at-arms'.[14]

MUNDAY'S LOST ORIGINAL

Apart from the rewriting by D, and the evidence of Munday's practice in the other scenes of the play, there is another means of getting a sufficiently clear idea of how this scene was constructed in the lost original version. It is well known that the first part of *Sir Thomas More*, up to and including what Greg called scene 7, is a reinterpretation of the role (in fact a minimal role) that More, as one of the under-sheriffs of London (he is promoted to sheriff in the 'book'), played during the repression of the anti-alien riots in 1517, culminating in what came to be known as 'the evil May Day'. This part of the play – with the one exception of scene 2 – is in fact an extremely able rehandling of historical events and incidents of early 1517 as reported by a specific source: pages 840–4 of the 1587 edition (augmented by Abraham Fleming, John Stow and others) of the third volume of Holinshed's *Chronicles*. The fact that most of the material of the chronicles is derived from Edward Hall's history is irrelevant: a study of the surviving scenes of the play's original version shows that the author was following Holinshed closely even in matters of spelling and punctuation, as well as wording.[15] Not a single incident reported by the historian in connection with the insolence of the strangers and with the Londoners' early reaction is left out of scenes 1, 3 and 4 of *Sir Thomas More*, though the last mentioned scene anticipates as well the attack on the houses of 'maister Mewtas, a Picard borne' (Holinshed, p. 842; *More* l. 419), which Holinshed includes in the report of the riot proper. The account of 'Euill Maie daie' in the chronicle

begins with the beating up at the hands of prentices of the alderman Sir John Munday – the subject of the suppressed scene 5 of the play – and contains the 'councell taken by the maior' in consultation with More (which inspired what Greg calls scene 5a in the addition in Hand C, but must closely reflect Munday's lost original version of it), as well as the breaking into the Counters and Newgate and the freeing of the prisoners (also reported in 5a). Holinshed goes on (p. 842):

The maior and shiriffes were present there, and made proclamation in the kings name, but nothing was obeied. Herewith being gathered in plumpes, they ran thorough saint Nicholas shambles, and at

---

[13] The first stage direction reads: 'Enter at one end Iohn Lincolne with [*words unreadable*] / together, at the other end enters ffraunces de [*words unreadable*] / a lustie woman, he haling her by the arme', while that opening scene 4 reads: 'Enter *Lincolne, Betses, Williamson, Sherwin* and other armed, doll in a shirt / of Maile, a head piece, sword and Buckler, a crewe attending.' Note that 'Betses' is plural, and in scene 1 (l. 63) Lincoln speaks of 'these two bretheren heere (*Betses* by name)'; since Munday gives speeches to only one of them, George, the reviser B decided to develop the other, mute, Betts into the figure of the Clown.

[14] Such a stage direction would explain D's failure to mention in speech headings Williamson together with Lincoln, 'betts' (meaning George Betts), Sherwin and Doll: he may have taken Williamson simply as Doll's surname instead of that of a separate character. Greg believed that the omission by C of the name of Sherwin in the additional stage direction to the scene, as well as C's substitution of the speech heading 'Williamson' for D's 'Sher' at l. 152 were both intentional. In his transcript of the 'ill May Day scenes' (*Shakespeare's Hand in the Play of 'Sir Thomas More'*, p. 208) Greg notes: 'This attempt to get rid of a minor but still important character can only be due to difficulties of casting and corroborates that evidence offered by the occurrence of Goodal's name (fol. 13★a) that the parts were actually assigned.'

[15] The original version's dependence on Holinshed rather than Hall (as M. Shütt, 'Die Quellen des *Book of Sir Thomas More*', *Englische Studien*, 68 (1933), 209–26, and all subsequent editors maintain) is briefly discussed in the appendix to the already mentioned edition of *Sir Thomas More* by V. Gabrieli and myself; we have provided more evidence for it at a Shakespeare Association of America seminar held in Ashland in April 1983, and this will be incorporated in the new edition of the *Book* that we are preparing for the Revels Plays.

saint Martins gate there met with them sir Thomas
More, and others, desiring them to go to their
lodgings. And as they were thus intreating, and had
almost persuaded the people to depart, they within
saint Martins threw out stones, bats and hot water; so
that they hurt diuerse honest persons that were there
with sir Thomas More, persuading the rebellious
persons to ceasse, insomuch as at length one Nicholas
Downes a sergeant of armes being there with the said
sir Thomas More, & sore hurt amongst others, in a
furie, cried; Downe with them. And then all the
misruled persons ran to the doores and windowes of
the houses with[in] saint Martins, and spoiled all that
they found.

There is little doubt that the original version of
scene 6 was strictly based on this passage, except for
its conclusion, when, in the play, More succeeded in
what Holinshed said he failed to do, persuading the
people and preventing further harm to the sergeant-
at-arms Nicholas Downes. It is More himself who,
in scene 13 of the original text, reminds Downes,
now a mace-bearer come to arrest him, of the past
event (fol. 19b, †1560–2):

> I *Downes*, ist thou? I once did saue thy life,
> when else by cruell riottous assaulte
> thou hadst bin torne in pieces: ...

I shall now attempt a reconstruction of the five
main situations of this scene as they must have been
presented in the original version:

1. The rioters, at the opening, meet with More's
party coming straight from the consultation at the
Guildhall which is the subject of scene 5a. The
difficulty lies in the fact that More is the last speaker
in 5a, and an immediate re-entry of the same
character just after his exit is unlikely. Presumably
in the lost original version of the Guildhall scene
there was further consultation between the Lord
Mayor and the two earls after Palmer, who had
advised 'to call [the people] to a parley' (Add. II, l.
109), and More himself, had left in order 'to calme
oᵉ privat foes / wᵗʰ breath of gravitie not dangerous
blowes' (Add. II, 119–20). More's party entering at
the beginning of scene 6, then, would include
Palmer as well as the other sheriff and the sergeant-
at-arms Downes, both indicated by Holinshed, and
possibly Cholmley.[16] The location of scene 6 had

been firmly established, following Holinshed's suggestion, as far back as scene 4, when Lincoln had
stated: 'This is Sᵗ. Martins / and yonder dwelles
Mewtas a wealthie Piccarde' (ll. 418–19).

2. The sheriffs and Downes begin to 'intreat'
with the crowd, offering the King's pardon. I suspect
that what went wrong when they 'had almost
persuaded the people to depart', was not the behaviour of 'they within saint Martins', but the
'frantike furie' of Sir Roger Cholmley, described by
Holinshed (p. 842) as 'no great freend to the citie',
so that 'he wan much euill will for his hastie
dooing'. But this is a mere hypothesis with no shred
of evidence: it is safer to surmise that the anger of
the people was roused by some words of Sergeant
Downes.

3. In the following turmoil, Downes is 'sorely
hurt' and, losing control, exclaims, as in Holinshed,
'Down with them'. It is this phrase that makes him
run the risk of being 'torne to pieces'; and that the
exclamation was in the original text is indirectly
witnessed by the version in Hand D. The reviser of
the scene, wishing to put all the blame exclusively
on the rioters, transferred it from the Sergeant to
Lincoln who, taking offence at Downes's definition
of the prentices as 'the simplest things', exclaims
'prentisses simple downe wᵗʰ him' (Add. II, 144).

4. At this crucial moment More intervenes

---

16 Cholmley was not necessarily present in the original
version of the Guildhall scene, since also in its revised form
(Addition II, 66–120) he is not mentioned among the
followers of the earls and never speaks: his name in the
entrance stage direction at line 95 may be an arbitrary
addition by C. In the edition of *Sir Thomas More* that I
am preparing together with Vittorio Gabrieli for the
Revels Plays we argue that at first the revisers of the play
meant to leave out the Guildhall scene (5a), though such
scene was present in the original version, so that the action
would continue uninterrupted from scene 4 (the rioting
in St Martin's) to 6 (More's intervention); D wrote his
addition assuming that Lincoln and the rest were still on
the stage at the beginning; only later there came a change
of mind and the Guildhall scene was reinstated with
several changes from the original: C was given the task of
copying out the new version of the scene, but found it
difficult to join it up with scene 4 and even more with
scene 6.

saving Downes's life, and upon the arrival of the Lord Mayor and the Earls of Shrewsbury and Surrey with reinforcements, first invites them to use persuasion rather than force, and then addresses the crowd – although more briefly and without the eloquence displayed in the revised version by D – to make them realize the enormity of their offence.

5. After More has pacified the crowd, the offer of royal pardon already advanced earlier in the scene (see point 2 above) is reformulated as an official promise not by More himself, but by a representative of the King's authority, such as Palmer – who has the same function as the King's mouthpiece in scene 10. This exonerates More from making a promise that in his position as Sheriff of London he could not be sure of keeping: he simply expresses shortly afterwards (fol. 10a, ll. *477–9) his opinion that the King is very likely to grant the pardon announced in the official proclamation, which, as is the case with most announcements of the kind in Elizabethan drama (see for instance the Herald in *Lear*, 5.2.110–14, or the Duke himself in *Othello*, 1.2.221–8), is in prose. This explains why the three lines of the original version containing the offer of royal mercy, which have survived albeit marked for deletion at the top of fol. 10a (ll. *473–5), are in fact in prose.

I have been adding up a number of conjectures: the sum total cannot be a single certainty. All the same, there is enough convergence between what can be gathered from the revised version in Hand D of the first part of scene 6 and the source passage in Holinshed to make this reconstruction at least plausible.

THE EDITOR'S PROBLEM

More relevant is the demonstration of the fact that the bookkeeper C, being ignorant of the original which was the starting point for D's addition, misinterpreted the latter's intentions. This poses a serious problem for the modern editor who wishes to provide a readable (and performable) text. S. McMillin[17] is not alone in arguing that *Sir Thomas More*, once the additions are put in their proper places, is by no means an accumulation of fragments,

a poor example of dramatic patchwork, and unfinished at that, but a complete and perfectly constructed theatrical piece. And surely Harold Metz[18] is right in maintaining that the different 'additions' are actual improvements of the structure of the play from a theatrical point of view, and that they were made essentially for aesthetic rather than 'political' reasons. My only reservation is against the three pages in Hand D – whether Shakespeare's or no – of which I contest the fitness to the rest of the play not on theatrical, aesthetic or structural, but merely on ideological grounds: the 'addition' contradicts the way in which the citizens (whom he calls 'prentices') had been presented up to that moment, and are to appear again in scene 7. D's obviously careless treatment of Lincoln and company as a bunch of fools, in contrast with their painstaking individual characterization in the original version, may be at the root of the bookkeeper's misunderstandings, when he tried to fit this section to the rest, to give names to characters, to decide upon their entrances, etc.

Now, the modern editor of *Sir Thomas More* who intends to present it as a viable stage play is very much in the position of the bookkeeper C, who prepared the prompt-book to be submitted first of all to the Master of the Revels. In fact the modern editors of the play, in old or modern spelling, from Alexander Dyce in 1844 to Vittorio Gabrieli and myself in 1981, have, one and all, accepted C's decisions. In scene 6, though, they were confronted with two inconsistencies: the two entrance directions for the Sergeant, both in Hand C, at lines 122 and 139, and the absence of an entrance for More, Palmer and Cholmley. They could not help, in these two instances, emending Hand C. But, not realizing

17 S. McMillin, ' *The Book of Sir Thomas More*: a theatrical view', *Modern Philology*, 68 (1970–71), 10–24; cf. J. Doolin Spikes, ' *The Book of Sir Thomas More*: Structure and Meaning', *Moreana*, 11 (1974), 25–39; and C. R. Forker and J. Candido, 'Wit, Wisdom, and Theatricality in *The Book of Sir Thomas More*', *Shakespeare Studies*, 13 (1980), 85–104.

18 G. H. Metz, 'The Master of the Revels and *The Booke of Sir Thomas Moore*', *Shakespeare Quarterly*, 33 (1982), 493–5.

the reason for C's errors of duplication and omission, they simply deleted the Sergeant's entrance in the opening stage direction, developing instead the one indicated at l. 139, and they unobtrusively added the names of More, Palmer and Cholmley to the existing entrance direction at ll. 146–7.

Was this the correct decision? I submit that, since these very emendations show that C was in some way mistaken, we should go to the root of those mistakes and, rather than patch them up with a minimum of interference, make an effort to restore D's original intentions misinterpreted by C, not only in the text of speeches, but also in stage directions and speech headings. If, as seems likely, D envisaged the presence of More, Palmer, Cholmley and the Sergeant on the stage from the beginning of the scene, why should we adopt later entrances for them? If D considered most of the rioters an anonymous rabble, why should we give names to them? The director will decide the question when staging the play – he must have this freedom. I would make one exception: D had not thought of a part for the clown, since there was none in Munday's original, and he was unaware that in the meantime the reviser Hand B had created such a part and was to introduce it by adding speeches for him to scenes 4, the last part of 6, and 7 of the play. C instead knew it, and made the right decision in assigning to this actor, who must be present on the stage, two of the speeches that D had destined to an anonymous 'other'; after all, as we noticed, most of the 'others' for D were clownish characters.

Here, in conclusion, is what I think the first part of scene 6, which I reproduced as it was before C's interferences, should be like in a modernized edition:

Enter [at one end] Lincoln, Doll, Clown, George Betts [, Sherwin,] Williamson [and] others; and [at the other end] a Sergeant-at-arms [followed by More, the other sheriff, Palmer and Cholmley]

Lincoln. Peace, hear me: he that will not see a red herring at a Harry groat, butter at elevenpence a pound, meal at nine shillings a bushel, and beef at four nobles a stone, list to me.

Another citizen. It will come to that pass, if strangers be suffered: mark him.

Lincoln. Our country is a great eating country, *argo,* they eat more in our country than they do in their own.

Clown. By a halfpenny loaf a day troy weight.

Lincoln. They bring in strange roots, which is merely to the undoing of poor prentices, for what's a sorry parsnip to a good heart?

Another. Trash, trash! They breed sore eyes, and 'tis enough to infect the city with the palsy.

Lincoln. Nay, it has infected it with the palsy, for these bastards of dung – as you know they grow in dung – have infected us, and it is our infection will make the city shake, which partly comes through the eating of parsnips.

Clown. True, and pumpions together.

Sergeant.
    What say you to the mercy of the King?
    Do you refuse it?

Lincoln. You would have us upon th'hip, would you? No, marry, do we not; we accept of the King's mercy, but we will show no mercy upon the strangers.

Sergeant.   You are the simplest things
    That ever stood in such a question.

Lincoln. How say you now: prentices simple? Down with him.

All. Prentices simple, prentices simple!

Enter the Lord Mayor, [and the Earls of] Surrey [and] Shrewsbury

Sheriff.
    Hold, in the King's name hold!

Surrey.   Friends, masters, countrymen –

Mayor. Peace ho, peace! I charge you keep the peace.

Shrewsbury. My masters, countrymen –

Sherwin. The noble Earl of Shrewsbury, let's hear him.

George. We'll hear the Earl of Surrey.

Lincoln. The Earl of Shrewsbury.

George. We'll hear both.

All. Both, both, both, both!

Lincoln. Peace I say, peace! Are you men of wisdom or what are you?

Surrey.
    What you will have them, but not men of wisdom.

Some citizens. We'll not hear my lord of Surrey!

Others. No, no, no, no, no, Shrewsbury, Shrewsbury!

The arrangement of the Sergeant-at-arms's short interventions as a single three-line speech interrupted by Lincoln's rude reply has been suggested by Ernst

Honigmann, and is consistent with the Sergeant's status: only the populace use prose, while people in authority (the Mayor, More, Surrey, Shrewsbury, and even the Sheriff, whose half-line is completed by Surrey's speech) speak in verse. A final remark: if, as suggested in note 16, when D wrote his addition he thought that the Guildhall scene was being left out and the citizens were already on stage, the first part of the entrance stage direction referring to them should be omitted; but the modern editor must take into account the final form of the play with the reinstated scene.

LIVY, MACHIAVELLI, AND SHAKESPEARE'S 'CORIOLANUS'

ANNE BARTON

In Book 7 of his great history of Rome, from her foundation to the time of Augustus, Titus Livius recounts, with a certain admixture of scepticism, the story of Marcus Curtius. In the year 362 BC, a chasm suddenly opened in the middle of the Forum. The soothsayers, when consulted, declared that only a ritual sacrifice of the thing 'wherein the most puissance and greatnes of the people of Rome consisted' could close the fissure and 'make the state of Rome to remain sure forever'.[1] Much discussion followed, but no one could determine what that precious thing might be. Then Marcus Curtius, described in Philemon Holland's Elizabethan translation of Livy as 'a right hardie knight and martiall yong gentleman', 'rebuked them therefore, because they doubted whether the Romanes had any earthly thing better than armour and valor'. Armed at all points, he mounted a horse 'as richly trapped and set out as possiblie he could devise', and – like Hotspur at Shrewsbury – 'leapt into destruction' (*2 Henry IV*, 1.3.33).[2] The gulf closed.

In the Rome of Marcus Curtius, a century after the time of Coriolanus, it is by no means obvious that valour is 'the chiefest virtue', the one to which the city still owes her greatness. Times have changed. The Romans need to be reminded, by the gods and by the heroic action of one 'martiall yong gentleman', that formerly, as Plutarch asserts in his 'Life of Coriolanus', 'valliantnes was honoured in Rome above all other vertues: which they called *Virtus*, by the name of vertue selfe, as including in the generall name, all other speciall vertues besides. So that *Virtus* in the Latin, was asmuche as valliantnes.'[3] This passage, in North's translation, caught Shakespeare's eye. But the version of it that

he introduced into act 2, scene 2 of *Coriolanus* is qualified and uncertain. 'It is held', Cominius says as he begins his formal oration in the Capitol in praise of Coriolanus,

> That valour is the chiefest virtue and
> Most dignifies the haver: if it be,
> The man I speak of cannot in the world
> Be singly counter-pois'd.   (2.2.83–7)

'If', as Touchstone points out in *As You Like It*, is a word with curious properties and powers: 'Your If is the only peacemaker; much virtue in If' (5.4.102–3). Cominius' 'If', like Touchstone's, is a kind of peacemaker. Set off by the cautious appeal to an opinion in 'it is held', it introduces a slight but significant tremor of doubt into what in Plutarch had been fact, rock-hard and incontrovertible. Cominius goes on to celebrate Coriolanus in battle as a huge, irresistible force – a ship in full sail, bearing down and cleaving the aquatic vegetation of the shallows, a planet, the sea itself – but 'If' continues to mediate between martial prowess as a traditional all-sufficing good and the possible claims of other human ideals. It is as though Shakespeare's Cominius already had an intimation of that later Rome in which Marcus Curtius would be obliged

[1] *The Romane Historie Written By T. Livius of Padua*, trans. Philemon Holland (1600), Book 7, pp. 252–3.

[2] Quotations from *Coriolanus* refer to the Arden edition, ed. Philip Brockbank (1976). Other quotations from Shakespeare are based on *The Riverside Shakespeare*, ed. G. Blakemore Evans et al. (Boston, 1974).

[3] *Plutarch's Lives of the Noble Grecians and Romanes*, trans. Sir Thomas North (1579), in *Narrative and Dramatic Sources of Shakespeare*, ed. Geoffrey Bullough, 8 vols. (1957–75), vol. 5 (1964), p. 506.

to demonstrate to a forgetful city that valour was indeed her 'chiefest virtue'.

In writing *Coriolanus*, Shakespeare depended primarily upon Plutarch, as he had for *Julius Caesar* and *Antony and Cleopatra*. Once again, North's translation provided him with the dramatic skeleton, and even some of the actual words, of his play. But this time, he also had recourse to Livy, the chronicler of Coriolanus, Marcus Curtius, and the fortunes of republican Rome. It has long been recognized that lines 134 to 139 in Menenius' fable of the belly, those concerned with the distribution of nourishment through the blood, derive from Livy's, not Plutarch's, version of the tale. Those six lines are important in that they provide tangible evidence that Livy's *Ab Urbe Condita* was in Shakespeare's mind when he was meditating *Coriolanus*. But they matter far less than a series of overall attitudes, attitudes peculiar to this play, which I believe Shakespeare owed not to any one, particular passage in Livy, but to his history as a whole – in itself, and also as it had been interpreted by another, celebrated Renaissance reader.

As an author, Livy is likely to have impinged upon Shakespeare's consciousness at a relatively early age. Selections from his work were often read in the upper forms of Elizabethan grammar schools, ranking in popularity only behind Sallust and Caesar.[4] As a young man, Shakespeare drew material from Book 1 in composing his 'graver labour', *The Rape of Lucrece*, published in 1594, six years before Philemon Holland's translation made the whole of Livy available in English. Shakespeare customarily consulted more than one historical source. He had never, before *Coriolanus*, written a play set in republican Rome, in a mixed state of the kind that, for various reasons, was attracting considerable attention in Jacobean England. Livy was the acknowledged, great repository of information about this republic, as well as its fervent champion. It was almost inevitable that Shakespeare should return to *Ab Urbe Condita*, now handsomely 'Englished' by Holland, in order to remind himself of what was happening in Rome at the beginning of the fifth century BC. What he found there was an account of Caius Martius which, although the same

in its essentials as that of Plutarch in his 'Life of Coriolanus', was different in emphasis, and radically altered by a context from which it could not be disentangled.

Unlike Plutarch, the biographer of great men, author of *Lives* carefully paired for moral and didactic purposes, Livy was pre-eminently the historian of a city. Throughout the thirty-five extant books of his history, he never breaks faith with the intention expressed in his very first sentence: to record the *res populi Romani*, the achievements of the people of Rome. By '*populi*', Livy does not just mean plebeians. He means everyone, all classes, the rulers and the ruled, the leaders and the led. In Livy's eyes, no man, no matter how great, should regard himself as superior to the state, or even coequal. Plutarch consistently plays down the political concerns of Dionysius of Halicarnassus, one of his main sources of information as to the nature of Rome's past. Livy, by contrast, is far less interested in individual destiny than he is in the changing character of Rome's institutions, her expansion through the Mediterranean, and the increasingly complex social and economic equilibrium worked out within the city over a long period of time. So, characteristically, he does not find it especially important to determine whether Coriolanus himself was, in fact, killed by his Volscian allies after he turned back from the gates of Rome, or whether he survived, eating the bitter bread of exile, into old age. Either ending is possible. What really matters to Livy in the Coriolanus story is, first, that thanks to the intervention of the women, Rome herself escaped destruction and even acquired a fine new temple dedicated to Fortuna Muliebris. Secondly, that a new stage was reached in the protracted but necessary struggle between patricians and plebeians – a struggle in which there was right on both sides.

Although Collingwood perversely tried to deny it, Livy is essentially a developmental historian. As T. J. Luce writes in his recent study of the composition of Livy's history, 'the central theme of his narrative is that the growth of Rome and the genesis

---

[4] T. W. Baldwin, *Shakspere's Small Latine & Lesse Greeke*, 2 vols. (Urbana, 1944) vol. 2, pp. 573–4.

of her institutions was a gradual, piecemeal process that took many centuries'. Book 2, in which the story of Caius Martius is told, addresses itself specifically to the question of how *libertas* was achieved, actually, and in men's minds. It begins with threats from without: Lars Porsinna of Clusium and the attempt of the exiled Tarquins to regain control of the city. It ends with the overcoming of threats from within, represented by Spurius Cassius, and by Coriolanus.[5] In describing the arrogance of Coriolanus, his stubborn refusal to countenance the tribunate, Livy writes with the Tarquin kings and their tyranny in mind, and also in full awareness of what (historically) was to come: an increase in the number of tribunes to ten, publication of the laws, permission for plebeian/patrician intermarriage, and the opening of the highest civic offices, including the consulship itself, to plebeians. Livy himself went on to chronicle these changes, leaving Coriolanus almost entirely forgotten in the past, except as the focus (intermittently remembered) of a cautionary tale. However useful in time of war, men like Coriolanus are a threat to the balance of the state, to an evolving republic which must try to take them with it but, if it cannot, has no option but to discard them by the way.

Although the populace in *Julius Caesar* includes one witty shoemaker, and there are — temporarily — two sceptics among the followers of Jack Cade, it would be hard to claim that Shakespeare displays much sympathy for urban crowds in the plays he wrote before *Coriolanus*. In depicting the fickle and destructive mob roused so skilfully by Mark Antony, the ignorant and brutal rebels of *2 Henry VI*, even those xenophobic Londoners rioting over food prices in the scene he contributed to *Sir Thomas More*, he is savagely funny, but also almost wholly denigratory. That is no reason for assuming, as critics tend to do, that his attitude in *Coriolanus* must be similar. In fact, this play is unique in the canon for the tolerance and respect it accords an urban citizenry. The very first scene of the tragedy presents plebeians who arrest their own armed rebellion in mid-course, not because of outside intervention by a social superior — the persuasive tactics of a Flavius and Marullus, a

Lord Clifford or a Sir Thomas More — but freely, of their own volition, because it is important to them to inquire exactly what they are doing, and why. The Roman people here are not distinguished by personal names. They speak, nonetheless, as individuals, not as a mob. They care about motivation, their own and that of their oppressors, and they are by no means imperceptive. Even the belligerent First Citizen thinks it important to establish that hunger has forced him into violence, not a 'thirst for revenge' (1.1.24). Not one of the citizens attempts to deny that Caius Martius has served Rome nobly, whatever his attitude towards them, nor do they make the mistake of thinking that he stands out against a distribution of surplus corn to the commons because he is personally covetous. The First Citizen contents himself with suggesting that this man's valorous deeds have been performed for suspect reasons: out of pride, and a desire to please his mother, rather than from disinterested love of his country. This is not very far from the truth. The Second Citizen has already cautioned the First against speaking 'maliciously' (l. 34), and yet the events of the play will, to a large extent, justify the latter's analysis.

The Roman people in this play are politically unsophisticated and, sometimes, confused and naive. Like Williams and Bates confronting the disguised Henry V on the eve of Agincourt, they can be blinded by rhetoric, even though theirs is in fact the stronger case. The English common soldiers allowed themselves to be diverted from the crucial issue of whether or not Henry's cause in France was 'good'. The citizens of Rome are so impressed by the fable of the belly that they fail to detect the logical flaw in its application: the fact that in the present famine the senators are indeed selfishly 'cupboarding the viand' (1.1.99) of last year's harvest in their storehouses, that the belly, by withholding nourishment from the rest of the body politic, has ceased to perform its proper social function. They also allow themselves to be manipulated by their tribunes. And yet it matters that, unlike the crowd in *Julius Caesar*, a

---

5 T. J. Luce, *Livy: The Composition of His History* (Princeton, 1977), p. 238 and *passim*.

crowd which has no opinions of its own, merely those which are suggested to it, first by Brutus and then by Mark Antony, the citizens of the republic can think for themselves. They draw their own conclusions, quite unaided, about the behaviour of Coriolanus when he stands in the market-place and insultingly demands their voices. If, as the First Citizen says in that scene, the price of the consulship is 'to ask it kindly' (2.3.75), Coriolanus at the end of it has been given something for nothing. The people sense this, although even here a dissenting voice is raised: 'No, 'tis his kind of speech; he did not mock us' (2.3.159). 'Almost all' the citizens, we are told – not all, because there are other, independent opinions – 'repent in their election' (ll. 252–3). The tribunes deliberately inflame the commons against Coriolanus, finally transforming them from angry but rational individuals into 'a rabble of Plebeians' (3.1.178 SD). They are right, however, when they claim that they have a mandate from the people, that the sudden reaction against Coriolanus is 'partly...their own' (2.3.260).

The worst thing the plebeians ever do is something for which Coriolanus himself never berates them. He is not present in Rome to witness their panic-stricken reaction to the news of his league with Aufidius, or the irrational fury they unleash upon Junius Brutus, their own tribune. This is almost the only occasion on which their behaviour can be said to approximate to that of Shakespeare's earlier crowds. In this play, it is exceptional rather than characteristic. It is true that, when cunningly prompted to do so by the tribunes in act 3, the plebeians claim that they alone embody Rome: 'the people', they shout, 'are the city' (3.1.198). This is patently false, as they themselves know in their calmer moods. Rome cannot be identified solely with her commons. But then, the assumption with which Menenius begins the play is equally false, when he tells the citizens that, however great their sufferings in the present dearth, they cannot strike against

> the Roman state, whose course will on
> The way it takes, cracking ten thousand curbs
> Of more strong link asunder than can ever
> Appear in your impediment.   (1.1.68–71)

The Roman state, according to this formulation, is not only exclusively patrician, excluding the proletariat, it resembles Coriolanus himself on the field of battle: a titanic machine, its motion timed with dying cries, mowing down every human obstacle in its path. Of course the city is not the exclusive property of the people, but neither does it belong solely to the upper class.

In the course of the play, Menenius, Cominius, their colleagues in the Senate, even Volumnia, will be forced to recognize that this is so. Although a few young hot-heads among the patricians may flatter Coriolanus that he does the 'nobler' to tell the mutable, rank-scented meinie just what he thinks of them, how unworthy they are to possess any voice in the government of Rome, although a few may toy with the idea, after his banishment, of abolishing the newly established institution of tribunes, these are not serious or consequential responses. Brutus and Sicinius are scarcely lovable men. There is a world of unsavoury implication in Brutus' reaction to the news of Coriolanus' alliance with the Volscians in act 4: 'Would half my wealth / Would buy this for a lie' (4.6.160–1). But they are clearly right in their belief that, once established as consul, Coriolanus would wish to strip from the people the hard-won concessions they have just gained. Such a course of action could only be disastrous. The tribunate, however selfish or inadequate their own performance in the office, is now a political fact. Once granted, however reluctantly, the right of the Roman people not just to rubber-stamp a consular election by exercising their ancient and vulgar prerogative of examining patrician scars in the market-place, but to make their own needs and wishes felt through their representatives, cannot be withdrawn.

Significantly, in the crisis of act 3, Menenius stops talking about a patrician juggernaut flattening dissenting plebeians like so many weeds. He asks rather that there be 'On both sides more respect' (3.1.179), begins to refer to 'the whole state' (3.2.34), appeals to 'good Sicinius' (3.1.190), 'worthy tribunes' (3.1.263), and admits that the division which has cleft the city 'must be patch'd / With cloth of any colour' (ll. 250–1). The tribunes, he admits, are the 'people's magistrates', and likely to remain so (3.1.200–1). When Sicinius says to him, 'Noble Menenius, / Be you then as the people's officer' (3.1.326–7), he accepts the designation without demur, and goes off to plead with Coriolanus to submit himself to judgement. Of course Menenius, like the other patricians, is trying to be tactful and conciliatory in what has suddenly become a desperate situation. Although it amuses him to observe the ebb and flow of popular life in the market, Menenius' basic contempt for the 'beastly plebeians', Rome's 'rats', her 'multiplying spawn', is deep-rooted. Attitudes like these are not changed overnight. Yet he recognizes, like all the patricians except Caius Martius, that a change in the structure of government has become inevitable. Not one of them welcomes the innovation, but they also see that if civil strife is not to 'unbuild the city and to lay all flat' (l. 196), to 'sack great Rome with Romans' (l. 313), they have no alternative but to move with the times.

Only Coriolanus refuses to accept that a new stage has been reached in the evolution of Rome.[6] In act 1, he affirmed bluntly that he would rather 'the rabble...unroof'd the city' (1.1.217) than that any concessions to them should be made. He never relinquishes this opinion. For him, the patrician compromise of act 3, the refusal of the nobles to entertain the prospect of such destruction, take his advice, and try to trample the new power of the tribunes in the dust, constitutes a betrayal both of himself, personally, and of an older Rome to which, in his eyes, only he now remains true. This is why, despite the manifest loyalty and grief of Cominius, Menenius, and the young nobility of Rome, those 'friends of noble touch' (4.1.49) – Cominius even tries to accompany him into exile – he can tell Aufidius later that 'our dastard nobles' have 'all forsook me' (4.5.76–7). Menenius, in act 1, made the mistake of reducing the Roman state to her patrician members. The plebeians, briefly, were persuaded to identify the city with themselves. But only Coriolanus ever deludes himself that he, a single individual, constitutes Rome's best and only self. It is a delusion which manifests itself in the magnificent absurdity of his response to the tribunes' sentence

of banishment in act 3 – 'I banish you!' (3.3.123) – where he effectively tries to exile most of Rome's population, that plebeian majority he detests. Because he thinks in this way, it is possible for him to betray his country without ever admitting to himself that he is, like the petty spy Nicanor, introduced (significantly) just before Coriolanus' arrival at the house of Aufidius in act 4, a Roman traitor.

In a sense, the possibility of such a betrayal has been present throughout Coriolanus' adult life. It is bound up with his essential and crippling solitariness, and also with his failure ever to consider how much his heroism has truly been dedicated to Rome as a city, and how much to his own self-realization and personal fame. Never, it seems, has it occurred to him that the two motives, the public and the private, might under certain circumstances conflict, or that the one might require adjustments and concessions from the other. Of course, he did not mean to be taken literally when he declared of Tullus Aufidius in act 1 that,

> Were half to half the world by th'ears, and he
> Upon my party, I'd revolt to make
> Only my wars with him.   (1.1.232–4)

The lines are revealing, nonetheless, in the way they elevate a purely personal competition above the claims of a country or a cause. Rome will always need great soldiers, dedicated generals and strong defenders. Livy makes this quite clear. Nonetheless, it is an urban republic, not the plains of Troy, a society which no longer, whatever may have been

---

[6] In the discussion which followed this paper as originally presented at the 1984 Shakespeare Conference in Stratford-upon-Avon, Professor John W. Velz drew my attention to contemporary knowledge of Lucius Annaeus Florus' *Epitome Bellorum Omnium Annorum*, with its account of Rome's passage through infancy, youth and manhood, to old age. Velz's own article, 'Cracking Strong Curbs Asunder: Roman Destiny and the Roman Hero in *Coriolanus*' (*English Literary Renaissance*, 13 (1983), 58–69), examines Shakespeare's indebtedness to Virgil in *Coriolanus* in ways that are important and persuasive, arriving at a reading of the play similar, in some ways, to my own.

the case in the past, is based exclusively, or even primarily, upon an ethos of war.

One of the great themes running through and unifying Livy's history of Rome is that of the gradual adjustment over the centuries of the claims of peace and war. Numa Pompilius, as the tribune Brutus reminds us in Shakespeare's play (2.3.235–8), was one of Coriolanus' ancestors, that legendary king of Rome who decided in the eighth century BC that it was time steps were taken to civilize his people. Accordingly, as Livy writes (in Holland's translation), he began

by good orders, lawes, and customes, to reedifie as it were that cittie, which before time had been new built by force and armes. Whereunto he, seeing that they might not be brought and framed in time of warre, whose hearts were alreadie by continuall warfare growne wild and savage: and supposing that this fierce people might be made more gentle and tractable through disuse of armes, he therefore built the temple of *Janus* in the nether end of the street of Argilentum, in token both of warre and peace.[7]

Shakespeare could have read about Numa, the great lawgiver and architect of a social and religious order, in Plutarch. There, Numa has a 'Life' of his own, paired with that of the Spartan ruler Lycurgus. He is also mentioned in the 'Life of Coriolanus'. But it is only Livy who patiently teases out the intimate connection, unfolding over a vast stretch of years, between Rome's need to cultivate the arts of peace as well as war, and the internal struggle between her patricians and plebeians. Over and over in the days of the republic, as Livy makes plain, the patricians depended upon war as a way of stifling civic dissension, busying giddy minds with foreign quarrels in order to keep them distracted from injustices and inequalities at home. Sometimes, this strategy worked, uniting Rome temporarily against a foreign foe. But increasingly, over the years, it did not. Rome could not wage war without the help of common soldiers, could not (indeed) even protect her own frontiers. And so, unhappy and mistreated plebeians either declined to enlist or, if impressed, refused once they arrived on the battlefield to fight. It was virtually the only weapon they possessed in

their attempt to wrest some rights and privileges from the ruling class.

In Shakespeare's play, Caius Martius appears, significantly, to be the only patrician who still believes that the internal difficulties of the city can be resolved by a Volscian war. The fact that the people are starving need not oblige the patricians to diminish their own stores: 'The Volsces have much corn: take these rats thither, / To gnaw their garners' (1.1.248–9). Plutarch, in his 'Life of Coriolanus', describes how at this time the patricians as a group hoped to rid the city of its difficult and seditious elements by way of a military campaign. But, in Shakespeare, it is only Caius Martius who welcomes war with the Volscians, for its own sake, but also because enforced national service may annihilate 'Our musty superfluity' (1.1.225), by which he means the commons, not the stored-up corn. Moreover, Shakespeare altered the order of events as they occur in both Plutarch and Livy. It is plain in *Coriolanus* that only after tribunes have been granted them do the citizens stop stirring up strife in the city and agree to provide soldiers for the Volscian campaign.

In that campaign, although Coriolanus – not to mention many of the play's critics – later chooses to forget this fact, the plebeians acquit themselves with credit. Cominius is forced initially into an honourable retreat, but he judges that the field has been 'well fought' (1.6.1). When, beyond all hope or probability, Coriolanus reappears through those gates of Corioli which he entered by himself, the soldiers are galvanized into action: they not only rescue him but take the city. Coriolanus could not have done this alone – even though later, just before his death, he seems to think that he did. A thing of blood, looking, as Cominius says, 'as he were flay'd' (1.6.22), Caius Martius then becomes a deadly weapon in the hands of common soldiers who, because they possess him, like a living icon of War, become for a crucial moment heroes too. And so the Roman victory is assured.

This is the one instance of real communion and understanding between Coriolanus and the Roman

---

[7] Livy, *Romane Historie*, p. 14.

plebeians in the tragedy, but it is ephemeral and special. Upon it, nothing can be built. Later, back in Rome, he will remember only that 'being press'd to the war, / Even when the navel of the state was touch'd, / They would not thread the gates' (3.1.121–3). He neglects to remember – even as he neglects to remember the name of the poor citizen of Corioli who once used him 'kindly' (1.9.81) – that the common soldiers did in fact enter the gates of Corioli, at the second opportunity, if not, in response to his threats and insults, at the first. Or how men who seemed to him at the time each worth 'four Volsces' (1.6.78) caught him up in their arms and cast up their caps in their eagerness for action. The only memory that sticks with Coriolanus is the initial prudence (for him, cowardice) of these soldiers, and the contemptible concern of poor men, after the battle is over, for plunder, in the pitiable form of cushions and leaden spoons. A biased, an unfairly selective representation of the campaign, it does nonetheless point to something that is true about the Roman plebeians.

From an early age, as Volumnia tells us, Caius Martius has been dedicated to war, and to achieving excellence in it. It is his metier, his life's work. But the attitude of the Roman people – even, to a large extent, of his fellow patricians – is different. Although the commons can, under exceptional circumstances, be fired with martial enthusiasm, they would really prefer, in Sicinius' words, to be 'singing in their shops and going / About their functions friendly' (4.6.8–9). For these small shopkeepers and traders, orange sellers, makers of taps for broaching wine-barrels, military service is something they are obliged to undertake from time to time, when the necessities of the state require it. But they had far rather pursue their normal, peacetime occupations than be out slitting Volscian throats. For Coriolanus, such a preference is contemptible. His view, however, is not endorsed by the play as a whole. The fact is that in an increasingly complex and finely balanced society, one in which even Cominius can hint that valour may not any longer be the chiefest virtue, Volumnia's son is something of an anachronism, out of line even with the other members of his class. Like that dragon to which he

likens himself in act 4, and to which Menenius and Aufidius also compare him, he is an archaic, semi-mythical creature, armour-plated, gigantic, corporeally invincible, a bulwark for the city in war, but something of an embarrassment in peace, because given then to blundering about the market in a bellicose fashion, breathing fire not on Rome's enemies but on the members of her own lower class.

In the second scene of act 3, after Coriolanus has been forced to take refuge from the crowd in his home, Volumnia (who is in large part responsible for her son's scorn of the people, 'woollen vassals', as she has taught him to call them, 'things created / To buy and sell with groats' (ll. 9–10), and who also recognizes that, as consul, he would quickly show them how he is really 'dispos'd' (l. 22), nonetheless begs him now to speak to them not 'by th'matter which your heart prompts you', but falsely, in 'syllables / Of no allowance to your bosom's truth' (ll. 54–7). The only hypocrisy that Coriolanus manages to utter, before anger and his bosom's truth overtake him, is this:

> Th'honoured gods
> Keep Rome in safety, and the chairs of justice
> Supplied with worthy men, plant love among's,
> Throng our large temples with the shows of peace
> And not our streets with war.   (3.3.33–7)

His sarcasm is barely concealed, but the First Senator responds enthusiastically, 'Amen, Amen', and Menenius, 'A noble wish' (ll. 37–8). Both of them, unlike Coriolanus, mean what they say. The Rome they want is the one set on its course by Numa: vigilant, strong in its own defence, but also a citadel of justice and religion, and paying equal honour, as befits worshippers in the temple of Janus, to the claims of war and peace. What Coriolanus disdainfully fabricates has become for the rest of the city, including the patricians, a genuine political and social ideal, even if tribunes are now required to help achieve it.

I have been trying to argue that, although Shakespeare is unlikely, while actually writing *Coriolanus*, to have kept a copy of Livy open beside him, as he apparently did with Plutarch, nonetheless the attitudes and interests of *Ab Urbe Condita*, as we understand that work now, live to a striking extent in this last of his Roman plays. But, it might be asked, is it reasonable to assume that Shakespeare in 1607–8 would have read Livy in at all the manner we read him today? As a man of his time, would Shakespeare not have been more likely to value the book for the individual stories embedded in it, for what it had to say about the lives of great men, than for an overall historical view of the kind I have been concerned to stress? Not, I think, necessarily. Here, it seems important to point out that Shakespeare's understanding, in *Coriolanus*, of the development and strengths of the Roman republic, as outlined by Livy, is markedly similar in many ways to that of his great Italian contemporary, Niccolo Machiavelli.

Machiavelli's *Discorsi*, his commentary on the first ten books of Livy, was not published in English until 1636. It circulated widely, however, in Elizabethan and Jacobean England in Italian (a language which, on the evidence of his use of Cinthio for *Othello*, Shakespeare could read) and also in various manuscript translations, three of which survive.[8] The notion that Machiavelli reached sixteenth-century England only as a stock stage villain, a caricature agent of hell, has long since been exploded. Among Shakespeare's contemporaries, Sidney, Spenser, Gabriel Harvey, Nashe, Kyd, Marston, Bacon, Fulke Greville, Ralegh, and Ben Jonson, to name only a few, were clearly familiar not only with the devilish practices and opinions popularly attributed to Machiavelli, but with what he had actually written. Neither then nor, indeed, at any time is a first-hand knowledge of Machiavelli tantamount to approval of what he has to say. The commentary on Livy is morally less outrageous than *Il Principe*, yet even Edward Dacres, its seventeenth-century translator, felt constrained to announce on his title-page that he was presenting this work, designed to instruct its dedicatee James, Duke of Lennox in how best to cope with the perils of the political world, fenced round 'with some marginall animadversions noting and taxing [the author's] errours'.[9] It seems to have been relatively common in Elizabethan and Jacobean England for writers to allude to Machiavelli as a caricature bogeyman or as a serious thinker, according to the needs of any specific occasion. The case of Spenser is especially inter-esting. In one work, *Mother Hubberds Tale*, it suited him to present the stereotype Machiavel – irreligious, perjured, self-seeking, hypocritical and cruel. But later, in his *View of the Present State of Ireland*, Spenser could, without a flicker of irony, offer Elizabeth's government detailed counsel as to the best way of pacifying that unhappy colony which he took straight out of *The Prince* and, to a lesser extent, the *Discourses*.[10]

I think myself that it would be more surprising if it could be proved that Shakespeare had managed to avoid reading Machiavelli than if concrete evidence were to turn up that he had. Certainly, the example of Spenser ought to caution one against believing that York's reference in *1 Henry VI* to Alanson as 'that notorious Machevile' (5.4.74), or the intention of the future Richard III to 'set the murtherous Machevil to school' (*3 Henry VI*, 3.3.193), in any way precludes the demonstration of genuine understanding elsewhere in the Shakespeare canon. (Significantly, when the Host in *The Merry Wives of Windsor* asks the rhetorical question, 'Am I politic? Am I subtle? Am I a Machivel?' (3.1.101), he has just rendered a signal service to the community, using deceit – the end justifying the means – in order to prevent Windsor's parson and her physician from trying to kill each other in a foolish cause.) There is, however, no real need to make an issue of Shakespeare's actual acquaintance with the *Discourses*. What matters is the way Machiavelli's interpretation of Livy bears upon *Coriolanus*, however the parallels between the two works arose.

Even critics fundamentally unsympathetic to Coriolanus as a character have a way of applauding the supposed political wisdom of his tirade in the first scene of act 3:

> when two authorities are up,
> Neither supreme, how soon confusion
> May enter 'twixt the gap of both, and take
> The one by th'other, (ll. 108–11)

---

8 Felix Raab, *The English Face of Machiavelli* (1965), pp. 52–3.

9 *Machiavels Discourses upon the first Decade of T. Livius*, trans. Edward Dacres (1636).

10 Edwin A. Greenlaw, 'Machiavelli and Spenser', in *Modern Philology*, 7 (1909), 1–16.

his attack upon what he scorns as 'this double worship...where gentry, title, wisdom, / Cannot conclude but by the yea and no / Of general ignorance' (ll. 141, 143–5). But what Coriolanus is repudiating here is in fact precisely the equilibrium in which, for Machiavelli, Livy had located the strength of the Roman republic. It is one of the central themes of the *Discourses* that the struggle between patricians and plebeians was positive, not negative, that indeed, as the heading of Chapter 4 in the First Book announces, 'the disagreement of the People and the Senate of Rome made the Commonwealth both free and mighty'.

Machiavelli is careful to distinguish dissension from faction. Faction finally destroyed the republic, in the time of the Gracchi, when the attempt to enforce the old agrarian laws split the city into two warring camps between whom communication and compromise became impossible. The result was a blood-bath, of just the kind that senators and tribunes alike, in *Coriolanus*, fear and make concessions to avoid, 'Unless by not so doing, our good city / Cleave in the midst, and perish' (3.2.27–8). But between the expulsion of the Tarquins in the sixth century BC and the end of the second century BC – over three hundred years – dissension between patricians and plebeians was not only relatively bloodless, compromises made on both sides ensured a balance of aristocratic and popular interests in which each individual, however humble, while subordinating his private interests to those of the state, was nonetheless able to cultivate his own *virtu*. It was a balance brought to perfection when, at just the right moment, tribunes of the people were added to the pre-existing political institutions of consuls and senate. Then, for a while, Rome had almost within her grasp that ideal condition of which Machiavelli dreamed, even if he was sadly aware that it was never likely to be realized in his own Italy: that of a free and stable state, the potential insolence and disorder of its people restrained by the power of the nobles, aristocratic ambition and arrogance checked by the people, a state so strong that it could afford to live at peace, with no need to expand, and no neighbour so foolhardy as to molest it.[11]

Although he recognizes that Livy grumbles from time to time about the inconstancy of the multitude,

their inadequacies and failings, for Machiavelli the merits of the Roman people are vindicated in the great sweep of Livy's history as a whole. They were, to an extent which perhaps Livy himself never consciously recognized, essential to what the republic achieved. As Machiavelli writes at the end of Book 1: 'the Cittie that imployes not their people in any glorious action, may treate them after their owne manner, as otherwise it was argued. But that, which will take the same course Rome tooke, must make this distinction'.[12] Even the humblest citizen of the Roman republic was given his chance to achieve 'glory', whether military or civic. As for the desire of the commons to conclude military campaigns as speedily as possible and return to their peacetime occupations, Machiavelli regards it as entirely proper. In his eyes, a man who is a professional fighter, a soldier and nothing else, is valueless to the state and may even endanger it. In the Roman republic, although every able-bodied man was expected to help fight her wars, war was nobody's occupation. And there were so many brave and victorious commanders all serving at one time (as do Cominius, Titus Lartius and Coriolanus), that the people did not need to worry about one of them making himself pre-eminent and so possibly tyrannical.

Machiavelli believed that no human being was either wholly good or wholly bad. An individual's natural qualities, his bent, shape themselves early and cannot thereafter be changed. People also, as they mature, learn certain ways of proceeding, accustom themselves to particular patterns of behaviour. States do this too. But around both, times and circumstances change. It is extremely difficult for individuals, and also for political institutions, to vary at need, to accommodate themselves to the demands of new situations. And yet their failure or success depends, ultimately, upon their ability to do so. A republic, Machiavelli suggests in the *Discourses*, is likely to fare better in this respect than a monarchy,

---

[11] In his essay, 'Machiavelli's Use of Livy' (Chapter 4, in *Livy*, ed. T. A. Dorey, 1971), J. H. Whitfield stresses the importance of the passage in Chapter 6, Book 1 of the *Discourses* in which Machiavelli formulates this ideal. Cf. pp. 83–4.

[12] Machiavelli, *Discourses*, Book 1, Chapter 60, p. 243.

because shee can better fit her selfe for severall accidents, by reason of the variety of her subjects, that are in her, then can a Prince: for a man that is accustomed to proceed in one manner, never alters, as it is sayd, and must of necessitie, when the times disagree with his waye, goe to wracke.[13]

In effect, once again, the pluralism, the contentious but firmly shared responsibility of the mixed state, work to its advantage.

As might be expected, Machiavelli's view of Coriolanus himself is harsher than Livy's, and much more dismissive than that of Shakespeare. Machiavelli deals with Caius Martius in Book 1 of the *Discourses*, in Chapter 7, entitled: 'How useful accusations are in a Republike for the maintenance of liberty'. For him, the story of Caius Martius was interesting simply because it displayed the triumph of democratic law. Coriolanus aroused the indignation of a famished populace by declaring in the Senate that corn ought not to be distributed gratis until the people agreed to subject themselves to the nobles and relinquish the tribunate. But the very tribunes Coriolanus wanted to abolish saved his life. If they had not intervened, accused him formally, and summoned him to appear before them and defend himself, he would have been slain in what Machiavelli's seventeenth-century translator calls 'a tumult', as he left the Senate. This episode, Machiavelli declares, shows 'how fit and useful it is that the commonwealths with their laws give meanes to vent the choler which the universalitie hath conceiv'd against any one citizen. For when they have not these ordinarie meanes, they have recourse to extraordinarie; and out of question these are of worse effect than those.'[14] In exiling Coriolanus, and never permitting him to return, the Roman state was guilty of no error or ingratitude, 'because he alwayes continued his malicious mind against the people'.[15]

It is true in general that 'contempt and contumely begets a hatred against those that use it, without any returne of advantage to them'.[16] But in a republic, above all, the man who is proud and uses insulting language, who openly displays his contempt for the commons, is intolerable: 'for nothing is more odious to the people, especially those that injoy their liberty'.[17] There is only one further reference to Coriolanus in the *Discourses*, a passing mention of how his mother persuaded him to turn back from the gates of Rome, used to introduce a debate on the relative merits of a good army or an able commander. Machiavelli does not bother to comment directly on Coriolanus' league with the Volscians. What he thought about it, however, can fairly be deduced from the heading to Chapter 47 near the end of Book 3: 'That a good Citizen for the love of his country ought to forget all private wrongs'.

Although Machiavelli took no interest in the nature of Coriolanus' life in exile, Shakespeare did. Caius Martius cannot possibly 'banish' the people who have driven him out of the city, restoring Rome to the condition of an ancient, warrior state. On the other hand, I believe, contrary to most critics, that he does find 'a world elsewhere' (3.3.135). Historically, the Volscians were a semi-nomadic, cattle-raiding people, hill-dwellers to the south, who envied the rich lands of the Latin campagna. From Livy, Shakespeare would have learned that Rome was at odds with them, off and on, for some two hundred years. She crushed them in the end, but the struggle was long and hard. What seems to have mattered most to Shakespeare, working on hints provided by both Livy and Plutarch, was that in the time of Caius Martius, Volscian society was clearly different and far simpler than that of Rome. According to Plutarch, Corioles was the 'principall cittie and of most fame'[18] – modern archaeologists, by the way, still cannot discover where it was – but it clearly had nothing like the centrality and importance for this nation that the seven-hilled city on

---

[13] Machiavelli, Book 3, Chapter 9, p. 498. In *Machiavelli* (Oxford, 1981), Quentin Skinner describes Machiavelli's conviction, established early in his life, that 'the clue to successful statecraft lies in recognising the force of circumstances, accepting what necessity dictates, and harmonising one's behaviour with the times' as his 'central political belief' (p. 38).

[14] Machiavelli, Book 1, Chapter 7, pp. 38–9.

[15] Machiavelli, Book 1, Chapter 29, p. 125.

[16] Machiavelli, Book 2, Chapter 26, p. 398.

[17] Machiavelli, Book 3, Chapter 23, p. 559.

[18] *Plutarch's Lives*, in Bullough (vol. 5), p. 511.

the Tiber had for the Romans. Antium, indeed, where Tullus Aufidius presides as a kind of feudal lord, seems equally prominent. This is why Shakespeare can so blithely confuse the two places in the final scene. According to Plutarch, Coriolanus was killed in Antium. That is where Shakespeare's scene begins. But by line 90, Antium has turned into Corioli: 'Dost thou think', Aufidius exclaims, 'I'll grace thee with that robbery, thy stol'n name / Coriolanus, in Corioles?' (5.6.88–90). Shakespeare is being careless, but it is a carelessness made possible by the fact that whereas Rome is unique, one Volscian town looks much like another.

Neither in Antium nor Corioli are there tribunes or aediles. There most certainly is an upper class, designated almost invariably in speech prefixes and in the text as 'lords'. (Only once, from Aufidius, do we hear the term 'senators', 4.5.133.) There are also 'people'. If there is the slightest friction between the two, we are never told about it. Moreover, in this society, everyone seems to regard war as a natural and even desirable condition of existence. In Shakespeare's play, the Volscians are always the aggressors, never the Romans. According to Plutarch, the Volscian lords were in fact reluctant after the sack of Corioli to break the truce agreed so recently with Rome. They had to be tricked, by Aufidius and Coriolanus, into renewing hostilities. In Livy, it is the Volscian commons, broken and dispirited by plague and by the loss of so many young men in the last war, who need to be deceived into resuming arms. Shakespeare ignored both accounts. When Coriolanus arrives, in act 4, at the house of Aufidius, the Volscian lords have already assembled there to plan a new campaign. While the plebeians, represented here by the servingmen, are overjoyed to hear that there is like to be 'a stirring world again' (4.5.225–6). War, they declare, 'exceeds peace as far as day does night . . . Peace is a very apoplexy, lethargy; mulled, deaf, sleepy, insensible; a getter of more bastard children than war's a destroyer of men' (ll. 228–32). Moreover, as the First Servingman maintains, 'it makes men hate one another'. The Third Servingman knows the answer to this apparent paradox: 'Reason: because they then less need one another. The wars for my money' (ll. 236–8).

In effect, the Volscian plebeians freely accept what in Rome has become a desperate and doubtfully successful patrician strategy: that you can hold a society together, create a bond more important than any social, political or economic inequalities by involving the whole nation in war.

As representatives of the Volscian commons, the three servingmen at Antium do not emerge well from a comparison with their equivalents in Rome. Their behaviour, in fact, on a smaller scale, resembles that of Shakespeare's earlier crowds. Some of the Roman citizens in this play (the Second Citizen in the third scene of act 2, for instance) are slower-witted than others, and likely to be teased about it by their companions. But they are consistently shown as capable of holding an intelligent discussion, and they do not all think alike. The Volscian servingmen, by contrast, constitute a miniature herd. All three of them treat the meanly-dressed stranger who has invaded the house with the same high-handed contempt – giving Coriolanus his first taste of what it is like to be thought poor and unimportant. When they discover who he is and how highly their master and the other lords regard him, they swing immediately, and in unison, to the opposite extreme:

Second Servant. Nay, I knew by his face that there
 was something in him. He had, sir, a kind of face,
 methought – I cannot tell how to term it.
First Servant. He had so, looking as it were – would
 I were hanged, but I thought there was more in him
 than I could think.   (4.5.157–62)

The general drift is plain enough, but these men are not very successful at putting their considered opinion of Coriolanus into words. Not, at least, by comparison with the Roman citizens of the first scene, or the two anonymous officers laying cushions in the Capitol in act 2 who can discern both that Caius Martius 'hath deserved worthily of his country' and that 'to affect the malice and displeasure of the people is as bad as that which he dislikes, to flatter them for their love' (2.2.21–4). When the third Volscian servant tries to impress his companions with a big word, he immediately gets it wrong: 'Directitude!', the First Servant asks, 'What's that?' (l. 215). 'Discreditude' seems to have been what his friend was trying to say. Mistaking of words is a common enough lower-class phenomenon in Shakespeare. It does not, however, seem to afflict the citizens of Rome.

Among the Volscians, Coriolanus is universally admired. The common soldiers 'use him as the grace 'fore meat, / Their talk at table and their thanks at end' (4.7.3–4). They flock to him, 'He is their god', following him

> with no less confidence
> Than boys pursuing summer butterflies,
> Or butchers killing flies.   (4.6.91, 94–6)

This is not the kind of special, momentary blaze of admiration that Coriolanus was able to strike out of Roman soldiers in an extremity, in the heat of battle. In this less complicated, archaic warrior state, it surrounds him every day and it is bestowed by nobles and commons alike. Only Tullus Aufidius resists. A man significantly out of touch with the simplicities of his society, even as Caius Martius was with the comparative sophistication of his, this Volscian lord is reflective and intelligent as his rival is not. Ironically, Aufidius would have found it perfectly easy to be politic in Rome, to 'mountebank' the loves of her people, and do all those compromising, diplomatic things at which Coriolanus rebelled. What he cannot do is overcome the Roman hero in a fair fight, and he has apparently tried no fewer than twelve times. His own retainers know this: 'here's he that was wont to thwack our general, Caius Martius' (4.5.182–3). Among the Volscians, such physical supremacy counts for much more than it does in Rome. It means that Coriolanus, for the first time in his life, becomes genuinely 'popular'. It also means that Aufidius, who stumbles on a real truth when he says, 'I would I were a Roman, for I cannot, / Being a Volsce, be that I am' (1.10.4–5), who decided after his defeat in act 1 that he could maintain the heroic reputation so important in his society only through guile ('I'll potch at him some way, / Or wrath or craft may get him', ll. 15–16), becomes desperate to destroy his new colleague: a man now worshipped by a nation savagely widowed and unchilded at his hands as he never was in his own country.

'Bring me word thither / How the world goes, that to the pace of it / I may spur on my journey' (1.10.31–3). Those seemingly casual words which Aufidius addresses to a soldier at the end of act 1 are telling. Aufidius is adaptable. Like Machiavelli, he understands the importance of accommodating one's behaviour to the times. He has also divined (as, for that matter, did the Second Citizen in the opening scene) that his rival is fatally inflexible, that he cannot move 'from th'casque to th'cushion', cannot 'be other than one thing' (4.7.43, 42). In this judgement, Aufidius is almost, if not entirely, right. Coriolanus in exile is a man haunted by what seems to him the enormity of mutability and change. This is the burden of his soliloquy outside Aufidius' house: 'O world, thy slippery turns' (4.4.12–26). The commonplaces upon which he broods – dear friends can become foes, former foes, dear friends; it is actually possible to hate what one once loved, love what one hated – have just struck him, as the result of his recent experiences in Rome, with the force of revelation. But fundamentally, nothing has altered in his own nature. Menenius may be puzzled when Coriolanus does not keep his parting promise to write to his family and friends – 'Nay, I hear nothing. His mother and his wife / Hear nothing from him' (4.6.18–19) – and initially incredulous that he could have joined with Aufidius. But the Coriolanus who has found a home and adulation among the Volscians remains, in this other country, the man he always was.

Only the embassy of the women can shatter his convictions, force him into a new way of seeing. The scene with the women, outside Rome, when Coriolanus holds his mother by the hand 'silent', when he recognizes that he is not, after all, 'of stronger earth than others' (5.3.29), has been written about often and well. It is, of course, the moment when Coriolanus finally recognizes his common humanity, the strength of love and family ties. But the victory won here is not, I think, as so often is assumed, that of a private over a public world. Shakespeare is at pains to assert that, in republican Rome, the two are really inseparable. Hence the mute, but important presence of the lady Coriolanus greets as

The noble sister of Publicola,
The moon of Rome, chaste as the icicle
That's curdied by the frost from purest snow
And hangs on Dian's temple.   (5.3.64–7)

Valeria is a character many critics have felt Shakespeare would have done well to jettison, most especially here. (I have even seen it suggested that the only excuse for her existence in the play is to show us the sort of strong-willed woman Coriolanus ought to have married, if only jealous Volumnia had let him.) But, surely, Valeria accompanies Coriolanus' wife and mother on their mission – even though she is not allowed, as in Plutarch, to initiate it – because Shakespeare meant it to be clear that this is by no means a strictly family affair. Valeria, 'greatly honoured and reverenced amonge all the Romaines', as Plutarch puts it,[19] is there to represent all the other women of Rome, those 'neighbours' among whom Volumnia, when she believes her plea has been rejected, is prepared (along with Virgilia and the little Caius Martius) to die.

In the triumphal honours accorded the women on their return to Rome, Valeria has her place, reminding us that although the family of Coriolanus have figured as the crucial agents of persuasion, succeeding where Cominius and Menenius failed, ultimately the victory belongs to the city they have placed above family ties, the Rome for which they spoke. Patricians and plebeians, senators and tribunes have already joined together to pray for the success of this embassy. Now, in celebrating that success, Rome is united as never before in the play. Not even Sicinius thinks of anything but of meeting Volumnia, Valeria and Virgilia to 'help the joy' (5.4.63). That scene of welcome, with its flower-strewn streets, its sackbuts, psalteries, tabors and fifes, contrasts sharply with its equivalent in Antium/Corioli: the parallel entry of Coriolanus bearing the terms of peace.

We are surprised, surely, to learn from Aufidius that Coriolanus means 't'appear before the people, hoping / To purge himself with words' (5.6.7–8), that there is (as the Third Conspirator fears) some danger that he may 'move the people / With what he would say' (ll. 55–6). The Folio stage direction following line 70 of this final scene indicates that

Coriolanus enters 'with drum and colours, the Commoners being with him'. Coriolanus has found it easier to get on with the Volscian commons than with their more pacific but demanding equivalents in Rome. It is striking, nonetheless, that he is prepared now to explain himself and his actions to lords and people alike, that he presents himself initially not as an heroic individual, but as the servant of a common cause: 'I am return'd your soldier' (5.6.71). Although he has not been able to make 'true wars', he has at least framed a 'convenient peace' (5.3.190–1). The attempt fails. Coriolanus tries here to do something which is new to him, but (as Machiavelli knew) the habits of a lifetime cannot be transformed overnight. Aufidius has only to produce that old, inflammatory word 'traitor', so effective before on the lips of the tribunes, and Coriolanus is lost. He reacts just as he had done in Rome. And, at last, all the Volscian people remember what, in their adoration of this man, they had been able for a time to forget: the sons and daughters, the fathers and friends he once slaughtered. Here, as Machiavelli would have noted, there are no tribunes to put a brake on their violence as they demand that Coriolanus be torn to pieces, no intervention of law or legal process to thwart the conspirators and enforce a compromise verdict. Coriolanus is simply slain, in 'a tumult', while the Volscian lords look helplessly on.

There is a sense in which the characteristically shrewd perception of Aufidius – 'So our virtues / Lie in th'interpretation of the time' (4.7.49 –50) – might stand as the epigraph for this play as a whole. Whatever the case in the past, or among the Volscians of the present, valour in this Rome is no longer 'the chiefest virtue', over-riding all the rest. It must, as Coriolanus himself finally discovers, learn to coexist with the values of peace and, even in war, modify its antique, epic character. There is something both touching and full of promise in the prayer Coriolanus offers up in act 5 at his last meeting with his son. He asks that little Martius, the soldier of the next generation, should

---

19 *Plutarch's Lives*, in Bullough (vol. 5), p. 537.

prove
To shame unvulnerable, and stick i'th'wars
Like a great sea-mark standing every flaw
And saving those that eye thee.   (5.3.72–5)

Shame here is more than a strictly military consideration. Coriolanus is thinking of his own, complicated misfortunes, of what may befall a man in peace as well as war. But while the great sea-mark, the lighthouse beacon standing firm in the storm, remains extra-human, its prime function is not to destroy but heroically preserve. It is an image closer to the one old Nestor finds for Hector on the battlefield in *Troilus and Cressida* – a god 'dealing life' (4.5.191) – or to Marcus Curtius dedicating himself to death in the chasm that all of Rome might live, than it is to that of the juggernaut, the mechanical harvester, the Caius Martius who was a savage and undiscriminating agent of death.

Coriolanus is a tragedy in that its protagonist does finally learn certain necessary truths about the world in which he exists, but dies before he has any chance to rebuild his life in accordance with them. Paradoxically, it is only in his belated recognition and acceptance of historical change, of that right of the commons to be taken seriously which the other members of his class in Rome have already conceded, that he achieves genuinely tragic individuality. The play is predominantly a history – indeed, Shakespeare's most political play, the only one specifically about the *polis*.[20] I believe that Livy's account of an evolving republic and also, in all probability, Machiavelli's commentary on *Ab Urbe Condita*, helped to shape it, that although it is certainly a better play than Jonson's *Catiline*, or even his *Sejanus*, it is perhaps more like them in its focus upon Rome herself at a moment of historical transition than is usually thought.

To the question of why Shakespeare should have felt impelled to write such a play at this particular moment, there can be no confident answer. The corn riots in the Midlands and, more especially, the anti-enclosure riots of 1607 which affected his native Warwickshire may well have had something to do with it. It is clear too that there was considerable interest in Jacobean England at this time in classical republicanism, in theories of the mixed state. In his book *Coriolanus in Context*, C. C. Huffman assembles an impressive amount of evidence to show that as James's absolutism declared itself more and more plainly, an educated minority came to believe that the King was trying to tamper with the fundamental nature of English government. England, they argued, was a tripartite state, composed of king, nobles and commons. In it, each element had its rights, with Parliament standing as the safeguard against tyranny. James was entirely aware of this line of thought, and of its roots in republican Rome. In 1606, he was fulminating against what he called 'tribunes of the people whose mouths could not be stopped' – by which he meant his antagonists in parliament. His concern, and the terms he chose to express it, were prophetic. In the great clash that was to come between king and parliament ('the injustest judgement seate that may be', as James protested) the theory of mixed government was to become a deadly weapon in the hands of the opposition.[21]

Unfortunately, Huffman uses all this historical material to introduce a reading of *Coriolanus* as Shakespeare's apology for Jacobean absolutism, even going so far as to suggest that the dramatist believed Rome would have been better off in ashes, with Volumnia, Virgilia and little Martius dead, than left at the mercy of an institution so wicked as the tribunate. As so often, the settled conviction that Shakespeare's view of history was orthodox, conservative, rooted in the political theories expounded in the Homilies, has blinded the critic to what is actually there on the page. But why should we assume that, in the words of a well-known essay on *Coriolanus* and the Midlands insurrection, 'Whether or not Shakespeare had been shocked or alarmed by

---

20 In her essay 'To Starve With Feeding: The City in *Coriolanus*' (*Shakespeare Studies*, 11 (1978), 123–44), Gail Kern Paster points out that the Spevack Concordance lists 88 uses of the word 'Rome' in *Coriolanus* as against 38 in *Julius Caesar* and 30 in *Antony and Cleopatra*. The word 'Capitol' occurs 15 times, against 2 instances in *Julius Caesar* and only 1 in *Antony and Cleopatra*.

21 C. C. Huffman, *Coriolanus in Context* (Lewisburg, 1971), *passim* but especially pp. 148, 169.

the 1607 rising is anyone's guess; but it is fairly certain that he must have been hardened and confirmed in what had always been his consistent attitude to the mob'?[22] Assertions like these encouraged Edward Bond to interpret the extremely ambiguous documents relating to the Welcombe enclosures of 1614 entirely to Shakespeare's discredit. One may dislike Bond's *Bingo*, with its portrait of a 'corrupt seer',[23] a brutal and reactionary property-owner victimizing the rural poor, but there is a sense in which it simply spells out and exaggerates the received notion about Shakespeare's political attitudes. There is no reason why such a view should persist. Although he remained as fascinated by history as a process in 1607 as he had been in the early 1590s, when he was writing the *Henry VI* plays, the man who conceived *Coriolanus* gives every indication of being more tolerant of the commons than before. He looked attentively at the young Roman republic delineated by Plutarch and by Livy, and chose to emphasize what was hopeful, communal and progressive in it, when writing his interpretation of the time.

---

[22] E. C. Pettet, '*Coriolanus* and the Midlands Insurrection of 1607', in *Shakespeare Survey 3* (Cambridge, 1950), 34–42.

[23] Edward Bond, in his Preface to *Bingo* (1974), p. xiii.

'HENRY VIII' AND THE IDEAL ENGLAND

ALEXANDER LEGGATT

At the end of *Henry VIII* Cranmer delivers a prophecy of the golden age of Queen Elizabeth, in a speech that seems designed both as the last in a series of striking set-pieces and as the culmination of the play's action. The elaborate and sometimes devious historical process the play has shown has been designed, we now realize, to allow Elizabeth to be born and to make this golden age possible. For the characters in the play, however, the age of Elizabeth lies in the future and, we are told, 'Few now living can behold that goodness' (5.4.22).[1] For the audience it lies in the past. Like all golden ages it is just the other side of the horizon.[2] If the author had been content to leave it there we might have been content to accept the convention. But Cranmer extends his idealizing vision to the present, to the reign of James; this too is part of the golden age. At this point the more realistic spectators might have reflected on the difference between dream and reality, and concluded that nothing gold can stay. The same train of thought might have prompted memories of the dark, unsettled end of Elizabeth's reign, memories against which Cranmer's vision could be tested. Cranmer is not just taking his audience somewhere over the rainbow; he is also asking it to see its own present, and its own immediate past, as a golden age. Outside the special conditions of court masque and complimentary verse, that takes some doing. And it was not what Jacobean drama normally did. Cranmer's speech, then, may look like an exercise in nostalgia; but it allows us, even encourages us, to set his ideal vision against our sense of the world as it really is.

There is one respect, however, in which Cranmer's speech might have evoked a simple nostalgia. Whether or not it recalls a past history, it certainly recalls an older drama. The cult of Elizabeth in her lifetime took many forms, and one of them was the custom of ending plays with a tribute to the Queen, often in terms quite similar to those Cranmer uses here. Sometimes the effect is a little perfunctory: when in the Epilogue to *The Rare Triumphs of Love and Fortune* Fortune declares,

And sith by Love and Fortune our troubles all do
    cease,
God save her majesty, that keeps us all in peace,[3]

we may not feel that the entire play has led us to that moment. But references to the Queen can be more than just courteous gestures. *A Looking Glass for London and England* badgers its audience with threats and exhortations, the last of which is:

Repent, O London, lest for thine offense
Thy shepherd fail, whom mighty God preserve
That she may bide the pillar of his Church
Against the storms of Romish Antichrist.
                  (5.5.91–4)[4]

---

[1] All references to Shakespeare are to *The Complete Works of Shakespeare*, ed. David Bevington (Glenview, Illinois, 1980).

[2] See Frank V. Cespedes, '"We are One in Fortunes": The Sense of History in *Henry VIII*', *English Literary Renaissance*, 10 (1980), 413–38; p. 436.

[3] *A Select Collection of Old English Plays*, ed. Robert Dodsley, revised by W. Carew Hazlitt, 15 vols. (1874–6), vol. 6, (1874), p. 243.

[4] References to Greene and Lodge's *A Looking Glass for London and England* and to Greene's *Friar Bacon and Friar Bungay* are to the texts in *Drama of the English Renaissance, I: The Tudor Period*, ed. Russell A. Fraser and Norman Rabkin (New York, 1976).

And we are warned that only the prayers of the Queen are averting the plague London so richly deserves. In other words, the tribute is put in terms that relate logically to the play's main business. The similar tribute at the end of *Friar Bacon and Friar Bungay* is presented as the last use of Bacon's magic, and the only unequivocally good one. In the main play Edward, as part of his development from playboy to prince, becomes a figure of martial prowess. Elizabeth will embody an opposite but complementary princely virtue in a reign of peace:

From forth the royal garden of a king
Shall flourish out so rich and fair a bud,
Whose brightness shall deface proud Phoebus'
   flower,
And overshadow Albion with her leaves.
Till then Mars shall be master of the field;
But then the stormy threats of wars shall cease.
The horse shall stamp as careless of the pike;
Drums shall be turned to timbrels of delight;
With wealthy favors plenty shall enrich
The strand that gladded wand'ring Brute to see,
And peace from heaven shall harbor in these leaves,
That gorgeous beautifies this matchless flower.
(scene 16, 45–56)

Brute's delight in his new kingdom also connects this tribute to Elizabeth with the note of cheerful patriotism that runs through the whole play. In several respects, then, Bacon's compliment to the Queen is not just in the play but of it.

In the original ending to *Every Man out of his Humour* Ben Jonson showed Elizabeth as the only power capable of curing the envious Macilente, in the last and most spectacular of the play's dishumourings:

So, in the ample, and vnmeasur'd floud
Of her perfections, are my passions drown'd:
And I have now a spirit as sweet, and cleere,
As the most rarefi'd and subtile aire.
(Epilogue, 12–15)[5]

The last line suggests that Elizabeth has purified not just Macilente but the whole climate in which she moves, and the speech continues with a vision of peace and glory similar to Cranmer's. Jonson was persuaded to change this ending; but he continued to defend it, he preserved Macilente's speech, and he

returned to the idea in *Cynthia's Revels*, where the entrance of the Queen, accompanied by one of Jonson's most graceful lyrics ('Qveene, and Huntresse, chaste, and fair', 5.6.1), produces a sudden and dramatic purifying of the play's atmosphere.

We see how far this kind of tribute can go in George Peele's *The Arraignment of Paris*. The title, and a number of formal statements early in the play, suggest that the subject will be the tragedy of Troy, and up to a point it is. But the story splits two ways. Paris is sent to Troy to endure his fate, accompanied by Apollo's grim prediction,

From Ida woods now wends the shepherd's boy,
That in his bosom carries fire to Troy.
(4.4.169–70)[6]

Meanwhile the Apple of Discord, imagined here as a golden ball, is awarded on appeal to Queen Elizabeth. When it is placed in her hands a number of things happen. The barrier between stage and audience is broken down, so that performers and spectators are aware of being together in a single room. The conventions of theatre are replaced by those of masque or pageant. More important for our purpose, the ball will look, in Elizabeth's hands, like the royal orb; it will be purged of its tragic associations and become simply a sign of her royalty. Paris must endure his destiny; but the Fates lay down their attributes at Elizabeth's feet. At the start of the play Ate's prologue announces a tragedy; the play then abruptly switches to the pastoral mode. So at the end tragedy is again replaced, this time by a court celebration.

Diana first introduces Elizabeth as a nymph who serves and honours her; she dwells in a secluded grove within the play's pastoral landscape. But as Diana describes it the secluded grove becomes

A kingdom that may well compare with mine,
An auncient seat of kings, a second Troy,
Y-compass'd round with a commodious sea.
(5.1.69–71)

---

[5] References to Jonson are to the texts in *Ben Jonson*, ed. C. H. Herford and Percy and Evelyn Simpson, 11 vols. (Oxford, 1925–52).

[6] References to *The Arraignment of Paris* are to the text in *English Drama 1580–1642*, ed. C. F. Tucker Brooke and Nathaniel Burton Paradise (Boston, 1935).

England is a magic place of paradoxes: the small, secluded island we hear of in *Cymbeline* – 'In a great pool a swan's nest' (3.4.140)[7] – and a majestic kingdom, a second Troy. That last identification is particularly important for the play. *The Arraignment of Paris* presents not just a compliment to Queen Elizabeth but the redemption of Troy from its own tragic history – just as in *The Faerie Queene* Arthur is to be redeemed from *his* tragic story by marrying not Guinevere but Gloriana. The presence of Elizabeth, here as in Spenser, is enough to change the ending of a famous story, enough to change the genre of a work in mid-action.

This reveals one of the most interesting and important features of sixteenth-century drama: its free handling of genre. The function of this freedom, very often, is to reshape reality in quite a radical way, taking us from the world as we know it to a sharply idealized vision. We see how purposeful this can be in John Bale's tragical–historical–polemical morality play *Kyng Johan*, in which the shifting between historical and allegorical characterization allows a pointed identification of Stephen Langdon with Sedition, and in which King John – for Bale a Protestant martyr – can be destroyed in the world of history and vindicated in the world of allegory. By the desertion of his followers, he is forced to a tragic choice between submitting to the Pope and having England destroyed by war. He submits, for the sake of his country. He is then poisoned by a monk, and dies in the arms of Widow England, a Christ-like figure in a Protestant *pietà*. He is then replaced on stage by Imperial Majesty, who may be Henry VIII or Elizabeth depending on the date of performance, but who is perhaps best seen as the King's other body. This ideal monarch gets from the Estates figures the obedience John could not command, and sets England to rights. Here, as in *The Arraignment of Paris*, we see an interplay between an established story with a fixed end – history, in fact, though of a different kind – and an ideal vision of things as they ought to be. This too is background for *Henry VIII*.

But before turning to *Henry VIII* we should look at the relation between the ideal and historical visions in some of Shakespeare's earlier history plays. Whatever he may do to the facts Shakespeare

generally preserves historical decorum. Nobody seems to know, as even minor characters in *Henry VIII* seem to know, that Elizabeth is on the way and everything will be all right. There are no magic visions of the future. One exception occurs in *Henry VI, Part 3* when King Henry, with the prophetic insight bestowed on him as compensation for his political incompetence, addresses the young Earl of Richmond as 'England's hope' and declares, 'This pretty lad will prove our country's bliss' (4.6.68, 70). This anticipates the ending of *Richard III*, in which the hero kills the demon king and we forget the deviousness of the Tudor claim, not to mention the Tudor character, as we contemplate a satisfying picture of England restored and at peace. History at this point stops and is replaced by myth.

There is a much subtler handling of the ideal England in *Richard II*, in Gaunt's tribute to the royal throne of kings. I call it a tribute because that is how it is remembered. Literally it is a complaint:

This royal throne of kings, this sceptred isle,
This earth of majesty, this seat of Mars,
This other Eden, demi-paradise,
This fortress built by Nature for herself
Against infection and the hand of war,
This happy breed of men, this little world,
This precious stone set in the silver sea,
Which serves it in the office of a wall
Or as a moat defensive to a house,
Against the envy of less happier lands,
This blessed plot, this earth, this realm, this
    England,
This nurse, this teeming womb of royal kings,
Fear'd by their breed and famous by their birth,
Renowned for their deeds as far from home,
For Christian service and true chivalry,
As is the sepulcher in stubborn Jewry
Of the world's ransom, blessed Mary's Son,
This land of such dear souls, this dear dear land,
Dear for her reputation through the world,
Is now leas'd out – I die pronouncing it –
Like to a tenement or pelting farm.
England, bound in with the triumphant sea,
Whose rocky shore beats back the envious siege
Of wat'ry Neptune, is now bound in with shame,

---

[7] I have discussed the function of Britain as a special, magic place in this play in 'The Island of Miracles: An Approach to *Cymbeline*', *Shakespeare Studies*, 10 (1977), 191–209.

With inky blots and rotten parchment bonds.
That England, that was wont to conquer others,
Hath made a shameful conquest of itself.

(2.1.40–66)

As in *The Arraignment of Paris*, only paradoxes will express the nature of England – a garden, a fortress, a moated country house; fertile, protecting, aggressive; a place enclosed and defensive, a place that sends forth heroes to conquest. But what interests me particularly is the grammar of the speech. With one exception, there are no verbs attached to this ideal England. Gaunt does not say, England was a royal throne of kings but is now leased out like a tenement; he says, this royal throne of kings is now leased out. The effect is that Gaunt's England is not located in the past; it is protected from the sceptical voice that asks if the reign of, say, Edward III, was really that glorious, the voice we may hear at the end of *Henry VIII*. (The exception that proves the rule is the line, 'That England, that was wont to conquer others', which refers to a verifiable historical fact.) All through the history plays people lament the good old days, and Shakespeare could be ironic about this sort of nostalgia – as in *Richard III*, where the Third Citizen fondly recalls the golden age of Henry VI, when 'the King / Had virtuous uncles to protect his Grace' (2.3.21–2). Gaunt's speech is not an exercise in nostalgia. It proclaims an ideal England – the true, inner England, if you like – that does not belong to history at all, but is always elusive and always available.

It is an ideal not just to lament but to live up to. On the whole Gaunt's idea of England as a crusading nation does not seem to touch Shakespeare's imagination very deeply. But Mowbray, who feared that his exile would result in 'speechless death' (1.3.172), dies after a noble career as a crusader. When he hears of this the new king Henry IV, for the first time since his return from exile, loses his poise ('Sweet peace conduct his sweet soul to the bosom / Of good old Abraham!', 4.1.104–5); and for the rest of his life he is haunted by the dream of leading England to the Holy Land. It is typical of his character that he expresses different motives for this at different times, and he himself may not know which (if any) is the

true one; but the desire to give England its ideal role in the Christian world may be one of them. He never succeeds, of course; for Shakespeare the world of history is anything but ideal. The vision of peace and reconciliation we get at the end of *Richard III* sometimes appears at the *beginning* of a play – as in *Richard III* itself, or *Henry IV, Part 1* – and is immediately eroded by irony. Even the achievement of Henry V is touched by reservations. He orders the garden of England only by ruining the garden of France, and as the Epilogue reminds us his successors destroyed everything he built. When Henry, courting the French Princess, looks to the future – 'Shall not thou and I, between Saint Denis and Saint George, compound a boy, half French, half English, that shall go to Constantinople and take the Turk by the beard?' (5.2.207–10) – we remember, and are I think meant to remember, that what they got was Henry VI. The condition of man in history is perhaps best summed up in *Richard II* by York's bitter words, 'Comfort's in heaven, and we are on the earth' (2.2.78).[8]

The tributes I have discussed – to an ideal England or an ideal Elizabeth – are, at their most accomplished, relevant to the plays in which they appear, and not just isolated gestures of courtesy. This is certainly true of Greene and Peele, as it is of the more glancing compliments in *A Midsummer Night's Dream*. But we are also aware of a change of gear, a shift to a different *kind* of vision. And the sharpness of the transition, as in the last act of *Cynthia's Revels*, can be an exciting and dramatic effect in its own right. We are learning to enjoy the way Spenser keeps changing the rules in *The Faerie Queene*; similar pleasures await us in the drama of his contemporaries. According to Clifford Leech, 'The Elizabethan way of writing is to put things together.' (One could say, for example, that Gaunt's England is put together with Richard's in the mind of the audience.) Leech added 'the Jacobean way is to fuse'.[9] We may now turn to *Henry VIII* with this

---

[8] On the significance of this line for the history plays as a whole, see John Wilders, *The Lost Garden* (London and Basingstoke, 1978), p. 63.

[9] *The Dramatist's Experience* (New York, 1970), p. 159.

question in mind: is it, in Leech's terms, a Jacobean play or an Elizabethan throwback? How, in other words, does it present the relation between the ideal vision and the world of history? Are they put together, or are they fused?

At first glance we seem to have, as in *Richard II*, juxtaposition, not fusion. While Cranmer speaks of a golden age in which everything is clear and in order the play as a whole shows the world of history to be complex, elusive and rather untidy. Indeed, it goes as far in this direction as any play of Shakespeare's. Following Wolsey's changes of policy is like following the plot of *The Way of the World*; it can be done, but it requires concentration. He arranges the Field of the Cloth of Gold and then contrives to break the league with France; he encourages the King's divorce and then delays it. At least we can be reasonably sure that he is following what he sees as his own advantage; but his sense of where that lies keeps shifting. What Henry wants is clear: he wants to divorce Katharine and marry Anne. But the question of why he wants it is more elusive. Three minor figures try to help us out:

Chamberlain.
It seems the marriage with his brother's wife
Has crept too near his conscience.
Suffolk.   No, his conscience
Has crept too near another lady.
Norfolk.   'Tis so.
This is the Cardinal's doing.   (2.2.16–19)

At different points in his last scene Wolsey attributes his fall to Anne, and to his own ambition (3.2.407–9, 439–42). The effect is of a multiple-choice history exam in which the candidate tries to tick all the answers.

In his long self-defence at Katharine's trial (2.4.165–228) Henry presents the official case for the divorce. His principal evidence of heaven's will in the matter is that the marriage has failed to produce a surviving male heir. Yet when, at the end of the play, Anne produces yet another girl Henry is more than content: 'Never, before / This happy child, did I get anything' (5.5.65–6). We might have expected Shakespeare to cover Henry's frustration with a dramatist's tact; instead he calls attention to it, when

the garrulous Old Lady – taking her life in her hands, we might think – teases the King by pretending for a moment the child is a boy (5.1.162–6). Motives are mixed, cause and effect are not related in a straightforward way, and our judgement of the characters is often pulled in contrary directions. The clearest example of split judgement is our double vision of Wolsey, whose fall produces both satisfaction and unexpected pity, whose accusers are at once honest Englishmen despatching a nuisance and jackals pulling down a wounded lion. But split judgements are pervasive. We wait for a clear defence of Buckingham's innocence, but it never comes and we begin to wonder.[10] Katharine storms out of her trial in a blaze of pride and anger, and Henry immediately praises her 'sweet gentleness' and 'meekness saint-like' (2.4.135–6). She refuses the jurisdiction of the English court and announces she will appeal to the Pope. In her next scene she appears as an honorary Protestant heroine, insisting the Cardinals, whom she calls 'cardinal sins' (3.1.104), address her in English, not Latin. Then at the end of the scene she submits to their counsel. Anne is a simpler figure, but the Second Gentleman gives two views of her in a few lines:

Heaven bless thee!
Thou hast the sweetest face I ever look'd on.
Sir, as I have a soul, she is an angel;
Our King has all the Indies in his arms,
And more and richer, when he strains that lady.
I cannot blame his conscience.   (4.1.42–7)

We go in a breath from worship to chuckling appreciation. If heaven has anything to do with it it must be 'A heaven like Mahomet's Paradise'.[11]

If we did not know that the play was once titled *All is True*, we would still have the Prologue's claim,

Such as give
Their money out of hope they may believe,
May here find truth too.   (ll. 7–9)

---

[10] See Lee Bliss, 'The Wheel of Fortune and the Maiden Phoenix of Shakespeare's *King Henry the Eighth*', *ELH*, 42 (1975), 1–25; pp. 4–5.
[11] Donne, Elegy 19, 'Going to Bed', l. 21.

The 'truth' the play may claim is not always that of literal historical fact; but it gives us a convincing account of the historical process as a devious, winding current and of historical characters as driven by contradictory motives and inspiring contradictory judgements. We accept the account as true because we recognize that the truth is rarely pure and never simple. In that respect the simplified golden age of Elizabeth seems juxtaposed with the rest of the play rather than fused with it; it belongs to a different order of reality.

But Cranmer prefaces his speech with the claim, 'the words I utter / Let none think flattery, for they'll find 'em truth' (5.5.16–17). As in the opening scene of *Cymbeline*, or the conclusion of *The Winter's Tale*, there is an insistence that the incredible is true:

Second Gentleman.
  That a king's children should be so convey'd,
  So slackly guarded, and the search so slow,
  That could not trace them!
First Gentleman.   Howso'er 'tis strange,
  Or that the negligence may well be laugh'd at,
  Yet it is true, sir.
Second Gentleman.   I do well believe you.
                   (*Cymbeline*, 1.1.63–7)

       That she is living,
  Were it but told you, should be hooted at
  Like an old tale; but it appears she lives.
         (*The Winter's Tale*, 5.3.115–17)[12]

All is true, not just the historical action but the mythical vision as well. We may ask, jestingly, what is truth? and not stay for an answer. We may say that there are two different kinds of truth, and leave it at that. But on closer inspection we may see that the play, having shown the difference between the two visions, also tries to bring them together in a single reality, so that the claim 'All is true' applies in the same way throughout.

In *Friar Bacon* and *A Looking Glass for London and England* the final tribute to the Queen picks up material from the play as a whole. The same is true here, but the connections are more subtle and pervasive, and are made at a deeper level. Elizabeth, as I have already suggested, is connected to the rest

of the play at the level of action; every important event leads to her birth. James has no such connection, and here the links are established by imagery. Wolsey falls 'Like a bright exhalation in the evening' (3.2.226); James 'Shall star-like rise... / And so stand fix'd' (5.5.47–8). Henry's worry about over-taxing his subjects is expressed in the image of a damaged tree:

        Why, we take
From every tree lop, bark, and part o' th' timber;
And, though we leave it with a root, thus hack'd,
The air will drink the sap.   (1.2.95–8)

James, on the other hand,

        shall flourish,
  And, like a mountain cedar, reach his branches
  To all the plains about him.   (5.5.53–5)

Such echoes might not mean very much by themselves, as the images are commonplace. But some of the speech's most important ideas can be traced earlier in the play. Perhaps the most striking and attractive of Cranmer's pictures of the golden age is that of the peaceful, self-sufficient householder:

  In her days every man shall eat in safety
  Under his own vine what he plants, and sing
  The merry songs of peace to all his neighbors.
                     (5.5.34–6)

The emphasis on domestic happiness is very different from Gaunt's vision of heroic action. The idea that every man should enjoy his own, obviously in a world without tax collectors, has been prepared for earlier in the play. Wolsey's taxation has robbed men of their earnings and forced employers to lay off their workmen (1.2.31–7). Enforced contributions

---

[12] Behind both these moments may lie the waking of Titania in *A Midsummer Night's Dream*:

  My Oberon! What visions have I seen!
  Methought I was enamour'd of an ass.
Oberon.
  There lies your love.   (4.1.75–7)

See also Cleopatra's debate with Dolabella (*Antony and Cleopatra*, 5.2.73–99).

to the Field of the Cloth of Gold have caused similar damage:

Abergavenny.   I do know
  Kinsmen of mine, three at the least, that have
  By this so sicken'd their estates, that never
  They shall abound as formerly.
Buckingham.   O, many
  Have broke their backs with laying manors on
    'em
  For this great journey.   (1.1.80–5)

The complaint that land is going into clothing is a familiar Jacobean one; we meet it, for example, in *The Revenger's Tragedy*. Here it is opposed by Cranmer's vision of the self-sufficient Englishman, contentedly enjoying his estate – whom we have seen before in the person of Alexander Iden in *Henry VI, Part 2*.

Such greatness and honour as men enjoy in Elizabeth's kingdom, they will enjoy through the Queen herself:

              those about her
From her shall read the perfect ways of honor,
And by those claim their greatness, not by blood.
                                (5.5.37–9)

This not only suggests Elizabeth's use of 'new men' as her most important counsellors but gives us the true form of an ideal that has been perverted by Wolsey, the 'butcher's cur' (1.1.120) who apparently rises through the King's favour but really contrives his own career for his own selfish ends. The play as a whole shows the emergence of Henry as the clear centre of authority in his kingdom, and the frustration of Wolsey's attempt to usurp that position for himself. Early in the play everyone is obsessed with Wolsey; and this, as much as his actual power, seems to be crippling and distorting English political life. Suffolk at one point looks beyond this obsession to a healthier state of affairs:

              For me, my lords,
I love him not, nor fear him; there's my creed.
As I am made without him, so I'll stand,
If the King please.   (2.2.49–52)

This does not prevent him from joining enthusi-astically in the final attack on Wolsey; Shakespeare

understood very well men's inability to act on their own best insights. But Suffolk, if only for a moment, has pointed to the England we hear of in Cranmer's speech, in which the sources of a man's position in the world will be his own independent integrity and the favour of the prince.

We feel King Henry's authority lock into place in his rescue of Cranmer. When he says of Cranmer's enemies, 'there's one above 'em yet' (5.2.27) he is actually speaking from a window above, his new dominance established by a striking visual effect. This introduces the question of the Anglican religious settlement, with the monarch as head of the Church, Cranmer's prayer book as the liturgy, and the Bible as the source of all necessary knowledge and belief. As in *King John*, Shakespeare makes much less of the Catholic–Protestant dispute than most of his contemporaries would have done. But he does make something of it. Cranmer's vision of every man under his own vine echoes, closely and clearly, a recurring prophecy of the peaceable kingdom in Scripture.[13] It is immediately followed by the words, 'God shall be truly known' (5.5.37). The juxtaposition suggests that the source of this truth will be a religion centred on the Bible. The historical Cranmer's contribution to this was to be a liturgy closely based on Scripture, with a thorough and extensive plan of daily readings.

The fact that we are witnessing the birth of the Church of England as well as the birth of Elizabeth, and that the two events are connected, is conveyed largely through suggestion; but the suggestions are clear and reasonably consistent. By a variety of devices Anne and Cranmer are seen as parallel characters. Wolsey's principal reason for opposing the King's marriage to Anne is that she is 'A spleeny Lutheran' (3.2.99). In his next breath he complains of the rise of Cranmer (3.2.101–4). He does not make the connection explicit himself, but we are allowed to see it. In the long night sequence of act 5, Anne and Cranmer are endangered together: Anne in a difficult childbirth, Cranmer set upon by his enemies. Henry appears in this sequence both as the

---

[13] 1 Kings, 4: 25; 2 Kings, 18: 31; Isaiah, 36: 16; Micah, 4: 4.

King rescuing his archbishop and as an anxious husband waiting for news; he says to Suffolk, 'Charles, I will play no more tonight. / My mind's not on 't' (5.1.56–7). The birth of Elizabeth and the rescue of Cranmer, who is then named her godfather, are thus seen as parallel actions, part of the same dramatic movement.

When Cranmer is brought before the Council it is clear that the issues are those of the Reformation. The Chancellor, Sir Thomas More, accuses him of

filling
The whole realm, by your teaching and your chaplains –
For so we are inform'd – with new opinions,
Divers and dangerous; which are heresies,
And, not reform'd, may prove pernicious.

(5.3.15–19)

When Henry rescues Cranmer and insists on a general reconciliation he does not refer to this kind of question at all;[14] for him the issues are the Council's shabby treatment of Cranmer and, behind that, the all-important question of the King's own authority. But the religious issue has not been altogether forgotten: when we see the King cracking the whip over his bishops we are reminded of his role as head of the Church.[15] Shakespeare does not, however, bring these matters too close to the surface. This may be dramatic tact, or political tact, or both. It may even reflect a desire to probe more deeply than mere sectarian debate would allow. By his ready forgiveness of his enemies Cranmer emerges from the scene as something more important than a Protestant hero; he is simply a good Christian. Henry's slightly bemused appreciation of this, 'Do my Lord of Canterbury / A shrewd turn, and he's your friend forever' (5.3.175–6), is among other things a way of indicating that he has picked the right godfather for the new princess. With all this in mind we may see that those five words, 'God shall be truly known', draw an extra depth of meaning from the play as a whole.

It is worth noting in this context that while Gaunt imagines an England regularly, heroically, at war, Cranmer's vision (like that of Bacon in Greene's play) is of a kingdom in which every man will 'sing / The merry songs of peace to all his neighbors' (5.5.35–6). The Queen will have enemies of course, but they will 'shake like a field of beaten corn, / And hang their heads with sorrow' (5.5.32–3). Even the imagery of war is agricultural and lightly touched with pathos. And while James's reign will be marked by the spread of empire, this is seen as a natural organic growth:

Wherever the bright sun of heaven shall shine,
His honor and the greatness of his name
Shall be, and make new nations. He shall flourish,
And, like a mountain cedar, reach his branches
To all the plains about him. (5.5.51–5)

This too is in keeping with the manner of the play as a whole – a history play without battles or even soldiers, in which the conflicts are civil and generally end in reconciliation, and in which there is a recurring interest in the contrast between worldly pomp and inner peace. When Katharine, in a scene parallel to Anne's coronation, sees a vision of heavenly spirits honouring her and presenting her with garlands, she calls them not spirits of glory or honour but 'spirits of peace'. So Elizabeth will be, in a secular sense, a prince of peace.

Katharine's full speech, however, is

Spirits of peace, where are ye? Are ye all gone
And leave me here in wretchedness behind ye?

(4.2.83–4)

If there is a split between an ideal vision and the world we have to live in, it is reflected not just in the contrast between Cranmer's speech and the rest of the play but in a number of smaller moments that repeat the main effect with variations. What we see, I think, is not a sharp break near the end of act 5 but a series of fissures running all through the work. Katharine's heavenly vision is succeeded by frank reminders of her mortal frailty:

Do you note
How much her Grace is alter'd on the sudden?
How long her face is drawn? How pale she looks,
And of an earthy cold? (4.2.95–8)

---

14 See Cespedes, p. 414.

15 On the importance of this theme in the play, see John D. Cox, 'Henry VIII and the Masque', ELH, 45 (1978), 390–409; pp. 399–400. This is a necessary modification of Cespides's generally valid claim (n. 14, above) that Henry never speaks as a Protestant reformer.

The effect is first introduced in a slightly debased form when Buckingham complains of having to miss the Field of the Cloth of Gold:

> An untimely ague
> Stay'd me a prisoner in my chamber when
> Those suns of glory, those two lights of men,
> Met in the vale of Andren.   (1.1.4–7)

It turns out that he has not missed anything worth seeing: in the rest of the scene the language is heavy with the effort to describe the competitive and finally pointless display of worldly pomp, in striking contrast to the smooth flow and easy clarity of Cranmer's speech.[16] But Buckingham's experience, unable through frailty to see the vision, takes more serious forms elsewhere. With clockwork regularity the various characters who fall try to move from this world to the next before they die, and they all find it difficult to do. Buckingham's description of himself, in his farewell speech, as 'half in heaven' (2.1.88) is exact: the other half is still on earth. He tries hard to speak charitably of his enemies but cannot keep the bitterness out of his voice: 'Yet I am richer than my base accusers, / That never knew what truth meant' (2.1.104–5). Wolsey in his farewell calls his honours 'a burden / Too heavy for a man that hopes for heaven' (3.2.384–5) but cannot suppress a flash of irritation at the speed with which the burden of the Chancellorship has been picked up by Sir Thomas More: 'That's somewhat sudden. / But he's a learned man' (3.2.394–5).[17] Katharine, having had her heavenly vision and been reconciled with her earthly enemy Wolsey, appears quite ready for the next world; but then she snaps irritably at a messenger who seems to her disrespectful, and will not accept the man's apology (4.2.100–8).[18] Like the others she is half in heaven, but only half.

We are told that Anne at her coronation 'kneel'd, and saint-like / Cast her fair eyes to heaven and pray'd devoutly' (4.1.83–4). But she is doing this in the midst of a scene not just of worldly pomp but of vulgar physical energy:

> Great-bellied women,
> That had not half a week to go, like rams
> In the old time of war, would shake the press

> And make 'em reel before 'em. No man living
> Could say, 'This is my wife' there, all were woven
> So strangely in one piece.   (4.1.76–81)

This double effect in the coronation fits the Second Gentleman's description of Anne as a heavenly angel who must be good in bed. It is also part of the strain of bawdy comedy that runs through the play, and about which Wilson Knight has written so eloquently.[19] It represents, as he suggests, a communal energy – 'all were woven / So strangely in one piece' – which we may set against the isolation of Wolsey, who operates 'spider-like, / Out of his self-drawing web' (1.1.62–3). (Richard III, we remember, is also called a spider.) In the golden age every man will sit under his own vine, but he will also sing the merry songs of peace to all his neighbours, and Henry's final instruction to his people to make holiday includes the admonition, 'This day, let no man think / H'as business at his house' (5.5.75–6).

That is in the last scene, however; the penultimate scene with the Porter and his man gives us a distinctly coarser view of this communal spirit:

Is this Moorfields to muster in? Or have we some strange Indian with the great tool come to court, the women so besiege us? Bless me, what a fry of fornication is at door! On my Christian conscience, this one christening will beget a thousand; here will be father, godfather, and all together.   (5.4.32–7)

---

16 I have avoided – some would say evaded – the authorship question on the grounds that the play is what it is no matter who wrote what. But one reason why there is not the consensus about this play that there is about *The Two Noble Kinsmen* is that here the changes from a difficult style to an easy one are more obviously deliberate and functional, suggesting either a close collaboration or a single mind at work. On the authorship question see R. A. Foakes, Introduction to the (revised) Arden edition (1964), pp. xvii–xxviii.

17 Douglas Rain, in George McCowan's production at Stratford, Ontario in 1961, made the first words of the passage an unexpected flash of anger, and then showed Wolsey recovering his balance.

18 See G. Wilson Knight, *The Crown of Life* (1947; repr. 1965), p. 295.

19 *Ibid.*, pp. 304–6.

We are never allowed to forget that the play's final miracle is the product of an adulterous passion. In Eliot's words, 'in sordid particulars / The eternal design may appear'.[20] And before we get too metaphysical about this we should acknowledge that the force that brings Henry and Anne together is the force that brings Sweeney to Mrs Porter in the spring. They meet at Wolsey's banquet, not one of the play's more salubrious occasions. The atmosphere is set by Lord Sands's jokes about lay thoughts, running banquets and easy penances (1.4.10–18). Anne participates in this atmosphere, letting Sands kiss her and encouraging his jokes:

Anne. You are a merry gamester,
My Lord Sands.
Sands. Yes, if I make my play.
Here's to your ladyship; and pledge it, madam,
For 'tis to such a thing –
Anne. You cannot show me.
(1.4.46–9)

In this atmosphere Henry's infatuation flowers instantly. As Wolsey remarks, 'Your Grace, / I fear, with dancing is a little heated' (1.4.100–1).[21] Some of the bawdy joking is quite clever, as when the Old Lady teases Anne with a reference to two kinds of royal orbs: 'In faith, for little England / You 'd venture an emballing' (2.3.46–7). But if we are to judge the final placing of this element in the play we have to notice that it stops short of the last scene. As Autolycus is instrumental in creating the finale of *The Winter's Tale* but is not present at the unveiling of the statue, so the bawdy energy of *Henry VIII* in general takes us to the birth of Elizabeth but has no place in the ideal vision that follows. There may be more than simply practical reasons for Anne's absence from the final scene – which, after all, celebrates a virgin. We see a relationship between the earthy vigour of the mob and the high ceremony of the final scene, but they do not finally come together. The Porter and his man have · great difficulty keeping the people in their place; but it seems they finally succeed.

In the play as a whole, and in individual scenes, the ideal vision and the mortal world are closely related yet finally separate. It is the condition of the major characters at their highest moments to live in both worlds at once, half in heaven, and to be constantly subject to the incongruities of that condition. In the last scene Henry imagines that even after his death his eyes will be fixed on earth:

This oracle of comfort has so pleas'd me
That when I am in heaven I shall desire
To see what my child does, and praise my Maker.
(5.5.67–9)

In heaven Henry will be half on earth. This double vision, this constant intersection of time and eternity, is pervasive. And however sordid the particulars may occasionally be, there *is* a design at work. We do not take a sudden leap out of ordinary history and ordinary time in the last scene when Cranmer begins to speak. Even the bawdy comedy contributes to this. It seems at first to put us in touch with low, particular reality; but as the play progresses it acquires an almost visionary force, and the shading from one to another is remarkably subtle. The play's view of history is finally paradoxical: it is, as I suggested earlier, a complex and untidy process. But it is a process with an end, and the longer we look at it the more clearly we discern a pattern. Even a spectator who has slept an act or two will notice the rhythm of alternating rise and fall on which the play is built. The three gentlemen who take us through Anne's coronation remind us that the last time they met was at Buckingham's execution (4.1.4–5). As they talk of Katharine's divorce and her sickness, they conclude, 'Alas, good lady! / The trumpets sound. Stand close, the Queen is coming' (4.1.35–6). There is a sharp juxtaposition of the old Queen and the new. The Third Gentleman's difficulty in remembering that York Place is now called White-hall (4.1.93–8) not only suggests how fast the world is changing[22] but reminds us of Wolsey's fall. (We may even remember that it was at York Place that Henry and Anne first met.) As Katharine falls, Anne

---

[20] *Murder in the Cathedral*, in *Collected Plays* (1962), p. 37.
[21] At this point in George McCowan's production Henry's hands were on Anne's breasts.
[22] See Bliss, pp. 13–14.

rises; as Wolsey falls, Cranmer rises.[23] And finally those who fall,

> and those who opposed them
> And those whom they opposed
> Accept the constitution of silence
> And are folded in a single party.[24]

Katharine is reconciled with Wolsey across the barrier of death, and imitates his concern for Cromwell in her concern for her daughter and her attendants. Wolsey and Buckingham, antagonists and opposites in life, are surprisingly similar in their ends.[25]

The pattern of rise and fall, in which those who fall begin to look alike, is only the most obvious instance of a general sense of predictability that hangs over the play. Characters as powerful as Henry and Wolsey seem at times to be groping in the dark, not really knowing where they are headed; but minor characters who have no particular ends, or characters who have surrendered their wills, can seem almost supernaturally in tune with what is coming. As *Richard III* is haunted by the past, this play is haunted by the future. The language of Buckingham's farewell anticipates both Katharine's fate and her reward:

> Go with me, like good angels, to my end;
> And, as the long divorce of steel falls on me,
> Make of your prayers one sweet sacrifice,
> And lift my soul to heaven.   (2.1.75–8)

Long before Katharine's divorce is anything but a rumour, Norfolk says that she 'when the greatest stroke of fortune falls, / Will bless the King' (2.2.35–6). She does; so does Wolsey; so has Buckingham. The Lord Chamberlain is almost embarrassingly prescient about Anne:

> And who knows yet
> But from this lady may proceed a gem
> To lighten all this isle?   (2.3.77–9)

Suffolk has a similar moment:

> I persuade me, from her
> Will fall some blessing to this land, which shall
> In it be memoriz'd.   (3.2.50–2)

There are some important events that look like sheer

fluke – so much so that the characters suspect some power is at work. Wolsey asks,

> What cross devil
> Made me put this main secret in the packet
> I sent the King?   (3.2.214–16)

The fact that Dr Butts just happens to pass by the Council chamber in time to see Cranmer's disgrace and report to the King may give an extra meaning to Henry's line, 'there's one above 'em yet' (5.2.27).

The shaping, idealizing vision that produces Cranmer's prophecy is already at work, fitfully but unmistakably, in the main play. The result is that for all the weight of circumstantial detail the England of this play seems suspended a degree or two above ordinary reality, as the England of (say) *Henry IV* never does. Nor is Cranmer's speech in its turn entirely isolated from time and mortal circumstance.[26] In common with others who have discussed this speech I have kept referring to it as a speech about Elizabeth, and have had to remind myself that James is in there too. We all seem to resent his presence, and to resist it instinctively. But he is there. He reminds us of the Queen's mortality, and of the fact that the rhythm of rise and fall we have seen in the play will be repeated even in this golden future. In earlier tributes it was customary to regard Elizabeth as immune from the workings of time. Even Jonson was enough of an idealist to have Macilente pray that the Queen would 'neuer suffer change', though he was enough of a realist to change the line, after her death, to 'suffer most late change' (Epilogue, 19). Cynthia was a mortal moon after all. Cranmer's speech not only admits this but

---

[23] Ronald Berman, '*King Henry the Eighth*: History and Romance' (*English Studies*, 48 (1967), 112–21; pp. 117–18), compares this pattern to a dance in which individual dancers are expendable and are constantly being replaced.

[24] T. S. Eliot, *Little Gidding*, in *Collected Poems 1909–1962* (1973), p. 220.

[25] See Eugene M. Waith, *The Pattern of Tragicomedy in Beaumont and Fletcher* (New Haven, 1952), pp. 121–2.

[26] For a contrary view, see Edward I. Berry, '*Henry VIII* and the Dynamics of Spectacle', *Shakespeare Studies*, 12 (1979), 229–46; pp. 242–3.

emphasizes it. At first, through the image of the phoenix, Elizabeth's death is seen as a triumph:

Nor shall this peace sleep with her; but as when
The bird of wonder dies, the maiden phoenix,
Her ashes new create another heir,
As great in admiration as herself,
So shall she leave her blessedness to one,
When heaven shall call her from this cloud of
    darkness,
Who from the sacred ashes of her honor
Shall star-like rise, as great in fame as she was,
And so stand fix'd.   (5.5.40–8)

Here the play's pattern of fall and rise seems to be replaced by two kinds of rising: Elizabeth to heaven (like other characters we have seen) and James to an earthly majesty with heavenly attributes, like Anne.

But Cranmer returns later in the speech to Elizabeth's death, as though to deal with unfinished business. Indeed, at its second appearance Elizabeth's death seems a new idea, as though the first time it had not really been faced at all. Now beneath the idealizing vision we glimpse the old Queen of the 1590s; and Cranmer's voice, for once in the speech, hesitates for a pulse-beat before resuming its normal tone of exultation:

She shall be, to the happiness of England,
An aged princess; many days shall see her,
And yet no day without a deed to crown it.
Would I had known no more! But she must die,
She must, the saints must have her; yet a virgin,
A most unspotted lily shall she pass
To th' ground, and all the world shall mourn her.
         (5.5.57–63)

This time, we note, her death is also a fall.

Beneath the confusion of history we sense a deeper order; through the account of the golden age we hear the rhythms of time. And Cranmer's vision of Elizabeth (and James) embodies, I have tried to show, many of the themes and images of the play as a whole. The fusion may not be perfect, but I think it is close enough to make the play, in Leech's terms, a Jacobean work. And through it all we detect the shaping hand of the artist. If we are to consider the play's Jacobean qualities, not to mention its Fletcherian ones, we need to notice its theatrical

self-consciousness, its overt manipulation of its audience. Just as in *The Arraignment of Paris* a mighty kingdom is contained within a sheltered grove, so here a grand and sweeping vision is contained within a small artefact, a stage play for a particular audience. In *Henry V* the 'small time' of the hero's life and the 'small time' of the play's duration seem an appropriate match, despite the Chorus's complaints that this cockpit cannot hold the vasty fields of France. In *Henry VIII* the tension between the great theme and the theatrical occasion is a little more acute, and the sense of the play's artifice is if anything more pervasive. The Prologue has designs on us: 'I come no more to make you laugh.... Be sad, as we would make ye' (ll. 1, 25). This emotionally manipulative quality is picked up by some of the characters, notably Buckingham: 'Farewell! And when you would say something that is sad, / Speak how I fell' (2.1.134–5). Katharine and Griffith construct a formally balanced obituary for Wolsey, making the play's usual process of split judgement quite conscious and overt. None of this is disturbing; but we may be a little disconcerted by the flippant tone of the Prologue's ending. Having been promised

    Things now
That bear a weighty and a serious brow,
Sad, high, and working, full of state and woe,
         (ll. 1–3)

we are told

    And, if you can be merry then, I'll say
A man may weep upon his wedding-day.
         (ll. 31–2)

The author, having offered to make our eyes flow with tears, allows us to see the twinkle in his. This anticipates the surprising light-heartedness of many of the following scenes, which break quite free of the sombre tone promised (or threatened) by the Prologue. The Epilogue seems frankly designed to make us laugh:

'Tis ten to one this play can never please
All that are here. Some come to take their ease,
And sleep an act or two; but those, we fear,
W' have frighted with our trumpets...   (ll. 1–4)

This jocular tone follows naturally from the joyful celebration that ends the play. But if this is the same actor who began the play with the portentous statement, 'I come no more to make you laugh' – and it seems natural that it should be – then we may suspect that behind all the pomp and grandeur, even the tragedy, there is an author playing tricks on us. Like Wolsey when he started the divorce, like Henry when he impregnated Anne, we do not get quite what we expected.

This final sense of artifice contributes to the play's unity. Tributes to Elizabeth in earlier drama, however well integrated they may be, have also the quality of a freely available convention that comes from outside the play and did not have to be invented by the individual writer. In that they resemble the now abandoned custom of playing the national anthem at the start of a performance; *Henry VIII* is, as it were, a play in which the author has decided to include the national anthem. The revival of an old custom is something peculiar to the needs of this play, a part of its conscious art. In that sense too Cranmer's vision is contained within the play's world and not extraneous to it. This air of artifice may leave us feeling a little detached. We may feel not that all is true but that all is rather contrived. But if we remember that this is not just a Jacobean play, or a Fletcherian one, but in some measure at least Shakespearian, we may be prepared to see, here as elsewhere in Shakespeare, the truth behind the contrivance. Katharine, at odds with fortune, listens to a song of Orpheus and the power of his art to order a disorderly world, to stop time and remake nature:

> Orpheus with his lute made trees,
> And the mountain tops that freeze,
>   Bow themselves when he did sing.
> To his music plants and flowers
> Ever sprung, as sun and showers
>   There had made a lasting spring.

(3.1.3–8)

This is an art that coerces reality, changing it virtually by force: the art of Peele when he changes the ending of the Troy story and gives the apple to Elizabeth; the art of Bale when he vindicates King John by taking England out of history; the art of Jonson when Macilente is dishumoured on the spot by the sight of Elizabeth. The ordering power of Shakespeare's art does not refashion the world so radically as this. It shapes and structures familiar material firmly but gently, so that the artifice is not a way of escaping reality but a way of understanding it more closely:

> This is an art
> Which does mend nature, change it rather, but
> The art itself is nature.

(*The Winter's Tale*, 4.4.95–7)

Henry VIII is the work of a writer fresh from *The Winter's Tale* and *The Tempest*. Few would put it at the same level; but we see in it the same imagination at work. *The Winter's Tale* leads to a double vision of Hermione as a miracle of art who is also (like Elizabeth) a mortal woman. Prospero's magic, for all its transforming power, works not through some arcane mumbo-jumbo (like that of Jonson's alchemists) but through the ordinary things of nature: 'Ye elves of hills, brooks, standing lakes, and groves' (5.1.33). The greatest moments of wonder come when mortal characters look at each other: Ferdinand at Miranda, Miranda at Ferdinand, Caliban at his master when he first appears in ordinary clothes. In *Henry VIII* the equivalent of this interplay between the familiar and the wonderful lies in the depiction of two different reigns. The reign of Henry seems to belong to ordinary history, the reign of Elizabeth to a world of miracle. Yet each participates to a surprising degree in the nature of the other. The tangle of history reveals an underlying pattern; Cranmer's vision is shaped and coloured by the conflicts and anxieties of the world it seeks to purify. *Henry VIII*, though it is a late, odd, neglected work, offers one more illustration of Shakespeare's abiding interest in the difficult but close relationship between what we dream of and what we are.

THE STRANGENESS OF A DRAMATIC STYLE: RUMOUR IN 'HENRY VIII'

PIERRE SAHEL

Henry VIII is a strange play which has not given rise to especially abundant criticism. If the bibliography of studies on *Hamlet* is about twice the size of the telephone book of a large city,[1] the complete list of writings on *Henry VIII* will hardly fill a volume as slender as the staff directory of a provincial university. This neglect can, in part at least, be traced back to James Spedding's doubts about the authorship of the play.[2] That question, for long a critical crux – and, in these days of newly acquired stylometric habits, soon to become a critical fashion – has presumably obliterated some of the play's other specific issues[3] which might well provide different clues to account for the reticence of critics: its moral confusion, for instance (though Spedding himself was by no means unaware of this), or its heterogeneous nature, for it is a history play written in the period of the romance plays, or its very strangeness, which has occasionally led its most serious readers plainly to wonder what *Henry VIII* is about.[4] Some attention has been paid to its weird, and probably cynical, structure;[5] but, with its series of sad downfalls punctuated by the tears that the characters shed even over those whose doom they have caused and concluded by Cranmer's enthusiastically optimistic tirade, the play seems to take pains to nonplus the readers and spectators of later ages: judging by the limited numbers of the critical platoon, this strategy of bafflement has not proved ineffective. It seems that if we try to analyse and explain its unwonted dramatic style, which is obviously in agreement with its strange structure, we may pluck out *one* of the hearts of this mysterious play.

Most of the events of *Henry VIII* are echoed – more or less unfaithfully – within the play itself. They are not dramatized but reported after having passed through distorting filters. Characters present incidents and occurrences – or, often, their own versions of incidents and occurrences.[6] Although a specialist of the study of reported scenes calls attention to only four 'typical and important' such scenes in *Henry VIII*,[7] the use of this technique or of similar devices is in fact so frequent in the play[8] that it may account for its extremely bizarre scenic language. It even seems that the images of the dramatized events themselves have deliberately been

---

[1] Jan Kott, *Shakespeare Our Contemporary*, trans. B. Taborski (1967), p. 47.

[2] 'Who Wrote Shakespeare's *Henry VIII*?', *Gentleman's Magazine*, 178 (Aug. 1850), 115–22.

[3] Edward I. Berry, '*Henry VIII* and The Dynamics of Spectacle', *Shakespeare Studies*, 12 (1979), 229–46: 'The question of authorship alone is likely to keep the play in a critical limbo' (p. 245).

[4] Frank Kermode, 'What is Shakespeare's *Henry VIII* About?' *Durham University Journal*, NS 9 (1948), 48–55; Tom McBride, '*Henry VIII* as Machiavellian Romance', *Journal of English and Germanic Philology*, 76 (1977), 26–36; p. 26.

[5] Norman Rabkin, *Shakespeare and the Common Understanding* (New York, 1967), p. 230.

[6] R. A. Foakes, *Shakespeare: The Dark Comedies to the Last Plays: From Satire to Celebration* (1971), p. 176: 'The "truth" of an event or action is not clear, but remains to be assessed in the light of differing views and interpretations of it.'

[7] Georg von Greyerz, *The Reported Scenes in Shakespeare's Plays* (Bern, 1965), p. 85.

[8] Herbert Howarth, *The Tiger's Heart: Eight Essays on Shakespeare* (1970), p. 39, finds that some of these devices add to the poetry of the play.

put slightly out of focus. In act 3, scene 2,[9] for example, as Wolsey is asking Cromwell to *report* the King's reaction at the reading of a packet of letters, he is himself being watched by several courtiers ('Observe, observe, he's moody', l. 75). The latter become involved in a strange scenic pleonasm since they describe the prelate's behaviour (ll. 75, 91, 104) while this is directly 'observed' by the spectator. But, whereas the courtiers are ignorant of what causes Wolsey's preoccupations (ll. 91–2), the spectator is provided with better information by Wolsey's long aside on Anne Bullen (ll. 94–104). Thereupon the King enters and, presumably standing a little aside on the stage, asks whether his lords saw the Cardinal. To answer him, Norfolk embarks upon the description of the man who is still before us – a new reported scene, and an extraordinary new pleonasm:

> My lord, we have
> Stood here observing him. Some strange
>   commotion
> Is in his brain; he bites his lip, and starts,
> Stops on a sudden, looks upon the ground,
> Then lays his finger on his temple; straight
> Springs out into fast gait, then stops again.
>
> (ll. 111–16)

What is wrong is thus inextricably mingled with what is correct: the spectator does behold Wolsey's 'strange postures' which are twice reported with profuse details by other beholders who are mistaken regarding the causes thereof.

The manifest superiority of the spectator of act 3, scene 2 unfortunately is a privilege which the play is chary of granting. No political leader, for example, discloses for us, in soliloquy or otherwise, the grievances and claims of the adversaries of the existing order. The most clearly voiced resistance to Wolsey is set forth by Queen Katherine who confines herself to repeating the complaints of the taxpayers – and she, obviously, is not one of them. All that we discover about these opponents is that they are numerous ('not by a few', 1.2.18; 'The many', 1.2.32). Elsewhere, criticism against Wolsey is not even expressed in the spoken words of a *persona*. An anonymous letter refers to the high-handed requisition of thoroughbred horses for the

Cardinal's personal service (2.2.1–9), thus illustrating the man's often-mentioned haughty pride. Other letters expose his intrigue with Rome (3.2.30–3) – but who intercepted them, we do not know. Nor shall we ever know who 'put unwittingly' the inventory of the Cardinal's abnormally great wealth among the King's papers. 'Some spirit', Norfolk suggests (3.2.129). As if wantonly, the play also multiplies fragmentary or doubtful pieces of information which we are not able to declare true or false, deprived as we are of the status of supreme judge usually bestowed on the spectator of Renaissance theatre. Soon after the news that Henry VIII has married Anne Bullen (3.2.41–2), for example, we are told of the King's projected union with the Duchess of Alençon (3.2.85–6). In another instance, Surrey and Suffolk recite *from memory* some of the articles collected against Wolsey: since these articles are in the King's hand (3.2.299) and will never be given *in extenso*, and since Wolsey protests he is not guilty (3.2.301), we are compelled to consider the charges made by his arch-enemies as, at least, questionable.

In act 3, scene 2, admittedly, our ignorance of what some nobles are happily whispering together – a stage direction merely mentions that they are *smiling and whispering* - is counterbalanced by a new pleonasm implying that the characters' low-voiced satisfaction is caused by intimations of Wolsey's imminent downfall: the beginning of the stage direction is totally unambiguous (*Exit King, frowning upon the Cardinal*, l. 203), and Wolsey correctly interprets his master's glare: 'He parted frowning from me, as if ruin / Leap'd from his eyes' (205–6). But the meaning of glances is often misunderstood. Cranmer shivers as he watches Henry's 'aspect of terror', and he reflects: 'I am fearful: wherefore frowns he thus / . . . All's not well' (5.1.87–8) – just before he hears the King call him 'my good and gracious lord of Canterbury' (92). In the following scene, Butts, the King's physician, unexpectedly revealed to be his confidant also, looks at Cranmer – who is meekly waiting in the anteroom of the Council chamber – before he reports to his master

---

[9] Edition cited: Arden Shakespeare, R. A. Foakes (1964).

the unfitting treatment inflicted upon the Archbishop. This report, which we can only suppose to be moving and convincing, will lead the King to intervene on behalf of his minister. Yet Cranmer is anxious lest Butts's glance may mean his doom:

> How earnestly he cast his eyes upon me:
> Pray heaven he sound not my disgrace.
>
> (5.2.11–12)

Such uncertainties and hesitations may well, to a large extent, be ascribed to the playwright's stylistic attempt to describe a realistically darksome political world – not a world, that is, of idealized heroes and plain villains but one where 'the fumbling inadequacies of men and their laws' or 'the failures and limitations of governors'[10] are normally inconspicuous yet none the less real. In any case, those struggles, the manifestations of which are so maturely and flexibly instilled into the very language of the play, are by some characters sensed to be fought with a strange weapon – rumour. Early in the play, Wolsey protests, or pretends to protest, against the onslaughts of an unnamed opposition:

> if I am
> Traduc'd by ignorant tongues, which neither know
> My faculties nor person, yet will be
> The chronicles of my doing, let me say
> 'Tis but the fate of place. (1.2.71–5)

The character here expresses his consciousness of a political fact. Whatever their circumstances, a statesman's acts are maligned by the public voice and sifted even by those who are not entitled to judge them. The circumstances of act 1, scene 2 are the consequences of the heavy taxation imposed, apparently without the King's knowledge, by Wolsey upon the clothiers and others. The hostile voice is heard at court, but it rises from the street against King and minister alike:

> My good lord cardinal they vent reproaches
> Most bitterly on you, as putter on
> Of these exactions, yet the king, our master
> ...escapes not
> Language unmannerly, yea, such which breaks
> The sides of loyalty, and almost appears
> In loud rebellion. (1.2.23–9)

Even though it is here described as less dangerous than open revolt, rumour is often regarded as the enemy of Henry's regime. And since the regime will fight back, the whole fabric of the play can be seen to echo the struggle between place and rumour.

Wolsey, as the prime mover of his country's political life, is the main target of the arrows of outrageous rumour. He is reported to have been responsible for the costly peace with France (1.1.50–1). It is alleged it was later bribed by the gold of Spain to breach that same peace (1.1.185–90). Some there are who claim that he urges the King to divorce Katherine of Aragon because he resents her imperial nephew's refusal to grant him the archbishopric of Toledo (2.1.163–4). In fact, rather than any particular political initiative, it is the exalted position of the man in power that arouses bitter reflections upon him, the more so as he is of humble birth. The entire nobility at Henry's court envies this butcher's son who has managed to dominate. The angry voice of rumour is as much a cause as a symptom of the governor's solitude. It cements, as an opposition group, the aristocracy whose members all feel equally overpowered by the Cardinal. Malicious reports and hostile murmurs undoubtedly have a cohesive force, for whoever circulates a rumour communicates his own emotions of jealousy or of hatred to his listeners. Yet the humble stock of the political master, however much it exacerbates rancour, is by no means the sole cause of the general enmity since Cranmer, once in power, also experiences the noblemen's hostility; all his virtues, as he well knows, will not be sufficient to silence the voice of discontent:

> Men that make
> Envy and crooked malice nourishment,
> Dare bite the best. (5.2.77–9)

The image here is that of the dog, or rather of the pack; dogs will howl when other dogs do. As the King rightly diagnoses:

> you have many enemies that know not
> Why they are so, but like to village curs
> Bark when their fellows do. (2.4.156–8)

---

10 R. A. Foakes, *The Dark Comedies to the Last Plays*, pp. 174–5.

The animal imagery aptly stresses the irrational quality of the hostile rumour whose critical bias may well outlive the specific motivations of any precisely defined opposition. It also suggests the contagious propagation of rumour which never convinces but conquers, which instils half-truths or glaring lies, which both insinuates[11] and insinuates itself, and which by its own insinuation grows. That is why it may also develop among the common people, and not only among the aristocracy. Indeed 'All the commons hate [Wolsey] perniciously' (2.1.49–50). The populace may, in the atmosphere of general disease caused by economic problems and imminent dynastic and religious upheavals, disparage great men and great men's actions, and, like an echo chamber, amplify political events. It uses rumour as a means of expression and communication, being too weak to voice its concerns and grievances differently. Wolsey was aware of one specific weakness in his anonymous opponents – that of ignorance (1.2.72–3). And yet any weakness can give birth to a rumour. Passing strictures on the government, even *sotto voce*, is a manner of self-exaltation, since the government is thereby demeaned and debased in the minds of the critics or of their listeners. Agreeing with or propagating hostile or derogatory comments satisfies other emotional needs. This tends in particular to balance the fear inspired by a too mighty power. It is hardly imaginable that the weak and powerless could openly challenge the masters of the kingdom. Even the great Duke of Buckingham is shortened his whole head's length for having rashly opposed Wolsey. Whether it be under Wolsey's rule or under Cranmer's, rumour is the voice of fear and the weapon of the poor hearts who curse not loud but deep:

> Th'archbishop
> Is the king's hand and tongue, and who dare speak
> One syllable against him? (5.1.37–9)

Fear does indeed prevail at Henry VIII's court or outside the palace, and anonymous gentlemen, numbers one and two (are they interchangeable? are they representative?), prefer to go on whispering in secrecy: 'We are too open here to argue this; / Let's think in private more' (2.1.168–9). The regime's adversaries cannot renounce this word-of-mouth medium and become explicit (or even simply articulate) so long as the regime does not discard its trappings and means of constraint. The latter alternative is vaguely contemplated towards the end of the play, when Cranmer is about to be impeached:

> 'Tis his highness' pleasure
> And our consent, for better trial of you,
> From hence you be committed to the Tower,
> Where being but a private man again,
> You shall know many dare accuse you boldly.
> (5.2.86–90)

Were the metamorphosis of public man into private man achieved, rumour would perhaps no longer be the fate of place – but then place and power would also cease to exist. It is *not* achieved, and rumour persists, a confused, indistinct threat, so scarcely perceptible at times that Cranmer is not even aware of its murmur (5.1.140–2). This force does not merely resist or check the rulers of *Henry VIII*. It triumphs over Wolsey who is cornered by the pack of his enemies at the moment of his downfall (3.2.228–349). Later Cranmer faces the same equivocal, relentless, and indeed mechanical opposition. The Lord Chancellor declares he is 'inform'd' of the Archbishop's heresies (5.2.51–3); but who informed him is not stated. Round the council-table, waiting to judge and assail the present minister, are sitting, among others, the very men who had judged and assailed the previous one. Such indeed is the fate of place, what Montaigne called 'l'incommodité de la grandeur': 'Puisque nous ne la pouvons atteindre, vengeons nous à en médire.'[12]

The obduracy of scandalmongering and censorious commentary paradoxically entails or reinforces the absolutism of the regime. Political repression is now legitimized and tries to muzzle the dogs of rumour:

> For...murmurers
> There's places of rebuke. (2.2.130–1)

---

11 See for example 2.2.26–8.

12 *Les Essais de Michel de Montaigne*, Book 3, Chapter 7, ed. Pierre Villey (Paris, 1965), p. 916.

[The king] sent command to the lord mayor
straight
To stop the rumour, and allay those tongues
That durst disperse it. (2.1.151–3)

And at the end of the play, the King's intervention in favour of Cranmer leads to the arbitrary interruption of a legal procedure. The coercive method, however, is fundamentally inefficient, for, while absolute government tends to limit or control the right of speech, rumour develops in an effort to compensate for the very lack of freedom of speech. Absolutism, therefore, entails rumour as much as rumour entails absolutism: a mouthless voice cannot be muffled. That is why the rulers of *Henry VIII* have recourse to more subtle techniques to suppress their monstrous adversary. Wolsey, after he has reluctantly executed the King's order to repeal the unpopular financial laws, adds in an aside to his secretary:

The grieved commons
Hardly conceive of me: let it be nois'd
That through our intercession this revokement
And pardon comes. (1.2.104–7)

To preserve or increase his personal prestige and be regarded as a benevolent statesman, he is using the very strategy of rumour by bruiting it abroad ('let it be nois'd') that it was he who took the merciful initiative. He is launching a counter-rumour. Elsewhere, we see that the men of place too can use cunning, go masked, and give unexpected blows ('where [Wolsey's sword] will not extend, / Thither he darts it', 1.1.111–12). Buckingham is overthrown by guile ('some trick', 1.1.128), and the most unfair denunciation is used against him to bring about his condemnation. Justice summons not so much false witnesses as witnesses of witnesses. The main indicter, a shady character who lost his office as Buckingham's surveyor 'on the complaint o'th'tenants' (1.2.173), claims to be reporting the words used by his ex-master quoting his chaplain as the latter was repeating the confidence of a 'holy monk' (1.2.168–71). Such defamatory arabesques are probably intended to underline the falseness of the surveyor's disclosure – all the more so since the Duke is not described as an ambitious, passionate man but as an actor playing ambition and passion, more or less ready to drown the stage with tears and cleave the general ear with horrid speech:

He stretch'd him, and with one hand on his dagger,
Another spread on's breast, mounting his eyes
He did discharge a horrible oath. (1.2.204–6)

In their struggle against rumour, the rulers further assert themselves as steerers of public opinion by making use of the people, that monstrous body,[13] source and proliferation of rumour. Crowds flock into the streets, now for Anne's coronation (4.1), now for the Princess Elizabeth's baptism (5.3). Though the exchange of act 5, scene 3 between the porter and his man presents a view from behind the scenes, the aim of such displays is to dazzle the mob so that the ostentatious events will be magnified in their successive reports.[14] The aristocracy itself, with its prestige, is enlisted on behalf of the State. Public ceremony and processions indeed can but serve the interests of the Crown. Particularly long stage directions describe the great noblemen as adherents of the King's power – instruments at the service of a policy *à la Louis Quatorze* (4.1: *The Order of the Coronation*; 5.4: *Enter Trumpets sounding...*; etc.).

Yet, though rumour is often viewed as the enemy of the established regime, it is much too neutral, much too elusive, to be counted merely as one more factor among the political forces at work in the play. *Henry VIII*, called or subtitled *All is True* in Shakespeare's lifetime,[15] refuses to be oversimplified; it does not do us the favour of ever allowing us to equate rumour with falsehood or biased distortion. A particular event proves to have actually taken place ('These news are everywhere', 2.2.38) though it was at first only announced by a confused murmur

---

13 See Frank V. Cespedes, '"We are one in fortunes": The Sense of History in *Henry VIII*', *English Literary Renaissance*, 10 (1980), 413–38; p. 435.

14 This is partly described in 5.3.66–8; but it is best illustrated by the account of the Field of the Cloth of Gold which transforms a diplomatic meeting into a myth. See 1.1.18–38.

15 See R. A. Foakes, introduction to the Arden edition, p. xxviii.

('buzzing', 2.1.148). Nor is rumour always mere slander. As it happens, even what was judged slanderous later appears to be correct ('that slander, sir, / Is found a truth now', 2.1.153–4). To be sure, only the student of the play feels himself caught on the horns of the dilemma between right and wrong. Within the play, rumour is not necessarily either true or false – it simply exists. It evolves, circulates ('it grows again / Fresher than e'er it was', 2.1.154–5), heedless of communicating any precise message, sometimes coactive with what is unreal, sometimes co-joining with something. Given the strange relations between the dramatic discourse and the dramatic action in *Henry VIII*, the evolution of a rumour cannot be accommodated within a logical pattern such as:

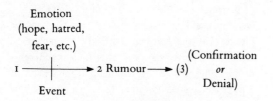

There is a constant interaction between events and reports. Rumour may seem to create reality. Words (whispered in hope or fear) may reify the very fact they evoke. This is so when Suffolk deems that Cranmer will soon be rewarded for his good services:

Suffolk. . . . we shall see him
For it an archbishop.
Norfolk. So I hear.
Suffolk. 'Tis so.

(3.2.73–4)

At the price of a singular scrimmage of tenses, where the present ('I hear') follows the future ('We shall see') and the past (''Tis so' – i.e. it has already been settled) follows the present, with run-on or truncated lines, the event is revealed to be an accomplished fact by the very man who had just

announced it as plausible. This astonishing dialogue may be set out as follows:

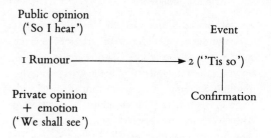

Another bizarre reversal of the logical pattern is noticeable at the time of the King's wedding:

Chamberlain. . . . The king already
Hath married the fair lady.
Surrey. Would he had.

(3.2.41–2)

Here it seems that, to exist, reality has to cast some shadow before itself, or even that a piece of information can only be the adumbration of a rumour. The emotion ('Would he had!'), normally at the origin of, or coupled with, rumour, follows the actual event: the wish comes after its fulfilment.

It is certainly wiser, as we study *2 Henry IV* – where the induction is given by Rumour (a clearly identifiable figure *'painted full of tongues'*) – to believe what we see the characters do than what is said of them.[16] But such a wise course is not open to us in *Henry VIII* where the dramatic action proper is very scanty. The various informative contents supplied by the rumours spread in the play are seldom in concordance, with the result that it is extremely difficult to appreciate adequately even public actions. Norfolk's eulogy of the ceremonies of the Cloth of Gold is initially extravagant. But we, who do not actually watch them, cannot share his enthusiastic praise, if only because Buckingham, his interlocutor, thinks the whole description bombastic ('O you go far', 1.1.38). And Norfolk himself is not

[16] Hugh Dickinson, 'The Reformation of Prince Hal', *Shakespeare Quarterly*, 12 (1961), 33–46; pp. 42–3.

long in reversing his own opinion and admitting the costly uselessness of the peace negotiation (1.1.87–9). We similarly tend to hesitate over the validity or nullity of Henry's marriage with Katherine. King, lawyers, and ecclesiastical courts now consider it as null and void. Yet Henry VII, the present King's father, and Ferdinand, Katherine's father, had consulted the wisest counsellors before deciding to celebrate the union. The past and its memories – which are perhaps the distorted echoes and rumours of bygone ages – thus seem to oppose the present-day views and their own wavering, contradictory, and occasionally self-contradictory voices.[17]

Another ambiguity prevails when we try to judge characters whose deeds are not frequently described by coherent testimonies. Wolsey, for example, has numerous enemies – and many a follower. He is highly praised during the banquet of act 1, scene 4; but his admirers are his guests. Norfolk defends him ('Say not treasonous', 1.1.156) when Buckingham refers to the Cardinal as a disloyal subject; but Norfolk, as we have seen, is not a trustworthy informant.[18] Of the prelate's disloyalty, Buckingham asserts that he has several proofs 'as clear as founts in July' (1.1.154), but gives none. Katherine, his steadfast enemy, draws of him a long unfavourable picture (4.2.33–4) which is immediately touched up by Griffith, her servant. But Griffith speaks late in the play – at the right moment, in fact, to deliver his praise of the Cardinal – and nothing is said of the possible links between a man who knows Wolsey's biography so well and Wolsey himself. In the time of his disgrace, the ex-minister admits he has committed numerous misdeeds, and even compares himself with Lucifer (3.2.371; 441) – but is not a fault confessed half redressed? He will have a glorious death, professing his faith, as one

says, or rather as Griffith says (4.2.68) – but then, besides the fact that (in Dr Johnson's words) in lapidary inscriptions a man is not upon oath, is not the report to be held in doubt? Many people in the play speak 'without knowing' – the very charge made by Wolsey against his opponents (1.2.72). But others know too many things. How can Campeius, for example, possibly be acquainted with his colleague's secret manoeuvring to oust a certain official who never appears in the play (2.2.120–35)? He alludes to a rumour ('ill opinion spread', 2.2.124). But how did rumour reach this stranger to Henry's court and country? Could the Renaissance *Curia* be as well informed as the Roman bankers with their newsletters and carrier-pigeons?

Henry VIII is contaminated by rumour, not only a political tool but also the syndrome of an unstable or even diseased community. The authorial effort, with the otherwise useless lights and shadows which are cast upon this or that passage, must have been concentrated upon rendering the dubious effects of rumours and counter-rumours in the scenic language of this highly theatrical and even pageant-like drama. Characters, actions, speeches, gestures, all have shaky and distorted doubles which the suggestion of dual authorship could hardly explain away. The spectator (or the critic, of course), plunged as he is into an atmosphere of doubts, will legitimately feel in a Joycian mood that 'the unfacts, did we possess them, are too imprecisely few to warrant our certitude'.[19]

---

17 Buckingham perceives another contradiction between past and present. See 2.1.112–18.
18 For a similar contradiction in Norfolk's assertions, cf. 1.1.193–4 and 2.2.19–21.
19 *Finnegans Wake* (3rd edn., 1964), p. 57.

'EDGAR I NOTHING AM':
'FIGURENPOSITION' IN 'KING LEAR'

MICHAEL E. MOONEY

Readers of *King Lear* must now 'acknowledge' the widely influential view of Edgar first proposed by Stanley Cavell, who questioned the sincerity and timeliness of Edgar's decision not to reveal himself to his grief-stricken, blinded father until it is too late to save him.[1] Cavell's opinion has affected the response of critics as widely divergent in their approaches as Janet Adelman and S. L. Goldberg,[2] and has taken hold in many quarters. It is a misleading view, in my opinion, not only because it ignores basic facts about the ways Shakespeare 'manages' his dramatic personae, but also because it fails to describe the relationship between a character's language and his stage location. It may be most mistaken, however, because it loses sight of the 'affective' response to *King Lear* that Shakespeare elicits from his audience.

Readers who share Professor Cavell's perspective overlook the functions Edgar performs as a 'choric' character and as the 'symbolic' figure of Poor Tom, preferring to limit their focus to 'psychological' examinations of his 'realistic' persona. This is surprising, especially in the light cast by Maynard Mack's suggestions about the ways Shakespeare 'manages' his characters in the play. 'At any given instant', Mack wrote in 1965, 'characters may shift along a spectrum between compelling realism and an almost pure representativeness that resembles... [the] *esse* [or being] of the Morality play...'[3] Indeed, as Mack sees the matter, *an audience* must be able to shift between the verisimilitude of Lear's passion and curse on Goneril in act 1, scene 4 and the representativeness of Edgar's stripping down to become Poor Tom in act 2, scene 3 (or the representativeness of Kent in the stocks at the end of act 2, scene 2).

Mack's judgement demonstrates the inadequacy of the 'realistic' approach by reminding us that characters in Renaissance drama are not just psychological states but also, at times, symbolic figures. When we add Edgar's third, choric and metadramatic function to his realistic and symbolic (or representative) roles, we may begin to sense the complexity of his depiction. Shakespeare utilizes Edgar in multiple ways, not the least of which is as a moral agent who tries to save Gloucester from despair. This is why any *one* approach to his character is necessarily reductive. But Mack's comments may be important in another sense, since the recognition that Edgar serves multiple functions also implies that he performs his roles from different figural positions in respect to the play's illusionistic frame. Each of Edgar's personae, that is, requires a different kind of audience awareness about the relationship among a character and his role(s), his stage position and the play's modes of presentation. The difficulty has been that literary criticism has yet to find a way to describe the relationship between language and staging in Renaissance drama. With the appearance of Robert Weimann's recently

---

[1] See 'The Avoidance of Love: A Reading of *King Lear*', in *Must We Mean What We Say? A Book of Essays* (New York, 1969).

[2] See Adelman's introduction to her *Twentieth Century Interpretations of 'King Lear'* (Englewood Cliffs, NJ, 1978), pp. 1–21; and Goldberg's *An Essay on 'King Lear'* (Cambridge, 1974).

[3] *King Lear In Our Time* (Berkeley, 1965), p. 67. Also see J. L. Styan's 'Changeable Taffeta: Shakespeare's Characters in Performance', in Philip C. McGuire and David A. Samuelson, eds., *Shakespeare: The Theatrical Dimension* (New York, 1977), pp. 138–9, for an assessment of the limitations of psychological-realistic approaches.

translated study,[4] however, we may well be at the point where such a description is possible.

Weimann's term, *figurenposition*, or the correlation of a character's stage location 'with the speech, action, and degree of stylization associated with that position',[5] promises to provide a means to relate our analyses of dramatic language to the flexible dimensions of the platform stage. In proposing such a term, Weimann carefully examines the influential role two earlier theatrical modes played in the formation of Elizabethan dramaturgy: the courtly or hall drama, with its illusionistic, 'representational' and self-contained frame, and the popular drama's illusion-breaking, 'presentational' focus. T. S. Eliot, of course, felt that the art of the Elizabethans was an 'impure art' because he believed dramatists confused the 'conventions' of popular staging with the 'realism' of totally illusionistic presentation.[6] But later critics have realized that the essence of this drama may well lie precisely in the mixture of 'naturalism' and 'conventionalism', representation and embodiment, that so often fuses in 'complementary perspective' (p. 237). In Weimann's view, this 'complementary perspective' may be discerned on stage in the 'traditional interplay between *platea* and *locus*, between neutral, undifferentiated "place" and symbolic location . . . [which] accommodates action that is both non-illusionistic and near the audience (corresponding to the "place") and a more illusionistic, localized action sometimes taking place in a discovery space, scaffold, tent, or other *loci*' (p. 214). But if, in earlier popular and illusionistic modes of staging, there is a clear distinction between non-illusionistic and illusionistic effects, this is not so clearly the case in Renaissance drama. In earlier drama, a character's delivery of illusion-breaking devices like asides, choric speeches or other kinds of direct or indirect address is facilitated by a downstage, *platea* position; 'realistic' dialogue, on the other hand, is often tied to a specific *locus* and held within the illusionistic frame of the play. In the more sophisticated Elizabethan and Jacobean theatre, however, a character's *figurenposition* may not, finally, be restricted to a particularized *locus* or to a generalized *platea* position. 'This *figurenposition*', Weimann points out, 'should not be understood

only in the sense of an actor's physical position on the stage, but also in the more general sense that an actor may generate a unique stage presence that establishes a special relationship between himself and his fellow actors, the play, or the audience, even when direct address has been abandoned' (p. 230). We need only think of Richard III's opening soliloquy or Hamlet's first punning aside to sense the way a character located within the illusion may yet 'establish a special relationship'. A character's *figurenposition* may 'thus be defined verbally as well as spatially' (p. 230), and even when he seems fixed within the illusion, an actor may figuratively 'step away' from that illusion through an aside or other 'extra-dramatic' device.

I am going to argue that Weimann's and Mack's views complement each other in a way which allows us a better understanding of the complex nature of Edgar's *figurenposition* in *King Lear*. I am going to argue that the three dimensions to Edgar's role correspond to different 'figural' positions within the play's illusionistic frame and to different 'realistic', 'representative', and 'choric' personae. These categories do not mean to ignore Mack's 'corollary peculiarity' in the language of Shakespearian character, in which speech is 'always yet more fully in the service of the vision of the play as a whole than true to any consistent interior reality'.[7] We need only remember the wisdom of Edgar's advice to Gloucester that 'Men must endure / Their going hence, even as their coming hither: / Ripeness is all'

---

[4] *Shakespeare and the Popular Tradition in the Theater*, ed. Robert Schwartz (Baltimore, 1978).

[5] Weimann, p. 224.

[6] 'Four Elizabethan Dramatists', in T. S. Eliot, *Selected Essays: 1917–1932* (1932), p. 114. Compare Weimann, pp. 220, 248–50.

[7] Mack, p. 68 and note. See Leo Kirschbaum, 'Banquo and Edgar: Character or Function?', *Essays in Criticism*, 7 (1957), 1–21, for a view of Edgar as a plot device; Hugh Maclean, 'Disguise in *King Lear*: Kent and Edgar', *Shakespeare Quarterly*, 11 (1960), 49–54, for a view of Edgar as a 'realistic' character; and Russell A. Peck, 'Edgar's Pilgrimage: High Comedy in *King Lear*', *Studies in English Literature, 1500–1900*, 7 (1967), 219–37, for a view of Edgar that mediates between Kirschbaum's and Maclean's.

(5.2.9–11)[8] to recognize that his language is in the service of the play's vision. Speech like this, to be sure, is one of Edgar's – and Kent's and Lear's – functions in the play. But this assessment does not so fully accommodate the sense we have that Edgar, in addition to playing a symbolic role as Poor Tom, is undergoing a number of changes in his character *at the same time* that he is guiding our response to the play. In my view, the contradictory feelings about Edgar that Stanley Cavell has engendered derive from the failure to distinguish his role as an active participant *in* the illusionistic action from his function as the symbolic figure of Poor Tom or as a commentator who stands, as it were, *outside* the play. These three dimensions of his role truly denote his *figurenposition*. They are also integrally related to Shakespeare's 'affective' manipulation of his audience in *King Lear*.

I. PRIVILEGED KNOWLEDGE: 'EDGAR I NOTHING AM'

The question of privileged knowledge is an important one in this respect, since the information that is given to an audience by a character – but which other characters on stage do not know – helps determine spectator response to the play. The giving of this kind of information may be noticed at the opening of *King Lear*. Cordelia's two asides while Lear attempts to measure his daughters' love for him separate her from the *locus* of the scene and invite us to see these events from a second perspective. They are not audience asides, but they do offer a privileged view on the action and prepare for Cordelia's apparent filial ingratitude. Banished Kent's opening soliloquy in act 1, scene 4 provides another, more obvious example, since from this point on until his appearance in act 5, scene 3 we know what no one on stage knows, that Caius is Kent in disguise. But a third example may determine our response to the play more than do the first two. Edmund's opening soliloquy in act 1, scene 2, with its invocation to 'Nature' and its announcement of his intentions, establishes his privileged relationship with the audience. Here Edmund's plot to 'trick' Gloucester into believing that Edgar intends to murder him

suggests his dominance, and the ease with which he accomplishes the deception makes us realize just how defective Gloucester's sight is and how naive is Edgar. In this scene Edmund behaves 'realistically', to be sure, but he also reveals his own symbolic nature as the Vice, so famous for and expert in engaging the audience's attention from the *platea* in countless earlier plays.[9] Edmund remains set *within* the illusion in this scene, but he also functions in a manner that overtly recalls his devilish theatrical predecessors. This revelation about Edmund's symbolic undertrappings, however, is linked to another revelation. By revealing his theatrical lineage, Edmund also provides Edgar with the representative role he will assume. Edmund 'cues' Edgar, who then appears 'like the catastrophe of the old comedy'. But if Edmund correctly identifies his own cue as 'villainous melancholy', he mistakenly adds that he will have a 'sigh like Tom o' Bedlam' (1.2.134–6). That, we know, is the role Edgar will play.

---

8 All citations from the play are taken from G. Blakemore Evans, textual ed., *The Riverside Shakespeare* (Boston, 1974). As my choice of text indicates, I have based my analysis on what is now recognized as one of the 'conflated' versions of *King Lear*. Steven Urkowitz, Peter W. M. Blayney, and Michael J. Warren have addressed the editorial and critical problems arising from conflation of the Quarto and Folio texts of the play. The issues raised *are* important, particularly in the cases of Edgar and Albany. For instance, Edgar's speech in 3.6.102–15 is found only in the Quarto; the Folio, on the other hand, expands his speech in 4.1.1–9, and assigns Edgar the play's final speech, which Quarto gives to Albany. Michael J. Warren has dealt with these matters incisively in 'Quarto and Folio *King Lear* and the Interpretation of Albany and Edgar', in *Shakespeare, Pattern of Excelling Nature*, ed. David Bevington and Jay L. Halio (Newark, Delaware, 1978), pp. 95–107. It seems clear, especially in terms of my argument, that Quarto and Folio 'flesh out' (albeit in different ways) Edgar's 'choric' and 'realistic' voices, with Quarto generally expanding his choric, Folio his realistic, personae. But I am aware that my attempt here ignores Warren's concluding demand: 'What we as scholars, editors, interpreters and servants of theatrical craft have to accept and learn to live by is the knowledge that we have two plays of *King Lear* sufficiently different to require that all further work on the play be based on either Q or F, but not the conflation of both' (p. 105).

9 Mack, pp. 56–62, and Bernard Spivack, *Shakespeare and the Allegory of Evil* (New York, 1958).

Edmund's theatrical metaphors are simultaneously thematic (Edmund sees himself and Edgar as playing parts in this deception) and metadramatic (in the sense that the lines are self-consciously theatrical). They are simultaneously self-enclosed within the illusion and self-consciously aware of this play as a play.

Many readers are aware of the similarity between this scene and the opening sequence of scenes in *Richard III* and *Othello*, where Richard and Iago also assert their dominance and establish a relationship with the spectators. But in *Othello*, Iago is the only character to maintain such a relationship. In *King Lear*, Edmund shares the audience with Edgar. In his soliloquy in act 2, scene 3, one that is approximately the same length as Edmund's in act 1, scene 2, Edgar announces his disguise. And like Kent, who remains on stage at the end of act 2, scene 2, stocked as Caius, Edgar provides us with a representative stage image. Kent's position on stage corresponds to a particularized *locus*, the stocks; and placed as he is within the self-contained illusionistic frame of the play, Kent remains unaware of Edgar's presence. By having both characters on stage at the same time, one in the background and one in the foreground, Shakespeare offers us two images, each of which depicts the disastrous consequences of loyal behaviour and filial faithfulness in Lear's shaken kingdom. By having Edgar appear between the end of act 2, scene 2, when Kent stoically accepts this turn of Fortune's wheel, and the beginning of act 2, scene 4, when Kent greets Lear ('Hail to thee, noble master'), Shakespeare conveys a sense of the passage of time. But Edgar's soliloquy, delivered from downstage, *platea* position, also has its own separate and distinct purposes. This pause in the forward movement of the action allows us to share in the predicament of one of the play's noble characters, one whose total number of lines will be second only to Lear's. More important, the soliloquy allows Edgar to establish his own privileged relationship with the audience.

In addition to adumbrating the large role Edgar will play in the events, this soliloquy also delineates Edgar's personae as a symbolic figure and as a commentator who will guide our response. As he establishes the fullness of his realistic role and intro-

duces his symbolic and choric personae, however, an audience must be able to attend to these disclosures with what S. L. Bethell called 'theatrical multi-consciousness'.[10] When Edgar grimes his face 'with filth', blankets 'his loins', elfs all his 'hairs in knots' and 'with presented nakedness' prepares to 'outface / The winds and persecutions of the sky' (ll. 9–12), he transforms himself into Poor Tom. And in his final words in this speech, he also adds his choric function to these two personae. The lines, 'Poor Turlygod! poor Tom! / That's something yet: Edgar I nothing am', indicate the kind of multiple awareness that is requisite. In saying 'Poor Turly-god! poor Tom!', Edgar may well speak with Tom's inflection, returning to his own voice when he considers the viability of the disguise: 'That's something yet.' The shift in inflection would thus suggest the two personae. As a realistic participant in the events, Edgar tells us that he has lost his identity as a son of Gloucester: 'Edgar I nothing am.' As a character who will next appear in Tom's visceral shape, Edgar now assumes a second persona. In these senses, Edgar shifts 'along a spectrum between compelling realism and an almost pure representativeness'. But implicit in the very nature of the soliloquy, in which an actor engages an audience's confidence, is Edgar's third persona as a commentator. As Kenneth Muir's gloss suggests, Edgar here figuratively steps outside the illusion to advise the spectators that, from this point, he will play the role of Tom: from now on, he tells us, 'Edgar I nothing am.'[11]

Understood in each of these three senses, Edgar's final lines delineate his realistic, symbolic, and choric personae – and their corresponding voices – in the play. The truth of the matter is that these personae

---

[10] *Shakespeare and the Popular Dramatic Tradition* (1944), p. 81. Also see Weimann, pp. 246–52, and Stephen Booth's '*King Lear*', '*Macbeth*', *Indefinition and Tragedy* (New Haven, 1983), p. 33 for discussion of the way 'an audience thinks in multiple dimensions'.

[11] See Kenneth Muir, ed., *King Lear*, the Arden Shakespeare (1952), p. 77n, who glosses the line by offering two 'realistic' and 'metadramatic' readings: 'There is some hope for me as Poor Tom; I am nothing, I am doomed, as Edgar. Or possibly the words mean merely "I am no longer Edgar."' Also see Styan, p. 138.

are not readily separable. At least not, that is, from the perspective of a reader in his study. Such a reader, envisioning the confrontation between Lear and Poor Tom in the 'to-and-fro-conflicting wind and rain' in act 3, scene 4, may accept that Edgar has undergone a transformation from earl's son to crazed Bedlam. An audience does not make the transfer so easily. Spectators must keep in mind that Edgar is now Poor Tom, but balance the identification with the knowledge dogging them that they are, nonetheless, still seeing Edgar. Movement on stage may well indicate that Edgar recoils more sharply than we can imagine when Gloucester includes him in pointedly asking 'What are you there? Your names?' (3.4.128). 'Poor Tom,' replies Edgar, who immediately plunges deeper into his disguise by cataloguing what he eats, swallows, and drinks (ll. 129–39). Although we cannot be sure Edgar recoils from Gloucester, certainly Gloucester has Edgar in mind here, as we later learn in the conversation the now blinded Gloucester has with the Old Man leading him:

Old Man.
  Fellow, where goest?
Gloucester.   Is it a beggar-man?
Old Man.
  Madman and beggar too.
Gloucester.
  He has some reason, else he could not beg.
  I' th' last night's storm I such a fellow saw
  Which made me think a man a worm. My son
  Came then into my mind, and yet my mind
  Was then scarce friends with him. I have heard more
    since.   (4.1.29–35)

But the double awareness we must maintain best emerges in Edgar's repetition of the phrase 'Tom's a-cold'. The phrase is repeated four times in act 3, scene 4 (ll. 58, 83, 146, 172). The first, second, and fourth times Edgar speaks it, he refers solely to his physical condition as Tom. The third time Edgar speaks these words comes after Gloucester has asked his name and commiserated with Lear's paternal misfortunes. 'Our flesh and blood, my lord,' he says, 'is grown so vild / That it doth hate what gets it' (ll. 145–6).[12] Lear does not answer. But Tom does, and for the second time in the scene Edgar adds the

word 'Poor' to the phrase. 'Poor Tom's' (l. 146) indeed impoverished and cold, beggared and outcast child that he is; and we shade into the area of Edgar's personal suffering.

In our analyses of act 3, scene 4 especially, we tend to overlook Edgar's own psychological dilemma in favour of stressing his symbolic function in the Lear plot. Lear's identification of Tom as the 'thing itself' rightly claims our attention as one of the recognitions at the heart of the play. But the importance of Lear's reaction obscures any sense we have that Edgar is still, in fact, Edgar. In the trial scene (3.6), however, we may more easily separate these two dimensions of his role – and add a third dimension to them. As the scene opens, Edgar continues to rave in the manner of Tom, but embedded in and introducing these maniacal outbursts are statements which suggest that Edgar drops Tom's mad idiom and speaks in his own voice. Let us consider one such sequence of comments. First, after taking his place at the mock trial, Edgar remarks, 'Let us deal justly' (l. 40), and follows the statement with a snatch of an old song. Then, when Lear starts to rage uncontrollably, Edgar echoes a line he had used earlier: 'Bless thy five wits!' (3.4.58; 3.6.57). Finally, as Kent intercedes to remind Lear of the 'patience...you so oft have boasted to retain' (ll. 58–9), Edgar speaks his first aside: 'My tears begin to take his part so much, / They mar my counterfeiting' (ll. 60–1).

Only the last of these lines is marked by editors as an aside, but they all may be considered 'asides' of sorts, delivered with increasing degrees of dissociation from the illusionistic action. Any reader of the play will grasp the thematic relevance of Edgar's 'Let us deal justly'; formalistic and spatial analyses link the line to any one of many references to justice in the play, particularly to Edgar's own assertion that 'The gods are just' in act 5, scene 3. Whether it be ironic or mocking, unconsciously significant or ominously foreboding, the line thus stands slightly apart from its context. The second of these utterances ('Bless thy five wits') raises a different sort of

---

[12] Muir, p. 118, cites the Cowden Clarke edition: 'Gloucester, reminded perhaps by some tone or inflection in his son's voice, links Edgar's supposed villainy with that of Goneril or Regan.'

problem. In repeating a line he had employed in a 'mad' context, Edgar seems to do little more than add to his string of nonsensical phrases. But the line does more. It not only anticipates, in its syntactic shape, a number of other 'blessings' to be given in the play; it also serves as Edgar's first choric comment, meant to guide audience response to Lear's plight. Although not, strictly speaking, an aside, the line reaches beyond the immediate to elicit an emotional reaction. It is important to note that when Edgar speaks in explicit aside, he uses language ('take his part', 'mar my counterfeiting') that separates him from the illusion, and accompanies his words with tears which reinforce the empathy he feels. The tears he sheds indicate his own emotional response and invite a similar response from the audience. Although Edgar clearly remains within the illusion here, he also steps outside the illusion to convey his feelings to the audience. His *figurenposition* may indeed be defined both spatially and verbally. When we hear his last line in this sequence, we more fully comprehend what we have hitherto only apprehended as a multiple and complex rendering of his role: 'Poor Tom,' he says to himself, 'thy horn is dry' (l. 75).[13]

2. MIXING PERSONAE: 'WHEN WE OUR BETTERS'

Edgar's comments in act 3, scene 6 are carefully modulated to evoke and ultimately to direct audience response. Their effectiveness depends on the acting skill with which he maintains a privileged relationship with the audience, and on the spectator's own privileged knowledge that Poor Tom is still Edgar, even though no one within the theatrical illusion is aware of the fact. But these statements are premonitory ones; Edgar's explicitly choric voice does not fully emerge until the conclusion of act 3, scene 6, when he remains on stage to deliver a scene-ending soliloquy. His speech on the value of community and the need for human compassion confirms our feeling that Edgar has been emotionally involved in the scene's mad proceedings:

When we our betters see bearing our woes,
We scarcely think our miseries our foes.

Who alone suffers, suffers most i' th' mind,
Leaving free things and happy shows behind,
But then the mind much sufferance doth o'erskip,
When grief hath mates, and bearing fellowship.
How light and portable my pain seems now,
When that which makes me bend makes the King
    bow:
He childed as I fathered! Tom, away!
Mark the high noises, and thyself bewray
When false opinion, whose wrong thoughts defile
    thee,
In thy just proof repeals and reconciles thee.
What will hap more to-night, safe scape the King!
Lurk, lurk.   (3.6.102–15)

In this speech, given while the Fool and Kent bear off the King, Edgar articulates what he feels and relates his misfortune to Lear's. He acknowledges the danger of too indulgent solipsistic suffering and recognizes the value of 'bearing fellowship'. He now sees his own 'pain' to be 'light and portable' compared to the King's burden, and he resolves to throw off ('bewray') his disguise when 'just proof' of his integrity recalls him to his rightful position. He lets us know, in short, what his psychological state has been since his soliloquy in act 2, scene 3. All this and more the soliloquy provides. But what has not been seen about the soliloquy is that Edgar here speaks in three voices, and that he slides from his choric to his realistic and finally to his symbolic persona during the course of the speech.

The soliloquy may be divided, in fact, according to these changes in voice and persona. The first six lines (102–7) are purely choric: Edgar comments on the larger significance of the King's plight by addressing his remarks directly to the spectators. His use of the pronouns 'we' and 'our' serves to join, rhetorically, his own experience to that of the outer audience. Both have, after all, been equal parties to the King's crazed delirium. Edgar's 'we' is thus inclusive and general. But in the next six lines

---

[13] Muir, p. 127, notes that Bedlam beggars wore a horn about their necks to put drink in, but he also cites the eighteenth-century editor Steevens: 'Edgar also means that he is unable to play his part any longer.' If we accept these two readings we acknowledge Edgar's three personae.

(108–13), the pronouns change from 'we' and 'our' to 'me' and 'my', signalling a shift into Edgar's 'realistic' persona which is accompanied by a corresponding modification in the tone of his voice: whereas before he spoke in a public and choric voice, he now speaks in a personal and reflective one. Now the magnitude of Lear's madness is applied to Edgar's specific dilemma. Only now does Edgar recognize that 'that which makes me bend makes the King bow' (109) and that Lear has been 'childed as I fathered!' (110). Influenced by the preceding trial, he goes on to use legal terminology (*opinion, just proof, repeal*) to express his hope that he will be given the opportunity to be reconciled with his father.

In these lines, clearly, Edgar remains a character *within* the play; in following his vocal shifts from choric character to realistic participant, we have, as it were, moved with him back into the illusion from his *figurenposition* 'outside' the play. As we might expect, the last stage of our reintegration into the theatrical illusion comes when Edgar reassumes his role as Poor Tom. This shift, too, is signalled by a change in voice. Perhaps Edgar speaks in Tom's mad idiom in saying 'Tom, away!' (110), but not until his final words here may we be certain Edgar has once again become Tom. While the words disturb us, since they abruptly change the tenor of the passage, an auditor will hear and understand that Edgar is once again Tom. 'Lurk, lurk' (115), he says to close the scene. He had, in his previous sequence of comments in act 3, scene 6, dissociated himself from the illusion; he now completes the process of reinvolvement in that illusion.

Despite these shifts in persona, there is an internal consistency to Edgar's character throughout the play. Shakespeare maintains this consistency by linking Edgar's thoughts and actions, even when a scene intervenes between his appearances. Such is the case when we next view Edgar in act 4, scene 1 and feel as if we had never left him. But an event of critical importance occurs in act 3, scene 7 – the blinding of Gloucester – and this action has a certain bearing on our response to Edgar. His brooding speech at the opening of act 4, scene 1 continues the thoughts expressed in the soliloquy that closed act 3, scene 6. It begins with an apparent non-sequitur,

'Yet', whose logical referent may well be his prior soliloquy, and which suggests that he has been brooding over his change in fortune:

> Yet better thus, and known to be contemn'd,
> Than still contemn'd and flatter'd. To be worst,
> The lowest and most dejected thing of fortune,
> Stands still in esperance, lives not in fear.
> The lamentable change is from the best,
> The worst returns to laughter. Welcome then,
> Thou unsubstantial air that I embrace:
> The wretch that thou hast blown unto the worst
> Owes nothing to thy blasts.   (ll. 1–9)

In further developing the topos implicit in the recognition that what 'makes me bend makes the King bow' (3.6.109), Edgar now explicitly associates his state with the fickle operations of fortune. He reasons that it is better to know he is 'contemn'd' than to allow himself to be self-deluded. Here we can discern the same mixture of choric and realistic speech: his lines are both choric *and* personal, and offer, as readers point out, a definition of tragedy based on the *de casibus* theme. When he welcomes the 'unsubstantial air', believing he has withstood fortune's vagaries, however, the lines now belong solely to Edgar's 'realistic' persona.

But we sense that Edgar is rationalizing. And when Gloucester enters, 'poorly led', Edgar absorbs one of the play's many shocks. He has learnt and grown from his suffering thus far, but his dearly bought knowledge is 'followed at once by an experience that explodes it'.[14] Presented with the sight of Gloucester, Edgar realizes the 'worst' may be worse still: 'I am worse than e'er I was' (l. 26), he laments. For the first time since act 2, scene 3, there is a separation between Edgar's and the audience's knowledge. Prior to this point, he has inhabited a privileged perspective with the spectators. They alone are aware mad Tom is Edgar in disguise and the fact grants them a degree of knowledge. But they have witnessed Gloucester's blinding, Edgar has not, and a rift now divides their understanding from Edgar's. Edgar's role as a character standing at a distance from the action now partly merges with his realistic persona, and his

---

[14] Mack, p. 62.

soliloquy on the vagaries of fortune becomes no more than a rationalization. Edgar's cry, 'O gods!' (l. 25), not only recalls Gloucester's three cries in act 3, scene 7 (ll. 35, 70, 92); it also delimits the extent of his ken in calculating the inscrutable ways of the gods in *King Lear*.

Although Edgar's limitations as a choric character make him an unreliable spokesman, there is a corresponding increase in his believability as a character in the play. And even if Edgar's views may now be seen as fallible, he still communicates with the audience through his asides, still maintains, qualified though it now may be, a privileged relationship with them. While Edgar may not, they hear Gloucester's thoughts about Poor Tom and his son (31–5). But Edgar responds as we would want him to Gloucester's despairing judgement that 'As flies to wanton boys are we to th' gods, / They kill us for their sport' (36–7). 'How should this be?' communicates Edgar in aside, and immediately he intuits that to reveal himself to Gloucester would serve no useful purpose: 'Bad is the trade that must play fool to sorrow, / Ang'ring itself and others' (37–9). He offers his father one of Tom's mad blessings: 'Bless thee, master!' (39).

At this point we begin to question Edgar's wisdom in remaining in disguise rather than re-vealing his true identity. Put another way, it is here we question Shakespeare's decision to allow Edgar to continue dissembling rather than to embrace his father. We will do so again when he admits his 'fault' in not revealing himself 'unto him, / Until some half hour past' (5.3.193–4). If he has not heard Gloucester speak about the way 'my son came into my mind' in the storm, Edgar *may* still be guarding his identity from discovery. But the interpretative controversy here hinges on the reason why Edgar feels he 'must' remain in disguise. After repeating the phrase he used twice in responding to Gloucester in act 3, scene 4 ('Poor Tom's a-cold'), Edgar himself seems convinced he 'cannot daub it further' (4.1.52). 'And yet', as he tells us, 'I must' (54), and he again shifts from talking in aside to speaking directly to Gloucester, blessing him a second time: 'Bless thy sweet eyes, they bleed' (54). But why 'must' he? In my view, Edgar here recognizes that

playing the 'fool to sorrow', that is, pandering to his father's despair, will not save the ruined earl. He decides, with the force of his realization that one's burden will be lightened when 'grief hath mates and bearing fellowship', to try to save his father. He decides that to reveal himself would *not* help Gloucester regain *his* self-esteem. Edgar fully re-assumes Tom's voice (56–63) and agrees to lead Gloucester, a man who has not seen because he 'does not feel' (69), to Dover Cliff, from where Gloucester will 'no leading need' (78). Edgar listens in silence as Gloucester gives the lie to his opening words in this scene: 'That I am wretched / Makes thee the happier' (ll. 65–6). But when the madman agrees to take the blind man's arm, he also agrees to take on the task of restoring Gloucester's faith.

3. DOUBLE READINGS: 'IN NOTHING AM I CHANG'D'

In act 4, scene 6, Edgar reveals to the audience that he trifles 'thus with [Gloucester's] despair...to cure it' (ll. 33–4). This aside should clarify, retrospectively, Edgar's earlier decision; for Cavellesque readers who object to Edgar's behaviour in act 4, scene 1, however, this 'cryptic' aside may sound like too little clarification come too late. But as Robert B. Heilman demonstrates,[15] in order to overcome the sin of despair, Gloucester must totally transform his ways of perceiving and understanding the world: he must deny the norms of sensory experience to reawaken his faith and to learn how to 'Bear free and patient thoughts' (4.6.80). As a moral agent, Edgar assists Gloucester in this task; and even though he 'tricks' him, the deception is not meant to harm Gloucester, as Edmund tricked him earlier. 'Trickery' itself is neutral; it gains meaning only with knowledge of the agent's intention. As Harry Levin suggested,[16] however, the molehill scene may

---

[15] *This Great Stage: Image and Structure in King Lear* (Baton Rouge, Louisiana, 1948).

[16] 'The Heights and the Depths: A Scene from *King Lear*', in *Shakespeare and the Revolution of the Times: Perspectives and Commentaries* (New York, 1976), pp. 162–86. Also see Alvin B. Kernan's 'Formalism and Realism in Eliza-bethan Drama: The Miracles in *King Lear*', *Renaissance Drama*, 9 (1966), 59–66.

well involve more than Edgar's educative deception of Gloucester. The audience is also nearly tricked into believing Gloucester has fallen so far down Dover Cliff that 'ten masts at each make not the altitude' he has 'perpendicularly fell' (ll. 53–4).

There is an immense deal of controversy surrounding the effect this scene has, with consensual opinion holding the view that an audience would not believe they were actually at Dover Cliff, about to watch Gloucester's suicide attempt.[17] As Levin points out, however, one thing is certain about the scene: here Shakespeare interweaves an audience's illusionistic assumptions with Gloucester's salvation. In this scene both are blind, after all, if in different ways: Gloucester believes the 'ground is even' (l. 3); given theatrical convention (and Gloucester's ruined eyes), the audience is prepared to accept 'Whatever is said on the subject of immediate place as the setting'[18] and instead *may well* believe Edgar when he tells Gloucester the ground is 'Horrible steep' (l. 3). After he 'falls', Gloucester questions, 'But have I fall'n, or no?' (l. 56); now aware Gloucester has been tricked, the audience knows he has, if only a few feet. But by the time the spectators fully comprehend Edgar's chicanery, Shakespeare has manipulated their expectations a number of times. On the relatively bare apron stage, the illusion must be established at the beginning of each scene, and here Shakespeare plays upon the very idea of an audience's illusionistic expectation. The powerful, 'vertiginous' impression Edgar's speech on the vista before them (ll. 11–24) has had on readers, at least since Samuel Taylor Coleridge's comments, *in fact* creates the illusion of sights and sounds Gloucester's – and the audience's – 'deficient sight' (l. 23) can only visualize:

Come on, sir, here's the place; stand still. How
    fearful
And dizzy 'tis, to cast one's eyes so low!
The crows and choughs that wing the midway air
Show scarce so gross as beetles. Half way down
Hangs one that gathers sampire, dreadful trade!
Methinks he seems no bigger than his head.
The fishermen that walk upon the beach
Appear like mice; and yond tall anchoring bark,
Diminish'd to her cock; her cock, a buoy

Almost too small for sight. The murmuring surge,
That on th' unnumb'red idle pebble chafes,
Cannot be heard so high. I'll look no more,
Lest my brain turn, and the deficient sight
Topple down headlong.

The pains Shakespeare takes to create the illusion of Dover Cliff have made many readers doubt whether they ever knew Edgar's intention.[19]

As critical testimony bears out, there are two possible responses to these events. If we do not sense Edgar's true purpose here, we are willing to believe we are on Dover Cliff. On the other hand, if we sense that Edgar intends to trick Gloucester as a way of saving him from despair, we go along with the deception. But it seems to me that the truth of the matter probably lies somewhere in between: individual audience members may feel one way or the other, but the majority of them find themselves moving between their illusionistic assumptions and their non-illusionistic knowledge. In this scene spectators participate in the programme of Gloucester's renewal, a process involving the denial of his accustomed ways of perceiving the world, and they do so in a way that places them in a position similar to Gloucester's. Indeed, the most revealing aspect of the scene could well be the realization that Shakespeare is consciously manipulating audience expectation.

The 'theatrical multi-consciousness' required here corresponds not only to different illusionistic and non-illusionistic affects in the theatre but also to the *figurenposition* implicit in Edgar's realistic and metadramatic personae. When Gloucester tells

---

[17] Alan C. Dessen argues that the 'fictional nature of the plummet from the cliff would be obvious to the audience' in 'Two Falls and a Trap', *English Literary Renaissance*, 5 (1975), 291–307; p. 303. Among other recent responses, see Derek Peat, '"And that's True too", *King Lear* and the Tension of Uncertainty', *Shakespeare Survey 33* (Cambridge, 1980), pp. 43–53; and James Black, '*King Lear*: Art Upside Down', *Shakespeare Survey 33*, pp. 35–42.

[18] Levin, p. 176.

[19] Stephen Booth, in '*King Lear*', comments that this description provides the most perfectly realized (imaginary) description of setting to be found in the play; see p. 165, n. 25. Booth's study, which appeared after this essay was written, complements my analysis in many respects.

Edgar, now dressed as a peasant, 'Methinks thy voice is alter'd, and thou speak'st / In better phrase and matter than thou didst' (ll. 7–8), an auditor is uncertain how to respond. Shakespeare has Edgar speak in blank verse, as opposed to his earlier prosaic language, to indicate his 'alter'd' voice. But Edgar, speaking *in* blank verse, immediately tells Gloucester 'Y' are much deceived. In nothing am I chang'd / But in my garments' (8–9). 'Edgar I nothing am' indeed. Gloucester here persists, 'Methinks y' are better spoken' (10), but to no avail.

The exchange raises two different sets of questions about Edgar's vocal shifts throughout the play. One set is related to Edgar's role *within* the illusion. A second set is involved with the relationship between his realistic and choric personae. The most glaring modification in Edgar's voice in the play comes when he adopts a 'Somersetshire' dialect at the end of this scene, but he may also speak in slightly altered voice when he appears to challenge Edmund in act 5, scene 3. These are but two examples, however. In fact, Edgar speaks with different inflection not only in these two instances, but also in his 'dispositions' as Poor Tom, as a peasant, and as the man who tells Gloucester his 'life's a miracle' (l. 55) after the supposed fall from the cliff. His is indeed a demanding theatrical role, perhaps the most difficult role to perform in the play. Only at the play's beginning and end can it be said he uses Edgar's 'true' voice, and even in this case the naive dupe of the play's opening has matured sufficiently to allow him to 'speak what we feel' at its close.[20]

These vocal changes are tied to Edgar's disguises and mark stages in his attempt to regain his true identity. They are recognizable in the text, and they occur within the illusion. But what of the less noticeable vocal shifts from his realistic to his choric persona? Quite apart from the questions raised by his changes within the illusion, Edgar's two personae also raise the issue of multiple meaning in his language. All good readers of Shakespeare are sensitive to and possess the ability to discern multiple meanings in language. But readers of a play do not often have the ability to link these meanings to an actor's performance or to an audience's 'multi-consciousness'. We teach students the way we

believe a line ought to be read, thereby 'fixing' its meaning, but all too often a performance of the play gives the lie to our surmises or makes us see there is more (or less) in the line than we originally thought. Such is the case with Edgar's response to Gloucester in 4.6.9–10. 'Y' are much deceiv'd', he tells Gloucester. But in what sense is Gloucester deceived? In a primary sense, Edgar instructs his father that he is wrong to think his voice has changed. Gloucester still believes, and the audience knows, differently. Although that audience may have to wait to be certain, they will discover that Gloucester has been correct three times: he is right in saying the ground is level, that he does not hear the sea, and that Edgar's speech is altered. But he is also 'much deceiv'd' in three roughly corresponding senses: his son is duping him as to his real identity, is duping Gloucester's ability to feel and hear, and is drawing attention to Gloucester's defective ways of perceiving the world. The line points in many directions at the same time: Gloucester has been self-deceived; Edgar is here deceiving him further; and the audience, whether it recognizes it or not, is a witness to deception.

Edgar's next words clarify the relationship between his multiple meanings and his different personae. As a character who shares a privileged perspective *with the spectators*, Edgar tells Gloucester he has not 'chang'd' in any way except 'in his garments'. Despite the apparent transformations in his state, he still remains Edgar, son of Gloucester. He plays upon the meaning of 'change' as indicating a modification in voice or tone *and* an alteration in condition, but his father cannot understand the line in both of these senses because of the deception. He must interpret it as a denial of his statement that Edgar's voice seems to have 'alter'd', and he responds by repeating his observation: 'Methinks

---

[20] See William R. Elton's perceptive comments in *King Lear and the Gods* (San Marino, California, 1966), p. 84n, where he relates these disguises to Edgar's quest for identity. Also consult Thomas F. Van Laan's 'Acting as Action in *King Lear*', pp. 72–3, and F. T. Flahiff's 'Edgar: Once and Future King', pp. 222–37, in Rosalie L. Colie and F. T. Flahiff, eds., *Some Facets of 'King Lear': Essays in Prismatic Criticism* (Toronto, 1974).

y' are better spoken.' Edgar's true identity as an earl's son has surfaced, if only for a moment, and Gloucester has noticed it. But spectators have a greater task here. To understand fully the dynamics of the exchange, an audience must not only attend to the immediate illusionistic context but also recall their prior, privileged knowledge. By using a line syntactically similar to the last line in Edgar's soliloquy in act 2, scene 3, Shakespeare at least assists them in their interpretative task: 'In nothing am I chang'd / But in my garments,' says Edgar, referring first to his change in dress and secondly to his unchanged identity. As Edgar exorcizes the spectre of Poor Tom and calls Gloucester 'thou happy father', we again attend to his words with the double awareness that he speaks of Gloucester as a fortunate old man the gods have preserved *and* as his natural parent.

4. MULTIPLE SHOCKS: 'SPEAK WHAT WE FEEL'

In convincing Gloucester that 'Thy life's a miracle' and in encouraging him to 'Bear free and patient thoughts', Edgar succeeds in restoring Gloucester's faith and sounds the note of romance that pervades the play's fourth act. We all feel, at this point, that all will be well. Immediately, we, Gloucester, and Edgar absorb another shock, the 'side-piercing sight' of Lear, '*crowned with weeds and flowers*'. Edgar will relate to the audience his own assessment of Lear's and Gloucester's meeting: 'I would not take this from report; it is, / And my heart breaks at it' (ll. 141–2). And he will tell us further that Lear's ravings mix 'matter and impertinency...Reason in madness' (ll. 174–5). But even after this scene of recognition we assume all may be well, since we see Edgar take his first decisive action by killing Oswald with a cudgel. Events in the play seem to show, as Albany comments when he learns about Cornwall's death,

> you are above,
> You justicers, that these our nether crimes
> So speedily can venge! (4.2.78–80)

And Edgar himself seems to have reached a plateau of understanding. Gloucester asks him 'what are

you?' (4.6.220).[21] In his reply, Edgar again lies to Gloucester about his identity, but he does so in a revealing way. In lines full of precipitates from earlier speeches ('a most poor man', 'fortune's blows') that now crystallize in his humble and mature awareness of his own 'possibilities', Edgar identifies himself as a man who has learned from the 'known and feeling sorrows' he has endured, and who is capable, above all, of empathy:

> A most poor man, made tame to fortune's blows,
> Who, by the art of known and feeling sorrows,
> Am pregnant to good pity. (4.6.221–3)

Oswald intervenes, but is quickly disposed of; and there is hope, when Edgar again takes Gloucester by the hand (4.6.284), that the virtuous characters in *King Lear* will thrive. Indeed, Lear's awakening in Cordelia's presence does nothing to change our feeling. All the virtuous characters have suffered and endured, and Lear's request to Cordelia to 'bear with me. / Pray you now forget, and forgive; I am old and foolish' (4.7.82–3) again sounds the note of romance. Even Nahum Tate would have been satisfied with *King Lear* had it maintained this mode. But the play has many further shocks in store. To this point, the experience of an audience has closely paralleled Edgar's experience throughout the play.[22] It has held on to his perspective and gone through what he has gone through. But it is also true, as Maynard Mack reasons, that 'three times' in the play 'a formula summarizing Edgar's present stage of learning is presented...only to be followed at once with an experience that explodes it':

He [Edgar] observes that to be mad Tom is to be at Fortune's nadir with no change possible except for the better, then meets his blinded father and knows 'I am worse than e'er I was.' He heals his father's despair at Dover Cliff, but finds him after the battle 'in ill thoughts again' and ready to 'rot' where he is. He pronounces judgment on his brother and on his father's act in begetting him, in full confidence, as we

---

[21] In asking the question, Gloucester echoes the similar question he asked Poor Tom in 3.4. Cf. Elton, pp. 84–8.

[22] See F. D. Hoeniger, 'The Artist Exploring the Primitive: *King Lear*', pp. 95–7, in Colie and Flahiff, eds., *Some Facets of 'King Lear'*.

have heard him say, that 'The gods are just,' only to learn in a few moments that Cordelia has been hanged at the order of that brother and under the countenance of those gods.[23]

As we have seen, in the first of these cases the audience is aware of Gloucester's blinding, while Edgar is not, and this fact separates its experience from his. But the shocks that come to Edgar after this point are shocks for everyone present, especially those who believe 'The gods are just' in *King Lear*. Edgar's career in the final act and one-half of the play thus parallels the audience's; he has taken them by the hand as well, and the sheer number of lines he has in the play only suggests his large role in guiding that response.

To be sure, there are other characters whose experience we share in *King Lear*. Kent immediately comes to mind. He explained to the spectators the purpose of his disguise in act 1, scene 4, and throughout the storm scenes we are aware he too is in disguise. But we do not get so personally involved with Kent as we do with Edgar. Although the two characters perform complementary roles in the Lear and Gloucester plots, there are important differences between them. Kent belongs to the symbolic Lear plot but acts concretely; Edgar belongs to the concrete Gloucester plot but functions symbolically as Poor Tom in the Lear plot. Kent represents the norms of manhood and service in the play; Edgar contributes to the play's use of clothing imagery and, in his external condition as Tom, parallels Lear's internal condition. It is Edgar, however, who also establishes much of the play's tone, Edgar who serves as the play's choric voice, Edgar whose experience we emulate in viewing the play. We are, in fact, even closer to Edgar than to Lear, who seldom responds to anyone (thereby increasing our sense of his isolation) and whose towering presence removes him from us. His tragedy is the one we must learn about, but it is Edgar who teaches us the way we should react.

Because we share so much of Edgar's perspective, however, we (and especially those readers Cavell has influenced) often find him wanting. We will not forgive him for being a less than perfect *raisonneur*,

forgetting to realize that he is himself learning and growing during the play and that his choric speeches are only *provisional* judgements on the significance of the action. We do not forgive his 'fault' in waiting until the last moment to reveal his true identity to Gloucester, when, hearing the truth, Gloucester's 'flaw'd heart... / 'Twixt two extremes of passion, joy and grief, / Burst smilingly' – even though Edgar tells us that he did save Gloucester 'from despair' (5.3.197–9; 192). We go through the play blaming him for not revealing himself and then hear what happens when he does. If Edgar and Cordelia had behaved differently, so the reasoning goes, this would not be the outcome.

These are impressionistic responses to the imagined moral efficacy of Edgar's revealing himself to his father. As such, they bear little weight. But the feeling that lies behind this impressionism may be more valid. *King Lear* demands an affective response from its audience; as Michael Goldman perceived, Shakespeare pushes our response to extremes at the end of the play.[24]

Readers who continue to fault Edgar and Cordelia for their actions are in error, but their response is understandable, as Samuel Johnson's well-known testimony makes abundantly clear.[25] Such a response

23 Mack, p. 62.
24 See *Shakespeare and the Energies of Drama* (Princeton, NJ, 1972), pp. 94 ff. Also see Booth, p. 57, on Edgar's decision not to reveal himself and on what happens when he does.
25 '...Shakespeare has suffered the virtue of Cordelia to suffer in a just cause, contrary to the natural ideas of justice, to the hope of the reader, and what is yet more strange, to the faith of chronicles....A play in which the wicked prosper, and the virtuous miscarry, may doubtless be good, because it is a just representation of the common events of human life; but since all reasonable beings naturally love justice, I cannot easily be persuaded, that the observation of justice makes a play worse; or, that if the other excellencies are equal, the audience will not always rise better pleased from the final triumph of persecuted virtue.
In the present case the public has decided. Cordelia, from the time of Tate, has always retired with victory and felicity. And, if my sensations could add anything to the general suffrage, I might relate, that I was many years ago shocked by Cordelia's death, that I know not whether I ever endured to read again the last scenes of the play until I undertook to revise them as an editor.' *Johnson on*

is understandable because it touches, subliminally, upon the most disturbing psychological fact about *King Lear*, the death of Cordelia. If there is a psychological truth about the play, it is that the experience of reading or viewing *Lear* is an unsettling, even distressing one. What occurs in the final scene indeed confounds 'the hope of the reader'. Such an affective response as Samuel Johnson's may miss the mark by expressing what one would have liked to happen, but it does aim at the heart of the matter. It may also partly explain the impetus behind, and the tremendous 200-year success enjoyed by, Nahum Tate's rewritten version, in which Lear lives to an even older age and in which Edgar and Cordelia marry and live happily ever after. To different degrees, Cavell, Johnson, and Tate have each imaginatively rewritten the play, in the hope that its 'shocks' might be softened, better endured.

But Edgar is not responsible for the play's most shocking event. He, Kent, and Albany constitute an on-stage audience less aware of what may occur to Lear and Cordelia than are the spectators in the theatre. Throughout act 5, scene 3, their privileged knowledge has granted them some measure of equanimity; this time, however, the greatest source of their anxiety derives from the privileged knowledge they once again possess. This knowledge they share not with Edgar but with the villainous Edmund; and it is Shakespeare's intention here to return the source of our privileged knowledge to Edmund, as was the case at the play's opening. They know Edmund has sent the Captain to do 'man's work' (l. 39), in some unspecified manner to dispatch Cordelia and, they must suppose, Lear. They may watch and applaud the way Edgar regains his lost name and title ('My name is Edgar', l. 170) and feel that the creaking and groaning wheel of justice and fortune 'is come full circle' (175) when Edmund is mortally wounded. But they must surely be put on edge when a Gentleman enters '*with a bloody knife*' crying 'Help, help! O, help!' (222). Edgar again responds as we would want him, asking 'What kind of help?' (222), but this time he lacks the knowledge to help. The audience is on its own. 'What means this bloody knife?' (224) demands

Edgar, the appropriate character to voice the question everyone on stage, and especially off stage, has on his lips. ''Tis hot, it smokes, / It came even from the heart of – O, she's dead!' (225–6), answers the Gentleman. The referent of 'she's' is ambiguous, and may well be a deliberate obfuscation on Shakespeare's part. 'Who dead? Speak, man,' asks Albany, increasing the anxiety of everyone present, but especially the spectator's, since the on-stage audience has simply 'forgot' (236) about Lear and Cordelia. But it is only the deaths of Goneril and Regan, not Cordelia, and we may all settle back. For a moment. The pacing here reveals Shakespeare at his finest, with lulls leading to frenzies as a result of the dextrous manipulation of the audience.[26]

All may yet be well. This 'judgment of the heavens' (232) is a reassuring one, and we greet Kent's arrival with composure. But once again, in keeping with the scene's – and the play's – alternating reassuring and tension-creating moments, our response is quickened. Edmund makes fully clear that the Captain has been sent

> To hang Cordelia in the prison, and
> To lay the blame upon her own despair,
> That she fordid herself.   (ll. 254–6)

We are all too familiar with what follows. Albany's hope that 'The gods defend her' (257) is devastatingly undercut by Lear's entrance with Cordelia in his arms; his lines only cruelly serve to cue Lear's entry. Our sustaining props throughout the play,

Shakespeare, ed. Arthur Sherbo, 2 vols., vols. 7 and 8 of the Yale Edition of the Works of Samuel Johnson (New Haven, 1968), vol. 8, p. 704. See Stephen Booth, '*King Lear*', pp. 5–6, 56–7, for a view similar to my own.

26 See William H. Matchett, 'Some Dramatic Techniques in *King Lear*', in McGuire and Samuelson, pp. 185–208. Matchett also writes of the way Shakespeare keeps us 'off balance' by manipulating 'audience responses' and by building that response around the 'rhythms of suspense and hope'. Stephen Booth, p. 10, comments that 'Edgar's questions are our questions.' Also see pp. 10, 11, 46 for relevant comments on Edgar and the 'affect' of *King Lear*. See Richard Fly, *Shakespeare's Mediated World* (Amherst, Massachusetts, 1976), pp. 90–1, 97–9 for a different view; and Nicholas Brooke, *Shakespeare: King Lear*, Studies in English Literature, 15 (1963), for an earlier opinion on Shakespeare's manipulation of the audience.

Kent and Edgar, are as helpless as we are, and only guide us to see these events as 'the promis'd end' or 'image of that horror' (264–5). There has been justice, but it has not, as it often is not, been equitable; and we realize that the gods have all along stood by simply waiting while Lear's tragic choices have brought on tragic consequences.

But it is correct that we return to Edgar in the play's last speech (provided that we follow the Folio text). Throughout act 5, scene 3, the audience has been separated from him, but it is fitting that the spectators, on and off stage, now share his mature vision. We may have blamed him for not guiding our response earlier, but in these lines he speaks yet again what we all feel:[27]

> The weight of this sad time we must obey,
> Speak what we feel, not what we ought to say.
> The oldest hath borne most; we that are young
> Shall never see so much, nor live so long.
>
> (ll. 324–7)

The new king's formal couplets and rhetoric do not disguise the intent of this speech by our voice of 'feeling' in the play. Edgar has helped us bear the 'weight of this sad time'. We may have blamed him for not knowing what was about to happen, but he has been as helpless and human as we have. Edgar's 'we' embraces everyone both within and without the play and is pointedly spoken to all. His realistic and choric voices are now one. His humane perspective is all the more affecting because of his *figuren-position* in *King Lear*. Reader and spectator, literary critic and theatrical interpreter, have been led to this point. Our knowledge of a character's *figurenposition* can help us link language, staging, and 'affect' in Renaissance drama.

---

[27] See Mack, p. 63; and Sheldon P. Zitner, '*King Lear* and its Languages', in Colie and Flahiff, eds., *Some Facets of 'King Lear'*, pp. 3–5, for further comment on Edgar's final speech and on the different 'languages' in *King Lear*. Also see Zitner, pp. 9–10, 16, 20, 21, for perceptive statements on other speeches by Edgar.

'VERY LIKE A WHALE': SCEPTICISM AND SEEING IN 'THE TEMPEST'

ROBERT B. PIERCE

Even among Shakespeare's plays *The Tempest* inspires an unusual amount of confusion and multiple interpretation. Mark Van Doren finds his way through all the commentary to a less than helpful conclusion: 'Any set of symbols, moved close to this play, lights up as in an electric field. Its meaning, in other words, is precisely as rich as the human mind, and it says that the world is what it is.'[1] Rather than offer still another reading, I want to look at the confusion as a phenomenon in the play itself, though some implications about meaning are likely to emerge despite my self-restraint.

One might consider the difficulty of *The Tempest* a non-problem, invented by modern hyper-ingenuity, but after all our difficulties of understanding are shared by the characters in the play. On looking from the critics back to the text, we may recognize ourselves in Prospero's diagnosis of Alonso's state: 'thy brains, / Now useless, boil'd within thy skull!'[2] Alonso is not alone. Repeatedly characters do not know what to make of what they see, and when they think they understand something, they are frequently wrong. In the Renaissance the *locus classicus* for analysing this kind of confusion in human affairs is Montaigne's *Apology for Raymond Sebond*, and it is a truism of modern criticism that Montaigne is one of the inspiring figures behind *The Tempest*.[3] In one of the grand passages of the *Apology*, Montaigne sums up his scepticism: 'In few, there is no constant existence, neither of our being, nor of the objects. And we, and our judgement, and all mortall things else do uncessantly rowle, turne, and passe away. Thus can nothing be certainly established, nor of the one, nor of the other; both the judgeing and the judged being in continuall alteration and motion.'[4]

Surely it is legitimate to see in *The Tempest* an expression of scepticism. One can apply the term either in the specific epistemological sense of the doubtfulness of human knowledge, not even knowing how much and how certainly we do know, or in a broader sense – doubting political enterprises, the trustworthiness of youthful exuberance, the power and virtue of magic, etc. But to grant the importance of scepticism in the play is to leave many questions unanswered, since scepticism is not one thing. Montaigne himself is capable of many different sceptical stances, from the detached *contemptus mundi* of the passage quoted, to the rigorous Pyrrhonism in his analysis of perception, and to the playfulness of another section: 'When I am playing with my Cat, who knowes whether she have more sport in dallying with me, than I have in gaming with her? We entertain one another with mutuall apish tricks. If I have my houre to begin or refuse, so hath she hers.'[5] Though it is part of an attack on human presumption, this passage is also an intellectual game, asking us to see simultaneously like the man and like the cat.

---

1 Mark Van Doren, *Shakespeare* (New York, 1939), p. 323.

2 *The Tempest*, ed. Frank Kermode, new Arden Shakespeare (London and Cambridge, Mass., 1954), 5.1.59–60). All quotations are from Kermode's edition and will be cited in the text.

3 For detailed consideration of Montaigne's influence, see John M. Robertson, *Montaigne and Shakespeare* (1909), and Kermode, pp. xxxiv–xxxviii. For a useful caution see Margaret T. Hodgen, 'Montaigne and Shakespeare Again', *Huntington Library Quarterly*, 16 (1952), 23–42.

4 'An Apologie of Raymond Sebond', *The Essays of Montaigne Done into English By John Florio*, Tudor Translations, 2 (1893), p. 329.

5 Montaigne, p. 144.

The Tempest is full of the difficulties of seeing, difficulties both in the thing seen and in the seer. At the beginning of the play we watch a shipwreck, which we recognize by all the conventions of Elizabethan drama, whatever the precise details of the staging. There is nothing in the text as we have it to suggest any doubt about what we are seeing, no visibly presiding Ariel nor any other deliberate undercutting of the realism. Indeed Shakespeare seems to have gone to some trouble to get his nautical atmosphere right, and the brief first scene is marvellously evocative as well as terminologically exact.

The second scene makes a striking transition in mood, form, and kind of reality, but at first nothing asks us to change our perception of what we have just seen. We share Miranda's perspective, partly because her language gives splendid expression to a natural human response to the shipwreck. But one phrase contrasts her view with ours: 'a brave vessel, / Who had, no doubt, some noble creature in her' (1.2.6–7). Coleridge remarks that only Miranda could have said that.[6] She is not only a creature to be wondered at, but also one full of wonder. Inevitably our cynical worldliness remembers the less than noble voices of the opening scene, but we later discover that Miranda is in a sense right: Ferdinand was aboard that ship.

Prospero then undertakes to correct Miranda's vision of the shipwreck (and thus ours):

> Wipe thou thine eyes; have comfort.
> The direful spectacle of the wrack, which touch'd
> The very virtue of compassion in thee,
> I have with such provision in mine Art
> So safely ordered, that there is no soul –
> No, not so much perdition as an hair
> Betid to any creature in the vessel
> Which thou heard'st cry, which thou saw'st sink.
>
> (ll. 25–32)

In the characteristically spare, packed poetic language of this play, Prospero's words express a mysterious calm that we are to find dominant in him. The syntax is remarkably twisted, yet ordered in a grand chiasmus, and each word carries an exact meaning and place. The speech heals Miranda's perception and ours, as much by its graceful music

as by what it says. Indeed the music helps to authenticate the claim to magical control.

Thus our original perception of the shipwreck is utterly gone, replaced by a new and equally sharp, compelling picture. In its very clarity it is disorienting, part of a larger confusion as we locate ourselves on this island of poetry and magic, where attention and comprehension demand a constant intellectual and imaginative strain. It is as though we were asked to attend to objects at the periphery of our vision instead of those on which our eyes were focused.

The play itself uses this theme of difficult perception and strange perspective. Prospero asks Miranda to think back to the limits of her memory, to images 'rather like a dream than an assurance' (l. 45). In his evocative phrase this past is 'in the dark backward and abysm of time' (l. 50). We may recall with a jolt that the remote land evoked is Italy, the real world, our world, as opposed to the magic realm of the island. In *The Tempest* the ordinary is remote, in contrast with the dreamlike clarity of the island.

Prospero is himself recalling the same past, and the recollection is painful to him. His speech acquires a tangled, abrupt syntax (see, for example, ll. 66–78) as he recalls his brother's treachery, and so we learn that the ordered calm of his earlier speeches is a precariously earned achievement. One function of the repeated questions to Miranda is to express this not-quite-conquered passion in him, though the strain on Miranda of hearing and absorbing his narration should also be apparent. She has been pushed to the limits of her perception and held there, and she has to undergo a complete reconception of herself, not just the daughter of a devoted and scholarly recluse, but a princess and also a victim of betrayal. The sleep into which she falls at the end of the narration is of course magical, a product of Prospero's art, but it is also a natural outcome of the strain expressed in a phrase like 'For still 'tis beating in my mind' (l. 176).

When Ariel appears, we get one more re-vision of the shipwreck:

---

6 Collier report of lecture, *Coleridge's Shakespearean Criticism*, ed. T. M. Raysor, 2 vols. (1930), vol. 2, p. 172.

I boarded the king's ship; now on the beak,
Now in the waist, the deck, in every cabin,
I flam'd amazement: sometime I'd divide,
And burn in many places; on the topmast,
The yards and boresprit, would I flame distinctly,
Then meet and join. Jove's lightnings, the
    precursors
O' th' dreadful thunder-claps, more momentary
And sight-outrunning were not: the fire and cracks
Of sulphurous roaring the most mighty Neptune
Seem to besiege, and make his bold waves tremble,
Yea, his dread trident shake.   (ll. 196–206)

Ariel is the agent of Prospero's art, and he makes the shipwreck his pageant, tagging each effect like a presenter full of the pride of his craft. Yet at the same time he pulls us back to the full imaginative force of the storm. It is not coincidental that the language reminds us of Lear's in the storm scenes. Our imagination responds once more to the art of the storm-painting even while we admire its artfulness. Prospero might almost be describing us: 'Who was so firm, so constant, that this coil / Would not infect his reason?' (ll. 207–8).

    Thus the opening of *The Tempest* is a virtuoso piece of different seeings, all of which we are asked imaginatively to share. We see a shipwreck for ourselves and then share that seeing with Miranda, but her perception is full of her own innocence, pity, and wonder, qualities that continue undiluted even while she has to invert her understanding of the shipwreck. Prospero is set apart from both her and us, with a stable, privileged view as the artist of the shipwreck. Then both Miranda and Prospero look to the past, which is our world, in contrast with the magic world of the island. To Miranda that past is almost unattainably distant, and her recollection of it is untainted by evil. Prospero sees the darkness that we are used to, the world of politics and betrayal, and even his calm and self-control are swayed by what he recalls. In this scene of perception and recollection, we are asked to participate in both the innocent and the wisely disillusioned vision, and then perhaps even to see with something of Ariel's aloof, slightly amused perspective.

    The pattern of shifting perception runs through the whole play, as appears with special interest in Ferdinand. After glancing at a silent and rather anonymous Ferdinand in act 1, scene 1, we hear of him in Ariel's amused report of his frantic response, the outcry giving still another interpretation of the shipwreck:

        The King's son, Ferdinand,
With hair up-staring, – then like reeds, not hair, –
Was the first man that leap'd; cried, 'Hell is empty,
And all the devils are here.'   (1.2.212–15)

Later Ariel leads him on stage, his frenzy subdued into grief, 'Weeping again the King my father's wrack' (1.2.393), but both the grief and the storm are transformed by Ariel's music. Ariel's second song invites him to envision his father's death by water:

    Full fadom five thy father lies;
        Of his bones are coral made;
    Those are pearls that were his eyes:
        Nothing of him that doth fade,
    But doth suffer a sea-change
        Into something rich and strange.

                  (ll. 399–404)

The description takes the form of a metamorphosis, a pattern that Shakespeare like many Renaissance writers draws from his beloved author Ovid. Ovidian metamorphosis embodies a sense of lost identity, but with two different possible implications: descent into a lower form, as in transformation into a plant or animal like Narcissus or Daphne, a stone like Niobe, or air like Echo; and ascent – stellification or even apotheosis. Ariel's song has Ferdinand imagine his father's death as a strange, grotesque transformation, clearly in the regressive pattern despite its haunting beauty.

    We later learn (as, presumably, does Ferdinand) that the opposite sense of metamorphosis is finally true. As Alonso descends into a madness that will turn out to be healing, his imagery echoes the picture that Ariel has evoked:

    O, it is monstrous, monstrous!
Methought the billows spoke, and told me of it;
The winds did sing it to me; and the thunder,
That deep and dreadful organ-pipe, pronounc'd
The name of Prosper: it did bass my trespass.
Therefor my son i' th' ooze is bedded; and
I'll seek him deeper than e'er plummet sounded,
And with him there lie mudded.   (3.3.95–102)

In his guilt he can imagine only the hostile, transforming sea with its staining and clasping mud at the bottom. Purged by his madness, however, Alonso becomes a new man, one who sees the world anew so that the words 'strange' and 'strangely' echo through his last speeches.

Father and son are separated from each other by Prospero's art, the one to be purged of guilt and the other to be altered in a subtler way, into new seeing. We first understand the goal of his transformation in Miranda herself, as she sees under her father's guidance, with both a literal and a figurative seeing: 'The fringed curtains of thine eye advance, / And say what thou seest yond' (1.2.411–12). What she sees is of course Ferdinand, and she perceives him as a spirit, a god, above all a creature superlatively noble. And Ferdinand's address to her shows how far he shares her kind of seeing:

> Most sure the goddess
> On whom these airs attend! Vouchsafe my prayer
> May know if you remain upon this island;
> And that you will some good instruction give
> How I may bear me here: my prime request,
> Which I do last pronounce, is, O you wonder!
> If you be maid or no? (ll. 424–30)

What can we infer from this speech? First, 'they have changed eyes': their love at first sight means by all the conventions of romantic comedy that she is to be his wife. Second, he intuitively knows Miranda's name in his very ignorance ('O you wonder!'), in the same sense as Florizel knows Perdita's nobility and Bassanio knows that Portia's image is in the leaden casket. Finally, he takes Miranda for a goddess, as she has taken him for a god.

Surely Shakespeare is imitating a famous incident in the *Aeneid*. Aeneas, like Ferdinand, has survived a sea voyage and a storm. He encounters a virgin huntress of extraordinary beauty and dignity, whom he addresses as a goddess: 'O dea certe!' In fact he is right: it is his mother, Venus, as he later recognizes:

> Thus having said, she turn'd, and made appear
> Her neck refulgent, and dishevel'd hair,
> Which, flowing from her shoulders, reach'd the
> ground,

> And widely spread ambrosial scents around:
> In length of train descends her sweeping gown;
> And by her graceful walk, the Queen of Love is
> known.[7]

Ferdinand, removed from everything ordinary on this magic island, stripped of family and friends, interprets Miranda as a goddess. Aeneas was right in his intuition. In Shakespeare's scene we may be amused at the young lovers' tendency to idolize each other, but in a sense Ferdinand is right too. Miranda is the supreme wonder of the island, and his immediate perception of that indicates his nobility, the nobility that Miranda has seen with her innocent clarity.

At the same time there is a difference between Miranda's swift, spontaneous utterance and Ferdinand's ornate formality, which verges on courtly gallantry. After all, there is something of a drop from his awed address to the blunt practicality of his 'prime request'. Ferdinand's vision has to be purged before he can see her fully, for reasons suggested in a later speech, his response to actually learning her name:

> Admir'd Miranda!
> Indeed the top of admiration! worth
> What's dearest to the world! Full many a lady
> I have ey'd with best regard, and many a time
> Th' harmony of their tongues hath into bondage
> Brought my too diligent ear: for several virtues
> Have I lik'd several women; never any
> With so full soul, but some defect in her
> Did quarrel with the noblest grace she ow'd,
> And put it to the foil: but you, O you,
> So perfect and so peerless, are created
> Of every creature's best! (3.1.37–48)

Ferdinand is sophisticated in both the good and bad senses of the word. He has known and lived in the Italian world, which provides the foil[8] to his perception of Miranda's uniqueness. This connoisseur of 'several virtues' has now encountered complete virtue and so must learn the transcendent meanings

---

[7] *Aeneid*, 1.556–61, *The Poetical Works of Dryden*, ed. George R. Noyes, 2nd edn. (Boston, 1950), p. 529.

[8] See Kermode's note at 3.1.46 on the implications of the word 'foil'.

of the conventional language of love: the images of financial value, harmony, bondage, grace, and divinity.

Impelled by his love for Miranda and guided by Prospero's educative plan, Ferdinand learns to see himself and the world around him anew, in the terms of these images. He sees himself by his father's supposed death as a king, one without realm or wealth. Almost immediately he takes on a literal bondage, Caliban's role as log-bearer. In place of the harmony of ladies' voices, he attends to Ariel's songs and the simple grace of Miranda's speech. And he learns how genuinely he must surrender his autonomy, accepting the seeming harshness of Prospero's control. Prospero both completes and honours Ferdinand's transformed vision by placing him and Miranda together as the audience for his marriage masque. With the 'blind boy' Cupid banished, the love of Ferdinand and Miranda is a match of untainted seeing.

One could trace the motif of different seeings through the other characters, but the pattern is clear enough without elaboration. Gonzalo sees a different island from Antonio and Sebastian; even their garments look different to him and to them. Trinculo and Stephano, confronted by Caliban, cannot decide what to make of him. They keep trying out different interpretations, which have in common seeing him as a potentially valuable commodity. Caliban when he looks at Prospero sees a Caliban given great power, and in Miranda he sees only a mate.

Thus the play encourages a sceptical sense of the varieties of perception, but the variety is not merely random. Whatever puzzlement there may be in what Prospero, Miranda, and Ferdinand think they see, the base and wicked characters are clearly and consistently wrong. What they see as a banquet is actually a punishment that drives them mad, and what the comic plotters see as rich garments are bait in Prospero's trap. With all our doubts, we know that they misperceive and especially that they flatten things out: they see without wonder – Miranda's vision – and without resignation – Prospero's.

Having looked at the characters' perceptions, we need to consider our own perceptions of them; it is by no means clear just what we see when we look at Prospero and Miranda. Prospero is especially difficult to interpret. Just to pose two among many questions, is he irascible, like the conventional stage magician, or has he attained the calm self-control of the philosophical mage? And is he a wronged man bent on vengeance so that he must learn detachment from his servant Ariel, or is he consistently benevolent and merciful?

Ferdinand and Miranda themselves struggle with those questions of definition and self-definition. Prospero casts himself in the stock comic role of the resistant father, like Egeus in *A Midsummer Night's Dream* and Old Capulet in *Romeo and Juliet*. Antiochus in *Pericles* is a monstrous version of the same role. But another father in *Pericles*, Simonides, plays the part of the resistant father as a trick before he gives his endorsement to the marriage of Pericles and Thaisa. Prospero is of course a deceiver in Simonides' vein, and he teaches Miranda and Ferdinand to see him as a generous father like Simonides, one who gives them to each other. But there is truth in the pose as well, the psychological truth of how painful it is for a father to renounce his claim on his daughter when she marries. Again there is truth in Prospero's deception of Alonso mourning his supposedly dead son: 'I / Have lost my daughter' (5.1.147–8). For the restoration of harmony to go on, both must renounce the primary love of their children. The benevolence of Prospero's intentions toward Ferdinand and Miranda seems unambiguous, but we can only guess at his exact mixture of grief and joy.

If critics split over a benevolent or angry Prospero in his attitude toward the plotters, the material for their disagreement is in the play, indeed in act 1, scene 2, and it reappears in act 4, scene 1. The magical masque of nuptial harmony is broken by his starting suddenly and recalling Caliban's conspiracy. When his visible anger moves Ferdinand and Miranda, he apologizes and offers a speech of consolation, 'Our revels now are ended' (ll. 148 ff.). Frank Kermode is puzzled by the anger, half-heartedly suggesting a structural reason: 'The apparently unnecessary perturbation of Prospero at the thought of Caliban may be a point at which an oddly pedantic concern for classical structure causes it to force its way through the surface of the play.'[9] But Prospero's vexation is not all that implausible. The harmony for which he has worked so hard and renounced so much is not after all complete. Some of his anger at Caliban may be transferred from the pain of renunciation, but it is also direct, its power implicit in his later remark about Caliban: 'this thing of darkness I / Acknowledge mine' (5.1.275–6). He is angry and dismayed, not because he cannot control Caliban, but because he cannot transform him.

A less noticed problem in this episode is the oddness of the speech itself as a consolation to Ferdinand and Miranda. It is not really an argument for calm at all; rather it is an enactment of attaining resignation. Prospero reaches stoical acceptance of the inevitable by focusing his mind on the evanescence of everything mortal. And indeed the speech only half-enacts that resignation, as Prospero admits:

> Sir, I am vex'd;
> Bear with my weakness; my old brain is troubled:
> Be not disturb'd with my infirmity:
> If you be pleas'd, retire into my cell,
> And there repose: a turn or two I'll walk,
> To still my beating mind.   (ll. 158–63)

He is making an excuse because he wants them out of the way while he deals with the plotters, but his irritation is real, as is suggested by Ariel's caution (ll. 168–9) and by the harshness of his exclamation against Caliban (ll. 188–93). Immediately afterward we see a parody version of Prospero's anger in Stephano's threats against Caliban.

Prospero struggles 'To still my beating mind', as he echoes the striking term from Miranda. Is it possible to see him now – or ever – as the philosophical sage, controlling himself as he controls others in his benevolent plan? For all the ambiguities in our perception of him, it may be possible to arrive at a tentative judgement. Surely he is not the irascible magician of the *commedia dell'arte*, yet that figure is in him. Probably we are to infer that twelve years of self-study and enforced renunciation have taught him self-control, but that it is still precarious enough to allow flashes of irritability. He has learned

self-control through renunciation, and it is constantly reinforced by new renunciations – of Miranda, of his magic power, of his superiority over Alonso, even of Ariel, whom he genuinely loves. Prospero, the master of illusions, allows himself no illusions, and so he turns his thoughts to his coming death. Though we cannot follow all the turnings of his thought, we imitate Ferdinand and Miranda in coming to trust it, all the more as we see the limitations of his power.

But if Prospero's wisdom is so imaginatively compelling, what are we to make of Miranda's innocence? The nineteenth century was drawn to an idealized version of her as a sort of Florence Dombey or Little Dorrit, a sweet maid whose goodness leaves wisdom to others. She is after all only fourteen. Yet there are elements of the characterization that do not fit that ideal pattern. The actress Sheila Allen commented that she saw Miranda as a tomboy, and there is much to justify that in the girl who offers (quite seriously) to carry logs for Ferdinand, who promptly disobeys her father to reveal her name to her lover, who rather bluntly proposes to him. And there is an edge to her voice that an older generation of editors often took from her[10] as she reacts angrily to Caliban's glee at the imagination of having raped her:

> Abhorred slave,
> Which any print of goodness wilt not take,
> Being capable of all ill! I pitied thee,
> Took pains to make thee speak, taught thee each
>   hour
> One thing or other: when thou didst not, savage,
> Know thine own meaning, but wouldst gabble like
> A thing most brutish, I endow'd thy purposes
> With words that made them known. But thy vile
>   race,
> Though thou didst learn, had that in 't which good
>   natures
> Could not abide to be with; therefore wast thou
> Deservedly confin'd into this rock,
> Who hadst deserv'd more than a prison.
>   (1.2.353–64)

---

[9] Kermode, p. lxxv.
[10] Kermode makes the case for giving the speech to Miranda in his note at 1.2.353. I would add that the passive construction at ll. 362–3 comes more naturally from her lips than from Prospero's.

Miranda is her father's daughter, with his educative impulse and his moral severity. Here she sounds rather like the Isabella of *Measure for Measure*, brisk and contemptuous in her dismissal of moral inferiority.

Miranda's innocence is not the same as ignorance, even though it does include an isolation from the world analogous to what is implied by Isabella's religious habit. She can perceive evil as long as it is the unambiguous evil of Caliban, whose outward ugliness fits his inward state. She has not seen the masked evil of civilization, though at least in theory she knows of that too: 'Good wombs have borne bad sons' (1.2.120).[11] Miranda has a youthful toughness and energy that coexist with her innocence, with everything that the nineteenth century saw as girlish sweetness.

Aldous Huxley's title for his anti-utopian novel embodies the cynicism that we are all tempted to feel at Miranda's exclamation when she first sees the collection of shipwrecked courtiers:

O, wonder!
How many goodly creatures are there here!
How beauteous mankind is! O brave new world,
That has such people in 't!   (5.1.181–4)

My impression is that modern audiences usually titter uncomfortably at her lines, even if the actress resists the temptation to play for a laugh. But surely by now we should have learned to distrust our own cynicism, and Prospero's response is a subtly defined pointer: ''Tis new to thee.' His words do not seem to me like a cynical dismissal but rather the poised, illusionless view characteristic of him. Kermode rightly compares his earlier comment on Ferdinand and Miranda's love compact: 'So glad of this as they I cannot be / Who are surpris'd with all' (3.1.92–3).[12] Probably it is wiser to look at Antonio and Sebastian with Prospero's eyes than with

Miranda's, but it is not clear that he sees all the truth. No doubt Montaigne was wiser than his cat, but every now and then it is worthwhile to see the game through the cat's eyes as well. There are clarities of innocence as well as clarities of wisdom.

The Tempest is surely a sceptical play. The characters are perplexed with ambiguities of seeing and judging, and we as audience are invited to share their perplexity. Even Prospero is not exempt from such difficulties. And parallel to the characters' confusion is ours as we try to see and judge for ourselves. Prospero, Miranda, and Ferdinand are in some ways puzzling figures, whose different facets inspire wildly different interpretations. But the kinds of scepticism in the play need to be distinguished. There is a playful scepticism based on the incompleteness of human perception, like the scepticism of Montaigne about his cat. There is a hierarchy of misperceptions dependent on the moral and intellectual qualities of the perceivers. And there is a deep-seated lack of illusion in Prospero, which modulates into a philosophical resignation based on seeing the world as evanescent. Like Jaques's melancholy, the prevailing scepticism of the play is 'compounded of many simples', and it is after all a pleasant compound, not to be confused with Beckett's dark view or even the bleak moral analysis of Donne's *Anniversaries*. If there is a hierarchy of perception in the play, it has two peaks, logically inconsistent with each other, yet bound together as a father and daughter are bound together. Characters and audience alike can deal with the rich and mysterious world of *The Tempest* to the extent that they can modulate between a lively innocence of seeing and a resigned wisdom of interpreting.

---

[11] Again Kermode resists some editions' transfer of these words to Prospero.

[12] Note at 5.1.184.

SHAKESPEARE'S MEDICAL IMAGINATION

MAURICE POPE

Shakespeare, unlike Chaucer, is still intelligible to us directly. But though his language in general needs no translation for speakers of modern English, his ideas often do. In particular his ideas about the hidden workings of our body were quite different from our own. For instance, he thought that sighing caused loss of blood, that tears were an overflow from the brain, and that falling in love was caused by the liver.[1] The temptation is to hurry over these oddities, understanding statements of fact in a metaphorical sense, or, where this won't do, glossing them with a synonym. So we may be told that 'spirits' means 'energy' or 'character' or 'resolve' as the context demands.[2] The deception works if the cases are far enough apart. But if allegedly different meanings for the same word come in the same line we lose confidence. Another kind of confusion can be caused by the gloss itself. For instance on one occasion we are told by Dover Wilson that 'blood' means 'spirit'.[3] But it does not. Blood was a kind of liquid in the veins and spirit was a kind of air in the arteries. It cannot be right to explain them as if they were interchangeable, even if in some situations they perform equivalent functions. We would hardly approve a glossator in the microwave future who explained to his readers a point that was obscure to them in a twentieth-century kitchen scene by cheerfully writing 'gas = electricity'. The only cure that will really work is to teach ourselves the necessary principles of sixteenth-century physiology. We shall then be able to take the hurdles in our stride instead of having to stop and move each one out of the way as we come to it.

In fact even the official commentators do not always manage to negotiate the hurdles as nimbly as they should. For instance the editor of the Arden *Coriolanus* tells us that 'The mysterious relationship between the brain and the heart often perplexes Shakespeare's language'. But this is not true. Shakespeare is always clear on the matter. The one who is perplexed is the editor.[4]

I shall begin by considering some particular lines in the plays where it seems to me that editors and commentators have erred or that a perceptible amount of new light may be shed by taking into account Shakespeare's physiological notions. After displaying these tangible fruits of a medically oriented approach, I shall turn to the abstract matter of the notions themselves and argue that they are to a large degree individual in both content and presentation and can therefore tell us something significant about Shakespeare's poetic personality.

But first the particular passages. To start with the most peripheral of them, there is a line in *Pericles* where Dionyza is planning to murder Marina. She tells Marina to take a walk along the beach and says with affected solicitude 'Pray walk softly; do not heat your blood' (4.1.50). Shakespeare refers to the blood over six hundred times, but this is the only

---

[1] 'Blood-drinking sighs', *2 Henry VI*, 3.2.63 (see also *A Midsummer Night's Dream*, 3.2.97, and *Romeo and Juliet*, 3.5.59); 'brain's flow', *Timon of Athens*, 5.4.76; 'liver', *Twelfth Night*, 2.4.97, 2.5.88.

[2] 'Energy', *All's Well that Ends Well*, 5.1.2; 'character', *2 Henry IV*, 5.2.125; 'resolve', *Macbeth*, 3.1.127.

[3] *Antony and Cleopatra* (Cambridge, 1950), p. 246. The full gloss reads 'ardent spirit, mettle'.

[4] At *Coriolanus* 1.1.135. He is also perplexed by the brain nourishing the nerves in *Antony* 4.8.22 though this is a perfectly orthodox way of expressing the orthodox theory.

occasion where it is suggested that blood may be heated by exercise. Admittedly there is no rule that authors must always repeat themselves and never say anything only once. However our suspicions may be aroused by the presence of other unique uses of blood in the play. When Thaisa asks Pericles if he loves her he replies 'Even as my life the blood that fosters it' (2.5.88). Nowhere else in Shakespeare is blood said to 'foster' life nor to have a love relationship with it. A little earlier in the same act there is another *hapax*. Thaisa tells Pericles that when her father drank a toast to him he wished it 'so much blood unto your life' (2.3.78). No such wish is to be found elsewhere in Shakespeare and moreover it contradicts, as we shall see, Shakespeare's normal view of what wine does to the blood. The extent of Shakespeare's share in *Pericles* is an uncertain question. These observations cannot settle it, but they can provide some new islands of fact in the ocean of debate.

Next a question of interpretation. Towards the beginning of *Antony and Cleopatra* it is reported to Octavius that piracy is so rife off the south Italian coast that 'the borders maritime / Lack blood to think on't, and flush youth revolt' (1.4.50–1). 'Revolt' is generally explained as signifying mutiny or defection.[5] But the idea that there was any kind of secession movement among the young in south Italy has no warrant in Plutarch whom Shakespeare is closely following at this point, nothing in the previous part of the sentence leads one to expect it, and it is not followed up in any way. How could a messenger skip so lightly over such news? In truth, however, he never introduces the idea of rebellion. The second part of the sentence repeats the first with stronger emphasis but with the same medical metaphor. The coastal regions of Italy, he says, turn pale with fear at the thought of the pirates, and even young men, who are normally of ruddy complexion, go green. The physiological explanation, quite orthodox, is that the outside of the body loses blood to the central areas round the heart when danger threatens. The word 'flush' indicates blood-filled cheeks, and 'revolt' means 'do a volte-face' or 'execute an about-turn', a sense of the word which is as frequent in Shakespeare as that of 'mutiny'.[6]

Thirdly, 'spirits' in the Prologue to *Henry V*:

> But pardon, gentles all,
> The flat unraised spirits that hath dar'd
> On this unworthy scaffold to bring forth
> So great an object.

This is normally glossed as 'The author and the company', 'spirits' being taken to stand for 'people', like the French *esprits*. But in all other passages where Shakespeare uses 'spirits' to mean persons there is always some hint of superior mettle. The people so described are suitors, wits, knights in armour or political leaders, not actors or stage-hands.[7] Moreover 'flat' and 'unraised' are strange epithets for people, whereas if 'spirits' is taken in its ordinary sense they make a perfectly appropriate point. The essence of spirits is to rise upwards, but mine, says the playwright, are unable to ascend to the height of their great argument. The correct gloss will therefore be something like 'My heavy, pedestrian Muse' as opposed to the 'Muse of fire' in the first line of the play. In *King John* 'spirits' is likewise used by the speaker of himself and is likewise construed as singular. John, addressing the citizens of Angiers, asks them to distrust the French

> And let us in – your King, whose labour'd spirits
> Fore-wearied in this action of swift speede,
> Craves harbourage within your Citie walles.[8]

Finally two passages from the scene in *Coriolanus* between Menenius Agrippa and the ringleader of the mob. Menenius Agrippa tells the fable of how the other members of the body threatened to rise against the Belly. According to the punctuation of the First Folio the Belly answered its accusers:

> True is it my Incorporate Friends (quoth he)
> That I receive the generall Food at first
> Which you do live upon: and fit it is,

---

[5] 'The meaning is that hot-headed youth revolt to join the pirates' writes Munro in the London Shakespeare; Dover Wilson in the Cambridge Shakespeare glosses by 'desert'.

[6] See for example *Love's Labour's Lost*, 5.2.74, *Cymbeline*, 3.4.53, Sonnet 92.10.

[7] *The Merchant of Venice*, 46, 2.7.46, 2.9.32; *Othello*, 2.3.51; *Lover's Complaint*, 236; *Henry VIII*, 1.1.35; *2 Henry IV*, 5.2.18; *Julius Caesar*, 3.1.164.

[8] *King John*, 2.1.232–4 (First Folio text, a3). The Folio puts a stop after 'let us in'. This punctuation makes a final sentence that is unsatisfactory in several respects, and it is not generally followed.

Because I am the Store-house, and the Shop
Of the whole Body. But, if you do remember,
I send it through the Rivers of your blood
Even to the Court, the Heart, to th'seate
    o'th'Braine,
And through the Crankes and Offices of man,
The strongest Nerves, and small inferior Veines
From me receive that naturall competencie
Whereby they live. And though that all at
    once...cannot
See what I do deliver out to each,
Yet I can make my Awdit up,...

                (1.1.128–42; aa1ᵛ)

Modern editors without exception print a colon or full stop after 'braine'. This creates a sentence that is impossible in form and inappropriate in emphasis. English usage demands 'I send it to *a*, to *b*, and to *c*'. The only time one can say 'I send it to *a*, to *b*' is when *b* stands in apposition to *a*, as for example in 'I am sending him to Brussels, to the seat of the European economic bureaucracy'. But heart and brain cannot be in apposition to each other as they were quite distinct organs for Shakespeare just as they are for us. So the sentence cannot be rescued in this way. It is simply not proper English. It is also inappropriate to the argument. The stomach is not trying to convince the unruly members that he serves the leading organs of the body but that he serves them all. This sentence therefore (which, we must remember, is created by the editors not by the Folio) cannot be right. Nor can the next. For consider 'the Crankes and Offices of man' through which the nutriment is said to pass on its way to the nerves and the veins. Are they different from the 'rivers of blood' through which it passed on its way to the heart? If so, what are they? Or are they the same? If so, all one can say is that the change of expression is not credible.

    Luckily for once the path of truth is as smooth as the path of error, and two plausible sentences can be created as easily as the two implausible ones of our published editions. All we need do is to strengthen the stop after 'man' instead of that after 'braine', and the Stomach will be speaking both good English and good sense. 'I send the food through the blood to the heart and brain and the rest of the body: the most active nerve and the most passive vein alike

receive their nourishment from me.' The second sentence is now a straightforward statement without physiological puzzles. The first takes on the natural form 'I send it to *a*, to *b*, and from end to end of *c*'.[9] 'The Crankes and Offices of man' is a satisfactory way of describing the other parts of the body and are moreover mentioned in their proper place as the final recipients of nourishment. The order of feeding is the same as that imagined in *Antony and Cleopatra* where the nerves are said to be nourished via the brain (4.8.22).

    A few lines later Menenius Agrippa turns to the ringleader of the riot and asks him:

          What do you think,
    You, the great toe of this assembly?
First Citizen.   I the great toe? Why the great toe?
Menenius Agrippa.
    For that being one of the lowest, basest, poorest,
    Of this most wise rebellion, thou goest foremost,
    Thou rascal, that art worst in blood to run,
    Lead'st first to win some vantage.

                (1.1.152–8)

Commentators worry about 'in blood', giving it psychological interpretations as if it meant 'on form' or 'in character'. But there is no need for a second metaphor to blur the first. All we need do is to remember the blood-supply as Shakespeare conceived of it. The joke, or paradox, is that the big toe always goes first when we walk, yet it is at the very end of the line as far as the venal system is concerned and gets the worst of the nutritional blood, or, to use the Belly's previous phrase, the least 'natural competency'.

    In the foregoing exegesis I have made one over-riding assumption, which is that Shakespeare's view of the human body and of how it may be imagined to operate is clear and self-consistent. I believe this to be true, though to justify it *in toto* would need more space than I have. Luckily it is not necessary, and I can refer readers who are sceptical on the point to a thorough article by Patrick Cruttwell devoted to Shakespeare's physiology and

---

9 'From end to end of' is the first definition of 'through' in Dr Johnson's dictionary; another Shakespearian instance after 'send' occurs at *Troilus and Cressida*, 1.3.257.

psychology,[10] and also to the conclusions of R. R. Simpson in his book *Shakespeare and Medicine* (1959). What I do wish to do, however, is to take issue with a secondary moral drawn by Cruttwell in the article I have just mentioned.

The age of Shakespeare [he writes] had still the integrated medieval view of the world and of man's place in it...Shakespeare is not really a philosopher; he had no philosophy of his own. He didn't need to have one; it was given him. He had simply to describe human life as honestly, vividly, and completely as he knew, and then, through the very terms of reference by which alone he *could* describe it, a philosophy emerges.

This is a special case of a popular image of Shakespeare, the romantic anti-intellectual who with his 'small Latin and less Greek' learned from nature rather than from books and who even preferred ready-made plots however humdrum to the mechanical labour of making them for himself.[11] But it is a more than usually dangerous version of the image in that being put forward with the authority of medicine, or at any rate of medical history, it seems to carry with it a scientific or technical flavour, and the general reader may be too over-awed to disagree. But the matter is not that recondite, and there are good grounds for disagreement.

The first is a straightforward observation. If there was a single 'integrated medieval view of the world' in Shakespeare's plays, then the characters in them should never have philosophic doubts. But they do. They can talk about miracles and modern sceptics, ask whether fancy, that is *fantasia*, is bred in the head (Galen) or the heart (Aristotle), and air the question of whether the soul is the same as the spirit in the brain.[12] The questions are all mentioned lightly enough, but in a tone that suggests they are genuine questions, not ones for which there is an obvious right and wrong answer.

Another way we can try to test the hypothesis that Shakespeare took over lock, stock, and barrel an 'integrated view of the world', whether medieval or Tudor, is to look at his contemporaries. If they all present the same ideas, then the hypothesis of an integrated view might be tenable. But if not, not. I should like to suggest that a provisional exploration of Spenser and Marlowe does not support the hypothesis. These are the two poets who may be judged most significant for our purpose since both were men with university learning. Should any Elizabethan poets have been articulate on these matters it is they.

In making a comparison of this nature one must have a common theme, and in order to eliminate chance as far as possible it must be a theme of common occurrence. I have therefore chosen blood, blood being mentioned some 140 times in Marlowe, 215 times in Spenser, and over 600 times in Shakespeare. Most of these references of course refer to the visible reality of blood or to blood as the symbol of battle or death, but there is a substantial minority of instances that refer to its supposed physiological or psychological functions. The results will be easier to present if I first say a word about what these were. The primary role allotted to the blood was nutritional. The food and drink we ingest was thought to be concocted in the stomach to become chyle. This chyle passed to the liver where it underwent a second concoction and became blood. As blood it was conducted from the liver through the veins to the rest of the body, where in the natural course of events it was absorbed. However, over-indulgence in food or drink could lead to trouble – a plethora of blood might be created, and this could bring all kinds of undesirable consequences ranging from minor pimples to major fevers. Abstinence was the obvious cure, for without food the blood level in the body would begin to drop until it was down to the correct amount. This theory of the blood formed part of a general system of physiology according to which the body, apart from the bones and the actual organs, consisted of a triple network of veins, arteries, and nerves. The veins contained blood, as

---

[10] Patrick Cruttwell, 'Physiology and Psychology in Shakespeare's Age', *Journal of the History of Ideas*, 12 (1951), 75–89.

[11] On the vanity of this quest see E. A. J. Honigmann, 'Shakespeare's "Lost Source-Plays"', *Modern Language Review*, 49 (1954), 293–307.

[12] *All's Well*, 2.3.1–35; *Merchant of Venice*, 3.2.63; *King John*, 5.7.3.

we have seen, and led from the liver; the arteries contained air and led from the left side of the heart; the nerves contained a more refined form of air and led from the ventricles or cells inside the brain. The purpose of the veins was nutrition, of the arteries ventilation, and of the nerves sensation and voluntary motion. The pulse was the air being pumped through the arteries, and it was air which inflated the muscles and caused them to work. This explains why when we are exerting ourselves we pant and our hearts beat faster. (It is not altogether clear whether the air that inflated the muscles was supplied directly from the arteries or whether it came through the nerves, but the latter is more likely.) The air in the arteries was called life-breath or vital spirit (*zotikon pneuma* in Greek), while the air in the nerves and in the ventricles of the brain was called soul-breath or animal-spirit (*psychikon pneuma*). This physiological system was due to Erasistratus, the anatomist of the third century BC, and formed the tap-root of Galenic and medieval theory. Naturally enough there was some alteration in it over the years. First, bleeding came in (during the first century AD) as a short-cut cure. For if a plethora of blood was the cause of disease why not get rid of it at once instead of waiting for starvation to take effect? Second, the theory was counter-intuitive in its demand that the arteries contain only air. Punctured arteries very obviously pour out blood. The Erasistrateans accounted for this by saying that all veins and arteries were joined (invisibly) at their tips, and that as soon as an artery was holed the air escaped and the blood rushed in on the principle of 'follow-through into an emptying space' (the origin of our proverb 'Nature abhors a vacuum'). This explanation sounds like special pleading to us, and perhaps it sounded equally unconvincing in antiquity too. At any rate Galen reports a series of experiments and arguments designed to prove that blood was indeed present in the living artery. The demonstration should have been a mortal blow to the system, and perhaps would have been if it had been pressed home. But Galen never makes it clear how much blood he believed the arteries to contain and indeed often talks as if he still assumed that their main content was spirit. So the Erasistratean system continued for an

amazingly long life, through the Middle Ages, through the Renaissance, and even for a century or more beyond. Harvey's discovery of the circulation of the blood in 1628 should have killed it, but parts of it managed to survive even that. The angel Raphael in the fifth book of *Paradise Lost* gives a great lecture on the progressive refinement of spirit from plant through man to angel, and Dr Johnson in his dictionary quoted, without any indication that he considered it obsolete, Locke's definition of 'spirit' as 'a substance wherein thinking, knowing, doubting, and a power of moving do subsist'.

In Galen we find superimposed on this Erasistratean physiology the more ancient but quite un-Erasistratean doctrine of the four elements, hot, cold, wet, and dry, and their manifestation in the humours 'blood', 'phlegm', 'yellow bile', and 'black bile'. This doctrine persisted through the Middle Ages and the Renaissance and though it now may be dead in our minds it is far from dead on our tongues. We have been taking each other's temperatures for over a hundred years and finding them steady at around 98.4 °F,[13] but we still use and understand the language of humoral psychology. The only difference is that when we describe somebody as having hot blood or a cold heart or a dry wit we realize that we are talking metaphorically whereas in the past we would have believed ourselves to have been talking about physical qualities. Even then though they were hidden. It could be debated about many things, for example nitre, whether they were hot or cold, and in defiance of immediate sensation wine off the ice was considered to be hotter than fish from the oven. The natural quality was more real and more permanent than the acquired one. Women were cold even in summer and men hot even in winter, and in procreation cold seed generated a female, hot seed a male. The ageing process was understood in these same terms. The young were hot and wet: the longer they lived the more they dried out until in old age they became cold and dry. And if it were

---

[13] The earliest quotation given in *OED* for laymen taking temperatures is 1888 (*s.v. temperature*, 7).

objected that old people dribble, no matter. A bottle may contain liquid, but it is still a dry bottle![14]

A third role played by the blood was in generation. The habit of describing kindred as being related by blood or as sharing the same blood is as old as Homer and we cannot tell how it originated. But it was given anatomical justification in antiquity and even more strongly in the Renaissance. For instance Vicary, writing in 1548, told how 'sparme' is 'gathered of all the best and purest drops of blood in all the body' and how the testicles are supplied by sinews from the brain, by arteries from the heart, and by veins from the liver, which bring 'feeling and steering, lyfe and spirite, and nutrimental blood, and the most purest blood of al other members'.[15]

There were minor functions, too, in which it is apparent that blood plays a part, and these were duly given their physiological explanations. For instance, blood suffuses our cheeks when we feel shame and deserts them when we feel fear. The explanation offered by Thomas Bright in 1586 in *A Treatise of Melancholy*, a book thought to have been used by Shakespeare, goes like this. Blushing is caused by shame, and shame is 'an affection of grief, mixed with anger against ourselves, rising of the conscience of some knowne, or supposed to be knowne offence'. What happens is that the heart first 'maketh a retractation of blood and spirit, as in feare and griefe', but when it realizes that there are to be no consequences more serious than some laughter or a verbal rebuke, it no longer feels an urgent necessity for the extra blood and spirit, so that they 'breake forth again more vehemently, and fill the parts about the face more than before' and this is what 'causeth the rednesse'.[16] But of course such functions of the blood as this were minor and derivative. Its major importance in Renaissance theory was its role in nutrition, its role as one of the humours, and its role in generation.

Let us now return to our poets and see what they make of these doctrines. First Spenser. We should not be surprised if so philosophic a poet were to display perfect familiarity with them and to be exceptionally clear in his presentation. On the other hand we should be surprised, very surprised, if he were to show himself ignorant and confused. But the latter is the case, not the former. He thinks that the pulse is to be felt in the veins, and seems uncertain whether its beat is caused by blood or spirit.[17] He talks as if 'vital air' was what one breathes out when it should have been what is contained in the arteries.[18] He is fond of the meaningless phrase 'vital blood'.[19] These are not shortcomings which Spenser can be forgiven on the ground that he is being forced against his will into alien territory. He often goes out of his way to talk in physiological terms. When Una sees her Knight in deadly peril, we are told what happened in her body.

> Through every vaine
> The crudled cold ran to her well of life
> As in a swowne.   (I. ix. 52.1–3)

But 'crudled' implies stiff – Banister, in his *Historie of Man*, called the liver 'crudded blood'[20] – and it is inept to specify the blood as curdled at the very moment when it is said to be 'running' back to the heart. However, Una can be forgiven her confusion when one considers what she has been looking at. The Red Cross Knight had been given a dagger and was about to commit suicide. He was nervous, and his hand 'did quake and tremble like a leafe of Aspin greene', and more surprisingly

> Troubled blood through his pale face was seene
> To come and go with tydings from the hart
> As it a running messenger had beene.
>   (I. ix. 51.5–7)

A similitude worthy of Macaulay's victim, Robert Montgomery, and equally deserving of the lash. Why should the heart be sending messages to the

---

[14] Ambroise Paré, *Les Oeuvres...* (Paris, 1575). I have used Malgaine's collected edition (Paris, 1840); the analogy of the bottle is on p. 37.

[15] Thomas Vicary, *A profitable Treatise of the Anatomie of mans body* (1577), repr. EETS, extra series, 53 (1888), pp. 79, 82–3.

[16] Thomas Bright, *A Treatise of Melancholy* (1586), pp. 161–4.

[17] *Faerie Queene*, II. i. 43.4, III. iv. 41.7, III. v. 31.4.

[18] *Ruins of Time*, 304; cf. *Faerie Queene*, II. i. 43–9.

[19] *Faerie Queene*, III. vi. 5.9 (unless here it means milk!), III. ix. 49.9, IV. x. 46.7 (nothing to correspond in Lucretius), and cf. II. i. 43.4.

[20] John Banister, *The Historie of Man...* (1578), p. 76a.

face, and what could possibly be their content? And what two things could be more unlike than a single messenger coming and going and a continuum such as blood? It is noticeable too that the lines are vapid as well as confused, and this is usually the case when Spenser touches on physiology. For instance he has some twenty instances of the word 'blood' in its genetic signification, and they are all unexciting – 'gentle blood', 'noble blood', 'Greek blood', 'Trojan blood' and suchlike. There are about the same number of what I may call moral uses – 'innocent', 'guiltless', 'guilty' blood – and a handful of humoral ones of the type 'hot blood'. The epithets are few and unimaginative. Above all there are virtually no instances of the phenomenon that we shall see is so characteristic of Shakespeare, the simultaneous exploitation of 'blood' in its different aspects. Finally we should note that all these medical and moral uses of the word form only a small portion, a quarter, of its total occurrences. In 160 of the 215 instances blood in Spenser means either the blood that comes from a wound or the idea of fighting or death associated with bloodshed. We shall see that Shakespeare presents a strong contrast with Spenser in this respect too.

Marlowe is as gory as Spenser or more so. He brackets war, blood, death, and cruelty. He makes his Tamburlaine proclaim that 'Blood is the God of War's rich livery';[21] and he himself both in his plays and in his poetry uses the word in this connotation for between 80 and 90 per cent of the time. But when he speaks of blood in a medical context he is quite unlike Spenser. There is clarity and orthodoxy instead of confusion and error. Food is concocted into blood, which fills the veins: the veins then carry the blood from the liver round the body to nourish it.[22] In youth the blood is hot, and it is the blood which keeps the body warm: but it becomes cold in old age.[23] Accidental heat dries it up in fever. The arteries, which run alongside the veins, carry the vital spirit ('the lively spirits') which is engendered in the heart and which is the agent by which the soul effects movement. The heart is fed by spirit, vein, and artery.[24] In short, Marlowe is fully aware of the physiological role attributed to blood by the academic opinion of his day, and states it firmly and correctly whenever occasion demands. But this is all. Of its psychological function and of the doctrine of the humours in so far as it relates to the blood there is no trace: people's temperaments and dispositions are never described by reference to their state of blood.[25] This is remarkable. Equally remarkable is the almost complete absence of the genetic use of blood. Except in two passing phrases in *Edward II* (4.6.16, 5.2.88) 'blood' in Marlowe never denotes family or race. Normally we might be tempted to dismiss such an absence in an author's vocabulary as due to accident or at best to a kind of mental quirk without intentional significance. However, with Marlowe we can be fairly sure that this particular absence was intended. For he translated a substantial amount of Latin poetry – Ovid's *Amores* and the first book of Lucan's *Civil War*. In them the words *cruor*, *sanguis*, and their associated adjectives occur over twenty-five times, and Marlowe regularly renders them by the English 'blood'. But he does not do so on the one occasion in Ovid and on the two occasions in Lucan where the original Latin has *sanguis* in a genetic sense. On these occasions he translates with 'line', 'son' and 'race' respectively.[26] This suggests that Marlowe had some positive objection to using blood to indicate kinship, and this is confirmed by a passage in *2 Tamburlaine*. Speaking about paternity to his sons, Tamburlaine makes no mention of blood, but only of spirit, as the genetic constant:

> My flesh, divided in your precious shapes
> Shall still retaine my spirit, though I die
> And live, in all your seedes, immortally.
> (5.3.369–71)

We can now consider Shakespeare. If we take first the purely physiological, or Erasistratean, theory of

[21] *2 Tamburlaine*, 3.2.119.
[22] *Ibid.*, 2.2.108, 3.4.6–7.
[23] *Lucan*, 363; *Dido*, 2.1.260.
[24] *2 Tamburlaine*, 5.3.84–5, 96, 4.1.185.
[25] Even 'hot' and 'cold' are rarely used by Marlowe in a psychological sense, and then only in such commonplace phrases as 'hot love', 'cold virginity', and the like. The blood itself is never said to take part in psychological activity, except for being shed by the heart in grief (e.g. *2 Tamburlaine*, 2.3.123, 5.3.265).
[26] Ovid, *Amores*, 1.3.8; Lucan, *De bello civili*, 1.112, 248.

the working of the body, we shall find that he was as much in command of it as Marlowe was, and that he was not confused like Spenser. The liver, the heart, and the brain are the principal organs.[27] The veins contain blood, the arteries spirit, and the body can be summed up as 'a confine of blood and breath'.[28] The nerves are nourished from the brain, which is supposed by some to be the residence of the soul, but which can also be likened to a limbeck and may contain fumes rather than pure spirit.[29] Unlike Marlowe and Spenser he does not explicitly refer either to animal or to vital spirits. But it is possible that in this he was not being ignorant but up to date, for there was a school of thought in the late sixteenth century according to which there was only one spirit.[30]

Second, blood in relation to the humours. We may remember that this psychological use is absent from Marlowe. But in Shakespeare, at least after the early comedies, it is absolutely regular, occurring over a hundred times. Hot blood implies quickness (especially to anger, love, and laughter) and readiness to rebel against reason and sound judgement. The blood is naturally at its hottest in youth. But it may be heated by accidental factors, for example by wine and food, by insults, and even by hot weather.[31] The opposite of hot blood is cold blood. Instead of alacrity it creates sluggishness and dulls our emotional responses; but it can also make us prudent. It is characteristic of old age, but can also be induced by hunger, by sadness, by sex, and above all by fear.[32] The word 'blood' in itself may be enough to signify a psychological state, either of age – 'young bloods look for a time of rest' says Brutus when he sees Lucius drowsy[33] – or of mood – the thoroughly dependable man is

> spare in diet,
> Free from gross passion or of mirth or anger,
> Constant in spirit, not swerving with the blood.[34]

The frequency and richness of Shakespeare's exploitation of 'blood' in psychological contexts presents the sharpest possible contrast to the paucity and banality of such passages in Spenser, while with Marlowe of course there is no comparison since

Marlowe offers no psychological uses of the word at all.

The occurrences of blood in its genetic sense are almost as numerous in Shakespeare as those that are psychological. It indicates rank, when it can be called 'royal', 'princely', 'noble', 'high', 'well-born', or 'true', and very occasionally the reverse, 'gross', 'false', or 'bastard'. It also indicates family connection without implications of rank: fathers, mothers, sons, daughters, brothers, sisters, recognize themselves as being of the same 'flesh and blood', or 'next in blood' or 'consanguineous'. The moral problem of blood's intrinsic value is sometimes glanced at,[35] but normally blood and personal merit are accepted without question as forming separate categories of excellence. In *King John* Lady Blanche has blood, beauty, and virtue – but her virtue is assumed to be the result of her education not her birth: in *All's Well that Ends Well* Bertram is exhorted to cultivate virtue to match his blood; in *The Merchant of Venice* Jessica hopes she is the daughter of her father's blood but not of his manners.[36] In all this the seriousness with which

---

27 *Twelfth Night*, 1.1.37.

28 *King John*, 3.3.44; *Love's Labour's Lost*, 4.3.302; *King John*, 4.2.246.

29 *Antony*, 4.8.22; *King John*, 5.7.3; *Macbeth*, 1.7.67; *Antony*, 2.1.24, 2.7.98.

30 Johannes Argenterius, in *In artem medicinalem Galeni* (Mons Regalis, 1566), pp. 186–7, puts forward nine arguments for there being only a single spirit, which he would name *spiritus influens*. Bernadinus Telesius, in *Quod animal universum ab unica Animae substantia gubernatur* (Venice, 1590), argues that this single spirit should be identified with the substance of the soul.

31 Numerous passages allude to the causes and effects of hot blood, the most notable being *Merchant* 1.1.80–6, *Henry V*, 3.5.19–23, *Coriolanus*, 5.1.50–6.

32 *Measure for Measure*, 1.3.52; *Much Ado*, 1.1.110–11; *Comedy of Errors*, 5.1.312; *Coriolanus*, 5.1.52; *The Taming of the Shrew*, Induction, 2.129; *Julius Caesar*, 4.3.278; etc.

33 *Julius Caesar*, 4.3.260.

34 *Henry V*, 2.2.131–3; cf. *Julius Caesar*, 3.1.58, *Henry VIII*, 2.3.103, *Troilus*, 4.1.17.

35 *All's Well*, 2.3.126–9; *Henry VIII*, 1.1.123, 5.5.38; *Troilus*, 4.1.16.

36 *King John*, 2.1.432 (cf. 493); *All's Well*, 1.1.55–7; *Merchant*, 2.3.18.

Shakespeare treats the supposed genetic function of blood is obvious. He presumably believed it was a fact, not just a metaphor. He makes Bolingbroke address his father, John of Gaunt:

> O thou, the earthly author of my blood,
> Whose youthful spirit, in me regenerate,
> Doth with a twofold vigour lift me up.
>
> (*Richard II*, 1.3.69–71)

And he himself says that to have a child is to 'bestow blood' and 'to be new made when thou art old, / And see thy blood warm when thou feel'st it cold' (Sonnets 11.3, 2.13–14).

Finally, there is a clear-cut difference between Shakespeare on the one hand and Spenser and Marlowe on the other in the ratio of medical to non-medical usage of the word 'blood', the latter being what I have called its gory aspect.[37] In Marlowe we saw that in over 80 per cent of his uses of the word bloodshed is what he had in mind. For Spenser the comparable figure was 75 per cent. But for Shakespeare I calculate it to be some 65 per cent in the works normally accounted early, 35 per cent and 38 per cent in the works of the middle and late period, that is to say after 1594 and after 1599. (The absolute number of occurrences of the word is around 200 for each of these three periods.) It is something of a surprise to find that Shakespeare, who is traditionally considered very much less intellectual than Spenser or Marlowe, makes more use of the word 'blood' in its medical and psychological senses than either of them.

Our comparison has shown that Shakespeare does not reproduce the same 'integrated view of the world' as his contemporaries. The view he presents is his own and this makes it much more interesting. It is not a maverick view in that it is consistent in itself and is in broad conformity with the medical opinion of the time; but it does have some individual features, and one is inevitably curious about their source. Was Shakespeare following some single medical authority who has hitherto lain unrecognized? Or was he an eclectic in the sense of somebody who had formed his own opinions?

Although it is not possible to say for certain I shall argue that the latter is the more likely.

The simple fact that no such single source has yet been recognized is in itself quite a strong argument in favour. For such a treatise, if found, would certainly be distinctive enough. It would have to agree with Argenterius about there being only one spirit. It would mention the view found in Telesius that the spirit in the brain was the substance of the soul. It would stress the idea – orthodox enough, but not usually dwelt on – that animals have the same spirits as us, one of the points made by Lorenzo in his speech to Jessica in *The Merchant of Venice* about the effects of music. In its account of tears it would agree with Thomas Bright that they consist of 'the excrementitious humiditie of the braine', but not in its account of sighs, because Bright's explanation of sighing does not suggest that it causes loss of blood, whereas this is several times assumed in Shakespeare.[38] Finally it would contain one major departure from orthodox physiology. Blood was generally considered the end product of our food and drink. Botello, in 1577, had attempted to quantify the rate of production and arrived at the figure of 8 to 10 ounces per day.[39] But Shakespeare and Shakespeare's characters never talk in this way. For them blood is like capital that can be used up rather than like income which is always being

---

[37] For the sake of completeness I should mention instances of very rare types of usage of the word blood that I have left out of the count: *Richard II*, 1.1.104 (Old Testament); *King John*, 5.7.48 (Christian?), and 5.1.11 (Neoplatonist?); *Lucrece*, 1736 ff. (her tainted blood turns black); and references to Christ's redemptive blood in Marlowe's *Dr Faustus*.

[38] For Argenterius and Telesius see n. 30. Telesius' disciple Thomas Campanella discusses the effects of one's spirits being 'attentive' (*Prodromus philosophiae instaurandae* (Frankfurt, 1617), pp. 70–1, *De rerum natura* (Frankfurt, 1623), pp. 161–2) as well as stressing the possession of spirits by animals (*Prodromus philosophiae instaurandae*, 61–2, *De rerum natura*, 94–8). Thomas Bright discusses tears in the *Treatise of Melancholy*, 140–1, and sighs, pp. 153–4.

[39] Leonard Botello, *De curatione per sanguinis missionem* (Lyons, 1577), discussed by Jerome J. Bylebyl in *Bulletin of the History of Medicine*, 51 (1977), 369–85.

replenished. It is often called 'dear' or 'costly', and no fighting man ever scorns the loss of blood on the ground that he will soon make it up again. On the contrary, it is consistently and on many occasions assumed to be a diminishing asset.[40] What food and drink are said to provide is not the body's nourishment but the body's heat.[41] Shakespeare's *obiter dicta* on the matter hang together as a theory, and a theory that in one respect at least has more common sense in it than the orthodox one. For the role of blood as a temporary concoction of the food one eats is not easy to reconcile with its role as the hereditary constant of one's personality. This function (accepted by Shakespeare) is easier to understand if our stock of blood remains the same throughout our lives subject only to the diminutions wrought by time and chance.

But, as I have said, it does not seem to me likely that there was a single, hitherto unrecognized, source for all Shakespeare's medical and physiological beliefs. Such a source might account for them being self-consistent, but it would hardly account for the vivid and original way in which they are handled. It seems far more plausible to give Shakespeare the credit for this than an unknown hack compiler of an anatomical digest. I should like to quote with approval Dr Simpson's conclusion that though some of his contemporaries may approach Shakespeare in the number of medical references 'they lack the inspired imagery, the quality of metaphor and simile, the dramatic use of the medical situation, and the accurate, tense, descriptive power of Shakespeare' (*Shakespeare and Medicine*, p. 114). And I should like to suggest that the reason for this is that Shakespeare was not handed a doctrine ready-served on a medieval platter, but that he pursued his curiosity for himself until he reached a view of the subject that he found satisfactory, acting in this not like a man of the Middle Ages ready to accept traditional authority nor even like a man of the Renaissance eager to search out new and more genuine sources but like a man of the Reformation who felt an obligation to form his own opinions for himself. In saying this I must stress that I do not for one moment wish to imply that Shakespeare was an academic by temperament. There is nothing neces-

sarily academic about the attitude I have described and no reason why it should lead to academic inhibitions. Having arrived at his conclusions either as a result of reading or of conversation or of reflection or most likely as a result of a combination of all three, then, like Mark Antony, he needed only to 'speak right on'.

The evidence which permits one to take this view is the easy mastery with which Shakespeare exploits different aspects of the concept of blood in the same passage and which could not have come from an anatomical text-book. The kind of combined usage I have in mind, though not unique to Shakespeare, is highly characteristic of him. In other authors it is perhaps rare. I have not found an instance in Marlowe. In Spenser, Artegall, confronted by a lawless multitude, was much troubled,

> ne wist what to do
> For loth he was his noble hands t'embrew
> In the base bloud of such a rascall crew.
> (*Faerie Queene*, V. ii. 52.3–5)

Here blood is used simultaneously in its visible and in its genetic sense, but though the weld may not seem to us to be one that needed any high degree of creative heat to achieve, the fact is that it stands alone or almost alone in the whole of Spenser's work. But in Shakespeare I count over a hundred instances like this where different concepts of 'blood' are fused. In each case of course the point, whether it be a joke or the thrill of horror which is the tragic equivalent of a joke, depends on immediate recognition. Both classes of effect vanish if one has to make a conscious effort. Let me quote some examples, beginning with a joke in *Love's Labour's Lost*:

Dumaine.

I would forget her; but a fever she
Reigns in my blood, and will rememb'red be.

Berowne.

A fever in your blood? Why, then incision
Would let her out in saucers. Sweet misprision!

(4.3.91–4)

---

[40] *Much Ado*, 4.1.193; *Winter's Tale*, 2.3.165; *Coriolanus*, 3.1.299, 5.2.56; *Troilus*, 1.3.301; *Timon*, 3.4.94; *Macbeth*, 5.1.38; *Cymbeline*, 1.1.157; Sonnet 67.10.
[41] e.g. *Troilus*, 3.1.122–4, 5.1.1.

And this exchange from *The Merchant of Venice* after Shylock has heard of Jessica's elopement:

Shylock. My own flesh and blood to rebel!
Salarino. Out upon it, old carrion! Rebels it at
these years?   (3.1.30–1)

Grim humour in *3 Henry VI*, when Gloucester has just murdered the King:

> What, will the aspiring blood of Lancaster
> Sink in the ground? I thought it would have
>   mounted.
> See how my sword weeps for the poor King's
>   death.[42]

Righteous indignation, also Gloucester's, when he thinks of his services to Edward IV: 'To royalize his blood I spilt my own' (*Richard III*, 1.3.124). A chilling touch in the sleepwalking scene in *Macbeth* when Lady Macbeth says: 'Yet who would have thought the old man to have had so much blood in him?' (5.1.36–7). The point is not simply, or perhaps not at all, 'What a mess he made!' It is a detached observation. Lady Macbeth had been dispassionate enough to be curious in the very act of murder. Old men ought to have very little blood: Duncan however had a great deal. Lady Macbeth was surprised by this as she might have been surprised to notice that he was wearing a wig.

Lastly the passage from *Coriolanus* about the big toe that we have already quoted (p. 177). This is a particularly good instance and provides a kind of spotlight on Shakespeare at work. The source for the fable of the Belly is unquestionably North's Plutarch. Not only is the order of narration the same but so are many words and phrases. There are possible verbal reminiscences of other writers, of Sidney, of Camden, and of Philemon Holland's translation of Livy, but they cannot be considered certain. What can be considered certain, however, is that Shakespeare in writing the passage somehow remembered a dramatized version of the fable published at the time of the Armada by a Winchester schoolmaster, William Averell, called *A Marvailous Combat of Contrarieties*.[43] Over twenty words in Shakespeare's version occur in Averell's and in none of the others. And they are not just ifs and ans but words of length and substance and individuality.

There also occurs in Averell and in none of the others the contrast between the head as the sovereign or Queen and the heart as the place where the counsellors forgather. Yet, and this is the remarkable thing, the whole framework of Averell's presentation is quite different. Averell gives the fable as a dramatic debate between Tongue, Hands, and Feet on the one side and the Belly and the Back on the other; the order in which the shared words appear is different; and in several cases though the words are the same Shakespeare has used them in a different context. It is extremely interesting to speculate on how this could have happened. Did he compose the scene like the compiler of a Variorum edition, surrounded by his sources open on his desk, choosing a word from this and a phrase from that? It would be grotesque to imagine any such procedure. So what should we imagine? That somebody told him of Averell's treatment of the fable, that he read it for inspiration, and that having read it he gratefully borrowed a large number of Averell's words and phrases? Perhaps. But there is an alternative. Two possible echoes of Averell occur in *1 Henry IV*, 'when *theeves* cannot be *true one* to *another*' and 'a shottened herring'.[44] If this is not a coincidence it means that Shakespeare had read Averell's little tract a great deal earlier, which is in itself a reasonable thing to suppose. Lively as it is, it is of the nature of ephemeral literature, and most people would have read it when it came out or not at all. Of course Shakespeare may have reread it before writing *Coriolanus*. We cannot possibly tell. But the fact that on several occasions words are transferred to quite different contexts may suggest not. It is an effect that would seem more likely after a lapse of

---

[42] *3 Henry VI*, 5.6.61–4: the echoing Marlowe passage (*Edward II*, 5.1.14) carries no such play on the word 'blood'.

[43] First published 1588, reprinted 1591. Attention was first drawn to it by E. A. J. Honigmann. K. Muir (*Notes and Queries*, 198 (1953), 240–2) listed the formidable number of verbal echoes which seem to put it beyond doubt that Shakespeare had read Averell's tract.

[44] *1 Henry IV*, 2.2.27 and 2.4.122, cf. Averell's 'when *Theeves* attack *one another true* men come by their goods' (B1 – my italics) and 'buttons, this yeere bumbd like a barrell, the next *shottend* like a *herring*' (B1ᵛ).

time. And why not fifteen years? Needless to say the remembering of so many words and phrases after so long would be remarkable. But Shakespeare must have had a remarkably retentive and quick-access memory for what he had read. Otherwise how could he have acquired his vast vocabulary which is as rich in literary as it is in colloquial words? Still, whatever the truth of this general question may be, Shakespeare must have told this particular fable with his 'poet's eye in a fine frenzy rolling' not from North's text to Averell's but from Menenius Agrippa to the ringleader of the crowd. The proof is the mention of the big toe. It is a joke, and a good joke too; it is totally integrated into the context of the scene; and it is also absolutely right in the context of Galenic medicine. Yet – and this is the point – it does not come, not even the word 'toe' comes anywhere, in any of the sources that have been suggested for the scene. Shakespeare's imagination must have supplied it, and there is no way this could have happened unless Shakespeare was in command of his own physiological knowledge.

Sir Vavasour Firebrace, a baronet in Disraeli's novel *Sibyl*, believed that baronets were the true hereditary champions of the crown and the body destined to save England. A medical historian championing Shakespeare must beware of Vavasourism. Physiology is not the central concern of Elizabethan literature, and no poet will have his reputation made or broken by it. Nevertheless by virtue of the very fact of its being in the wings and not on the centre of the stage it can provide some useful sidelighting. In the far from exhaustive look we have taken it has illuminated a few minor points in Shakespeare's text, exposed some weaknesses in the aesthetic approach according to which he was a kind of Bunthorne, free to poeticize because the drab work of philosophy had been done for him, and revealed an unfamiliar aspect of his imagination. These are not negligible gleanings and I suspect that further search could increase them significantly.[45]

---

[45] This is the revised text of a paper read to the Pybus Club of the University of Newcastle in 1983. I must thank its members, and particularly Mr James Longrigg, not only for inviting me to address them but also for the many helpful comments and suggestions that they made to me in the subsequent discussion.

SHAKESPEARE IN THE THEATRICAL CRITICISM OF HENRY MORLEY

RUSSELL JACKSON

Henry Morley (1822–94) is best known as a tireless editor and introducer of the classics of English literature – the 64 volumes of his *Universal Library*, published between 1883 and 1888, and the 209 volumes of *Cassell's National Library*, which appeared between 1886 and 1890, together with other, shorter, series designed to introduce the great (and minor) writers to as large a public as possible. His *Tables of English Literature* (1870), *A First Sketch of English Literature* (1873), and the ten completed volumes of his *English Writers* (1887–95) place him in the same league as the Cowden Clarkes and Charles Knight as a promoter of the study of good literature. His appetite for the rediscovery of unfamiliar books suggests comparison with the labours of the Reverend A. B. Grosart and his army of editing curates. He was a professor of English Language and Literature in the University of London – first at King's College, later at Queen's – and earned an honourable place in the history of the rise of English studies and the development of adult education. As a University Extension lecturer he toured the country by train, enduring inconvenience and fatigue in the cause of popular education. His biographer, Sir Henry Solly, cites a timetable from the 1870s, from which the following is a representative day's schedule:

Friday. – Leave Stockton 6.30. York: Dryden; Defoe's Early Writings. Leave York, London and N.W., 12.40, via Leeds; Liverpool 4.15 Lecture New Brighton 8: Ideal Commonwealths. Leave Lime Street 11 p.m., Birmingham 2.30 [a.m.].[1]

Sometimes Morley's life was positively dangerous: 'He once had a narrow escape of his life when the floor of the railway carriage came out while the train was travelling at a considerable speed, and he had to mount the seat and hold on by the hat-rail till they came to the next station.' He also enjoyed at least one of those encounters with vivid eccentrics which seem to be intensified by the privacy of the compartments in non-corridor carriages:

On another occasion he had for a companion an old gentleman who had been trying to make himself more comfortable with the aid of a somewhat deflated air-cushion. Professor Morley was going to blow it up for him; but his action was arrested by the exclamation, 'Stop, sir, stop! that cushion contains my deceased wife's breath!'

Morley abounded in qualities which we might regard as characteristically Victorian: earnestness, industry taken to the point of obsession, veneration for the great literary works, and faith in the centrality of literature in the definition of culture. We might be inclined to associate these attitudes with a certain lack of humour and proportion. The very copiousness may prompt a degree of condescension in our treatment of Morley – much as it does, quite wrongly, in the case of George Saintsbury. The essential simplicity of the task of writing literary history, as conceived by Morley,

[1] Henry Shaen Solly, *The Life of Henry Morley, LL.D.* (1898), pp. 297–8. Solly's biography is the principal source of information on Morley's career, together with Morley's reminiscences in *Early Papers and Some Memories* (1891) and James Gairdner's article in *The Dictionary of National Biography*, vol. 13 (1894), pp. 975–6. Morley trained and practised as a doctor before taking up education and journalism: David Palmer (*The Rise of English Studies*, 1965) suggests that with Morley 'English studies became fully professional' (p. 50).

may seem touching and naive. He has few of the methodological inhibitions that vex many modern scholars and critics.

Whatever Morley's limitations as a critic and historian, his fifteen years as a drama critic, between 1851 and 1866, show that he was neither naive nor humourless, that he had a breadth of learning and the sympathetic good sense to use it well, and that if his capacity for work was prodigious, it was in proportion to his appetite for enjoyment.

I

The most important feature of Morley's theatrical criticism is his insistence that the theatre is a social and cultural institution of great importance, and that for the educated middle classes to ignore it is an abdication of responsibility. If the theatre is in a poor way, it is our duty to support it and improve it by active influence. Morley sees his role as that of a physician, watching at the bedside: 'desiring to see our Drama, with a clean tongue and a steady pulse, able to resume its place in society as a chief form of Literature, with a stage fitly interpreting its thoughts and in wide honour as one of the strongest of all secular aids towards the intellectual refinement of the people' (p. 9).[2]

The diagnosis is familiar from other commentators of the 1850s and 1860s. The increase in London's population created a new market for entertainment which the two 'patent' houses, Covent Garden and Drury Lane, failed to satisfy. They had been rebuilt to a size no longer conducive to the effective performance of intimate, spoken drama, and had gone into competition with the 'minor' houses in providing musical, melodramatic and spectacular shows. The compromise between commercial pressure and artistic standards had become less and less tenable: Macready's two periods as a manager had shown that the repertoire based on Shakespeare and the 'legitimate' no longer paid well enough. In the 1840s it had seemed that the idea of a 'national' theatre no longer held out any hopes of success. In response to this dismaying state of affairs, two managements had managed to establish companies which gave regular perfor-

mances of the 'legitimate' repertoire. In the West End, Charles Kean's Princess's Theatre gave 'revivals' of Shakespearian and other drama, whose specially prepared scenery and costumes of unimpeachable historical accuracy, spectacular displays of pageantry, and expert stage management gave them an attraction comparable to the best contemporary melodramas and Christmas pantomimes. In Islington, Samuel Phelps had taken Sadler's Wells Theatre, and transformed it from a melodrama house of doubtful respectability to a prodigy of popular, educational entertainment. Kean's Princess's was popular in the sense of appealing to a fashionable, unintellectual, West-End clientele for basic economic support. Phelps's Sadler's Wells was popular in the sense of being a people's theatre: aimed primarily at the respectable artisan and the literate middle classes. Although their audiences overlapped (playgoers being to some extent a class on their own), the social emphasis of the two theatres was seen as distinctively different: West-End as against People's Theatre. But it is the similarities that we should attend to. Both theatres had a strong bias towards efficient stage management, historical accuracy, the excision of conventional accretions from Shakespeare's text and an appeal to the desire for educational information presented through the medium of entertainment. Kean's theatre seems more showy and pretentious, with its triple-size playbills and its more limited repertoire; Phelps's more appealing in its populist aims and more conscientious in the pursuit of *ensemble* and harmonious stage-effects. Phelps was a better actor than

---

[2] Reference is made throughout to the page-numbers of the second edition (1891) of *Journal of a London Playgoer, from 1851 to 1866*, which was first published in 1866. The second edition constituted the second volume of a projected multi-volume collection of Morley's papers (*Early Papers and Some Memories* being the first), but the series was not continued. The 1891 *Journal* has a useful index, and has been reproduced in 'The Victorian Library' with an informative introduction by Michael R. Booth (Leicester, 1976). Morley made minor adjustments of style and content in the articles selected for reprinting in the *Journal*. Among the reviews he omitted were notices of *The Tempest* at the Princess's (18 July 1857) and Charles Dillon's *Othello* (6 December 1856).

Charles Kean, he put on more Shakespeare and encouraged better new writers.[3] Kean drew the carriage trade, and was patronized by royalty; Phelps's theatre was remarkable for its earnest, enthusiastic audiences, often book in hand, following the play so intently that, in the words of Morley's notice of *A Midsummer Night's Dream* (1854), 'many a subdued hush arose, not during, but just before, the delivery of the most charming passages' (p. 58). The comparison between East End and West End, to the discredit of the latter, had become a commonplace of theatrical commentary by the time Blanchard Jerrold and Gustave Doré published their *London: a Pilgrimage* in 1872:

The Stage has not progressed with the spread of education – that is, not in fashionable parts of London. This is not the place to develop the reasons why; but it may be noted that the drama is spreading through the poorer and less educated portions of society who always crowd to the theatres where classic or sterling modern drama is played. (p. 173)

The development of these two managements, and the continuing debate about their merits and the implications of their success, are important to our understanding of Morley's Shakespeare reviews. Other elements of the mid-century debate concerning the state of the Drama are also relevant, and these must be referred to briefly.

Like many other writers, Morley was anxious to encourage new dramatic authors, and correspondingly harsh in his comments on the practice of buying-in cheap and shoddy adaptations from the French. The originals of these, he complains, were themselves 'based not even on a true study of French life, but only upon a shrewd perception of the French varieties of stage-effect and of stage-character' (p. 21).

He expresses the commonly held concern over the direction taken by burlesque and extravaganza, away from acceptable absurdities and the mockery of subjects worthy of ridicule, and towards senseless puns, the display of female legs and the travesty of works of drama and literature that should be above parody. The use of slang in burlesques is similarly to be deplored.

Morley joins in the debate about 'sensation' drama, and makes the important distinction between the reprehensible dependence of some new plays on spectacle and extreme physical violence, and the legitimate use of complicated plots and violent action in well-devised melodramas where some element of human character-drawing and motivation is at issue:

A good story cannot be the worse for taking a very strong hold upon the attention. They are the crimes and mysteries of life that stir the depths of human character and bring into play all the passions. If plays and stories turning with strong interest upon incidents of crime are to be put down as 'sensational', let us bury our Shakespeares fathoms five, cry 'Out upon Marlowe, Ford, Massinger, and all the rest of them,' and burn half the best novels in our language. (p. 302)

He is not anxious to do away altogether with absurdity in burlesque or even in melodrama: 'As for improbability of incident, he is a dull fellow who does not sometimes like it' (p. 239). In reviewing melodramas of the old-fashioned sort – where an unequivocal appeal is made to the emotions and sympathies of the audience – Morley evidently relishes the familiar improbabilities even as he catalogues them. In his account of T. P. Cooke, the famous impersonator of nautical heroes, for example, he shows his affectionate regard for the appropriate clichés:

The acting is...full of quiet touches that bespeak the actor's genius, and for all that belongs to the stage-sailor – love of salt-water, grogs, quids of tobacco, devotion, patriotism, power of engaging in terrific combat any dozen of another nation, dying true to his ship, and recovering suddenly from death at the call

---

[3] For a scholarly account of Phelps's management, see Shirley S. Allen, *Samuel Phelps and Sadler's Wells Theatre* (Middletown, Conn., 1971). Between the seasons of 1844–5 and 1861–2 Phelps staged thirty-one of Shakespeare's plays, a total of 1,632 performances. Non-Shakespearian drama accounted for 1,860 performances (figures from Allen's Appendix I, 'Chart of Shakespearean Performances'). In the course of his tenure as sole manager of the Princess's (1851–2 to 1858–9) Charles Kean revived twelve of Shakespeare's plays (figure derived from J. W. Cole's record in his *The Life and Theatrical Times of Charles Kean, F.S.A.*, 2 vols., 1859).

of duty – Mr Fitzball has determined that the gods shall accuse him of shortcoming in no one particular.

(p. 164)

He is alive to the 'good or bad habit that an English audience has of looking out for something upon which to feed its appetite for the absurd' (p. 190) and the care required in melodramatic writing to keep this tendency in check with the judicious use of comedy. Wilkie Collins's drama *The Red Vial* had been condemned, Morley points out, 'not for any serious demerit, but for a defect arising from misapprehension of the temper of an English audience'. It was perhaps the appreciation of this desire for humour that led Shakespeare to put the fool in *King Lear*. 'Such plays as *Jane Shore*, or Otway's *Orphan*, never had a healthy life upon our stage; and as a nation we have for the style of the serious French drama an ingrained antipathy' (p. 191).

This distinction between French and English taste suggests one aspect of Morley's implicit definition of the audience for whom the modern playwright should be working. Another is to be found in his rejection of Hérold's opera *Zampa* as a Frenchman's *Don Giovanni*, full of stock operatic situations 'all set to good light music, which should please a Frenchman, but which, because there is not a spark in it of fun or feeling . . . is received with dulness by an English audience' (p. 187).

In fact, Morley makes quite clear in his 'Prologue' the standard he wishes to set for the new Theatre:

Our model manager should take for standard of the people he would please an honest Englishman of the educated middle-class, akin to all that is human, trained not only in school and college, but in daily active stir of life, to interest in all true thinking and true feeling, to habitual notice of varieties of character, and to a habit of noting its depths in real life.   (p. 20)

It is from this assumption that many of Morley's specific criticisms of theatrical practice and organization derive. As we shall see, the emphasis on 'all true thinking and true feeling' and on 'depth' of character are of considerable importance in reading Morley's criticisms of Shakespearian performances.

They are also representative of the values of other Victorian commentators on Shakespeare, and it is especially valuable to find them here in the context of a critique of the contemporary theatre and its plays.

Behind this ideal figure of the humane, educated middle-class Englishman, Morley's passion for the bourgeois revolutions of the 1840s may be detected. He had, indeed, hailed the Italian uprisings of 1848 with a poem entitled *Sunrise in Italy*, and he made no secret of his faith in the middle class as upholders of the values neglected in fashionable society. In his comments on opera – which are in themselves a fascinating account of operatic acting and taste in the mid-century – Morley suggests that the popular taste is for the true composers: Mozart, Mendelssohn, Rossini. The fashionable world, by contrast, is preoccupied with Verdi and Donizetti, for whom Morley has scant regard. *La Traviata* he condemns on the grounds of its immorality and musical ineptitude: 'an opera very far inferior in value to the worst of Mr Balfe's' (p. 115). He looks on the Restoration as a period of decadence for English drama: 'It was dependence upon courtly favour that destroyed in the stage of the Restoration its old national character' (p. 15). He believes firmly in the popular nature of Shakespearian drama:

That bowl of small-change taken at the play-house door gave a more sure support to men of genius who earned their share from it, than Royal favour and the being in high fashion among courtiers.   (p. 15)

In Morley's opinion, the Theatre thrives as a healthy cultural institution by attracting and entertaining intelligent middle-class paying customers, not by reliance on 'a large half-intelligent population now in London that by bold puffing can be got into a theatre' (p. 19). He welcomes improvements in front-of-house conditions: comfortable chairs, the discontinuing of 'fees' (gratuities) to attendants, and so forth. At the same time, he does not intend the theatre to become the exclusive preserve of the educated middle class: he hopes to entice the working man to it, to use it as an instrument of education. Morley wants a Theatre that will civilize the proletariat, not revolutionize it or feed its grievances.

In addition to these social ideals, Morley holds firmly to the general principle that drama can elevate as well as entertain. Tolerant as he is of 'fun', he is unequivocal in stating his preferences when he is in the presence of a masterpiece of idealized humanity. *Fidelio* elicits from him a comparison with Shakespeare that reminds us of the importance attached, in the last analysis, to *depth*:

The most exquisite of Mozart's melodies have no such life in them as this, but are as the fancy of Spenser, pure fancy unsurpassed, beside Shakespeare's sounding of all notes that are to be drawn out of man's heart.

(p. 210)

Leonore is 'a heroic wife, with all the tenderness and purity of Shakespeare's Imogen' (p. 211).

II

The principal characteristic of Victorian Shakespeare productions which we confidently point to as having been discarded early this century, and having distorted the plays' form and meaning, is pictorial realism. It is not surprising that Morley should welcome the opportunity offered by some plays for this kind of display. Of *King John* he observes 'There is not a play of Shakespeare's that more admits or justifies a magnificent arrangement of scene...' (p. 30). In Charles Kean's production,

We see revived the rude chivalric grandeur of the Middle Age, the woes and wars of a half-barbarous time, in all its reckless splendour, selfish cruelty, and gloomy suffering. (p. 30)

Richard II gives the same manager 'reasonable opportunity' for such shows as the 'complete spectacle of lists set out for a tournament on Gosford Green' and the 'triumph of the entry of Bolingbroke with Richard into London' – the latter being 'a fine piece of stage-effect'. 'Of course,' Morley admits, 'it is necessary to make room for stage-appointments and processions by omissions from the poetry, and *Richard II* was well chosen as a play from which certain omissions may be made

without serious damage to its effect for acting purposes' (p. 142).[4] At the end of Kean's 1856–7 season, Morley complimented him on his creation of 'a brilliant museum for the student' in which the antiquities of the various ages 'were presented, not as dusty, broken relics, but as living truths, and made attractive as well by their splendour as by the haze of poetry through which they were to be seen' (p. 163). The Princess's Theatre gave to *The Merchant of Venice* 'the local colouring that was in Shakespeare's mind' (p. 174). Shakespeare's plays gave a legitimate and satisfying pretext for scenic art. Commenting on the failure of a 'great Egyptian spectacle', *Nitocris*, at Drury Lane in 1855, Morley observes that 'To connect spectacle with one of Shakespeare's plays ensures a certain degree of success', but that without 'some matter that the public thought worth hearing' it had little chance (p. 109). The production at the Princess's of Kotzebue's *Pizarro* – an old-fashioned, heroic melodrama – suggested that 'Mr Charles Kean is right in thinking that there is no Atlas except Shakespeare for the world he fashions' (p. 163).

All this is mid-century orthodoxy, appreciation that would have gratified Kean by its correspondence to his motives in staging Shakespeare plays as historical spectacles. But Morley's enthusiasm for the 'museum' is qualified by an appreciation of visual effect on a smaller scale. In Samuel Phelps's production of *Coriolanus* (Sadler's Wells, 1860) he compared 'the view of Antium by the light of the rising moon', evidently 'contrived to give colour to the poetry', with the less pretentious *tableau* that followed:

...There is no scene in the play more impressive to the eye than the succeeding picture of Coriolanus, seated by the glowing embers of the brazier that represents his enemy's hearth. (p. 217)

---

4 Charles Kean's acting version is described by G. C. D. Odell, *Shakespeare from Betterton to Irving*, 2 vols. (New York, 1920) vol. 2, pp. 292–4. The revival of what was, in the nineteenth century, a 'rare' play, was given on 85 nights in a season which lasted nearly a year (1 September 1856 to 21 August 1857) and included 290 nights of Shakespeare.

Morley applauds Phelps's skill in making the 'pomp of processions with the constant noise of drum and trumpet...follow instead of leading the march of the poem' and in remembering 'in the action of Coriolanus himself . . . that heroic pride is self-contained' (p. 216). In contrast to Edmund Kean's 'ungovernable passion', Phelps summons a 'sub-limity of disdain' for 'I banish you'. When Caius Martius receives the name Coriolanus and is ex-horted to 'Bear the addition nobly ever',

Mr Phelps represents him stirred by the warning into a large sense of what is in his soul, and lifted upon tiptoe by his soaring thought. The same action gives grandeur to the words,

> I'd rather be their servant in my way
> Than sway with them in theirs,

and is afterwards more than once used, not osten-tatiously, and never without giving the emphasis intended.   (p. 216)

The *Journal* has many of these vivid sketches of acting technique. Phelps's Falstaff, in *1 Henry IV*, has a 'lively intellect that stands for soul as well as mind in his gross body' and shows his 'determination to cap every other man's good saying with something better of his own' by his tendency to 'thrust in with inarticulate sounds, as if to keep himself a place open for speech while he is fetching up his own flagon of wit from the farthest caverns of his stomach' (p. 275). In the same actor's Timon Morley notices that 'As the liberal Athenian lord, his gestures are large, his movements free – out of himself everything pours, towards himself he will draw nothing', whereas in the second half of the play 'he sits on the ground self-contained, but miserable in the isolation, from first to last contrasting with Apemantus ...who is a churl by the original sourness of his nature, hugs himself in his own ragged robe, and worships himself for his own ill manners' (p. 132).

In the case of Phelps, these appreciations are connected with approval of the management's policy. It is characteristic of Morley, though, to perceive the significance of a subtlety in an actor's personal performance for the overall interpretation of the play, and to relate it to the principles on which the whole staging has been conceived. His strictures on bad acting are often amusing and always un-equivocal. Thus, after a second visit, Mlle Stella Colas's ill-advised attempt on Juliet did not seem as bad as it had been on first viewing because she had by now got rid of 'some of the worst absurdities of action':

the upward gesture of snipping with scissors, for example, that accompanied Juliet's suggestion con-cerning Romeo, that Night, when he died, might 'take him and cut him out in little stars', a line that, to a dressy second-rate French ingénue, inevitably sug-gested millinery, and Night as the editor of *La Belle Assemblée*.

But, unfortunately, 'bad as it was, this Juliet [was] still abominable', because the 'innocent Italian child' was transformed into a French *ingénue*, 'in her stage-innocence the most self-conscious of all forms into which the front of womanhood has ever been recast'. Morley discusses in some detail the actress's misreading of Juliet's speech before she drinks the potion, and points out that any apprehension of the ghostly form of Tybalt ought to be outweighed in the character's mind by her imagining the promised union with Romeo.

A long and carefully argued critique of the French actor Charles Fechter's Othello notes the misplaced emphasis on the Moor's 'quick impres-sionable character' at the expense of his dignity, applauds the subtlety and ingenuity of the reading, but insists that it confers on the character a Gallic quality at variance with Shakespeare's intentions. In the rendering of Othello's description of his wooing, Morley finds 'a colloquial ease that is most clever and agreeable, though not at all "unvarnished"' (p. 228). Here the point is Fechter's conferring a self-consciousness on Othello, rather than a com-plaint of the same quality as objectionably present in the mimetic technique. Fechter throughout en-gaged the audience's sympathy for Othello, with the consequence that 'the fifth act [became] very pain-ful' to a degree not intended by the dramatist. His business of looking in a mirror to point 'It is the cause...' as a reference to Othello's dark skin is part of the same approach. The total effect of the final act is 'full of passion and emotion, and the audience is deeply stirred, but the effect belongs rather to

French melodrama than to English tragedy' (p. 232). The effect is strengthened by 'a melodramatic but false reading' in which Othello's '...and smote him, thus' leads to his stabbing not Iago but himself – 'to flash surprise', after dragging the villain around and holding a dagger above him.

Both these examples of Morley's close attention to physical action show a keen eye, and for the contemporary reader they would have had special interest as part of the debate on the relative merits of French and English acting in tragedy and melodrama. They also show an appreciation of the fine distinction between tragic and melodramatic acting. Although Morley liked good melodramatic writing and performance (a taste not at all incompatible with affectionate amusement at its absurdities) he evidently felt that the analysis of such performances as Fechter's put on his mettle an English critic with literary pretensions. The review of Fechter's Othello is one of the longest of its kind in the collection. In the case of Mlle Colas, Morley is anxious to distinguish what is vicious in the taste that applauds such performances. Elsewhere he is splendidly brutal when he feels that some theatrical infamy needs to be crushed. For such absurdities as the appearance of two little girls as Richard III and Richmond he has no words to waste. The performance by the Bateman sisters (at the St James's Theatre in 1851) was simply 'a nuisance by no means proportioned to the size of its perpetrators' (p. 27).

Like the social significance of Phelps's work at Sadler's Wells, these performances are judged in the light of general issues important in the eyes of Morley and his more thoughtful contemporaries. The visits of French and German actors raise wider questions of artistic policy, as well as points of the interpretation of the text. Shakespearian productions are discussed as part of a wider repertoire, which shapes the actor's craft and represents the scope allowed to contemporary dramatists. Morley's detailed reviews of the acting in French, Italian and German opera (where, unlike some of his colleagues, he had the advantage of knowing what the words meant) show a similar desire to go beyond the closed world of the 'points' traditionally established by performers. He is not concerned with the actor's or

singer's significance as a public personality, except in so far as their status reflects the public's attitudes. He admires the openness of Emil Devrient's Hamlet, remarkable for its lack of strongly enforced 'points', making it difficult for a critic to extract 'any one-sided theory of Hamlet's character' from the performance (p. 41). This was as much a sign of the difference between German and English technique as of Devrient's undoubted personal ability: the casting of the piece showed 'the even excellence characteristic of the German company'. Where Morley comments that with Devrient, 'many passages which on our stage are especially made to stand out, of course fell back into the ranks', one senses that he perceives a connection between the 'points' system and the deadening effects of the British hierarchy of actors. In a similar vein he comments on the ensemble achieved by Sadler's Wells casts. Devrient impresses by his ability to play a range of parts beyond the 'line' which one would expect of an English tragedian, and which the latter would insist on as his prerogative. Phelps is applauded for effecting a compromise whereby he does not put aside his responsibility as actor–manager:

If Mr Phelps takes upon himself the character which needs the most elaborate development, however carefully and perfectly he may produce his own impression of his part, he never by his acting drags it out of its place in the drama. (p. 129)

Even the smallest part is given the importance accorded to it by Shakespeare 'in his plan' – a phrase which indicates belief that a 'plan' is to be discerned in the works. In fact, Morley believes such performances as Phelps's to be true to the technique of the dramatist: 'Shakespeare appears in his integrity, and his plays are found to affect audiences less as dramas in a common sense than as great poems' (p. 130). The Sadler's Wells Midsummer Night's Dream is praised for its emphasis on one main idea:

[Phelps] knew that he was to present merely shadows; that spectators, as Puck reminds them in the epilogue, are to think that they have slumbered on their seats, and that what appeared before them have been visions. (p. 57)

The achievement of this effect – aided by the use of a gauze drop which 'subdue[d] the flesh and blood of the actors into something more nearly resembling dream-figures' – was made possible by 'the poetical feeling prompting a judicious but not extravagant outlay' (p. 58). Consistency, harmony, the subordination of the parts to the whole – these qualities seem to require the extraordinary conditions offered by the German state theatres or the idealism of Phelps. The review of Kean's production of the same play notes the lack of harmony between poem and scenery, and the irrelevance of some of the spectacular effects. One, a shadow-dance of fairies, is cited as 'a sacrifice of Shakespeare to the purposes of the ballet-master' (p. 134). After pointing to the encore given to the elaborate finale – 'a ballet of fairies round a maypole that shoots up out of an aloe, after the way of a transformation in a pantomime, and rains down garlands' – Morley suggests that its being encored 'is evidence enough of the depraved taste of the audience'. But he ends on a conciliatory note:

I make these comments in no censorious mood. It is a pleasure to see Shakespeare enjoyed by the large number of persons who are attracted to the Princess's Theatre by the splendours for which it is famous. I do not wish the splendour less or its attraction less, but only ask for more heed to the securing of a perfect harmony between the conceptions of the decorator and those of the poet.　(pp. 134–5)

Three years separates these reviews, and no explicit comparison with Phelps is made in that of Kean's version of the play. Nevertheless, it is clearly implied that the Princess's needs to attract an audience less attentive than they should be to the play as poem. Kean's sins of commission and omission (the latter include the Helena–Hermia quarrel), the lack of careful thought in his overly balletic treatment of the fairies, the introduction of an impressive but too specific background representing ancient Athens – these are signs of a false taste imposed on him by a 'depraved' audience. If the review of the Sadler's Wells presentation can be read as a reply to Hazlitt's famous conclusion (in his *Characters of Shakespear's Plays*) that 'the boards of a theatre and the realms of

fancy are not the same thing',[5] that of Charles Kean's *Midsummer Night's Dream* suggests that the mystical union can only be achieved under the right social conditions, which alone will produce the right artistic values. His enthusiasm for Kean's 'museum' was qualified by a sense of the showmanship it involved.

Morley's implicit comparison of Charles Kean and Samuel Phelps as actor–managers would have been more obvious to a contemporary, for whom the weighing of their complementary virtues in the balance was a commonplace of theatrical criticism and gossip. The two theatres had different economic bases – John Coleman claims that Kean could 'take as much money in two nights as Phelps did in six'.[6] Although the Sadler's Wells audience was rightly celebrated for its attentiveness and enthusiasm, and Phelps's productions were usually less ostentatious than those of Charles Kean, it must not be forgotten that each audience had a varied composition and that Phelps and Kean were both mid-Victorian actor–managers, with values in common. *The Times*'s review of Kean's *King John* is interesting in this respect, for it includes information omitted by Morley concerning the audience's response to the play. We are told that 'The determination to check Papal aggression met with all the accustomed cheers, the "Italian priest" coming in for his due share of vociferous defiance from boxes, pit and gallery' (10 February 1851). This somewhat old-fashioned response – recalling the Georgian audience's habitual turning of plays to account for political demonstrations – is interesting in its combining the different social levels within the auditorium. It serves to warn us against drawing simple conclusions from the Princess's social superiority. In a similar manner, *The Times*'s notice of Phelps's *A Midsummer Night's Dream* should remind us that the Islington management was bringing Shakespearian production in line with popular taste, as much as the reverse. At Sadler's Wells, we are told, 'decoration is an all-important matter,...it is a principle to bring out

---

[5] William Hazlitt, *Characters of Shakespear's Plays* (World's Classics edition, 1916: repr. 1955), p. 104.

[6] John Coleman, *Memoirs of Samuel Phelps* (1886), p. 214.

every season one work at least which, while it belongs to the highest dramatic literature of our country, shall also stand as a specimen of scenic art' (10 October 1853). Morley's commentary on Phelps and Kean in the 1850s and 1860s is part of a debate that gathered momentum as the Victorians took in hand the socialization of their culture. Morley was an enthusiast for sanitary reform, educational reform, and the Italian *Risorgimento*: Shakespeare and the theatre he took in his stride.

III

What qualities did Morley admire in the plays, and how did he like them to be brought out? We have seen that his criteria for successful stage production include the treatment of the play as a 'poem' – that is, acknowledging and expressing its essential unity and coherence as a work of art, and avoiding the false emphasis given to individual scenes, speeches, and characters by personal vanity or the cultivation of bad theatrical taste. But what are these poems? To what end have they been composed, and what pleasures can they afford when properly rendered?

Some of Morley's expectations leap out at the reader as characteristically Victorian. He seeks re-finement in Hotspur: Mr Montgomery, playing the part at Drury Lane in 1864, was able to give the contemptuous description of the fop with his pouncet-box 'with a manner simply of rough, violent distaste', but he missed in his 'impatient jesting at Glendower' the opportunity to 'speak lightly and with audacious gaiety on the quick impulse of young blood' (p. 276). Morley seems to want a Hotspur something like Steerforth in *David Copperfield*, minus the villainy. The 'gay untamed fancy, full of fresh life in mirth and sportive tenderness' was marked in Montgomery's scenes with Lady Percy, but elsewhere his manner was 'too much that of an unpleasantly headstrong boy' (p. 276). Even allowing for conventional expressions (such as 'mirth and sportive tenderness') this sounds a somewhat mawkish Hotspur. Similarly, Morley's description of Justice Shallow shows a Victorian appetite for pathos: 'There is nothing more sternly earnest in Shakespeare, and more tragic in its

undertone, than the dialogue between Shallow and Silence at the beginning of the second scene of the third act' (pp. 284–5). Morley renders a simpler and more solemn account of this scene than we might expect from a modern critic; mortality is a different subject for him. Because he sees the clear direction of the audience's sympathy as the overriding task of playwright and actor, Morley (like most of his contemporaries) has no taste for irony at the charac-ter's expense in such moments of crisis. This shows with particular clarity in his review of Charles Kean's *Richard II*.

There he objects to the omission of the final scene of act 1, 'in which the audience is prepared for Gaunt's death by tidings of his illness, and for Richard's seizure of his plate by a distinct knowledge of the King's sore poverty, his need of means to fight the Irish rebels, and his consequent wish that Gaunt may die, and leave his wealth behind him'. This scene prepares us to see 'with less surprise and abhorrence' the seizure of Gaunt's goods in the scene that follows. Similarly, Kean's Gaunt died on stage – ignoring Shakespeare's provision of an off-stage death. This further detracted from any sympathy the audience might entertain towards the King. Richard in this revision 'becomes immediately a bird of prey beside the corpse, and loses irretrievably the good-will of the audience' (p. 143).[7] The omission of act 3, scene 1 – the sentencing of Bushy and Green – also takes away a sequence 'cunningly preparing us for pity'. 'The effect . . . is to impede seriously the course of sympathy in the audience for King Richard's misfortunes, and to throw great difficulty in the way of the actor by whom it is the whole purpose of the play that sympathy should be excited' (p. 143). Charles Kean managed to 'win

---

7 A promptbook of Charles Kean's production (Folger Prompt *Richard II*, 2: Shattuck no. 7) shows that Gaunt's body was the focus of the conspiratorial scene with Ross, Willoughby and Northumberland that follows the exit of Richard and his entourage. In Terry Hands's production (RSC, 1980–1) Gaunt died on stage, was left in his chair for the remainder of the scene, and at its conclusion was allowed to remain on the stage after the other actors departed, as an emblem of the dying order.

some pity for his hero' by 'the skill with which he marked, as the turning point in Richard's story, the revoking of Bolingbroke's sentence of banishment', but it was not enough. Mrs Kean's pathos in the Queen's parting from Richard (5.1) 'conquered a few kind thoughts for Richard', but this too was insufficient.

Other cuts Morley thought quite justified, and he is not alone in wishing to be spared the Aumerle scenes in the fifth act. But his reading of that sequence is more serious than most of its detractors would accept: 'truly the most vigorous sketch ever conceived of the domestic misery that is among the incidents of civil war' (p. 142). Morley reads the play as a 'fine picture of the old, wild days of English civil war' in which 'a clash of arms' is 'blended with . . . incidents of grief and terror' (pp. 141–2), and through which we steer a course according to the careful direction of our sympathy for the principal character. He is a long way removed from twentieth-century readings of the play as a political tragedy, and from the concept of 'ambivalence'. Even the degree of detachment suggested later in Walter Pater's portrait of the King as aesthete is foreign to this view of the play. It is with Richard's feelings, not his perception, that we must identify. Similarly, Morley's reactions to King John – which we have glanced at as indicating his attitude to scenic embellishment – emphasize the grief of Constance and the effect of the crime against Prince Arthur on such hardened cases as Hubert and Faulconbridge. 'None of the characters of the tragedy are cast in an unyielding mould.' Although the King himself cannot be other than a villain in Kean's best style, the play itself has the requisite pathetic qualities: 'the heart heaves and throbs beneath its coat of mail' (p. 30).[8]

The political content of the histories is thus simplified: they present examples of human suffering and valour, against a background of colourful savagery. The twentieth-century rediscovery of Shakespeare as a political playwright has yet to take place. As one might expect, Morley's view of the tragedies is equally far removed from the analyses of Danish politics and the Lears who inhabit a recognizably cruel society that we are used to in the latter half of the twentieth century. Phelps, with all his sense of social duty and Morley, for all his revolutionary sympathy, would never have considered the Crimean war as legitimate, a conscious influence on their interpretation of King Lear. The plight of the poor naked wretches might be a sign of the playwright's sharing in the distress of all right-thinking men at the evils of indigence, but to produce in a performance an implicit commentary on the Poor Law reforms would have been inconceivable.

It should not surprise us, then, to find in Morley's reviews of the tragedies little evidence of the productions' representation of the milieu of the plays. A suitably realistic historical setting is taken for granted, but is not treated as a dominant feature. (With the Histories, the depiction of the Middle Ages is an end in itself.) Nor do the Tragedies elicit much general, interpretative comment: their importance and the chief grounds of their appeal are apparently well established, and require no introductory discussion. Morley discusses in some detail the actor's direction of the audience's sympathies – as the review of Fechter's Othello shows. Of the overall significance of the play he says little, except by implication. In a reviewer at this date we may count this as a virtue, for it yields a clarity of observation, unclouded by parti pris.

Perhaps the best example of Morley's reporting of tragic acting, apart from the description of Fechter's Othello, is to be found in his notices of Ristori and Helen Faucit as Lady Macbeth. Adelaide Ristori, the great Italian tragedienne, was appearing in an Italian translation of the tragedy. The emphasis was firmly on her role:

Madame Ristori conceives Lady Macbeth as a woman who pens up her emotions, who is watchful, self-contained, who fights against compunctious visitings of nature without letting a stir be seen or any note of

---

[8] Morley's phrasing, applied as it is to the whole play, is unusually warm: most Victorian critics admired the pathos of Constance and Arthur, but were alienated by the lack of sympathy in John and the cynicism of the play. See A. C. Sprague, Shakespeare's Histories: Plays for the Stage (1964), chap. 2.

aches within to escape her lips, until her heart too sorely charged gives way under the weight it is forced secretly and silently to bear.   (p. 158)

Her husband, by contrast, lacks altogether Lady Macbeth's capacity for self-containment. The contrast was in fact too crude. Signor Vitaliani, to whom the hapless task fell, gave 'a performance equalled only in its more frantic passages by the dancing of Mr Robson in the choruses of Vilikins and his Dinah' – 'He wriggles, leaps, and pirouettes, serving undoubtedly as a tremendous foil to the impassive figure of the lady who when his fits are most distressing commonly stands by his side' (p. 158). Having said this – and admitted that 'Lady Macbeth is, of course, the entire play at the Lyceum' – Morley can proceed to an examination of the 'main points in [Ristori's] conception of it'. In the reading of the letter she shows the 'deep awe which supernatural occurrences awaken in her. She is not less sensitive than Macbeth to the terror they produce' (p. 159). At 'We will speak further' she intimates her determination in contrast to her husband's misgivings: '...she has her hands upon him, and with a persuasive yet compelling force urges him on, smiling the while with firm-set lips and nodding satisfaction at her work. He is in her power; he moves at her urging.' (This effect is repeated in their exit after the final scene of act 1.) The welcome to Duncan conveys subtly her 'spirit of the fox'. Soon her hands are again on Macbeth, literally pushing him to the murder of Duncan in the first scene of act 2. The beginnings of her breakdown come with her 'real horror' at the description of Duncan's 'silver skin laced with his golden blood' (she 'passed rapidly over the admission to herself that she with her own hand would have killed Duncan "had he not resembled her father as he slept"'). In the banquet scene Macbeth's 'When now I think you can behold such sights...' conjures up in her mind the image of the dead King:

Those words...mark the turning point in Madame Ristori's personation of the lady's character. She meets them with the action of an eager, startled, 'hush!' ...Then, when she is alone with her husband, and he in his wild pacing up and down comes suddenly upon

her still face, over which a new expression is now creeping, he recoils as from another spectre. (p. 161)

Her expression becomes 'more and more spectral', and at the end of the scene her manner of leaving the stage suggests, as do her voice and expression, 'a weariness of soul and body'. This 'spectral' quality is seen again in the sleepwalking: 'Her exit, when her mind has recurred to the night of the murder, is with a ghostly repetition of the old gesture of urging Macbeth on before her' (p. 161).

Although there is no doubt that this adaptation acknowledged Ristori as the principal, if not sole, attraction in the play (the remainder of the action was disposed of in one page of the published acting edition), Morley is content to applaud the power displayed by the actress. For at least one night he allows the tragedy to be handed over to Lady Macbeth. His criterion of 'poetic' completeness in performance – the quality admired in Phelps's ensemble of decor and company – can be waived in favour of a truly great individual interpretation. In his critique of Helen Faucit's performances Morley is on different ground. This was a revival mounted in 1864 at Drury Lane, with Phelps as Macbeth ('a half-barbarous warrior-chief'). Because Drury Lane was considered the rightful home of Shakespearian drama – the 'National Theatre' – Morley finds it appropriate to attack the continuing use of the music by Locke, the flying and dancing witches and the presentation of Hecate, 'like a cross between a beefeater from the tower and a ghost from the Styx'. By 'untuning the key note' the 'singing and jigging corps de ballet' spoils 'the harmonies of the whole play' (p. 288). But again, after this preliminary grumble and a paragraph on Macbeth himself, it is Lady Macbeth who attracts his attention.

Morley saw the performance twice. In his first notice he wrote that Helen Faucit had made the Lady Macbeth of the first scenes too soft: 'passionately womanish and herself impulsive'. The reason adduced is Miss Faucit's well-known faculty of being 'too essentially feminine, too exclusively gifted with the art of expressing all that is most graceful and beautiful in womanhood, to succeed in inspiring anything like awe or terror' (p. 289). When she came, however, to the 'reaction of disappointment and hidden suffering after the crime' she was on firmer ground. Her detachment from the crimes subsequently perpetrated by her husband showed Lady Macbeth as a suffering, essentially compassionate woman. She had been praised by other critics for the evidence of 'smooth treachery' in 'the tender playing of her fingers about the head of the child Fleance' but Morley read this differently: 'The fingers of the woman who has been a mother, and has murder on her soul, wander sadly and tenderly over the type of her lost innocence' (p. 291). She excelled in the 'collapse into weariness of life-long torture' at the end of the banquet scene. If the actress failed in the sleep-walking it was the result of an overly self-conscious delivery which gave it 'too much the air of a well-studied recitation'.

On a second visit, Morley felt that much had been put right, perhaps in response to critical reactions. The performance of the first part of the play was now of a piece with that of the second. Miss Faucit's former excessive loudness had gone, to be replaced by 'methods of expression perfectly within her range and far more impressive' (p. 292). It was now clear to Morley that Lady Macbeth's fainting after the discovery of the murder of Duncan and the grooms was not only genuine, but was specifically in response to the description, 'Here lay Duncan, / His silver skin laced with his golden blood', which strikes her as a 'recurrence to the image which recalled her father when he slept' (p. 292).

This emphasis on the pathos that arises directly from the audience's sympathy with the character is characteristically Victorian, and many of Morley's most discriminating comments on the performance of the Tragedies turn on some such point. He notes, for example, how the final scenes of *Coriolanus* secure our feelings in the hero's favour by the sinking of Aufidius 'into the dastardly chief of assassins' (p. 218). Although Phelps misses the 'terrible' in Lear's early scenes, once he enters 'with his robes washed almost colourless by the rain' after his exposure to the storm, 'every thing is exquisitely done, the story being read wholly with regard to its pathos, not to its terror'. Lear has become an archetypal Victorian figure of the pathetically senile

parent: 'The king is lost utterly in the father' (p. 227). Morley had the privilege – rare for a Victorian theatre-goer – of seeing *Timon of Athens* and *Pericles*. It is clear from his accounts of these plays that the pathos of Phelps's performances in the title roles appealed to the critic. But there is an important distinction. In *Timon* it is the generalized pathos of the human condition – a fable of the contrasts between riches and poverty and the vulnerability of the 'generous impulsive nature', presented 'as a poem' to the audiences at Sadler's Wells (p. 131). *Pericles*, on the other hand, offered spectacle as its principal claim to success, but Phelps impressed by 'true feeling for the pathos of the situation' in Pericles' recognition of his daughter – 'a triumph marked by plaudit after plaudit' (p. 82). In another play on the margins of tragedy, *Cymbeline*, it is the pathos of Imogen that is the centre of attention. Helen Faucit was remarkable for her 'simple presence' in court in the first scene, 'modestly clinging to her husband, shrinking from the rough life outside their love, and stretching out towards him, as he departs, the hands that return to her empty' (p. 292). This performance, in 1864, had lost some of the 'false touches' of the previous year's revival. Morley's praise of Helen Faucit is true to that actress's reputation, and to the current reading of the play, and shows him at his most 'Victorian':

It is no light honour to an actress, that the part in which she excels most should be that which represents the purest and most womanly of Shakespeare's women; in the whole range of poetry the most delicate embodiment of all the qualities that blend to form a womanly perfection – simple piety, wifely devotion, instinctive, unobtrusive modesty, gentle courtesy, moral heroism with all physical cowardice, – no thin ideal, but a very woman, who includes among her virtues aptitude for cookery.   (p. 293)[9]

---

[9] Mrs Jameson had noted the cookery in her *Characteristics of Women, Moral, Poetical and Historical* (first published in 1832 and better known under the title *Shakespeare's Heroines*): '...we must not forget that her "neat cookery" which is so prettily eulogized by Guiderius formed part of the education of a princess in those remote times' (edition of 1879, pp. 230–1).

Imogen, it will be recalled, had been compared by Morley to Beethoven's Leonore: 'Fidele', like 'Fidelio' was a 'heroic wife', disguised as a boy, a type of wifely devotion and a symbol of the redemptive power of woman.

Morley's reviews of the Comedies evince a corresponding desire for 'depth' even in amusing plays. In Phelps's *A Midsummer Night's Dream* one of the few jarring notes was the comedy of the four lovers: 'because the arguing and quarrelling and blundering, that should have been playful, dream-like, and poetical, was much too loud and real'. Helena's plight was farcical rather than, as it should be, pathetic: 'The merriment which Shakespeare connected with those scenes was but a little of the poet's sunlight meant to glitter among tears' (p. 60). When Fanny Kemble gave her programme of readings from the play at Exeter Hall, the right balance was struck, 'charm' was thrown over Hermia and Helena, and the latter's character was brought out 'as something true and womanly' (p. 92). The dreamlike quality which Morley so admired in Phelps's production, and which he clearly considered appropriate to every part of the play, was achieved in the actor's performance of Bottom. This Bottom was taken into the dream-world, 'made an essential part of it, as unsubstantial, as airy and refined as all the rest' (p. 60). Even the mechanicals' play was part of the dream, with 'Bottom as Pyramus ... more perfectly a dream-figure than ever' (p. 61). The more elaborate scenic devices and balletic episodes of Charles Kean's production were rejected, as has been noted, because they were illogical and inconsequential: they also broke into the dream-world, which was threatened by Kean's pedantic approach to the Athenian setting.

A similar seriousness marked Phelps's Malvolio and Don Armado, according to Morley's account. Morley was pleased by the gravity of a Malvolio dressed as a Spanish grandee: 'Such a man, as Mr Phelps represents him, walks not with a smirk and a light comic strut, but in the heaviness of grandeur, with a face grave through very emptiness of all expression' (p. 139). The ending had none of the hysteria nowadays associated with it. This Eminent Victorian has a boundless comfort in his self-contentment, which sustains him even when locked up as a madman.

...When at last he, for once, opens his eyes on learning how he has been tricked, they close again in happy self-content, and he is retiring in state without deigning a word to his tormentors, when as the fool had twitted him by noting how 'the whirligig of time brings in his revenges', he remembers that the whirligig is still in motion. Therefore, marching back with as much speed as is consistent with magnificence, he threatens all – including now Olivia in his contempt – 'I'll be revenged on the whole pack of you!' (p. 140)

Other Malvolios 'seen by the playgoers of this generation' had been 'more fantastical and caused more laughter', but the impression they made had been 'less deep'. Don Armado was treated, Morley claims, as a shallower creature than Malvolio, and 'carries all his bravery on the outside'. Although 'he talks conceitedly of love' in his soul he 'carries enshrined the image of a country drab, its best ideal' (pp. 166–7). Because Morley regards the role as the vehicle of Shakespeare's 'sharpest satire' against affectation, he sees it with less sympathy than we might expect. The Victorian admiration for sincerity appears to be at work in this: Don Armado is declared a sentimental hypocrite.[10]

In *As You Like It* Morley, like most of his contemporaries, finds an Arcadia: 'In *Love's Labour's Lost* Shakespeare jested at euphuism; in *As You Like It* he played euphuist himself in pleasant mood, and out of quips and fancies built a wise and tender day-dream of the world' (p. 294). Depths are near at hand of course, in the character of Rosalind as Helen Faucit plays her:

Girlish abandonment to exquisite delight, womanly depths of feeling shown from time to time when any rough wind sweeps across the rainbow mist, these lie together in her as the depths of its wisdom lie near to the playfulness of the whole exquisite dramatic show,

---

[10] A reviewer in the *Daily News* (1 October 1857) described Armado's 'tall, gaunt figure, point-device attire, pompous strut, and conceited drawl' (quoted by Edith M. Holding, '*Love's Labour's Lost* and the English Stage, 1762–1949', unpublished Ph.D. thesis, University of Birmingham, 1978, p. 115).

and through breaks in its golden cloud-world we seem to see all kingdoms of the world of thought spread out before us. (p. 295)

Again, this is Victorian orthodoxy regarding the play, in response to a fully orthodox performance (with such points as the Rosalind's being 'bashfully conscious of her mannish dress' at 'What shall I do with my doublet and hose?'). It is no surprise to find Morley appreciative of Amy Sedgwick's showing, as Beatrice, 'behind the mask of a gay mockery, the gentle spirit of a woman' (p. 171) or noting with approval the distinction made by Marion Terry between Viola's 'womanly fear' in the duel scene and the 'spirited display of firmness and skill in fence' shown by Sebastian, whom the actress doubled with his sister (p. 209). The 'depth' of these comedies is held by Morley to lie in their genial 'philosophy' and their touching portraits of womanly good-humour mingled with pathos.[11]

IV

The generalizations concerning Shakespeare's work that can be elicited from Morley's theatrical criticism are rarely original or penetrating. But the observation of stage business and the actor's art is shrewd and vivid. Morley's *Journal* should discourage any tendency to associate trenchancy and perception in the criticism of acting exclusively with such radical views as Shaw's. Morley is in fact very careful to keep his ideas about the plays very much in the background – perhaps just as well, if the platitudinous analyses published in his later books are a fair measure.[12] From Morley we can learn much about the taste of an educated Victorian theatre-goer, no enemy to spectacle and absurdity, but calling for sincerity, 'poetic' harmony and 'depth' when he knows it is appropriate to expect them from

an author and his interpreters. His social interests are linked to this open-minded approach. He is ambitious that Shakespeare should be freely available as heart-warming, popular entertainment. Shakespeare 'spoke home to the heart of the common man', Morley reflected as he considered the Sadler's Wells audience: 'It is hard to say how much men who have had few advantages of education must in their minds and characters be strengthened and refined when they are made accustomed to this kind of entertainment' (p. 138). In his 'prologue' Morley exhorts his public to encourage the theatre, and to make use of its potential as a secular means of enlightenment. He should be allowed to make his own conclusion in the earnest, dated but not unsympathetic vein of the lay-preacher exhorting his congregation:

God, who gave to the moth his dainty wings and to the violet a scent whose use is but the creation of pleasure, gave to man, with the delights of speech, faculties that weave them by the subtlest of his arts into a flower-world of intellect and feeling. At the playhouse-door, then, we may say to the doubting, Enter boldly, for here, too, there are gods. (p. 13)

---

[11] I have described some manifestations of this attitude to the 'mature' comedies in '"Perfect Types of Womanhood": Rosalind, Beatrice and Viola in Victorian Criticism and Performance', *Shakespeare Survey 32* (Cambridge, 1979), 15–26.

[12] Subtlety and intellectual agility may have been at a discount in the extramural teaching Morley toiled at, but in his synoptic historical-critical volumes one finds conclusions that might have seemed trite in the Mechanics' Institutes. For example, in his last completed book, the tenth volume of *English Writers, an Attempt towards a History of English Literature* (1893), Morley announces an insight he had arrived at much earlier in his career: 'Every play [by Shakespeare] represents some problem of life and its solution. All through his mature plays we learn the spiritual rule of three, by which alone the problems of life can be solved: Love God; love your neighbour; do your work.'

SHAKESPEARE PERFORMANCES IN STRATFORD-UPON-AVON AND LONDON, 1983–4

NICHOLAS SHRIMPTON

This has been a lively but uneven year for the English Shakespearian stage. It is not often, for example, that one can report not merely on exciting performances but also on two separate proposals to build scholarly reconstructions of Jacobean theatres. But the making of stages, as well as the playing upon them, has in 1983–4 involved an odd mixture of gratified hopes and worrying disappointments.

On 5 September 1984 the Royal Shakespeare Company announced that an anonymous benefactor had given all the money needed to build a third auditorium in Stratford. To be called the Swan, this 430-seat theatre will have a large apron stage surrounded on three sides by three tiers of galleries. First planned in the late 1970s, and long since despaired of for lack of finance, this approximation of a Jacobean indoor playhouse will be open from the summer of 1986.

Just three weeks after this exhilarating news came a rather different announcement. For fifteen years Sam Wanamaker had been fighting to build a replica of the Globe close to its original site on Bankside. Much, though not all, of the money had been raised. An impressive list of rich and royal patrons had been gathered to the colours. Scholars and architects had collaborated on a design for a building in which Shakespeare's plays could be rendered in something very close to their original conditions. The Globe Trust reached an agreement with Southwark Council and the developers Derno whereby the cost of the site for the theatre would be financed by the construction of an adjacent office block.

What happened next was a shift in the political complexion of Southwark Council and a sudden endorsement of the views, previously ignored, of a lobby called the North Southwark Community Development Group. Moving the road sweepers' depot (a caravan and some scruffy sheds) which at present occupies much of the site would involve sacrificing some land, otherwise available for council housing, elsewhere. In the last week of September the Council's ruling Labour group decided to oppose the Globe project. In early October their planning committee announced that negotiations would cease and the previous agreement be regarded as void. Once, the Globe Trust had hoped to start building in the autumn of 1984. Instead the matter passed into the hands of the lawyers, as Derno sued Southwark, and the Globe Trust issued writs against both of them.

On stage, fortunately, the year began with some gratified hopes. Adrian Noble had already begun to establish himself as the best of the group of young directors into whose hands the work of the Royal Shakespeare Company has now passed, with his *King Lear* and *Antony and Cleopatra* in 1982 and his *Comedy of Errors* in August 1983. He closed the 1983 Stratford season and opened that of 1984 with two productions which confirmed his status as a rising star.

Measure for Measure, in October 1983, was the first of these. Set in a baroque Vienna, it opened with an elaborate wordless tableau staged to music in the manner of Gluck by Ilona Sekacz. At the bottom, apparently, of a black cavern stood some gilded furniture, an iron spiral staircase leading to a tiny tower-room, a single strip of white carpet, a tailor's dummy and an enormous pier-glass. A red-coated figure got up from an elegant writing desk and walked slowly to this mirror, where a valet changed

8　*Measure for Measure*, Royal Shakespeare Theatre, 1983, and Barbican Theatre, 1984. David Schofield as Angelo and
Juliet Stevenson as Isabella

his red coat to a black one. The Duke of Vienna was shedding his robes of office and becoming a private man. At the end of act 1 a second strip of white carpet was laid, across the first, dividing the stage into neat quarters.

The white cross, the shifting vestments of authority, the mirror in which men find and lose themselves – the visual apparatus was serving a clear symbolic function. Emrys Jones, reviewing the production in the *Times Literary Supplement*, recognized its potency but deplored it:

The whole ensemble – light and darkness, robe, mirror, voice – creates a hypnotic image of baroque theatricality. For a few moments it exerts power; it fascinates and thrills. But it also makes one suspect that the director would have been happier with a sub-operatic 'show' like *Amadeus* (where frankly the words don't much matter) than with his present assignment.[1]

Once again, in other words, the gorgeous eclecticism of Adrian Noble's *mise-en-scène* (designed, here as in the case of *King Lear*, by Bob Crowley) was causing offence and raising problems.

Eclectic as well as gorgeous it most certainly was. Mariana's moated grange, with its blue sky and Japanese parasols, appeared to be a Jazz Age villa on the French Riviera. And though the actors retained their baroque costumes for the prison scenes, they seemed somehow to have wandered on to the set of an American *film noir*. This was the State Pen *circa* 1930 – a wall of grey bricks and steel bars, complete with gas lights and an electric chair on which the disguised Duke leant to speak of death to Claudio.

Mixed settings of this kind are an irritant which just occasionally, like grit in an oyster, produces a pearl. I was irritated at first, then slowly won to the

---

[1] *Times Literary Supplement*, 21 October 1983.

9 *Measure for Measure*, Royal Shakespeare Theatre, 1983, and Barbican Theatre, 1984. Daniel Massey as the Duke with Isabella

view that the disparities all, excitingly, made sense. In the final scene the Duke entered through the (hinged) mirror to find himself on a set consisting of a box of skyscaped walls and a baroque spiral staircase festooned with tiny lights like a Christmas tree. Surreal was the only word for this glittering incongruity, and surrealism was, one suddenly realized, a perfectly appropriate analogy for the fantastical quality of this play's conclusion. Certainly the crisis of the moral action worked quite grippingly in this ritzy playgound.

Critics who found the settings obtrusive tended, at the same time, to find the production's intellectual substance inadequate. Emrys Jones, for example, felt that a stress on 'the worldly and the social' had led to a neglect of the play's 'intellectual and spiritual dimension'.[2] It is true that one important performance was damagingly weak. David Schofield played Angelo as a dapper and dangerous little hypocrite, a sly court chaplain whose clerical dress reminded one of Tartuffe or Mr Slope rather than of a repressed puritan genuinely deranged by passion. Irving Wardle remarked in *The Times* that there is 'no justification for giving the idea that the austere Angelo is an old hand at criminal seduction'.[3] This insensitivity to the inner life of the character went hand in hand with a posturing and melodramatic treatment of his soliloquies. In the scenes with Isabella such nervous and over-acted attempts to impress were sometimes right. Elsewhere they were disastrous and left one with the feeling that, in a play where characters are frequently 'acting', Schofield lacked the technique to distinguish his own levels of artifice.

But if Angelo was weak, the Duke and Isabella

---

[2] *Ibid.*
[3] *The Times*, 5 October 1983.

seemed to me to be very strong indeed and to be part, what's more, of a production which laid considerable stress on the 'spiritual dimension' of the play. Daniel Massey's Duke was a fastidious and ascetic figure who seemed actually to relish his temporary status as a friar. His decision to deceive Isabella ('But I will keep her ignorant of her good') in 4.3, always one of the most difficult moments of the play, had as a consequence a credible religious basis. Massey knew what he meant when he proposed to 'make her heavenly comforts of despair' (4.3.109) and delivered the line with something of the thrilling conviction which Isabella brought to 'Why, all the souls that were were forfeit once' at 2.2.73.

As this suggests, Juliet Stevenson was fully up to Massey's weight and gave one of the year's most memorable performances. She was sometimes the victim of unsympathetic staging. But she thought and felt her way through the role with remarkable care and conviction, illuminating in the process not only the spiritual dimensions but also some neglected human aspects of the play.

Two of these were of particular importance. In 3.1, as the Duke finished his explanation to her of the bed-trick, they grasped at each other in a momentary embrace of triumph. Seconds later, remembering their status as novice and friar, they nervously disentangled themselves, having set up with the greatest possible delicacy the erotic charge which would make their eventual marriage credible. Still more interesting was the stress which this production placed on female friendship. Isabella and Mariana, played by Emma Watson, established a real sense of supportive intimacy. The silent decision before 5.1.442 which is the true crisis of the play did not here take the form of a long pause. Instead Isabella gave one anguished gaze about her then swept across the stage to kneel by Mariana in sisterly solidarity.

This subtly feminist shading went hand in hand with a distinctly hostile attitude to the play's low life. Despite a marvellous Mistress Overdone from Peggy Mount, the pimps and punters were played to frighten rather than to charm us. The human warmth and realism of Pompey's 'they will to't' (2.1.22) were here excluded by a sense of the threat posed to women by prostitution, pornography, and sexual harassment. As any staging of this play must be, the production was unsympathetic to the rigid application of the letter of the law; it remained, none the less, distinctly in favour of the assertion of moral and spiritual authority. The result may not be a *Measure for Measure* for all time. But its austere moral temper and stylistic eclecticism made it, in the early 1980s, quite remarkably of its age.

Adrian Noble and Bob Crowley were working together again, as director and designer, on *Henry V* which opened the new Stratford season in March 1984. Here the visual style was both more sombre and more single-minded. The French wore correctly fifteenth-century black velvet. The English sported baggy combat kit which, despite a slight air of having been purchased at the fashionable end of South Molton Street, remained passably medieval throughout.

At the beginning of 3.6 there were some hints of deliberate anachronism. With the English army in the fields of France, it came on to rain and the production's most memorable image – long lines of forlorn troops, huddling or marching under soaked tarpaulins – inevitably prompted associations with the First World War. But its purpose was less to draw specific parallels with 1917 than to establish a sense of the unchanging experience of the PBI in every age. The David Jones of *In Parenthesis* would have relished it.

This bleak stress on the horrors and discomforts of war did not, of course, leave much scope for the Muse of fire. Ian McDiarmid's Chorus was, accordingly, used to ironize the action rather than to stir the imagination. He haunted the stage throughout, like a Brechtian narrator, sending up his own speeches and occasionally drawing or withdrawing a flimsy curtain across the proscenium. At times his speeches were moved to new contexts to lend point to his presence. Thus 3.7 followed the act 4 Prologue, and 'The French, advis'd by good intelligence / Of this most dreadful preparation' (act 2 Prologue, 12–13) was ironized by being spoken after 2.1, with its far from dreadful picture of the makeshift preparations of Bardolph, Pistol, and Nym.

Inserted incident sometimes performed the same

10 *Henry V*, Royal Shakespeare Theatre, 1984. Kenneth Branagh as King Henry

function. Bardolph's death here took place on stage in 3.6, with the King staring directly into his old companion's eyes as a burly Exeter slowly strangled him. Naught for our comfort was the message of such staging, and it was against this dark background that Kenneth Branagh set his boyish and charming Harry. Brisk, sprightly, and sensitive, he fainted from the top of a siege ladder into the arms of his adoring troops after 'Once more unto the breach, dear friends', sank weeping to his knees for 'Not today, O Lord' (4.1.288), and swooned away completely after his victory at 4.7.100.

This innocent delicacy of spirit made him a persuasive wooer, if a slightly insubstantial military leader. It also contributed very directly to Adrian Noble's dialectical interpretation of the play. Unusually, a Stratford programme was on this occasion actually in tune with the production it accompanied, setting out in parallel columns contradictory views of Henry V as 'Hero-King' (by John Gillingham) and criminal 'Scourge of God' (by J. L. Bolton). The production, similarly, took the form of an open debate between alternative views of Henry's French wars. The sensitive boy-king who shrank from atrocities was seen to be, simultaneously, the noble leader of an inspired crusade and the commander of a ruthless gang of raggle-taggle mercenaries. Those mercenaries were, it should be added, played with great force. Bernard Horsfall gave Pistol's 'And Holdfast is the only dog, my duck' (2.3.52; see fig. 11) such resonance that it became, unexpectedly, one of Shakespeare's most moving articulations of marital fidelity.

The Royal Shakespeare Company returned to history in June, with Bill Alexander's production of *Richard III*. This was a show full of sound and fury, signifying that the director had chosen to treat the play on its considerable merits as a comic

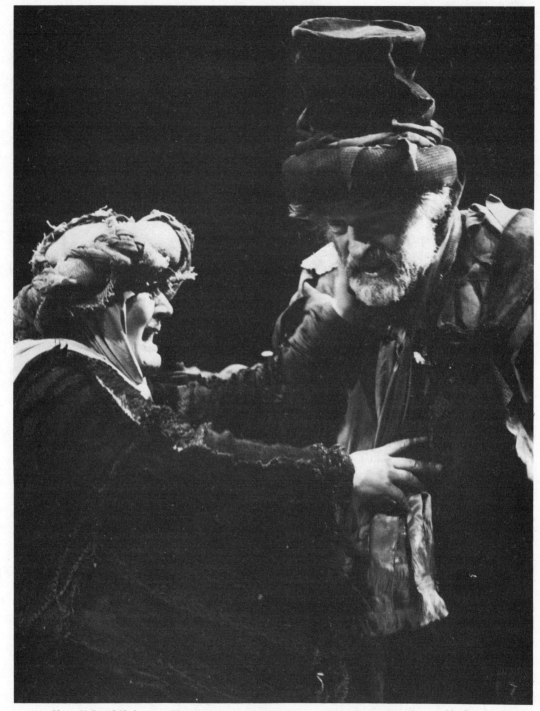

11   *Henry V*, Royal Shakespeare Theatre, 1984. Pistol (Bernard Horsfall) bids farewell to Mistress Quickly (Patricia
Routledge)

melodrama rather than as chronicle or embryonic tragedy. Where *Henry V* had handled history with a kind of hesitant intelligence, this production filled it with savage energy and made it the setting for a charismatic central performance. The set and the costumes were scrupulously Gothic; the mood and manner, on the other hand, were Gothick. Antony Sher's black spider of a Richard haunted a stage which was essentially a hall of tombs.

If such procedures had a somewhat nineteenth-century feel, the *mise-en-scène* had been planned to reinforce rather than to qualify that impression. At the end of the first half, following 4.1, an entire scene (without words) was inserted to show us Richard's coronation. Smoke, light, tumultuous music, and the assembly of nearly forty actors and musicians into a lavish tableau combined to produce an effect straight out of the Victorian Spectacular Theatre. As the lights went up for the interval, even the Stratford tourist with the most rudimentary command of English could feel that he was getting his money's worth.

The director was ably and amply supported in these intentions by his composer, Guy Woolfenden, his designer, William Dudley, and above all his lighting designer, Leo Leibovici. The lights had almost as much claim to be deemed the star of the production as Antony Sher himself. Gothick glooms alternated with the cold light of day in a manner which echoed Richard's shifts between monstrous malignity and engaging cynicism. Other tricks of the light enabled what were essentially only two sets – a Perpendicular stone screen flown in to isolate the forestage, and a tomb-filled apse of what might be Old St Paul's or Westminster Abbey – to function as a realistic setting for almost every scene. The Tower, the Palace, Baynard's Castle, Pomfret Castle, streets, dungeons and council chambers, all seemed different and all convincing.

Only in the final act did this cinematic style break down. Sher spoke 'Here pitch our tent, even here in Bosworth field' with the air of a man determined to reassert the Elizabethan bare-stage convention. It was, alas, a little late for eyes which had spent the previous two hours adjusting to a very different set of scenic assumptions. Splendid though the battle

was (both Richard and Richmond set off for it on life-size hobby-horses), it was hard to overlook the fact that it appeared to be taking place in Poets' Corner.

Inside this gorgeous packaging there were some striking performances. Brian Blessed followed up his powerful bully of an Exeter in *Henry V* with a big, bluff performance as 'th'adulterate Hastings' here. Harold Innocent was outstanding as an obese and irascible Edward IV, Yvonne Coulette almost equally effective as a rueful but dignified dowager Duchess of York.

Her comments on her wicked son's childhood ('Tetchy and wayward was thy infancy; / Thy schooldays frightful, desp'rate, wild, and furious', 4.4.168–9) had, indeed, a peculiar interest in this production. This Crookback Dick was genuinely crippled, and the effects of his handicap were seriously considered. Sher got about on a thoroughly modern pair of metal crutches, using them when appropriate as a weapon, as gymnastic apparatus, and as a rhetorical aid. Everything above the waist, including his brain, had been overdeveloped to compensate for his feeble legs. The result was a witty and winning imp of a man whose desperate need to outdo his healthy contemporaries left him empty and exhausted once he had achieved absolute power. Antony Sher brought a clinical delicacy as well as a furious energy to this interpretation and struck a clear note of human truth amidst the haste and splendour of a noisy show.

The three productions could all be put, without hesitation, into my category of gratified hopes. Their sequence had, unfortunately, been interrupted in April 1984 by a distinct disappointment, in the shape of John Caird's *The Merchant of Venice*. The design, by Ultz, was a text-book demonstration of the fact that a set can be expensive, carefully pointed, and at the same time wholly inappropriate. Swathes of red tapestry and carpet, together with three vast Chinese jars (the caskets) poised over the stage on industrial robot-arms, gave the impression that we were about to watch *The Merchant of Hong Kong*. But the costumes were conventional images of sixteenth-century Venice and the floor of the stage was dominated by two vast, baroque pipe organs.

12   *Richard III*, Royal Shakespeare Theatre, 1984. Antony Sher as Richard

Michael Billington observed that the effect was 'less of the Adriatic than of *20,000 Leagues Under The Sea*'.[4] This sensation was reinforced by the fact that the organs were motorized and powered their way about the stage, playing thunderously, to form such features as the outer walls of Shylock's house. Belmont was no less of a fairground. The mottoes on the caskets were spoken, over the tannoy, by a mysterious off-stage voice (described in the programme as the 'Ghost of Portia's Father'). The caskets themselves were side-show tricks, opening to reveal a pop-up skeleton, a laughing fool's head, and a life-sized, coloured effigy of Frances Tomelty in the role of Portia.

The trouble with all this was less its simple vulgarity than its active incongruity. Any sense of ideological distinction between Venice and Belmont was impossible when a single, sumptuous set was used for both places. In Venice the merchants' chance encounters and commercial conversations seemed to be taking place in a private drawing room. At Belmont Portia observed the light burning in her hall while already, apparently, within it, and Lorenzo might more properly have remarked how sweet the moonlight slept upon this carpet.

The playing was scarcely more satisfactory than the set. The casting gave the distinct impression that the company had kept its weightier, older and more experienced actors for other productions and the verse-speaking was rarely other than pedestrian. These were ominous circumstances in which to attempt a controversial reading of the play, but John Caird and his Shylock, Ian McDiarmid, did just that. The Jew was played in a wholly unsympathetic way. Malicious, playful, heartless and ultimately grotesque, he was denied any hint of tragic status.

This experiment was clearly inspired by a scholarly wish to reach back beyond the humane Shylocks of Irving and Charles Macklin to a sixteenth-century convention, identified in the programme with the attitudes of Marlowe's *The Jew of Malta*. In part, I suspect, because the production seemed in other ways so slightly conceived, the result was public denunciation. On the opposite leader page of *The Times*, on 17 April, William Frankel attacked the Royal Shakespeare Company

for its revival of an anti-semitic stereotype and took it as a sign that 'post-Holocaust inhibitions' on public anti-Jewish presentations were fading.[5] Responses as fierce as this might seem to suggest a performance of memorable, if unlikeable, power and originality. In fact the presence of this unconventional Shylock added to, rather than transcended, the production's problems, leaving it simultaneously lightweight and incapable of comic light-heartedness.

Ron Daniels's production of *Hamlet*, with Roger Rees in the title role, opened in September 1984 and provoked very varied responses from its original reviewers. My own feeling was that it fell into the same category of worrying disappointments as *The Merchant of Venice* and, more particularly, that it showed how the energy and splendour which can carry a production of *Richard III* will not suffice for this more sophisticated and intellectual text. Brian Blessed's playing in the two productions summed up the difference. As Hastings in *Richard III* he was appropriately hale and hearty. As Claudius in *Hamlet* he gave, in Michael Ratcliffe's words, 'a performance inexcusable in its coarseness from first to last'.[6]

The most immediately disappointing quality of this *Hamlet*, however, was the extent to which it represented a regression from Jonathan Miller's distinguished production of 1982. Miller's Ophelia was a genuinely disturbing mental case. His Osric was a tough royal 'minder'. His Claudius and Gertrude were middle-aged lovers caught up in a sensual fascination which they could not master. Some cobwebs at least, one felt, had been swept for ever from the face of *Hamlet*. Ron Daniels's production gave no sign that he was even aware of these perceptive innovations. At Stratford Ophelia was sweetly pretty even in her madness and delivered her songs in a ringingly operatic *bel canto*. Osric was a stock fop from the usual theatrical Never-never Land of affected behaviour, neither convincingly Jacobean (the context suggested by the costumes)

---

[4] *The Guardian*, 12 April 1984.
[5] *The Times*, 17 April 1984.
[6] *The Observer*, 9 September 1984.

13   *Hamlet*, Royal Shakespeare Theatre, 1984. Roger Rees as Hamlet

14   *Love's Labour's Lost*, Royal Shakespeare Theatre, 1984. The Princess of France (Emily Richard, far right) and her attendants, Katherine (Kate Buffery), Rosaline (Josette Simon), Boyet (Harold Innocent), and Maria (Alison Rose)

nor recognizably modern. Claudius was merely an irascible Old King Cole.

If Daniels's sense of character seemed oddly old-fashioned, his grasp of local detail was often positively wrong – and was so in a manner which varied from the ludicrously literal to the breath-takingly careless. Thus, Hamlet's hyperbolic declaration in his letter to Claudius that he has been 'set naked on your kingdom' (4.7.44) obliged him to appear in the graveyard scene clad only in a pair of improvised sailcloth underpants. On the other hand, his killing of Polonius was done, not through the arras, but after a chase which would make it obvious to even the most obtuse of assassins that it was not Claudius whom he was stabbing.

Act 3, scene 3 was perhaps the scene which most vividly demonstrated the production's inadequacies. Claudius entered his oratory through a pair of free-standing french windows ('Anyone for tennis?') and shuddered his way through a violent soliloquy. Hamlet spied him through the glass but came down-stage to deliver his speech only inches from the King's ear. Was this a realist stage convention we were watching? In that case, presumably, Claudius had gone into some kind of religious trance which left him unable to see or hear. Or was it, more plausibly, a piece of non-realist staging? Nothing in the manner of the rest of the production, unfortunately, had prepared us for such an assumption. In fact the presentation seemed neither thoughtful about the text nor truthful in its playing.

Amidst these unpropitious surroundings, Roger Rees offered a delicate, romantic, slightly posturing Hamlet. This was a sensitive soul, full of nervous energy and frequently on the verge of tears. Only once, in the prose speech 'If it be now, 'tis not to come' (5.2.212), did he give a real sense of

15 *Love's Labour's Lost*, Royal Shakespeare Theatre, 1984. Dull (George Raistrick), Holofernes (Frank Middlemass), and Sir Nathaniel (John Rogan)

intellectual depth to the character, and even the emotions were flaunted more often than they were probed. The result, despite an impressively fierce ghost from Richard Easton, a well-judged Polonius from Frank Middlemass, and a quirkily pedantic First Clown from Sebastian Shaw, was a production more pretty than penetrating. As a tour of the play's beauties it served well enough. But it was more that than an interpretation.

The qualities which did not quite suffice in Roger Rees's Hamlet worked very well indeed, a month later, when the same actor returned as Berowne in Barry Kyle's *Love's Labour's Lost*. This was a production which neglected the more intricate verbal wit of the play but achieved, none the less, a buoyant sense of physical and emotional fun. Rees was the figure primarily responsible for establishing this intoxicating mood, and he did so with that distinctive combination of energetic sentiment and wry

detachment which had served him so well in *Nicholas Nickleby*.

The setting was Late Victorian – part Proust, part *Tom Brown's Schooldays*, and part Chekhov (which served well for the Russian masque). The King of Navarre's academy seemed to be a sixth-form study at an English public school, with Berowne as a rebellious art student in a group of waistcoated prefects. If this youthful stress did something less than justice to the fear of 'cormorant devouring Time' (1.1.4), it made a crucial contribution to the high spirits of the show. Melancholy music and wistfully elegant exterior settings were intriguingly combined with a rousing and rapid verbal style.

The ladies, possibly because they were confronted with such conspicuously juvenile lovers, seemed slightly inhibited and Emily Richard's delivery of 'A time, methinks, too short / To make a world-without-end bargain in' (5.2.776–7) did not provoke quite the shiver of which, at their best, those lines are capable. But Edward Petherbridge drew an exquisitely understated portrait of Don Adriano de Armado, Harold Innocent showed us Boyet as a courtly Oscar Wilde, and Frank Middlemass and John Rogan as Holofernes and Sir Nathaniel (first seen as a pair of Victorian dons sharing a sandwich lunch on a park bench) gave an authentic comic warmth to the play's sense of 'recreation' (4.2.156).

Josette Simon's lively Rosaline in this engaging *Love's Labour's Lost* provokes a final note on what should perhaps be termed the social history of the English Shakespearian stage. For some years now the Royal Shakespeare Company has been edging to-wards racial cross-casting. Josette Simon is a black actress, and though neither of her parts this season seemed perfectly chosen (as Nerissa in *The Merchant of Venice* she was an odd recipient for Portia's abuse of the Prince of Morocco; as Rosaline she was more literally 'black as ebony' than 4.3.243 was ever intended to suggest), her arrival in significant speaking parts marks the opening of a new chapter in our attitude to what constitutes appropriate casting. This development was confirmed, in a rather different way, by the year's events in the stage history of *Othello*. Before 1984 the London stage had seen only three black actors take the part of Othello: Ira Aldridge in 1826, Paul Robeson in 1930, and Errol John in 1963. 1984 saw two such performances, by Rudolph Walker at The Young Vic in May, and by Joseph Marcell in the tiny studio at the Lyric Hammersmith in September. Whether literally cast or cross-cast, black actors and actresses will henceforth be a normal part of our experience of Shakespeare. In a year in which a production of a Shakespeare play raised questions of racism, it is I think a cheering thought.

THE YEAR'S CONTRIBUTIONS TO SHAKESPEARIAN STUDY

1. CRITICAL STUDIES

reviewed by BRIAN GIBBONS

To begin with, Rome, and two worthwhile books, Howard Erskine-Hill's *The Idea of Augustus in English Literature*[1] and Robert S. Miola's *Shakespeare's Rome*.[2] Erskine-Hill devotes only one chapter to Shakespeare, but the entire first half of his book is of interest to Shakespearians. It begins with a lucid and well-substantiated account of Augustus and his Rome, derived not only from classical but also from twentieth-century historians, and then traces the response of patristic, medieval, and European Renaissance writers, especially Bodin, Machiavelli, and Lipsius. Shakespeare himself is introduced by way of Donne and the satirists, and – interestingly – the Ben Jonson of *The Poetaster* and the royal entry entertainment of the Temple of Janus (1604). Parts of Erskine-Hill's account will be familiar to scholars, but the overall grasp is impressive: thorough scholarship, presented through a sturdy structure of argument, yields a great deal of significant information in a readily accessible form. Ideas of Rome's Augustan age, Erskine-Hill shows, 'have been a presence in English in all periods, reaching back even to the circle of King Alfred', but more importantly, we should note, a pattern of fairly stable associations concerning Augustus 'had been fully assembled by the sixteenth century'. The rise of satire in the last years of the sixteenth century shows London as 'a darker and more dangerous place than Augustan Rome'. The so-called Golden Age of Elizabeth as Astraea offered writers little support, security, or freedom of speech: Spenser had lamented in 1579 that 'Mecaenas is yclad in claye / And great Augustus long ygoe is dead'. It never ceases to impress one that, in the midst of what

Donne called 'our Age of Rusty Iron', Ben Jonson, single-handed, should have determined to generate a complete cultural reorientation towards Augustanism. *The Poetaster* (1601) is a remarkable *tour de force* in actually representing on stage Augustus, flanked by Virgil and Horace, as Erskine-Hill puts it 'enforcing upon the stage an Augustan judgement about writing, an opinion of Augustus himself'. Jonson's royal entry entertainment in the City of London on 15 March 1604, The Temple' of Janus, is an illuminating contrast to Shakespeare's treatments of Rome. As the King approaches the Temple a flamen and the Genius of the City meet at the altar: the flamen, roused by the tumult, finds the Ides of March come! The Genius of the City insists that the new power embodied in James I overrules 'All tumults, fears or other dark portents'. As he leaves, James shuts the temple gates, recalling 'the most important event for the Christian providential view of Augustus: the establishment of world peace'. Erskine-Hill observes that to make James I thus explicitly act out an Augustan role 'is what one might expect after nearly a century of serious political discussion of Augustus' (p. 129). Turning to Shakespeare at this point he notes the contrast: in *Antony and Cleopatra* Shakespeare uses the idea of *pax augusta* not to crown an action but 'to be countered by the surprising remaining resources of Antony, in military prowess and loyalty in the hearts of men'. In *Julius Caesar* Erskine-Hill notes comparable dialectic: a possible appeal to a

---

[1] Edward Arnold, 1983.
[2] Cambridge University Press, 1983.

conventional Elizabethan approach, simply taking Caesar as emperor; alternatively a view in touch with Bodin, seeing Caesar neither as king by divine right nor tyrant betraying the republic. A third view, deriving from Machiavelli and Renaissance Italian concepts of the republic, is apparent in Cassius. Erskine-Hill sees the play as confirming Bodin's verdict on Caesar, who 'embodies that logic of history' which led to 'the imperial theme'; yet, cut off in his hour of triumph, 'Caesar remains an enigma and is meant to be so: the speculations of Brutus as to how a crown might change his nature are never settled.' Erskine-Hill proposes *Antony and Cleopatra* and *Coriolanus* as studies in intemperance. The Caesar of *Antony and Cleopatra*, in his austerity, may recall the Augustus of *The Poetaster*, and we are invited to see that in some sense the play is an answer to Jonson's image of an ideally austere Augustus. Shakespeare counters Temperance with an affirmation that in 'hyperbole of action, licence, a conscious voyaging forth to the extreme there may be, far from weakness, Magnificence'. Erskine-Hill adds substance to the view that conscious Augustanism in English literature begins not in 1660 or 1700 but in the last years of Elizabeth, and he shows Shakespeare as a penetrating, dialectical explorer of this idea.

Robert S. Miola's approach to *Shakespeare's Rome* has the Augustan virtues of proportion, lucidity, and temperance, though Miola does take issue with the critical tradition which makes the reign of Augustus assume a climactic importance for Shakespeare. Miola asserts that Shakespeare nowhere portrays the transformation of Octavius into the prince of peace, the crowned Augustus. Rather, that coming apotheosis must only be inferred from 'hints and half guesses'. In a most instructive footnote (p. 162 – surely deserving promotion to the main argument), Miola points out that Seneca's *De Clementia* 1.11 influenced an Elizabethan tradition that sharply distinguished the ascendant Octavius, deceitful, ambitious, and tyrannical, from the crowned Augustus. Miola concedes that Shakespeare does allow Octavius in *Antony and Cleopatra* some magnanimity, both in his grief for Antony and his resignation at the death of Cleopatra; whereas 'Suetonius and Dio Cassius have Octavius employ-

ing Psyllian snake-charmers to suck the poison from Cleopatra's wounds, in an attempt to revive her for the triumphal procession'. As this instance may suggest, Miola takes pains to register the difficulty of Shakespeare's art, rather than to steamroller complexity which might offer resistance to an over-determined thesis. He notices that in *Julius Caesar* Shakespeare makes both Brutus and Caesar claim for themselves the virtue of constancy, which emphasizes their similarity in vacillating at crucial moments, and the interest they both have in seeking earthly fame and reputation. This ironic disparity between the characters' self-image and the reality alerts an audience to the difficulty of disinterested moral judgement. Then the assassination scene

> poses, dramatically, the problem of assessing and evaluating character. Just after Caesar imperiously sets himself apart from men who are flesh, blood, and apprehensive, the conspirators brutally stab him to death. This climactic moment paralyses an ability to make calm judgments...the blood does not indicate whether Caesar was tyrant or king, but only that he was a mortal human being not a marble Roman bust.
>
> (p. 100)

Miola compares the improvised ceremony, 'Let us bathe our hands in Caesar's blood / Up to the elbows', to the bloody slaughter of Lavinia and Thyestean banquet of *Titus*, gory spectacles clashing with the noble sentiments and abstract ideals producing them. Caesar had turned away from Calphurnia, his flesh-and-blood wife, to the insubstantial image of himself as the great mother of Rome. Such subordination of the claims of the private hearth and home to those of the city is presented in *Julius Caesar* as unnatural, inhuman, and doomed. Miola relates this to other episodes in the play, as when Portia rebukes Brutus for removing her to 'the suburbs / Of your good pleasure'. Here Portia sees the marriage bed (and by implication hearth, home and family) as a kind of city no less important than Rome. Brutus must choose between the vow of marriage and the conspiratorial vow, two 'incorporate' bodies. Miola recalls adroitly that both Lucrece and Titus also deny the claims of their private families in order to fulfil the claims of Rome. 'The paradoxes implicit in such action, however, first sketched in Titus' barbaric slaying of his children, receive sharper definition in *Julius Caesar*, particularly in confrontations between husbands and wives.'

These instances may suggest the book's main themes:'"*pietas*", an essential Roman virtue for Shakespeare as for Virgil; the vital relationship between Roman family and city; the interplay between honour and constancy; and the Roman body bruised to pleasure the Roman soul'. In *Lucrece* 'Images of the wild outdoors and animal predation suggest the cruel bestiality of the invading Tarquin. Lucrece's bedroom, situated at the centre of the concentric circles that encompass the family, household, and city, enclosed by civilising laws, becomes "the wilderness where are no laws"'.' Once invited, the reader will recognize in that line many pre-echoes of the subsequent Roman plays, not simply of the closest, *Titus Andronicus*; and later in the book we are invited to see in *Cymbeline* a close reworking of these motifs: 'the siege and invasion motif, appearing (in *Cymbeline*) on both the sexual and national levels, articulates no vision of impious violation...Romans may hold to '*suum cuique*' as their justice, but Britons...share their victories. In Shakespeare's Rome *pietas* demands the honouring of family, country and god. In Shakespeare's Britain, however, the smallest circle, the family, expands outward to include the rest' (p. 234). Miola leaves the reader with a lively comparison of *Cymbeline* to *Titus*. In *Titus*, on stage and in language, 'the pastoral world, symbolic of the non-urban, un-Roman, and therefore, private sphere, is repeatedly violated, its innocent life hunted and maimed, its branches lopped'. In *Cymbeline* the lopped branches of the stately cedar revive and are reunited to the old stock.

Miola certainly demonstrates that there are important large and small interconnections between Shakespeare's Roman works, and though the book is perhaps stronger in handling specific matters than larger-scale concepts, its general emphasis on Shakespeare's sustained response to Virgil is important, finding in *Coriolanus* a return to the stage world of *Titus* and a spacious concern with the central issues of the last six books of the *Aeneid*.

John W. Velz argues in an article[3] in *English Literary Renaissance* that critics of the Roman plays in the past have too much concentrated on Plutarch; Velz finds in the *Aeneid* an important influence on Shakespeare in *Coriolanus*, Virgil's teleological view of history being analogous to Shakespeare's 'diachronic vision'. Velz argues that Shakespeare chooses to set his Roman plays 'at the interface between' two periods of Roman history in order to pit his heroes tragically against the tide of the times, as Virgil pits Dido and Turnus against Roman destiny. Velz compares Coriolanus to Turnus, a splendid anachronism; he sees the comparison as lending a Virgilian quasi-cosmic dimension to the play. Yet when proposing sources and analogues it is always necessary to guard against the danger of underplaying Shakespeare's originality. Is there not something strangely *in*comparable, unique, in Coriolanus the hero, even by Shakespearian standards, a frighteningly original exploration of distortion, which is essential to *Coriolanus* the play, and may not be left out of account? As in *Titus*, in *Coriolanus* Shakespeare has an awesome power not only to defamiliarize but actually to uncover and present something new in new ways.

In an essay on tragic ritual from Aeschylus to Shakespeare to Soyinka, Philip Brockbank[4] considers the persistence at deep levels, in dramatic form and characterization, of remote and barbaric impulses and rites: tragedy in the western world being, in an anthropological perspective, quite a brief tradition. He insists that, because there are persisting strains in our nature, 'certain tragic structures are bound to recur, but it does not therefore follow that they are archetypal and unchanging. Tragic art is an instrument for changing human nature, not for impaling it on rigorously conceived necessities' (p. 11). Philip Edwards[5] is concerned to see the tragic quality of *Hamlet*, eroded by twentieth-century

---

[3] 'Cracking Strong Curbs Asunder: Roman Destiny and the Roman Hero in *Coriolanus*', *English Literary Renaissance*, 13 (1983), 58–69. Velz is acknowledged in the Preface to Miola's book.

[4] *Shakespeare Survey 36* (Cambridge University Press, 1983), 11–20.

[5] 'Tragic Balance in *Hamlet*', *ibid.*, pp. 43–52.

criticism, restored. This must involve the overthrow of the view, popular since 1930, that the Denmark of Claudius and Gertrude is healthy, while by contrast Hamlet is a figure of nihilism and death. Edwards argues that Shakespeare's Hamlet fiercely refuses to condone the blurring of recognized distinctions and differences which give his cultural order coherence. Hamlet's view of Claudius is clear: 'He that hath killed my king and whored my mother'. In Hamlet's sense 'the distinctions between persons are ratified by heaven, so that the killing of Claudius is as far removed from the brutal poisoning of the former king as can be. It would belong in an area of sacredness which is totally foreign to us.' Edwards comments that today

We can't possibly share Hamlet's sense of values ...But nor could Shakespeare necessarily or unequivocally share Hamlet's sense of values. It is in the moment of the weakening and questioning of distinctions that he writes his play. What Shakespeare could not do was to repudiate Hamlet's sense of values. We, having gone right down the road Shakespeare was on, have turned the corner, and can't see the place where the play happened, where blurring has just begun, and might perhaps be stopped.   (p. 49)

Edwards makes use of Tyndale as well as Kierkegaard to focus Hamlet's dilemma: obedience to God might transform a murder into a holy act, but 'if the individual has misunderstood the deity − what can save him?' Edwards wants Hamlet to vex and trouble us with the suspicion that he was 'after something worth having': 'Is't not to be damned to let this canker of our nature come in further evil?' This essay is valuable for what it demonstrates of modern critical inadequacy: critics are shown failing to rise to the full challenge of Shakespeare's *newness* in *Hamlet*, where he advances thought through his dialectical procedures (what Camille Slights in a recent book[6] terms 'casuistical'). Shakespeare here identifies a change in values within his culture; he represents it as it is experienced by his hero, through whom, if they allow themselves, audiences may in turn be changed. The antiquated theatrical device of the Ghost may stand in part for those seemingly remote and discarded cultural phases which so powerfully, if darkly, inform the present. Confronting the past and the old is, again, seen to be an essential part of making anything new.

Terence Hawkes warns in an article in *Encounter*[7] of a conspiracy; literary criticism in Europe is infected with concealed ideological bias, and literary texts are manipulated to impose repressive attitudes and discourage questioning, and hence subversive, habits of mind. Although his concern is situated in the present, and in Britain − 'the clear defining boundaries of an established island culture' − he embarks on an odd piece of local history from the beginning of the century, in order to unmask Dover Wilson, scarcely a virile presence in contemporary critical debate, though perhaps insidious, as having been repressively anti-socialist in his views on literature-teaching. This repressiveness is also to be seen in his anxiety that what Professor Hawkes ironically calls that 'central and monumental text' of 'English-speaking culture', *Hamlet*, be protected from suggestions of ambiguity or uncertainty.

Hawkes thinks 'We inherit, after all, a particular notion of *Hamlet* as a coherent story which runs a satisfactory, linear, sequential course', and he asserts that 'our' literary criticism, 'Eurocentred' as it is, allows only one coherent interpretation of a work at a time, requiring us to '*appease* a text whose vitality resides precisely in its plurality'. Hawkes contrasts America, where the text is a means, not an end.

At least E. A. J. Honigmann must be exonerated from this British disease, presumably, on the strength of his sparkling British Academy Lecture 'Shakespeare's Mingled Yarn and *Measure for Measure*' (read in 1981).[8] Honigmann's concern is with 'mixing' as a principle of Shakespeare's art, a principle often explicitly drawn attention to by the dramatist, as well as philosophically meditated upon by the Gentleman (in *All's Well that Ends Well*) who

---

6 See *The Casuistical Tradition in Shakespeare, Donne, Herbert and Milton* (Princeton University Press, 1981).

7 '*Telmah*: To the Sunderland Station', *Encounter*, April 1983, 50–60. An example of speculative discourse taking *Hamlet* in its stride is James L. Calderwood's *To Be and Not To Be: Negation and Metadrama in Hamlet* (Columbia University Press, New York), 1983.

8 *Proceedings of the British Academy*, 67 (1981), 101–21; the lecture was published separately in 1983.

speaks the words quoted in Honigmann's title. Shakespeare's 'mixing', then, is his 'expert interweaving of different views of the same person, of past, present, and future, of slow time and fast time, of conflicting motives, or the interplay of many emotions in a single phrase'. Furthermore, Honigmann pinpoints a procedural problem that still largely defeats criticism: how to grapple with a play as a whole, not simply with detachable units such as imagery, character, genre, plot. Why not indeed focus instead on the mixing principle, interaction. A play unfolds through time, and to that extent is linear, but 'the linear structure of events, of cause and effect, is not the only structure that concerns us' (p. 104). A play that lasts two or three hours can be held in the mind as a single experience somewhat like a painting, offering experience 'that remains present, like a painting, even as it unfolds, challenging us to connect the ends of opposed winds, a bear and a statue, Claudio's guilt and Angelo's, Angelo's ignorance of the world and Isabella's and the Duke's'. This 'present continuous' of drama, as Honigmann shows, this mixing of what we may have heard and seen already, makes a given moment throb with implications: Hamlet's interest in the question 'How long will a man lie i'th'earth ere he rot?' is related to an earlier topic, how long will a man's memory outlive his life; again, the play being filled with mock-interviews, in which the Prince pretends to misunderstand a questioner, now the First Gravedigger turns the tables on him, answers knavishly. The shape of their exchanges is another thread that hooks into a larger design. In a play where there has already been much talk of suicide and the hereafter, the gravediggers, says Honigmann, 'pick up these themes and fool around with them as naturally as [they] pick up bones' (p. 105). Contrasting the Porter in *Macbeth* and the Clown at the end of *Antony and Cleopatra*, Honigmann remarks how each clown scene is sewn into the fabric of the play, densely yet distinctively, 'mingled'. This leads to a defence of the 'bed-trick', often regarded as an error of Shakespeare, choosing to solve the problems of a realistic plot by resorting to pure folk-tale. Honigmann defends the device as fully 'mingled' in its surroundings in the play, which he shows to be far

from 'realistic', while bed-tricks in literature and history turn out to be more various than critics suppose. Shakespeare *chooses* to make the bed-trick have a jarring effect on his audience. He had already mingled his ingredients in this play densely and surprisingly; but, further, 'making an issue of it, challenging the audience to put the pieces together and to think critically about a "poem unlimited"'. 'The distinctive feature' of *Measure for Measure*, Honigmann suggests, 'is that it mystifies and keeps changing direction, both at the level of story and of seriousness, insisting on our revising our expectations to the very last' (p. 120).

Bernice W. Kliman, writing on 'Isabella in *Measure for Measure*'[9] has a simple opening statement: 'Seldom does a performance present the number of conundrums suggested by a reading. The reason is simple, of course. The high-density text contains an excess of what we need to know. It gives us (to take only one character) a duke both humorous and pompous, both Providence incarnate and Fool.' One can find diverse meanings in shifting tone and emphasis, but in Kliman's view performance requires selection from these conflicting signals to produce 'a unified, satisfying work of art'. In the case of this play at least such a procedure seems to beg the question. Why did Shakespeare make a high-density text if nobody was going to register its nature in performance? In the same volume Judith Rosenheim discusses 'The Stoic Meaning of the Friar in *Measure for Measure*'.[10] Do the 'providential nuances' of the role adopted by the Duke reflect a Stoic rather than a Christian idea of divinity? This article argues that they do, and that the play as a whole censures this Stoicism, showing it to collapse in the unhooding of act 5. Is it really so simple?

---

[9] *Shakespeare Studies*, 15 (1983), 137–48.

[10] Pp. 171–216. Among other articles in this annual are Richard Paul Knowles, 'Theophanies in the Last Plays' (269–80), and Bryan A. Garner, 'Shakespeare's Latinate Neologisms' (149–70), which reminds us that not all of Shakespeare's neologisms have stuck; for instance 'adoptious', 'bodements', 'conspectuity', 'imperceiverant', which nobody would wish away from their specific contexts in the plays, would not sound out of place in the mouth of Jonson's Crispinus.

Much good sense on the subject of cutting texts for performance is to be found in Alan C. Dessen's article 'Shakespeare and the Modern Director',[11] particularly when Dessen discusses the readiness of directors to cut what is deemed 'not to work'; he finds that material deemed unplayable, and cut, in one production, turns up as a successful part of another (pp. 58–9). Referring to *As You Like It*, Dessen argues that since, in scene 5 of act 2, a banquet is directed to be set up (lines 26–7) this should be done in productions; then scene 6 will be played with this banquet in full view, affecting our reaction to Adam's 'O, I die for food' and to Orlando's 'If this uncouth forest yield anything savage, I will either be food for it or bring it for food to thee'.

Joan Hartwig's subject in *Shakespeare's Analogical Scene*[12] is the contribution made by scenes which have not, primarily, a necessary place in the *narrative* sequence of a play; their function is to present analogy, sometimes through comedy, usually through a contrast in mode, tone, or attitude: she notes 'When modern producers...are puzzled by the presence of certain scenes (or think that their audiences will be), they use the cutter's knife. Their deletions imply that modern audiences no longer [respond to] the power of analogy' (pp. 3–4). Hartwig, in seeking to take account of the extreme pervasiveness of this feature of Shakespeare's artistry, is driven to multiply sub-categories lest her procedural technique ignore too much, but she succeeds in alerting a reader to the real complexity of interrelations between episodes in a play by Shakespeare: her subject is not merely 'mirror-scenes', because there is more involved than reflecting other action: analogous scenes 'build accretively' to the play's full exploration of an experience, reorienting and reshaping what we have seen, will see, or are seeing, but in Hartwig's formulation, they do so always 'in a literalising perspective'. The procedure in the main part of the book is to inspect categories: e.g. minor comic characters in major parodic scenes, parodic scenes in *Macbeth* (including Malcolm), the structure of *Romeo and Juliet*, and later, sub-plots in *Hamlet*, *Cymbeline* and *The Tempest*. It has to be said that the

book does not have much new in it, and its chief use will be in its assembling of many instances in one place. Hartwig writes with pressured concern for detail, and can sometimes seem over-ingenious; but the subject is an important one.

Frederick Kiefer[13] approaches Shakespearian tragedy by way of Senecan and Christian medieval ideas of Fortune, and a chapter analysing Lodge, Marlowe and Kyd, whose plays are seen as presenting a capricious Fortune surviving, 'after a millenium and a half', as essentially pagan. He then moves on to Shakespeare: *Romeo and Juliet*, *Richard III*, *Julius Caesar*, *Hamlet*, *Lear*, *Timon*, *Antony and Cleopatra*. Kiefer advances a thesis, which is that Fortune assumed greater, not less, importance as Elizabethan literature developed, and greater, not less, importance in Shakespeare's successive tragic plays. The book begins with substantial and serviceable chapters, on the *Mirror for Magistrates* and on Elizabethan translations of Seneca. Here there are well-found and significant conclusions: the tone of the translators is self-deprecating, but actually they made considerable changes, chiefly in the choric passages: what their translations offer is 'the representation of a world even more precarious and unstable than that of the original' (p. 67). This fresh examination helpfully supplements the standard accounts by such scholars as Willard Farnham, and Kiefer provides an excellent bibliography of recent Seneca scholarship. Later in the book – too much later, I find – there is another very useful, and interesting, chapter on Occasion, the modified image of Fortune which began to appear in the late fifteenth and early sixteenth centuries, with the new attributes of sail and dolphin and hourglass or clock, and a forelock taken from the Occasion of antiquity. Kiefer writes well of this Fortune of Machiavelli, of Prospero, of Renaissance emblematists such as Cor-

---

[11] *Shakespeare Survey 36* (Cambridge University Press, 1983), 57–64.

[12] Subtitled *Parody as Structural Syntax* (University of Nebraska Press, Lincoln, Nebraska, and London, 1983). Over half of the book has appeared previously in the form of articles in learned journals.

[13] *Fortune and Elizabethan Tragedy* (Huntington Library, San Marino, California, 1983).

rozet and Modena, of the rich Florentine merchant Rucellai, whose *impresa* designed in the 1440s by Alberti, with its sail and forelock, implies the pursuit of a vigorously active and adventurous career. Kiefer shows merchants, artisans, historians, emblematists, poets and playwrights responding enthusiastically to a concept of Fortune expressing not only its awesome power to change man's circumstance, but also confidence in his powers. In his chapters on the great plays *The Spanish Tragedy, Romeo and Juliet, Julius Caesar, Hamlet*, he risks, himself, becoming fatally dull – he finds in *Romeo and Juliet* an inexperienced Shakespeare guilty of mingling Fortune inconsistently with Fate, thereby failing to subordinate disparate materials to a consistent vision. Kiefer's own chapter on Fortune, Occasion and Time, inexplicably printed later in the book, might, had it preceded the discussion of the play, have yielded the subtler account which that masterpiece *Romeo and Juliet* certainly deserves. Altogether the book is too long. Fortune and Fate, however intelligent the strategy which deploys them, remain somewhat unwieldy instruments of critical analysis when insistently applied to Shakespeare's major tragedies. So many other issues clamour for attention while the author pursues his set task; but certainly, one freely allows, he does have his reward discussing the end of *Antony and Cleopatra*.

C. G. Thayer's discussion of *Shakespeare's Politics*[14] is too intelligently adult, well prepared, and responsive to the complexity of Shakespeare's art, to make its downright unfashionable, disambiguating thesis really easy to reject. Thayer makes good use of his knowledge of Elizabethan history and political theory, and is far from shy of confronting the many awkward problems the plays present. This is an honest attempt to find a coherent advocacy about government throughout the sequence *Richard II, Henry IV, Henry V*. He offers a conservative account, in the sense that it preserves much good critical counsel and hard scholarship from his predecessors, but it is also conservative in insisting on the integrity of the tetralogy, in restricting itself to this very familiar grouping of plays, and, on the whole, to very familiar questions about them. That this yields a sometimes absorbing, often mordantly

witty book, is all the more to his credit. His main thesis can be simply defined: he sees the four plays of the second tetralogy as constituting a group, integrated by Shakespeare's concern to 'Offer reasonable objections and suggest alternatives', as his contribution to the much-discussed subject of governors and governing which, Thayer argues, must have had for Shakespeare (as for his fellows) a special urgency at the end of the Tudor era. His overall argument is that Henry V is exhibited as 'the precise antithesis of Richard II', with 'none of Richard's illusions and none of Richard's problems'. Henry V, the 'mirror of all Christian kings', has nothing whatever to do with mystical doctrines of Kingship.

> The notion of the King as God's substitute is raised briefly, only to be discredited, in Gaultree Forest (*2 H IV*, IV ii 26–30), and it *is* discredited, by John of Lancaster's insufferable "God, and not we, hath safely fought today", (121), a mere hypocritical gloss on his own treachery. There is otherwise no hint of divine right, divine kingship, of the King's Two Bodies in *Henry IV*. Henry V represents the triumph of man-centred kingship in which the standard by which a king is measured is human. (pp. 144–5)

But Thayer believes this idea need not have been offensive to James: 'Man-centred kingship leaves plenty of room for authority (altogether too much for most modern tastes): it does come from God after all' (p. 163).

The epilogue to *2 Henry IV*, plays invites the audiences to come back for more, whereas the end of *Henry V*, on the other hand, is a sonnet asking us to contemplate this short-lived star of England: 'this ending is designed to separate history from its movement, time from its flowing…if we contemplate *this* history, and are properly instructed by it, then what followed need not necessarily repeat itself' (p. 149). Thayer argues that the chronology of Shakespeare's own works is what matters; *his*

---

[14] Ohio University Press, Athens and London, 1983. Shakespeare is taken as an example in A. D. Nuttall's wide-ranging and stimulating discussion of the problem of the literary representation of reality, *A New Mimesis* (Methuen, 1983). The account of Prince Hal as a 'White Machiavel' is well worth consulting (pp. 143–61).

history of Henry VI was in the past; what matters *now* is Henry V in the context of 1599.

Thayer pursues an argument with vigour and goes to considerable lengths to represent, fairly, views opposing his own. At the heart of his book is the conviction that the subject of justice and good government, of interest to Shakespeare the historical person, must be of interest to us as citizens today; but he would have us respect the particular historical circumstances in which Shakespeare lived, thought and wrote. Thayer readily recognizes that his late Elizabethan Shakespeare, with his fierce mockery of the Lollard martyr Oldcastle, his endorsement of social obedience and hierarchy as a means to justice, and his commendation of his creature Henry V as an ideal, not a real, ruler, may be unpalatable to many readers and spectators in the present. This book is worth consulting particularly for its discussion of Gaunt and political passivity in *Richard II*, of Lollardry as touched on in *Henry IV* and *Henry V*, and of Gaultree Forest in *Henry IV*. Its conclusion, that Shakespeare's irony is subdued to encomium in *Henry V*, is partisan, but honestly fought for.

Jonathan Dollimore's *Radical Tragedy*[15] includes some discussion of *Troilus, Lear, Antony and Cleopatra*, and *Coriolanus* in the context of a number of tragedies by various dramatists of the Elizabethan and Jacobean periods. Dollimore assents to the view which has become widely current in theatrical, as well as academic, interpretations of English Renaissance plays, which sees their political and social thrust as critical and questioning, and invokes with approval the practice and theory of Brecht: who commended Elizabethan/Jacobean drama's boldness in experiment, appetite for dialectic, and propensity for shock, scandal, and general all-round offensiveness. The structure of Dollimore's book displays his dual concern, on the one hand to stress the 'demystifying' of dominant ideology in these old plays, on the other to adduce from an eclectic, interesting selection of modern theorists, an apologia for a materialist 'anti-humanism'. Dollimore argues that this is closer to the Jacobean age than the 'essentialist humanism' which evolved in the in-

tervening period between then and now and which has coloured much criticism. This 'essentialist humanism', whereby 'the individual is understood in terms of a pre-social essence, nature, or identity, and on that basis s/he is invested with a quasi-spiritual autonomy', is seen as reflecting its religious antecedents. Dollimore's doctrine of materialism avoids the term 'individual', preferring 'subject', because it foregrounds the condition of man 'informed by contradictory social and ideological processes'; the 'subject' 'is never an indivisible unity, never an autonomous self-determining centre of consciousness'. Jacobean dramatists when presenting discontinuity and contradiction, have often been attacked for aesthetic failure. Dollimore defends these features as imitative of the real world and argues that 'To the extent that it posits an underlying primordial state of dislocation, the language of chaos mystifies social process. To the extent that it interrogates providentialist belief – robbing the absolute of its mystifying function – it foregrounds social process' (p. 44). The choice of *Troilus, Lear* and *Coriolanus* is clearly appropriate in this context, though the discussion of *Antony and Cleopatra* leaves a good deal out of account. It serviceably traces Shakespeare's ironic depiction of power politics and his critical treatment of the sublime, but it leaves the play all alienation, its persons the subjects of power-relations, to be erased when discarded by the power-structures. There is more dungy earth in the play, surely? Coriolanus may with more justice, perhaps, be described as 'the ideological effect of powers antecedent to and independent of him' (p. 219).

At the end of his essay 'Le discours de l'autre dans *Julius Caesar*' Pierre Spriet[16] stops and asks himself a question: 'Est-ce le sens de *Jules César*?' The unexpected answer is 'Non, bien sûr'! Spriet goes on to justify his 'Non', not as flippancy or an

[15] Subtitled *Religion, Ideology and Power in the Drama of Shakespeare and his Contemporaries* (Harvester Press, Brighton, 1983).
[16] *Coriolan, Théâtre et Politique*, Travaux de L'Université de Toulouse-Le Mirail, Série B, Tome 5 (1984).

assertion that all critical pronouncements are equally futile, but as follows:

'Un classique', écrit I. Calvino, 'est une oeuvre qui provoque sans cesse un nuage de discours critiques dont elle se débarrasse continuellement'. Il nous faut découvrir ce que nous savions ou nous croyions savoir, écrit-il encore. Il ne peut pas nous être indifférent parce qu'il nous permet de nous définir nous-mêmes par rapport à lui.

In the same volume there is a sheaf of essays on *Coriolanus* in which the altered meanings of such words as politics, democracy, election and tyranny are inspected from various points of view, some familiar to English-speaking criticism, some refreshingly different (if not *différant*). The articles by Raymond Gardette, '*Coriolan et le concept de la tyrannie*' and Jean Fuzier, '*Coriolan, tragédie de l'ambiguité*', are very substantial, and the volume as a whole is commendable. In another part of the field should be noted the lively use to which the current critical concept of 'la marginalité' is put, in discussing *1 Henry VI*. Pierre Sahel[17] writes (with restraint) about the depiction of the French in that play as a type of the marginal, the clown: 'le Français commet imposture sur imposture, n'adhère à aucun code, est incapable d'assumer une fonction reconnue par la tradition nobiliaire...les Français sont peut-être les clowns de la pièce...Pourtant, si le clown amuse, il lui arrive de faire peur' (p. 25). In other ways both King Henry VI and Joan of Arc are marginal, the one commending charity to vassals who have never included it in their code, the other ironic at the expense, not only of the English, but also of French untrustworthiness. The nobles are ready to exclude her; she is a woman in armour, intruding in a male domain; her origins are uncertain, even her name is varied, and she is compared to exotically remote figures, Mahomet, Caesar, Deborah, Hannibal, Hecate. The burning of Joan clearly fails to cancel the many kinds of threat she represents, which may be related to the play's process, 'multipliant les franges, les bordures, les zones-frontières, les gestes ségrégatifs, les processus de retrait ou d'exclusion'.

Also interested in disintegrative elements in early Shakespeare is Mary L. Fawcett, in her discussion 'Arms/Words/Tears: Language and the body in *Titus*'.[18] This is a lively application of various fashionable critical strategies to a play certainly robust enough to withstand such treatment. The play literalizes words by writing them out on the stage; Titus sends weapons wrapped in a text from Horace; and the silent Lavinia is a text for interpretation, a 'map of woe' we must learn to read. Whether we must learn to read the play's concern with words and bodily members in quite the following, post-Freudian terms, everyone may decide for himself (or is this a parody the editors of *ELH* failed to detect?). I quote:

Since it borrows from the past, language must finally be based upon incest; the mother tongue for this speaker is a father-hand inserted incestuously between the teeth of a ruined mouth, a vagina dentata. From one point of view the severed hand seems like a continuation and an enlargement (almost an erection) of the tongue-root; the hand completes the tongue. Language is thus manipulation – a handling of the tongue.

That qualified suggestion, 'almost', in the parenthesis, is prettily judged.

Little suspicion of irony, alas, is attributable to the joint authors, T. G. A. Nelson and Charles Haines, of an article on 'Othello's Unconsummated Marriage',[19] who assert that Othello failed to consummate his marriage with Desdemona 'because of the pressures placed upon him during the couple's turbulent first night in Cyprus'. So Desdemona is not merely faithful but immaculate, she lives and dies a virgin. When she orders 'Lay on my bed my wedding sheets' she is 'giving Othello another chance to achieve what hitherto he has failed to achieve'. So, they suggest, it is anxiety about failure

---

[17] *La Marginalité dans la Littérature et la Pensée Anglaises*, *CARA 4* (Publications Université de Provence, Aix-en-Provence, 1983).

[18] *ELH*, 50 (1983), 261–78.

[19] *Essays in Criticism*, 33 (1983), 1–18.

to consummate the marriage that 'fatally' impairs Othello's judgement.

In this context of slandered heroines, there is some very interesting material in Lisa Jardine's generally disappointing book *Still Harping on Daughters*.[20] The chapter on 'The Saving Stereotypes of Female Heroism' discusses Griselda and Lucrece before inspecting *The Golden Legend*, in which 'female saint's life after female saint's life involves a trial of sexual advance' – either her refusals inflame the man and lead to her martyrdom, or she adopts male dress and flees to a monastery, subsequently to be accused of fathering a child, submitting to punishment in silence, and found at death to be female and hence innocent. Lisa Jardine compares these chaste women falsely accused to Shakespeare's Hero, swooning at the altar into silence when accused, to Hermione, pattern of patience, but also to Isabella, in whom we see 'the full range of possibilities latent in these admirably steadfast and courageous assaulted (or at least slandered) women' (p. 190). 'Were Isabella a female saint in *The Golden Legend*...she would flee in disguise and do interminable servile penance ...Or she would stand firm and submit to torture ...Shakespeare's Isabella is belittled by the stereotypes to whom she so flagrantly fails to match up.'

Andrew Gurr, writing on 'The bear, the statue and hysteria in *The Winter's Tale*',[21] makes a number of excellent points which take account of the deliberate juxtaposition of 'crude' theatrical effects to highly sophisticated learned allusions. The bear and the statue are precisely matching counterparts at the end of the two parts of the play; a double-take is involved in both cases. The bear, if a real bear really on the rampage, will indeed dine on the actor of Antigonus; the spectator's shock at its appearance must be subsumed into a recognition that it is a bear in stage terms; a modulation from horror to comedy; though bears were the most familiar kind of wild beast in Elizabethan London, Gurr reminds us that in emblem tradition the bear licked its cubs into shape, a natural sculptor, and this makes a contrast with Giulio Romano and the sculpture of Hermione which comes to life, recalling Pygmalion

and Galatea. As nature and natural passions prevail in the Court in the first part, so art prevails in the natural world of the shepherds. Florio defined tragicomedy as half a tragedy and half a comedy; Evanthius, whose definitions of comedy and tragedy were cited in school editions of Terence, seems to be deliberately, trickily echoed in the shepherd's remark 'Thou met'st with things dying, I with things unborn': with classical forms and precepts so close to the surface, Gurr argues that Shakespeare is calling attention to his deliberate flouting of the Unity of Time on the seacoast of Bohemia, which, since it flagrantly does not exist, is no less deliberate a flouting of the unity of place. The play appears as a complex interweaving of conscious themes of art and nature, out-pastoralling Pastoral.

Meanwhile, in another part of the forest, A. Stuart Daley pays close, literal-minded attention to the rural settings of *As You Like It* and points out that the word 'forest' in Tudor times denoted a large untilled district composed of pastures, wastes and usually some woods; originally it denoted Crown lands used for hunting.[22] The real Forest of Arden, a dominant geographical feature of the central Midlands in England, was far from a continuous expanse of woodland. In the play there are two distinct milieux: a wildwood where the Duke is to be found ('these woods'), and where deer-hunting goes on. The two girls, on the other hand, are on a sheep farm; grazing being a principal land-use of forests, this is plausible. Celia says the farm is in a 'bottom', a fat valley pasture where woods would not be tolerated.

In *Cymbeline* Michael Taylor notes ('The Pastoral

[20] Harvester Press, Brighton, 1983. Cautious references to Courtesy Books by Marion D. Perret in 'Petruchio: the Model Wife' fail to support a gymnastically ingenious inversion, whereby supposedly Petruchio's governing of the domestic side of life shows Kate what a wife should do. *Studies in English Literature, 1500–1900*, 23 (1983), 223–35.

[21] *Shakespeare Quarterly*, 34 (1983), 420–5. This article should serve as a model of concise, pointed and significant communication in a journal whose standards in these respects are poor, aside from its theatre reviews.

[22] *Shakespeare Quarterly*, 34 (1983), 172–80.

Reckoning in *Cymbeline*')[23] that the pastoral experience is harsh: 'innocence (rather than happiness) has to be renewed on a daily basis in a spirit of absorbed self-negation in a more formidable landscape than the traditional *locus amoenus* of Greek pastoral'. This is put differently earlier in the article: 'The impression we have of something hyperbolically and unnaturally over-ripe, where...spring has become autumn, and where value can be expressed only in punitive terms, suggests a deeper

malaise' (p. 101). Taylor like Gurr demonstrates the extraordinary pressure which Shakespeare subjects pastoral to, and the surprising range of fashionable Renaissance theory Shakespeare is able to glance at – and with a quite un-British feeling for the Baroque.

---

[23] *Shakespeare Survey 36* (Cambridge University Press, 1983), 97–106.

2. SHAKESPEARE'S LIFE, TIMES AND STAGE

reviewed by LOIS POTTER

Like the 1984 International Shakespeare Conference at Stratford-upon-Avon (where some papers in this *Survey* were given), that of the Shakespeare Gesellschaft West for 1982 was devoted to Shakespeare and History. It seems appropriate, then, to begin with its *Jahrbuch*, which contains special contributions from historians. Two of these are of great interest. G. R. Elton asks how far recent work on the fifteenth century has modified the image offered in Shakespeare's two tetralogies.[1] The study of local records has shown, for instance, the fictitiousness of the image of an England ravaged by the Wars of the Roses: the struggle of a couple of claimants to the throne was *not* the whole history of England. This lively lecture (the *Jahrbuch*, more than the *Survey*, preserves the speaking voice) does however concede to Shakespeare an acute insight into the psychology of social types (such as Hotspur, whom he sees as a characteristic product of the feudal nobility) and a sense of concreteness and detail aspired to by, but lacking in, many historians.

Ulrich Broich, in one of the most sensible things I have read on the histories, examines the assumptions made in the plays about the knowledge and preconceptions of their audience.[2] He notes that, unlike, say, Peter Shaffer in *Amadeus*, Shakespeare always sets out to give the audience what it expects. At the same time, he transcends these expectations. If patriotism and optimism are not seriously brought

into question, views of history are. Because Shakespeare speaks only through characters, it is possible to hear pure Tillyard from the Bishop of Carlisle and something very close to pure Jan Kott nihilism from Richard II. Thus, Broich suggests, not only Shakespeare but his audience may have been prepared to entertain competing ideologies.

Another of Broich's points – that the theatre is far more aware than the scholarly world of the aspect of Shakespeare that is not 'timeless' – is brought out in a number of other *Jahrbuch* articles, for instance Horst Zander's account of the generally unsympathetic or downbeat treatment of Richmond in West German productions of *Richard III*.[3] Zander sees Richmond as the touchstone for a director's view of history; this perhaps explains why so few productions, including the 1984 RSC one, have allowed him to kill Richard in single combat. Rudolf Stamm discusses patterns of action and speech in *Richard II*: for instance, the wavering rhythms of the Duchess of Gloucester in act 1, scene 2, York's to-ing and

---

[1] 'Kann man sich auf Shakespeare verlassen? Das 15. Jahrhundert bei Shakespeare und in der Wirklichkeit', *Jahrbuch 1983*, 27–39.

[2] 'Shakespeares Historien und das Geschichtsbewusstsein ihres Publikums', *ibid.*, pp. 41–60.

[3] 'Die Darstellung Richmonds auf der West-deutschen Bühne', *ibid.*, pp. 111–24.

fro-ing, the Aumerle scenes, and the way in which all these hover daringly on the edge of comedy.[4]

Not on the history plays, but strongly aware of Shakespeare in history, are two other *Jahrbuch* pieces. Michael L. Greenwald compares Anne Barton's introduction to the Penguin *Hamlet* with John Barton's production of the play.[5] Avraham Oz, on the interesting subject of Israeli productions of *The Merchant of Venice*, tries less to convey a sense of the various interpretations than to explore concepts of 'intention' and 'authenticity'; he ends with the suggestion that Israeli audiences, by insisting on a sympathetic portrayal of Shylock, have refused to let the play speak to their own economic and political situation.[6]

It was a year in which the name of Tillyard was often invoked, rarely with affection. Two articles in *Literature and History*, 10 (1984), are a good example of the kind of thing that was also being said at Stratford, as no doubt at Bochum. Michael Tomlinson argues against the assumption that Shakespeare always agreed with the chronicles: 'The most extensive knowledge of the ideas he was familiar with would not tell us what his response to those ideas was.'[7] In support of an anti-Tillyard line, he argues that Shakespeare could have known of more liberal political views, that drama is a more popular form than the chronicle, and that a dramatist is particularly likely to find conflict fruitful rather than terrifying. Graham Holderness looks at three views of *Henry V* produced in 1944: Wilson Knight's openly patriotic effusions, the Olivier film, and Tillyard's book on the Histories.[8] Whereas the first two now seem dated, he claims, the Tillyard view remains as powerful as ever, its polarities of order and disorder built into the terms of exam questions and even into the structure of works which set out to attack it. The desire for a 'timeless' Shakespeare is itself the product of its own time.

I don't propose to show that the major reference works which have come my way this year were fully expressive of 1984, but they have benefited from new methods of data-gathering and book production. Ian Lancashire's *Dramatic Texts and Records of Britain: A Chronological Topography to 1558*, actually includes in its acknowledgements a com-

puter and three of its programs.[9] The book is a splendid example of modern technology, a handsome 600 pages, easy to read and well illustrated. Apart from Professor Lancashire's introduction, a compact summary of what is known and still needs to be known in the field, the contents are presented in tabular form: a chronological list of dramatic texts, a topographical list of dramatic records for Britain, and useful appendices listing playing companies, their locations and patrons, playwrights of the period, and records of theatrical sites. The list of doubtful plays and records has a curious fascination of its own, enabling one to follow the pattern of misinformation established by sub-scholarly work or by deliberate falsifications like Collier's. Completed by a full index and the cross-referencing which technology makes possible, the book is the more useful in that it doesn't do its readers' work for them but gives them the tools. It also makes demands on the judgement, since the computer net is made of very fine mesh indeed and Professor Lancashire has deliberately (and quite rightly, I think) allowed some small fry to remain. All libraries will need his book, and many individual readers will wish they could afford it.

Ronald W. Vince's *Renaissance Theatre, A Historiographical Handbook*, is also a useful reference tool.[10] Covering Italy (with a separate chapter on Commedia dell'Arte), Spain, England, and France, with a final section on Festival and Pageantry, it is partly a list of available sources and partly a critical history of relevant scholarship. Vince has definite ideas on the subject – for instance that scholars should be more willing to trust visual evidence about the theatre – and he also raises the question of what

---

[4] 'Die Theatralische Physiognomie der Haupt-und Nebenszenen in Shakespeares *Richard II*', ibid., pp. 89–98.

[5] The Marriage of True Minds: The Bartons and *Hamlet*, 1980–81', ibid., pp. 151–63.

[6] 'Transformations of Authenticity: *The Merchant of Venice* in Israel 1936–1980', ibid., pp. 165–77.

[7] 'Shakespeare and the Chronicles Reassessed', pp. 46–88.

[8] 'Agincourt 1944: Readings in the Shakespeare Myth', pp. 24–45.

[9] University of Toronto Press and Cambridge University Press, 1984.

[10] Greenwood Press, Westport, Conn., and London, 1984.

we mean when we try to establish the 'real' text of a play. Researchers who want to know what the 'Lansdowne MSS' are, or where to find masque music or illustrations of a royal entry, will find the answers here. Obviously, no one can be equally expert in all the areas of scholarship which he summarizes; I would have liked Professor Vince to point out that the newsbooks which he cites as sources for theatrical information started only after 1642, and that the works of John Bulwer, so often offered as evidence about acting conventions, are not about acting at all. But in my numerous areas of ignorance I found the book informative and pleasant to read. Despite the virtues of the computer, there is still a place for good continuous prose.

The Annotated Bibliography of *Henry V* by Joseph Candido and Charles R. Forker is the first of this Garland series that I have seen.[11] Editorial policy is to include not only summaries of scholarly and critical studies but also parodies, reviews of productions, and translations. I need only say that it seems to have achieved this aim admirably and that it's a pity to find camera-ready copy making possible a new type of error: the publishers have mixed up the General Editor's preface to this volume with the one for *Cymbeline*.

Of the shorter pieces dealing with documentary evidence, two are connected – somewhat tenuously – with Shakespeare's biography. Eric Poole traces the history of the property owned by Robert Arden and the tangled relationships in the Stratford area.[12] It is a record of nice people on the whole, apart from the poet's uncle Henry, who got into a fight in 1574. Noting the forbearance shown by other members of the Town Council when John Shakespeare began to absent himself from meetings in 1578, Poole suggests illness, perhaps a slight stroke, as a more charitable explanation than drink or riotous living for the decline in his fortunes after that date. More controversially, R. C. Horne offers 'Two Unrecorded Contemporary References to Shakespeare'.[13] The first is 'M.L.', regretting his attack on a 'reverend wit' whose 'verses live supported by a spear'; the second is to Lucrece, and doesn't seem to me necessarily to mean Shakespeare's heroine.

New transcripts of theatrical records, supplementing those of the Malone Society and Toronto's Records of Early English Drama, include David W. Blewitt's list of properties and expenses for Winchester and Eton productions (both long and short beards are mentioned)[14] and N. W. Bawcutt's two articles based on fragments of transcripts of Revels accounts with a complicated provenance, now in the Folger Shakespeare Library.[15] Most of the hitherto unpublished material relates to fringe activities like the showing of a three-headed child. William Ingram has compiled a useful finding-list of Elizabethan minstrels, with transcripts of all records in which they appear.[16] The careers of two minor players have been filled out a little more. 'Anthony Jeffes, Player and Brewer', is traced, mainly in his later career, by S. P. Cerasano, who notes that a number of players had connections with City guilds.[17] Willem Schrickx, continuing his study of English actors on the Continent, provides evidence that the original 'pickleherring' was George Vincent, an actor in John Green's company.[18]

Janet S. Leongard has discovered (and printed, with an English translation) the record of a lawsuit which appears to demolish the conventional view that The Theatre of 1576 was the first building of its kind and the first professional London playhouse.[19]

[11] Garland Publishing, New York and London, 1983.

[12] 'Shakespeare's Kinsfolk and the Arden Inheritance', *Shakespeare Quarterly*, 34 (1983), 311–24.

[13] *Notes and Queries*, NS 31 (1984), 218–20.

[14] 'Records of Drama at Winchester and Eton, 1397–1576', *Theatre Notebook*, 38 (1984), 135–43.

[15] 'Craven Ord Transcripts of Sir Henry Herbert's Office-Book in the Folger Shakespeare Library', *English Literary Renaissance*, 14 (1984), 83–94, and 'New Revels Documents of Sir George Buc and Sir Henry Herbert', *Review of English Studies*, 35 (1984), 316–31.

[16] 'Minstrels in Elizabethan London: Who Were They, What Did They Do?', *English Literary Renaissance*, 14 (1984), 29–54.

[17] *Notes and Queries*, 31 (1984), 221–5.

[18] '"Pickleherring" and English Actors in Germany', *Shakespeare Survey 36* (Cambridge University Press, 1983), 135–47.

[19] 'An Elizabethan Lawsuit: John Brayne, his Carpenter, and the Building of the Red Lion Theatre', *Shakespeare Quarterly*, 34 (1983), 298–310.

In 1569 John Brayne sued his carpenter for inadequately fulfilling the requirements which the document specifies (they include a turret and trapdoor) for a stage at the Red Lion – a house, not, as has been thought, an inn. As Brayne was a partner in The Theatre with his brother-in-law James Burbage, it is possible that he may also deserve the credit for the design of the later building.

John Orrell's article on 'The Private Theatre Auditorium' reproduces the design of 1605 for a polygonal theatre in Christ Church, Oxford, and goes on to argue that it might have been based on that of Blackfriars.[20] Assembling an impressive list of references to 'rounds' and 'spheres' in private theatre plays, as well as two mentions of 'this square' in Fortune plays, he makes a good case for the view that the private theatres of pre-war London anticipated those of the Restoration in their design. Orrell has also contributed more evidence about 'Sunlight at the Globe', based on experiments with a three-dimensional model which formed part of the research now going into the Bankside Globe.[21] It seems pretty well proven that the north-east orientation of the theatre, with its high superstructure (called a 'shadow' in the Fortune contract), was intended to allow the stage to be in shade for as much of the afternoon as possible.

Keith Brown argues on the basis of Orrell's findings that the outdoor theatres could have made more use of lighting than is usually thought: candles and torches would have showed up effectively in the shade as well as providing a warmer atmosphere in winter.[22] The absence of stage directions about lighting, he believes, reflects 'the invisibility of the familiar'. R. B. Graves provides evidence about the expenditure on candles and torches at court and at the Cockpit at Court, whose candelabra were specially gilded by John de Critz.[23] This article, which contains lots of interesting details, points out that the Elizabethan idea of magic was not romantically dim candlelight but rather the brightest possible illumination. Of course, what looked to contemporaries like dazzling radiance might not strike us that way: he calculates that 200 candles in a large hall would give about as much light as three or four 100-watt bulbs.

We continue to acquire new information about the Stuart audience and, perhaps, about the politics of theatre. Martin Butler's study of the backgrounds and connections of two men who are known to have attended a play in 1642 (because they fought a duel afterwards) provides one more piece of evidence against the view that only a narrow, cavalier section of the population was still going to the theatre at this date.[24] Herbert Berry prints a letter of 1634 describing a performance of The Late Lancashire Witches.[25] Part of its fascination is that it gives a rare glimpse of what a seventeenth-century spectator wanted – and was disappointed not to find: 'any poeticall Genius, or art, or language, or iudgement to state oᵣ tenet of witches (wᶜʰ I expected,) or application to vertue'. But Berry also argues, rather like Margot Heinemann with Middleton's Game at Chess, that the Heywood–Brome play was officially-inspired propaganda – in this case, against the accused witches (who were never brought to trial). The playwrights were given (perhaps by Pembroke) exclusive use of the documents in the case and a rival company was forbidden to deal with the topic. On the evidence of these two examples, the theatre was being used as a sinister form of thought-control. But the production's success was due not only to its topicality but also to 'odd passages and fopperies to provoke laughter'.

Berry's piece is one of the most interesting contributions to Medieval and Renaissance Drama in England, a new annual publication edited by J. Leeds Barroll III, which welcomes contributions on anything except Shakespeare. I must deal with non-Shakespearian material extremely briefly, to keep this review to manageable length, but it seems fair to say that the level of this first number (mostly

[20] Theatre Research International, 9 (1984), 79–93.
[21] Theatre Notebook, 38 (1984), 69–76.
[22] 'More Light, More Light!', Essays in Criticism, 34 (1984), 1–13.
[23] 'Stage Lighting at the Elizabethan and Early Stuart Courts', Theatre Notebook, 38 (1984), 27–36.
[24] 'Two Playgoers, and the Closing of the London Theatres, 1642', Theatre Research International, 9 (1984), 93–9.
[25] 'The Globe Bewitched and El Hombre Fiel', Medieval and Renaissance Drama in England, 1 (1984), 211–30.

on Renaissance authors) was quite high. The opportunity for long reviews and review articles on dramatists other than Shakespeare is particularly useful. Here it has resulted in Paul Werstine's rigorous examination of the textual scholarship of two Revels Plays editors and Doris Adler's review of Cyrus Hoy's commentary to the Fredson Bowers edition of Dekker ('Provenance and Printing History in Two Revels Editions', 243–62).

Among other periodical collections, *RORD* (*Research Opportunities in Renaissance Drama*), 26 (1983), focuses on Dekker and carries another piece by Doris Adler, this time on the history of Dekker bibliography. Further articles and reviews record performances of medieval and Renaissance plays, with a special checklist of professional performances of Webster's plays by David Carnegie. *English Literary Renaissance*, 14 (1984), is a special number on Renaissance drama dedicated to Virgil K. Whitaker. It has a slight Middletonian emphasis, with a bibliography of recent studies (by John B. Brookes); other contents will be discussed separately where relevant.

Books on Shakespeare's contemporaries have been particularly numerous this year. Charles Nicholl's *A Cup of News: The Life of Thomas Nashe*, is a lively account of one journalist by another.[26] Shakespearian scholars will be interested in his identification of all dark ladies in Shakespeare with Emilia Lanier, and the suggestion that she is also the original of Diamante in *The Unfortunate Traveller*, who is loved by both master and servant. There are some speculations about Ferdinando Lord Strange as a model for the King of Navarre and patron of the School of Night. Nicholl also suggests that the Nashe–Harvey controversy meant that the two men were so closely linked in the popular imagination as to be recognizable not only as Moth and Armado but even as Petruchio and Kate.

Johannes H. Birringer, *Marlowe's 'Dr Faustus' and 'Tamburlaine': Theological and Theatrical Perspectives*, also has a brief chapter on *Macbeth* but is mostly about *Faustus*.[27] It is an ambitious effort, in need of further editing, but the author's determination not to over-simplify Marlowe justifies to some extent his own over-inclusive approach, which is also well

substantiated by his grasp of the play's theological complexities. The discussion of the play in the theatre embraces even the most heavily adapted versions, and his own comments ('This dialogue calls for inspired acting') don't seem to me to get very far. There *are* good things in this book: readers should not be put off by the uninviting camera-ready copy, and should watch out for the transposition of pages 300 and 301.

Anne Barton's *Ben Jonson, Dramatist* has been eagerly awaited for some time and, in the form of chapters separately published, has already influenced other Jonson criticism (see below).[28] Essentially, it replaces the 'classical' Jonson with a romantic one, whose grotesque and fantastic imagination required the iron discipline of his literary theories. On her account, he was an earnest and sensitive man whose deepest feelings were for family ties, particularly those between father and son. Hence, she finds no difficulty in imagining him, as author of the additions to *The Spanish Tragedy*, entering into the spirit of the old play and the pain of a father's grief. In his later years, especially after the publication of the Shakespeare Folio, he is increasingly drawn back to his own real forebears, the popular and romantic Elizabethan dramatists from whom he had claimed to detach himself: the prodigal son returns home. Professor Barton's vast knowledge of the literature of the period allows her to trace the various branches of Jonson's spiritual family, and to make some fascinating connections, like the use of Camden's *Remains* in a chapter on the names of Jonson's characters. She is particularly good on the plays that have received the least discussion. Their political and historical context does not interest her much, nor, surprisingly, does their theatrical quality (there is no attempt, for instance, to explain *how* the actors of *Bartholomew Fair* coped with its exceptionally large number of characters). This is perhaps because the characters are, for her, autonomous beings: like Jonson himself, they are reticent about their feelings, not because they have none, but because they have

---

[26] Routledge and Kegan Paul, 1984.
[27] Trierer Studien zur Literatur, 10 (Peter Lang, 1984).
[28] Cambridge University Press, 1984.

too many. The book's stress on human vulnerability is sympathetic and appealing, but at times I was suspicious of my own response to it. Was I, perhaps, being made to like a Jonson who was what many readers would have preferred him to be: more Chekhovian, more *Shakespearian* even?

Other recent studies of Jonson also draw on comparisons with Shakespeare. Lawrence Danson's 'Jonsonian Comedy and the Discovery of the Social Self', at the opposite extreme from Barton, argues that, whereas Shakespeare's characters have a psychological identity, Jonson's exist only in their social selves; Jonson's plays, like Milgram's notorious electric shock experiments, reveal the extent to which the individual conscience gives way under social pressure.[29] Two essays from *Renaissance Drama*, 14 (1983) acknowledge Barton as a source for their view of the later Jonson turning back to the Elizabethans. Thomas Cartelli's discussion of *Bartholomew Fair* sees Grace and her suitors as sympathetic figures of romance, Overdo as a 'more sympathetic Prospero', and Joan Trash's gingerbread stuff as a parody of the stuff that dreams are made on.[30] Patrick Cheney links the philosophy of *The New Inn* to the idea of two souls becoming one: whereas *Epicoene* had satirized the love code of hermaphroditism, this play returns to the Spenserian vision.[31]

The collection '*Accompaninge the Players*': *Essays Celebrating Thomas Middleton, 1580–1980*, contains some intelligent studies of work not much written about previously, a well-written overview of his work by Roma Gill, an account of a production of *A Chaste Maid in Cheapside* (rather heavily adapted but intelligently thought about), a political/topical interpretation of *The Witch* in the light of the Essex divorce, and two interesting articles on *Women Beware Women*.[32] Peter Morrison, whose essay on *The Changeling* – 'A Cangoun in Zombieland' – lives up to its provocative title, also gives an annotated bibliography of the play.

Revenge plays have more obvious links with Shakespeare. Scott McMillin, 'Acting and Violence: *The Revenger's Tragedy* and Its Departures from *Hamlet*', makes the point that the absence of a Horatio to tell Vendice's story means that 'what is morally closed seems narratively unfinished'; the

double masque of revengers and the double identity of Vendice represent a threat to the individuality of the actor himself.[33] Kate G. Frost has found 'An Unreported *Hamlet* Allusion', in the 1614 edition of *The Philosophers' Banquet*, to 'What the Trag: Q. [not Gertrude but the Player Queen] but fainedly spoke'.[34] Sarah P. Sutherland's *Masques in Jacobean Tragedy* is a brief and elegant study of the masques in seven non-Shakespearian plays.[35] Paradoxically, her approach, a basically moral one, reaches the opposite conclusion to that of many moralist commentators: divine vengeance is brought on the murderer in due time, usually through his entanglement in his own snare, and such revengers as Vendice and Marston's Antonio are not meant to be seen in an ironic light. Reluctant to impose a rigid 'Revenge Tragedy' formula on these plays, Professor Sutherland nevertheless suggests that they all involve, as does the court masque itself, some kind of relationship between decorum and its violation.

This is also the theme of Angela J. C. Ingram's two-volume contribution to Salzburg Studies in English Literature, *In the Posture of a Whore: Changing Attitudes to 'Bad' Women in Elizabethan and Jacobean Drama* (no. 93, 1984). Immensely wide-ranging, it only slightly overlaps with the categories of Simon Shepherd's *Amazons and Warrior Women*. Professor Ingram explores the area between archetype and stereotype, noting how often potentially threatening figures, such as female politicians, are transformed into 'safer' categories such as those of shrews or adulteresses.

Minor examples of Shakespearian influence are traced by H. R. Woudhuysen, who offers one more piece of evidence that *Henry VIII* was generally known as *All is True*,[36] and Paul Dean, in '*The*

[29] *PMLA*, 99 (1984), 179–93.

[30] '*Bartholomew Fair* as Urban Arcadia: Jonson Responds to Shakespeare', pp. 151–72.

[31] '*The New Inn* and Plato's Myth of the Hermaphrodite', pp. 173–94.

[32] Ed. Kenneth Friedenreich (AMS Press, New York, 1983).

[33] *Studies in English Literature*, 24 (1984), 275–91.

[34] *Notes and Queries*, 31 (1984), 220–1.

[35] AMS Press, New York, 1983.

[36] '*King Henry VIII* and *All is True*', *Notes and Queries*, 31 (1984), 217–18.

Tragedy of Tiberius (1607): Debts to Shakespeare'.[37] R. P. Corballis has had the unusual idea of looking at 'The Name Antonio in English Renaissance Drama', to see whether the use of 'tony' as a synonym for simpleton in *The Changeling* might reflect a general attitude toward the name.[38] His theory works for some characters and, with a little stretching – extending the definition to cover the over-anxious, openhearted, fatherly type – can obviously be made to fit Shakespeare as well.

Of the various articles on context, always a mainstay of this review, I found the following most useful. Henry Saunders, in 'Staple Courts in *The Merchant of Venice*', argues that these London institutions, rather than those of Venice, were Shakespeare's model for the handling of the case of Antonio v. Shylock.[39] Thomas McAlindon has worked out a complex theory of number symbolism in *Julius Caesar*, based on fours and eights (the numbers of unity, friendship, and marriage, disrupted by the act of the conspirators).[40] Karl P. Wentersdorf, in 'Hamlet's Encounter with the Pirates', shows that Elizabethan experiences of piracy would have made Hamlet's letter to Horatio sound a lot more probable than it does now.[41] David Kaula starts from the antithesis in act I, scene I between two kinds of portents (for the death of Caesar and for the birth of Christ), suggesting that the play as a whole reflects Protestant belief in the conflict of the true and false churches, the latter of which descends from Cain and is based on Rome: fratricidal Claudius, with his Roman name, is thus an appropriate antagonist for the ex-student of Wittenberg.[42] Sharon L. Jansen Jauch sets the prophecies in *Macbeth* beside real ones of the period: Shakespeare's audience would have been familiar with such symbols as crowned heads and bloody children, and would not have taken them, as Macbeth does, to be favourable.[43]

After the explosion of writing on the visual arts last year, there is little to report this time. Two excellent papers from the University of Warwick's 1984 conference on English Arts and the Italian Renaissance – Leo Salingar's 'Shakespeare and the Italian Concept of Art' and M. M. Martinet's 'The Image of Italian Art in the English Renaissance Mind' – have been published as Supplements 3 and

4 of the *Renaissance Drama Newsletter*.[44] Sybil Truchet's 'The Art of Antiquity in Works by Lyly and Shakespeare' argues that Renaissance English writers got their ideas of art and artists not from the Italians but from ancient authors, especially Pliny; however, references to classical art (especially classical patronage) are often a way of making a point about the contemporary situation, and some Renaissance ideals, such as verisimilitude, are also classical.[45] This interesting article draws on Lyly's novels as well as on *Campaspe*, and finds Shakespeare's account of Lucrece before the painting of Troy an example of the collaboration of artist and spectator that brings art to life. Harry Morris, in a study of Holbein's Dance of Death pictures, shows their possible influence, and that of the essay which followed them, in the History plays.[46] His article should be read in conjunction with Marjorie Garber's piece on *Memento Mori* figures in Shakespeare, which I reviewed in *Shakespeare Survey 36*. A further contribution to this grisly but compelling subject, by John M. Bowers, considers what kind of monument Cleopatra was meant to have, and suggests that the clown bearing figs, who appears shortly after her cry, 'Where art thou, Death?', is a counterpart to the Death figure waiting on banquet guests in another Holbein scene.[47] Finally, though it is not illustrated, Phoebe S. Spinrad's '*Measure for Measure* and the Art of Not Dying' is a persuasive critical study which takes several *Ars Moriendi* themes – life as a prison, the contrast between

[37] *Notes and Queries*, 31 (1984), 213–14.

[38] *Cahiers Élisabéthains*, 25 (1984), 61–72.

[39] *Notes and Queries*, 31 (1984), 190–1.

[40] 'The Numbering of Men and Days: Symbolic Design in *The Tragedy of Julius Caesar*', *Studies in Philology*, 81 (1984), 37–93.

[41] *Shakespeare Quarterly*, 34 (1983), 434–40.

[42] '*Hamlet* and the Image of Both Churches', *Studies in English Literature*, 24 (1984), 241–55.

[43] 'Political Prophecy and Macbeth's "Sweet Bodements"', *Shakespeare Quarterly*, 34 (1983), 290–7.

[44] Available from the Graduate School of Renaissance Studies, University of Warwick, Coventry CV4 7AL.

[45] *Cahiers Élisabéthains*, 24 (1983), 17–26.

[46] 'The Dance of Death Motif in Shakespeare', *Papers on Language and Literature*, 20 (1984), 15–28.

[47] '"I am Marble-Constant": Cleopatra's Monumental End', *Huntington Library Quarterly*, 46 (1983), 283–97.

earthly and divine remedies – as its point of departure.[48]

Notes and Queries, 31 (1984) contains in its May number the usual range of brief notes on sources and analogues, some more convincing than others. Volume 14 of *Renaissance Drama* (1983), edited by Leonard Barkan, is devoted to 'Relations and Influences'. Its most provocative contribution, by James P. Bednarz, suggests that one of the 'rejected addresses' for Theseus' wedding celebrations was meant as a satire on Spenser's *Tears of the Muses*, which had lamented the silencing of 'our pleasant Willy' – Lyly, whose coterie drama Spenser supposedly preferred; Shakespeare was hitting back by making Bottom's dream a parody of Prince Arthur's.[49] Peter L. Rudnytsky finds some interesting links between *A Woman Killed With Kindness* and *Othello* as well as with the play which uses the proverbial tag, *The Taming of the Shrew*.[50] The general subject of Imitation is well covered by Paula S. Berggren in '"*Imitari* is Nothing": a Shakespearean Complex Word', whose starting point is the fact that the quotation of the title is spoken by a ridiculous character.[51] A wide range of reference is drawn on to show that, whereas 'counterfeiting' is always disreputable, 'imitation' is a word of enough dignity for Ulysses to be annoyed when Patroclus misappropriates it for his mimicry of the Greek leaders.

On the strength of some of the other source studies, it is hard to say whether Shakespeare was more involved in imitation or counterfeiting. When critics allow themselves to take into account every conceivable type of influence – positive, negative, out-of-context, visual as well as verbal – the result may do justice to the quirky way an author's mind really does work, but it looks suspiciously like a way of leaving themselves an absolutely free hand. I had both kinds of reaction to J. J. M. Tobin's study of the influence of Apuleius.[52] Shakespeare's enthusiasm for this particular source apparently led him 'to borrow material without respect to its tonal or story-line integrity': for instance, the bedchamber murder recalls Psyche with her candle bending over the sleeping Cupid; 'the owl was a baker's daughter' conflates two different Apuleian stories.

Some of these echoes seemed quite possible to me, others far-fetched. Moreover, the Apuleian story itself is ambiguous in tone; this is pointed out by Jan Kott, in a stimulating essay on *A Midsummer Night's Dream*.[53] Like *The Golden Asse*, Shakespeare's play has elements both of mystical allegory and of a carnival joke in its grotesque pairing of Bottom and Titania. In view of the connection often seen between Kott himself and the Brook *Midsummer Night's Dream*, it is interesting that the critic now feels that productions where Bottom wears a monstrous phallus distort the play as much as the traditional romantic ones. A complementary study by François Laroque interprets this double aspect of Shakespearian comedy in terms of a development in Shakespeare's concept of Ovidian metamorphosis: we move from Bottom's transformation to Falstaff's horns in *The Merry Wives* and thence to the reference in *As You Like It* to the exiled Ovid and the cynical possibility 'That any man turn ass'.[54]

Among other studies of classical influence, a sensitive and suggestive article by John Pitcher demonstrates how *The Aeneid* undergoes a sea-change in *The Tempest*, through images of the drowned man, grief at the transitoriness of human things, and the reworking of the story of Dido and Aeneas in Prospero's masque.[55] The most daring part of the argument is the relation of Shakespeare's

---

[48] *Texas Studies in Literature and Language*, 26 (1984), 74–93.

[49] 'Imitations of Spenser in *A Midsummer Night's Dream*', pp. 79–102.

[50] '*A Woman Killed With Kindness* as Subtext for *Othello*', pp. 103–24.

[51] *Texas Studies in Literature and Language*, 26 (1984), 94–127.

[52] *Shakespeare's Favorite Novel, A Study of 'The Golden Asse' as Prime Source* (University Presses of America/Eurospan, Lanham, New York, and London, 1984).

[53] 'The Bottom Translation', *En Torno a Shakespeare* (Shakespeare Institute, Valencia, 1982), 7–61.

[54] 'Ovidian Transformations and Folk Festivities in *A Midsummer Night's Dream, The Merry Wives of Windsor*, and *As You Like It*', *Cahiers Élisabéthains*, 25 (1984), 23–36. This number also includes Larry Langford, '"The Story Shall be Changed": The Senecan Sources of *A Midsummer Night's Dream*' (pp. 37–51), another attempt to show what might be called negative imitation.

[55] 'A Theatre of the Future: *The Aeneid* and *The Tempest*', *Essays in Criticism*, 34 (1984), 193–215.

play to Virgil's prophecies both of what might have been and what was still to be – particularly, to the projected theatre which Aeneas sees depicted in Carthage.

Gilles D. Monsarrat's *Light from the Porch: Stoicism and English Renaissance Literature*, brings precise definitions to a topic which has been badly in need of them.[56] The first part of the book traces the transmission of stoic ideals on the Continent and in England; the second part deals with plays usually taken to express stoic values. Monsarrat's definition of stoicism is so strict that it rules out nearly all of the latter. Even Brutus turns out to be a platonist (as Plutarch said he was) rather than a stoic; Hamlet's world-weariness in act 5 is not the same as the Stoic's identification of himself with the course of the universe. In fact, only private theatre plays (chiefly Marston's) depict pure stoicism; among Shakespeare's characters, only Horatio genuinely fits the description, and even he weakens at the end. Few English writers accepted the view that all passions were wrong, and thus stoicism in drama is presented chiefly as an ideal which characters find themselves unable to put into practice. In Ross Kilpatrick's 'Hamlet the Scholar', stoicism is connected with satire, and Hamlet's probable undergraduate reading in the Roman satirists is linked with the name of his closest friend, a possible allusion to the advocate of the golden mean.[57]

Peggy Muñoz Simonds suggests some 'Overlooked Sources of the Bed Trick' – I should prefer to call them analogues – which come from the Bible, Arthurian legend, and the story of Jupiter and Alcmena.[58] Two other studies of the problem plays draw usefully on earlier drama. Paula Neuss, in 'The Sixteenth Century English "Proverb" Play', makes a sensible distinction between plays which merely illustrate a proverb and those which, like *All's Well that Ends Well*, relate the proverb to a plot which eventually leads to a questioning of its adequacy.[59] Carol W. Pollard also treats *All's Well* as a morality, this time in relation to *The Dutch Courtesan*.[60] Both plays, she argues, are puzzling because they draw on two types of morality convention: the last-minute repentance of the Everyman plot and the deterministic plot which opposes

Worldly Man and Heavenly Man for all eternity. Thus, whether or not we believe in the promises of reform at the end will depend on our assumptions about the genre to which they belong.

Genre is also a significant factor in Jill L. Levenson's 'Romeo and Juliet before Shakespeare': the novella's concern with rational motivation and the opposition of reason to passion is, she argues, used in the play 'to produce contradictions, and thus ironies'.[61] The Nine Worthies in *Love's Labour's Lost* are part of a well-known tradition: Judith C. Perryman looks at earlier lists of Worthies and points out that the particular ones chosen to appear in this play had all been defeated, as have the four would-be 'brave conquerors' of Navarre's court.[62] Richard Proudfoot, who also sees the Worthies as an ironic comment on the four men, suggests a link between the comic characters who play these roles and the types described in Sidney's *Defence of Poesy*, first published in 1595; the comic types recur in Berowne's self-castigation.[63] Ironically, Armado is 'the play's one successful lover', and the silence of Jaquenetta in the final scene is one of several dramatic effects which will recur in later plays.

William Flygare's *Montaigne-Shakespeare Studies* contains tabulations of quotations from the two authors with cross-reference to possible parallels and a chronological table showing the biographical overlap between them.[64] It is privately printed, in a very limited edition, and the author writes as if from

---

[56] Collection Études Anglaises, 36 (Didier-Érudition, Paris, 1984).

[57] *Mélanges Offerts en Hommage au Révérend Père Étienne Gareau* (Société des études anciennes de Québec, 5th Series, 1983).

[58] *Shakespeare Quarterly*, 34 (1983), 433–4.

[59] *Comparative Drama*, 18 (1984), 1–18.

[60] 'Immoral Morality: Combinations of Morality Types in *All's Well that Ends Well* and *The Dutch Courtesan*', *Cahiers Élisabéthains*, 25 (1984), 53–72.

[61] *Studies in Philology*, 81 (1984), 325–47.

[62] 'A Tradition Transformed in *Love's Labour's Lost*', *Études Anglaises*, 37 (1984), 156–62.

[63] '*Love's Labour's Lost*: Sweet Understanding and the Five Worthies', *Essays and Studies*, ed. Raymond Chapman (English Association, John Murray and Humanities Press, 1984), 16–30.

[64] Apollon Press, Kyoto, 1983.

inside a bottle on the sea. Almost equally hard to get at the moment, but deserving of a wider audience, is Leo Salingar's 'King Lear, Montaigne, and Harsnett', a sophisticated and convincing study of the clusters of images and ideas which, more than isolated parallels, suggest the influence of the two other writers on Shakespeare's play.[65] The elaborate collection of parallels in A. Kent Hieatt's comparison between the Sonnets and Spenser's translation of Du Bellay's Antiquités de Rome draws attention to one important aspect of their imagery: 'Shakespeare might have been impelled to fuse praise of the beloved as a patron – a pattern of vulnerable, antique excellence – with similar and additional ideas in Ruines and to associate with the adored, socially superior youth certain features of the histories: veneration of a mythic past, hatred for modern time-serving Commodity, and the search for a new English hero.'[66]

The transition from history in Shakespeare to Shakespeare in history brings us to a somewhat miscellaneous group of works. Brian Loughrey and Neil Taylor, in 'Jonson and Shakespeare at Chess?', discuss a painting which probably has nothing to do with Shakespeare at all, and whose provenance is suspiciously obscure; that their article appeared in Shakespeare Quarterly rather than an art journal can be explained by the fact that the painting was on display at the Folger Shakespeare Library in 1984.[67] David Gervais's study of 'Delacroix's Hamlet' reproduces a number of the lithographs done between the 1830s and 1843, when they were privately printed.[68] Although Delacroix was present at the famous Paris Hamlet which set off the craze for Harriet Smithson, his images are independent of the stage performance. This, Gervais argues, is one reason for their excellence: he sees most theatrically inspired illustrations as 'translating what is already a translation from text to stage'.

This sense that we are always at one remove from the Shakespearian original is, not surprisingly, particularly acute in scholars who habitually work with translations. The Shakespeare Institute of Valencia devotes much of its time to collaborative translations of the plays, with an eye as much on the theatre director as on the scholar. The recent collection of essays by its director, Manuel Angel Conejero, stresses the interrelation of these topics.[69] His discussions of Shakespeare productions – Michael Pennington as Hamlet at Stratford; the Giorgio Strehler film of Lear, in Italian, at the Centre Pompidou in Paris; a French version of The Two Noble Kinsmen – focus chiefly on the contingent nature of the experience (the sense of linguistic displacement, the effect of the theatrical ambiance, the discrepant reactions of members of the audience), sometimes to the point of blurring the line between the theoretical and the anecdotal. The most complex of Conejero's essays are available in English in the Institute's biennial publication, En Torno a Shakespeare (1980 and 1982). His suggestion that much can be learned from 'a stylistic analysis of Shakespeare in Castilian or of Calderon in English' can be tested in his own discussion of the Valencian translation of 'If it were done when 'tis done' and in Juan V. Martinez-Luciano's 'El Termino "Time" in Macbeth' (both in the 1982 En Torno a Shakespeare). A similar example of the interdependence of theatrical and linguistic translation can be found in Ann Fridén's account of Ingmar Bergman's three productions of Macbeth in Stockholm: that of 1948 was the first one in which the translation permitted director and actors to stress the link between the witches' 'Fair is foul' and Macbeth's 'So foul and fair a day I have not seen'.[70]

I felt that S. S. Hussey's otherwise useful The Literary Language of Shakespeare suffered somewhat from its lack of a theatrical perspective.[71] There is much good material here: suggestions about possible Warwickshire dialect forms, Latin and

---

[65] Anglo-American Studies, 3 (Salamanca, 1983), 145–74.

[66] 'The Genesis of Shakespeare's Sonnets: Spenser's Ruines of Rome: by Bellay', Publications of the Modern Language Association, 98 (1983), 800–14.

[67] Shakespeare Quarterly, 34 (1983), 440–8.

[68] The Cambridge Quarterly, 13 (1984), 40–70.

[69] La Escena, El Sueño, La Palabra: Apunte Shakespeariano (Instituto Shakespeare/Instituto de Cine y Television, 1983).

[70] '"He Shall Live a Man Forbid": Ingmar Bergman's Macbeth', Shakespeare Survey 36 (Cambridge University Press, 1983), 65–72.

[71] Longman, London and New York, 1982.

English influences on vocabulary, grammar, and syntax; the use of special linguistic devices for character differentiation or the creation of a 'Roman' or 'theatrical' style; the nuances involved in choosing between 's' and 'eth' or 'thou' and 'you'; the difficulty of knowing whether a particular usage is or is not colloquial. But the discussion of Shakespeare's development assumes a pattern of continuing improvement, always in the direction of greater realism – for instance, Hussey prefers soliloquies to be introspective, and thus 'probable', rather than directed at the audience. It seems curious that someone so aware of the changing nature of language should not consider the importance of extratextual meanings. Even so, the book can be recommended to students who are having difficulty placing Shakespeare's language in context.

Among works on the context of performance, one of the most interesting is by William B. Hunter, Jr, who follows up the references to the moon in *Midsummer Night's Dream* to provide an occasion and a date for the play.[72] He argues that it was performed on St Valentine's Day of 1596, five days before the Carey–Berkeley wedding and the new moon, and would have ended with the Bergamask and Theseus' promise of a fortnight of revels; the final appearance of Puck, followed by the fairies, was a special epilogue for the day of the wedding itself.

The other studies of Elizabethan production focus on doubling. Scott McMillin has looked at plays published in 1594, with a view to determining the size of their casts.[73] He finds that published texts require anything from ten to twenty-three actors, but the three plays known to have been in the repertory of the Queen's Men – *The True Tragedy of Richard III*, *Friar Bacon* and *Selimus* – can be done with fourteen actors each, probably because they were taken on a provincial tour. John C. Meagher's enjoyable 'Economy and Recognition: Thirteen Shakespearean Puzzles' asks a number of intriguing questions (e.g. why doesn't Paris attend the Capulets' ball?) whose answers shed light on the doubling problem.[74] He points out various ingenious ways in which Shakespeare, having assembled all his actors to make a crowded scene, manages to get some of them off stage in time to reappear at the beginning

of the next scene in other roles. I'm not sure about some of the meanings he reads into doubling – for instance, that we are more ready to accept Paulina's union with Camillo because he is the double of her first husband Antigonus – though the possibility that Perdita is the double of Mamillius does suggest the potentialities of foregrounding a theatrical convention to make a symbolic point.

It is clearly difficult to distinguish between those doublings which are meant to be taken for granted and those which were intended to be funny or significant. This problem also arises in the other two essays on doubling, both by Giorgio Melchiori.[75] He and Meagher agree that Paris is absent from the Capulets' ball because he was doubling one of the other characters: Meagher thinks it was Mercutio, Melchiori that it was Tybalt. Both doublings can be shown to be thematically appropriate: as Stephen Booth has already suggested,[76] a Paris–Mercutio–Prince trebling would provide an extraordinary family resemblance among the three kinsmen; a Paris–Tybalt doubling makes both men victims of Romeo's love. But the trebling has been shown to be theatrically impossible, and the various symbolic pairings cancel each other out. Moreover, some of this neat patterning seems to have been forced on the company by the needs of their provincial tour.

An important, though only partly Shakespearian, book on Restoration theatre is Curtis A. Price's challenging view of Purcell's music drama as an important form in its own right rather than a staging post on the way to opera.[77] Unlike most writers on

---

[72] Appendix to *Milton's 'Comus', Family Piece* (Whitston Publishing Company, Troy, NY, 1983).

[73] 'The Queen's Men in 1594: A Study of "Good" and "Bad" Quartos', *English Literary Renaissance*, 14 (1984), 55–69.

[74] *Shakespeare Quarterly*, 35 (1984), 7–21.

[75] 'The Staging of the Capulets' Ball: Doubling as an Art', *En Torno a Shakespeare* (1982); an expansion of this article is 'Peter, Balthazar, and Shakespeare's Art of Doubling', *Modern Language Review*, 78 (1983), 777–92.

[76] In *Shakespeare: The Theatrical Dimension*, ed. P. C. McGuire and D. A. Samuelson (AMS Press, New York, 1979), cited by Melchiori in *Modern Language Review*.

[77] *Henry Purcell and the London Stage* (Cambridge University Press, 1984).

this period, he takes seriously the plays for which the composer wrote his music. His most interesting suggestions have to do with *Dido and Aeneas*: in its original context, the opera (with its sorceress who comes from *Macbeth* via Shadwell's *Lancashire Witches*) might have hinted at the connection between witchcraft and Catholic plots against the united reign of William and Mary. When Gildon incorporates the opera into *Measure for Measure*, however, Angelo identifies himself with Aeneas (Price even suggests that Mrs Bracegirdle may have doubled Dido and Isabella), thus becoming the 'hypocritical opportunist' which Dido calls him.

By contrast with the Shakespeare Jubilee organized by Garrick, the one of 1864 has been largely ignored. Richard Foulkes's monograph fills the gap admirably, but also shows why it was allowed to exist for so long.[78] Petty squabbling, financial incompetence, and broken promises make for dispiriting reading and are not unfamiliar enough to have an exotic appeal. But there are some attractive discoveries: the illustrations of the Pavilion erected for the entertainments at Stratford (a pity that it was only a temporary structure), the account of such quintessentially Victorian efforts as 'The Fairies' Festival in Commemoration of Shakespeare'. Foulkes points out that this festival, unlike its predecessor, rightly focused on performances of the plays (for both élite and popular audiences), and anticipated many subsequent cultural developments, particularly in Stratford itself.

Theatre Notebook, 38 (1984), contains two pieces on nineteenth-century theatre: Daniel Barrett's '"Refined Vivacity": The Acting of Leigh Murray' includes the actor's sensible comments on how to play Cassio's drunk scene (pp. 115–122); S. Wallace Roche's 'A la Langtry' (pp. 122–31) discusses 'the only genuine professional travesty' of *Antony and Cleopatra* in the nineteenth century.

P. C. Kolin's introduction to *Shakespeare in the South: Essays on Performance*, says that it is intended for 'anyone interested in the South, or Shakespeare or both'.[79] I think it is a collection of more interest to Southerners than to Shakespearians. Much of the first part (a historical survey of Shakespeare productions) tends to be not much more than a calendar

of performances, with occasional points of interest: the immense popularity of *Richard III*, the female Romeos, the child actors. Some of the articles on modern Shakespeare festivals in the second part are little more than a series of impressionistic comments, but the final chapter should be of interest to teachers, as it describes a workshop programme in Florida which seems to have had good results. The article of greatest general interest, Charles B. Lower's 'Othello as Black on Southern Stages, Then and Now', shows that, in pre-Civil War performances, the hero was played as black, and as a noble figure; the cuts made in the sexual language were no different from those made elsewhere. The immense popularity of this story of miscegenation, in such a time and place, casts an interesting light on the whole question of historical context. Lower sees it as proof that nineteenth-century audiences went to the theatre for escape rather than relevance.

Of the various studies of modern directors, Christopher Innes's *Edward Gordon Craig* is the most substantial, making the man's work sound much more coherent than it usually seems when writers concentrate on his stormy biography or quote his overstated, exclamatory style.[80] His account of the Moscow *Hamlet*, for instance, may usefully be set beside Laurence Senelick's (reviewed here last year), which was the chronicle of an egomaniac's disaster. Cary M. Mazer's 'Actors or Gramophones: The Paradoxes of Granville-Barker' is also a defence of a director often attacked for over-dominating his actors.[81] The evidence points both ways. On the first night of *The Winter's Tale*, we learn, Barker actually pushed Florizel and Perdita on to the stage as they were preparing to make their first entrance: the result was spontaneity and vitality – but it was still the director who had contrived it. Ralph Berry defends 'Komisarjevsky at Stratford-upon-Avon', calling him 'the jester as revolutionary' and noting

---

[78] *The Shakespeare Tercentenary of 1864* (Society for Theatre Research, 1984).

[79] University Press of Mississippi, Jackson, 1983.

[80] Directors in Perspective series (Cambridge University Press, 1983).

[81] *Theatre Journal*, 36 (1984), 5–23.

that his eccentricity allowed him to get away with many experiments which would now arouse critical hostility.[82]

The political context of two modern productions is considered in Ann Fridén's study of Bergman's increasingly dark treatments of *Macbeth* (see note 70, above) and Wolfgang Solich's analysis of Peter Brook's 1979 *Measure for Measure* at the Bouffes du Nord.[83] Solich argues that Brook's stress on Isabella's feminism, and such details as the homosexual attraction of the disguised Duke for the proletarian Lucio, denied the political realities of the play 'by forcing social conflicts into the arena of psychology'.

Macmillan's new 'Text and Performance' series, under the general editorship of Michael Scott, sets out to juxtapose the study of the text with the analysis and comparison of four modern productions. Of the first four volumes to appear, Peter Davison's *Hamlet* is the most wide-ranging in its choice of material (Garrick's adaptation, Gielgud rehearsing Burton, the Marowitz collage) as well as scholarly in its discussion of textual cruces and its suggestion that the examples of clownish ad libs recorded in Q1 might have been Burbage's own. T. F. Wharton, on the two *Henry IV* plays, begins by implying that he sees performance simply in terms of right or wrong delivery of a text, but in the second part he warms to his subject and, despite his avowed intention of making a 'commitment' to one of the four productions, actually succeeds in making them all vivid and attractive. Michael Scott's account of *Antony and Cleopatra* suffers, I think, from its almost exclusive concentration on hero and heroine. Roger Warren's *Midsummer Night's Dream*, firmly on the side of 'human', as opposed to symbolic, treatments of the play, shows a fine sense of verbal textures and the ability to describe a production. Neither he nor Scott likes Peter Brook's treatment of their play, but Warren's criticism is more convincing than Scott's, because based on a better understanding of what the director was doing.

Two 'Shakespeare Workshop' videotapes produced with schools in mind are a welcome change from the printed page. Both were written by David Whitworth and produced by Noel Hardy with members of the New Shakespeare Company. I found *The Comic Spirit* rather more successful than *The Tortured Mind*; it is in any case the more necessary of the two, since comedy is far harder than tragedy to bring alive. It gives a wide selection of Shakespearian comedy scenes along with a discussion of various levels of comedy from banana skin jokes to examples of verbal dexterity, sexual antagonism and near-tragedy. The *Much Ado About Nothing* sequence shows this approach at its most inventive. The introductory scene in which a reporter with notebook interviews Beatrice and Benedick during Leonato's cocktail party not only gives the plot of the play with remarkable economy but also picks up its often-noticed themes of reporting and noting. A serious treatment of the church scene is followed by the duel-that-might-have-been between Benedick and Claudio, with dialogue from *Romeo and Juliet*. I found this fantasy more effective than its counterpart in *The Tortured Mind* (a conversation between Ophelia and her psychiatrist). Some aspects of the tragedy tape need careful handling by the teacher – for instance, the use of eighteenth- and nineteenth-century theatrical illustrations without any explanation of their context, the casting of a white actor, un-made-up, as Othello, and the (I assume) unintentional implication that the Hecate scenes of *Macbeth* are by Davenant. The extracts are mostly performed in modern dress, apart from one rather conventional costumed scene from *Lear*. They are well done, and could be stimulating provided that the class is able to take them as a starting point rather than a definitive statement about the plays.

The release of John Barton's *Playing Shakespeare* during the showing on Channel Four of the workshops on which it was based meant that it was possible to compare the written and spoken dialogue, noting which bits were spontaneous and which scripted, and where Barton had used the book

---

[82] *Shakespeare Survey 36* (Cambridge University Press, 1983), 73–84.

[83] 'Prolegomenon for a Theory of Drama Reception: Peter Brook's *Measure for Measure* and the Emergent Bourgeoisie', *Comparative Drama*, 18 (1984), 54–81.

to set down apologies and second thoughts.[84] The book is least good where the series was best, in the comparison of various ways of speaking the lines. To be told that '*Patrick Stewart reads Salerio, and David Suchet Shylock. Then vice versa*' is about as helpful as reading an opera libretto when you don't know the music. But Barton's own personal credos and his discussions with the actors, which received a lot of criticism in reviews of the broadcasts, are effective on the page. Perhaps, as one of his actors hinted, he is too anxious to find irony and ambiguity (and hence 'balance') everywhere, but when it comes to discussing where to pause and breathe in a long and complex speech, or how much to load the key words in a passage, he is hard to beat.

Barton is a director who might have been an academic; Alan C. Dessen, author of *Elizabethan Stage Conventions and Modern Interpretations*, is an academic with some of the instincts of a director.[85] This close and detailed study of the whole corpus of Elizabethan plays, with special attention to their stage directions, can be seen as a continuation of M. C. Bradbrook's pioneering *Themes and Conventions of Elizabethan Tragedy* – based, as the earlier book could not be, on considerable experience of these plays in the theatre. Dessen identifies stage conventions, like the entrance 'as from' dinner, or

hawking, or a journey, and suggests that symbolic details of costume must have been used to establish location much more than props or bits of scenery. He frequently links Elizabethan practice with that of the popular moral play, and thus tends to prefer stylization to realism in, for instance, fight scenes. His examples are a persuasive argument for worrying out the meaning of difficult speeches and stage directions instead of assuming that they require emendation. He does not altogether come to terms with the problem facing the director who might wish to put some of his suggestions into practice: the modern audience's inability to know when a convention is not a convention. But, if he sometimes goes too far in thinking that there must always be a good reason for everything that a dramatist writes, this is a better working assumption than its opposite. 'History may be servitude, / History may be freedom.' Of this, though they differ in their emphases, Barton and Dessen are equally, and intelligently, aware.

---

[84] Methuen, in association with Channel 4 TV, London and New York, 1984.

[85] Cambridge University Press, 1984. An earlier version of its argument can be sampled in 'Shakespeare's Scripts and the Modern Director', *Shakespeare Survey 36*, pp. 57–64.

3. EDITIONS AND TEXTUAL STUDIES

reviewed by MacDonald P. Jackson

Oxford–Cambridge rivalry now extends to Shakespeare publishing by the two university presses.[1] The new Cambridge editions, like the Oxford ones, present modern-spelling texts and imitate the Arden layout, but their textual analyses are placed in appendixes and they offer reading lists of books and articles, not Oxford's indexes to the commentaries. Sketches by C. Walter Hodges re-

in the New Cambridge Shakespeare series, general editor Philip Brockbank. *Titus Andronicus* and *Julius Caesar* were published in 1984 by the Clarendon Press, Oxford. All editions are available both in hard covers and in paperback. Also received was a bilingual *1 Henry IV* (Aubier, Paris, 1983), edited and translated by Michel Grivelet. Stanley Wells's important *Re-Editing Shakespeare for the Modern Reader* (Clarendon Press, Oxford, 1984) arrived too late for this survey, but will be discussed in the next. My line references are to the edition under review or, in discussion of articles and notes, *The Riverside Shakespeare* (Houghton Mifflin, Boston, 1974), ed. G. Blakemore Evans.

---

[1] *The Taming of the Shrew*, *Romeo and Juliet*, and *Othello* were published in 1984 by Cambridge University Press

construct possible Elizabethan-Jacobean stagings of selected episodes. The pages are larger, though not more readable, than those in the Oxford and Arden series. The volumes are pleasant to look at and handle.

Ann Thompson's edition of *The Taming of the Shrew*, appearing soon after Brian Morris's new Arden (1981) and H. J. Oliver's Oxford (1982), is a worthy competitor. On the main scholarly issues she agrees with Morris against Oliver when they differ and with both men when they do not: she believes that the Folio text was set from a transcript rather than foul papers, that *A Shrew* (1594) derives from Shakespeare's play, that none of the discrepancies between the sub-plots of *A Shrew* and *The Shrew* imply major revision of the latter, but that *The Shrew* once contained equivalents of the additional Sly episodes preserved in *A Shrew*. Any pre-Folio version of Shakespeare's comedy 'would have been simply an uncut version of the play that we have, not a radically different version in any other respect' (p. 173). Her exposition of the evidence is lucid and her conclusions – reached independently of Morris and Oliver – are reasonable.[2]

The derivative nature of *A Shrew* is confirmed by Thompson's discussion of sources. Drawing on J. H. Brunwald's doctoral dissertation and article, which examine the folklore origins of the taming plot, she points out that at least six of the many elements that *The Shrew* takes from the oral tradition recorded as tale-type 901 in the Aarne-Thompson index are absent from *A Shrew*; it is much more likely that the theatre hacks who cobbled up *A Shrew* 'simply missed some significant traits out of the reconstruction...than that Shakespeare revised *A Shrew* with such detailed and pervasive reference back to the original tradition', to which his Katherina–Petruchio scenes are so clearly indebted (p. 13).

In an appendix Thompson prints from *A Shrew* not only the Sly material but also a sixty-line stretch of banter that may paraphrase a Shakespearian scene originally placed between 3.2.117 and 3.2.118. Speculating on why such cross-talk between servants should have been jettisoned from F, she suggests that either Shakespeare came to regard it as unfashion-

able or unfunny, or he cut it as a countermeasure to the lengthening of the play through 'the decision... to put Hortensio into disguise and generally complicate the sub-plot' (p. 180). Here logic momentarily deserts her: the second explanation is incompatible with her conclusion that no Shakespearian *Shrew* without a disguised Hortensio as wooer of Bianca ever reached the stage.

Thompson's discussion of evidence for dating *The Taming of the Shrew* and of its affinities with Shakespeare's other works 'cannot establish any clear sequence', but 'suggests that the play belongs to the earliest phase of his development' – perhaps 1590. She rightly refuses to be more definite.

'Since the late nineteenth century the movement for the liberation of women has done for *The Shrew* what reaction to the anti-semitism of our time has done for *The Merchant of Venice*: turned it into a problem play' (p. 21). Thompson admits uneasiness about its values, though enjoying its 'formal qualities, the sheer craft and detail of the construction' (p. 41). She surveys a wide range of expedients whereby actors, producers, and critics have sought to palliate the comedy's apparent barbarities and nullify its endorsement of male supremacy. In the theatre these have included freely adapting the script, insisting on a jolly, farcical atmosphere that discourages ethical and emotional involvement, hinting that Katherina falls in love with Petruchio at first sight, and undercutting Katherina's final speech by a knowing wink or an ironic tone. She points out that even the thematic approaches of twentieth-century criticism have worked to make the main action more acceptable. To treat the play in terms of 'acting', 'supposing', 'dreaming', or 'games-playing' is to distance and defuse the more problematic aspects of the taming plot; and Petruchio may be seen as a

---

[2] In arguing that the Folio *Shrew* was not set directly from foul papers, she might have mentioned that the ratio of *has* and *does* to *hath* and *doth* is wildly anomalous for an early Shakespeare play, being unmatched before *Twelfth Night*; a scribe appears to have introduced several instances of his own preferred forms, probably in the seventeenth century, when *has* and *does* first began to appear frequently in drama. Such high-handedness would be uncharacteristic of the Folio compositors.

benign and ingenious educator who cures Katherina's shrewishness by 'supposing' her 'a more promising candidate for wifehood than she seems to be' (p. 32). Thompson outlines the insights of recent feminist criticism by Dusinberre, Nevo, Garber, Novy, Kahn, and Cooper. She interestingly notes that Katherina is 'without a female friend at any point in the play' (p. 37), and that for her homily on marriage roles Shakespeare relies on secular arguments, spurning theological aid. She suspects that in performance 'the personality of the actor playing Petruchio is crucial to the play's success', and justly praises John Cleese in Jonathan Miller's intelligent BBC production (p. 41). As a guide to the play and the responses it has provoked, she is sensitive and open-minded. On one small point she seems wrong: she claims that for the original audience 'the romantic climax would . . . have been crowned by the ultimate ambiguity [irony?] that all the actors were male and Petruchio could no more "bed" his Kate in the sense intended than Christopher Sly could bed his "wife" in the Induction; the long-awaited consummation is indefinitely suspended, an impossibility in the real world' (p. 40). The fact that in the 1590s a boy would have acted Katherina is neither here nor there. Once the play is over Petruchio and Kate cease to exist, and it matters not a jot whether they were represented by Richard Burton and Elizabeth Taylor or two glove puppets.

Thompson continues her critical account of the play in her full and lively commentary, drawing attention to significant stages in the relationship between Katherina and Petruchio or in the exposure of Bianca's character, making cross-references between thematically and structurally related passages, considering the tone of the dialogue, and noting details of stage business. For example, Petruchio's statement to his wife that 'for this night we'll fast for company' (4.1.148) elicits a gloss on 'for company' ('together') and the comment: 'Many directors ignore this statement and have Petruchio eat his supper when he returns alone at 158. A Shrew has at this point the stage direction *Manent servingmen and eate up the meate.*' And the text takes on vivid theatrical life when we learn – apropos of Baptista's mysterious knowledge at 2.1.98 that he

is addressing 'Lucentio', whose name he has not heard – that while some editors and directors have Baptista read an inscription in one of the books that Tranio-alias-Lucentio has just presented, in the RSC's modern-dress production at Stratford in 1978 Tranio handed over a visiting card.

Textually this edition is orthodox, adopting an average number of emendations. Novelties are the amply justified naming of the character who enters at 4.2.71 SD as Merchant, not Pedant, and the retention of F's 'sir', normally taken as a misreading of 'for', at 5.2.65, where Petruchio, repudiating jibes about Katherine's shrewishness, proposes the wager on her obedience, with the words 'and therefore, Sir Assurance, / Let's each one send unto his wife'. 'Sir Assurance' (F lacks the capitals) she plausibly explains as an 'ironic form of address to the over-confident Baptista or Lucentio'. In Induction 2.94 SD and following speech-prefixes she gives the Page who is dressed as F's 'Lady' his name, Bartholomew, specified in Induction 1.101, and at 1.1.9 she prefers 'ingenuous' (or 'liberal') studies to 'ingenious' ones.

At 4.3.90–1 Petruchio comically disparages a gown made for Katherina: 'Here's snip and nip and cut and slish and slash, / Like to a censer in a barber's shop'. 'Censer' is Rowe's interpretation of F 'Censor'. Like other editors, Thompson explains that it is an incense-burner with holes in the lid, but admits that the use of perforated fumigators in barbers' shops of the time remains purely conjectural. So R. W. F. Martin's new proposal, 'scissor', deserves consideration.[3] 'Cizers' in *The Comedy of Errors* is the one other Shakespearian use of the word, but 'vnsistered' in *Pericles* is a certain misreading of 'unscissored' (perhaps spelt 'vnsissered'). The singular is unusual, but *OED* records examples in Cotgrave's dictionary of 1611, and gives various spellings. A possible argument against emendation is that another cryptic allusion to a censer appears in *2 Henry IV*, 5.4.18. Moreover, on Martin's interpretation Petruchio compares the results of the action of scissors in a tailor's shop with

---

[3] 'A Proposed Emendation for *The Taming of the Shrew*, IV.iii.91', *Notes and Queries*, NS 31 (1984), 184–6.

the action of scissors in a barber's shop, which seems rather lame.

'The textual situation in *Romeo and Juliet* is fraught with problems, some of them essentially insoluble.' G. Blakemore Evans seems in no danger of *hubris*, but few Shakespeare scholars could be better equipped to undertake even the most daunting of editorial assignments. His survey of facts and opinions about the early texts of *Romeo and Juliet* is terse and exact. There are no surprises: Q1 (1597) prints a 'reported' or 'memorially reconstructed' text; behind Q2 (1599) lay Shakespeare's foul papers; other texts are derivative, F being printed from Q3, 'with almost no attempt at correction apart from the addition of a few obvious stage directions' (p. 206).[4] Still in question is how and how much Q1 has contaminated Q2. At least one section of Q2 (1.2.50–1.3.35) is a straight reprint of Q1. Evans takes the majority view that elsewhere the Q2 compositors set directly from foul papers, but intermittently consulted Q1. So even readings common to both texts must be open to suspicion when links in punctuation and capitalization indicate localized Q1 influence on Q2. But Q1 can be used to repair Q2's deficiencies. Though conservative in his adherence to Q2, Evans accepts 'three-and-a-half additional lines and eighteen substantive readings' from Q1. 'These figures do not include further debts to Q1 in punctuation and stage directions or its occasional agreements with readings in Q3 and F which have been adopted here' (p. 212). The last half of that sentence is puzzling: Q1 surely claims precedence over Q3 and F as source of readings shared with those unauthoritative texts.

The half-dozen or so substantive readings in which Evans departs from his Riverside text are reversions to Q2. On the other hand, the 'letter' at 1.2.63–71, which he previously followed Q2 in printing as prose, he appropriately sets out as verse. The play's major crux is the near duplication of four lines in Q2 at the end of 2.2, where they are Romeo's, and the beginning of 2.3, where they are Friar Lawrence's, as in Q1, which omits the first version. Evans makes a good case for assigning the lines to the Friar, and accepts the second version as 'Shakespeare's rather careless revision' (p. 211). He

retains Q2's notorious 'runnawayes eyes' at 3.2.6, making runaways plural and interpreting them as 'the horses of the sun' or, more doubtfully, 'vagrant night wanderers'. This is better than the notion, first promulgated by the Reverend Halpin in 1845, that Runaway is a sobriquet for Cupid, but no explanation of Q2's word has yet yielded as much plain sense in context as the best of the numerous emendations, 'rumour's' (which assumes that 'rumoures' was misread as 'runawaies'). Virtually every Shakespearian textual crux stirs up associations that must be rigorously censored if we are to find meaning that is apt, sharp, and strong. Cupid runs away from Venus, and Phoebus' horses ran away while Phaëton was in charge, but these considerations cannot both be pertinent to 3.2.6 and the chances are that neither is. At 2.2.31 the choice is between two sets of associations, those centred on Q2's word and those centred on Q1's. Evans thinks of cumuli swelling as they drift ('lazy *puffing* clouds') and recalls maps picturing personified cloud-cheeked winds; others will imagine angels on horseback ('he *bestrides* the lazy *pacing* clouds') and note the passage's cluster of links with *Macbeth*, 1.7.19–23, and *Henry V*, 3.7.14–18; the misreading of 'pasing' (= pacing) as 'pufing', and normalization to 'puffing', would have been easy enough. Evans resists several customary metrical regularizations. At 3.2.19 he is right to insist on retaining 'new', and the line is metrically tolerable, but F2's change of 'upon' to 'on' has the dual merit of removing a superfluous syllable and remedying the obtrusive repetition of 'upon' from the previous line; 3.5.43, cited as no less 'hypermetrical' than 3.2.19, has ten syllables and sounds like a good Shakespearian pentameter to me. At 1.1.71 SD Evans's Prince is Escales (Q2–4 F 'Eskales'); other editors name him Escalus, as in Brooke's poem. Evans collates Q1 as fully as its extreme divergence from Q2 allows, and his commentary vies with that of the new Arden edition in thoroughness and interest. The Prologue's definition of the tragedy as both 'piteous' and 'fearful' within the space of three lines seems not to

---

4 But he notes that S. W. Reid has pleaded the value of F's changes.

have aroused his curiosity any more than it has that of previous editors.

Evans holds that *Romeo and Juliet* was written later than usually supposed, basing his view largely on J. J. M. Tobin's argument that the tragedy's characters and diction were influenced by Thomas Nashe's *Have with You to Saffron-Walden*, circulated in manuscript some three months before reaching the bookstalls some time in the period October 1596–March 1597.[5] Other evidence that *Romeo* was completed in 'the latter half of 1596' is, he concedes, 'either weak or ambiguous and would not seriously stand against a date as early as 1594' (p. 6). He is at pains to establish that the proposed date does not upset the orthodox chronology for Shakespeare's sixteenth-century plays.[6] However, he has been unable to take account of a later article that complicates matters: in it Tobin finds in *The Two Gentlemen of Verona* parallels with *Saffron-Walden* at least as striking as those in *Romeo*.[7] Yet Evans accepts the usual assignment of *Two Gentlemen*, in its final form, to 1593–4, and judges it earlier than *Romeo*. Tobin discounts the possibility that Nashe's language was affected by performances of the two unpublished Shakespeare plays, and Evans believes that in the case of *Romeo* 'a fair analysis of the evidence' makes Nashe's indebtedness to Shakespeare 'highly unlikely' (p. 4). Shakespeare may conceivably have seen *Saffron-Walden* during the two or three years that Nashe was intermittently engaged in writing it, but if so, his supposed borrowings from it are of little help in dating *Romeo* or *Two Gentlemen*. The most plausible resolution of this problem is that Shakespeare and Nashe mined the same Elizabethan vernacular, and that the vocabulary links between *Saffron-Walden* and the plays are fortuitous. *Romeo and Juliet* contains two hundred words that Shakespeare does not use elsewhere. This total would be greatly enlarged were we to count not only single words but uniquely used phrases, such as Tobin cites. Is it really significant that ten peculiar expressions used by Shakespeare only in *Romeo and Juliet* (twelve, if we include two words attested only by the Bad Quarto) should also appear in *Saffron-Walden*, a book of 166 lexically prodigal pages?

Evans deftly outlines Shakespeare's methods of 'tightening, focusing, and restructuring' Arthur Brooke's lumbering narrative poem, *Romeus and Juliet*, and his sense of the miraculous transformation wrought upon this primary source informs his critical account of the play. Addressing the question whether *Romeo and Juliet* is tragedy of Fate, of character, of both, or an experiment that fails to come off, he reasons that Shakespeare's handling of the paradoxically opposed concepts, Fate and free will, 'confused though it may be, is nevertheless an effective cause' of the play's enduring theatrical appeal. His sections on 'language, style and imagery' and 'the characters' pack in familiar material and get the emphases right. The young lovers, he points out, are the first of Shakespeare's characters to mature within the course of a play, and the catastrophe stems from their 'absolute commitment'. He is shrewd about Friar Lawrence (pp. 23–4), who behaves as the plot demands. His section on *Romeo and Juliet* in the theatre includes speculation about the Elizabethan staging and business, drawing on Q1's stage directions (many of which he incorporates in his text), is entertaining about the period following the Restoration when for close on two hundred years adaptations, such as the Garrick–

---

5 The later limit is the end of the legal year, the title-page's '1596' perhaps covering our January–March 1597. The earlier limit is set by Nashe's allusion to the 'late deceased' Countess of Derby, who died towards the end of September 1596 (McKerrow, IV, 302). Near the end of the text Nashe seems also, as McKerrow noted, to mention projected publication at the beginning of Candlemas Term (23 January–12 February): for what it is worth, this should point to late January 1597. The Bad Quarto (1597) of *Romeo and Juliet* was probably in press during this very month, though it may have been printed late 1596 (Evans, p. 207). The time-scheme for circulation of *Saffron-Walden* and composition, rehearsal, staging, memorial reconstruction, printing, and publication of *Romeo and Juliet*, is uncomfortably tight when the first and last stages of the sequence are assigned their most probable dates.

6 His discussion of the relationship between *Romeo and Juliet* and *Love's Labour's Lost* assumes 'a revision of the latter sometime between July–September and Christmas 1597' (p. 5), but John Kerrigan has cogently argued that no such revision took place; see *Shakespeare Survey* 37, pp. 216–17.

7 'Nashe and *The Two Gentlemen of Verona*', *Notes and Queries*, NS 28 (1981), 122–3.

Kemble version, prevailed, but, except in some sharp remarks on Zeffirelli, skims over the twentieth century: fuller description of a few major modern productions, or analysis of recurrent strengths and weaknesses could have further illuminated the play.[8]

Othello is really a trickier editorial proposition than *Romeo and Juliet*, since there are two good early texts, which differ in over a thousand readings. F, which nearly all editors consider superior, contains some 160 lines not in Q (1622). F has been purged of oaths, and both texts suffer from forms of minor error ordinarily perpetrated by compositors and copyists. However, some of the more significant variation can only have been produced by memorial contamination, scribal high-handedness, or authorial revision. Norman Sanders's predecessor, the Cambridge New Shakespeare editor, Alice Walker, thought that behind Q lay the corruptions of a transcriber who, working from a cut acting version, too often relied on his memory of the play and sometimes made deliberate alterations. She argued also that F had been printed from an annotated copy of Q, not directly from manuscript. This last claim has been disputed, and Nevill Coghill presented a strong case for supposing that most of F's unique passages were amplifications made by Shakespeare as he retouched his original text. E. A. J. Honigmann has supported the theory that authorial revision accounts for many of the major divergences between Q and F.

Sanders's discussion of the issues is sometimes muddled. Accepting J. K. Walton's rebuttal of Walker's case for F use of annotated Q copy, he cites as further evidence that F was set from manuscript the variant at 1.1.153 where Q reads 'hells paines' and F 'hell apines': 'here the F version is more likely to have been the result of a compositor's misreading of a manuscript than of Q1's type' (p. 200). F's nonsense is almost certainly due not to misreading but to mechanical error, 'a' and 'p' having been transposed. In the same paragraph he goes on to quote two undoubted misreadings *in* Q, claiming that they 'make it hard to sustain' Walker's hypothesis that F was set from a corrected exemplar of Q. They are, of course, irrelevant to the question. Adding to the confusion is Sanders's statement that in one of the instances the Q compositor probably

misread 'gastnes(se)' *for* 'gestures', when he means *as* 'gestures'.

Walker persuaded Greg, Philip Williams, and other astute scholars that F was set from an exemplar of Q mainly by means of her argument from the pattern of -t/-'d/-ed spellings for unvoiced preterites and past participles.[9] She argued that the variant spellings appear arbitrarily in Shakespearian texts, that the tendency was for -t endings in the quartos to be modernized as -'d/-ed endings in the Folio, that for the 72 such verbs shared by Q and F of *Othello* Q preferred -t (47 instances) and F -'d/-ed (48 instances), and that every one of F's 24 -t spellings was anticipated in Q. If Q and F were independent prints, F should, she maintained, sometimes have spelt -t where Q spelt -'d/-ed; the modernization must have been progressive. According to Sanders, Walker's argument 'cannot accommodate the evidence that three compositors and two scribes were responsible for Q1' (p. 201). What can be the reasoning behind this contention?[10] Honigmann's evidence that Q was set by three compositors from a manuscript prepared by two scribes has been challenged, but were it decisive it would form an obstacle not to Walker's argument but to the only alternative explanation that has so far been offered for the pattern to which she drew attention – Walton's suggestion that Q exactly reproduced the endings in Shakespeare's autograph (or perhaps in

---

[8] G. Melchiori's wide-ranging 'Peter, Balthasar, and Shakespeare's Art of Doubling', *Modern Language Review*, 78 (1983), 777–92, mingles astute observation and bold speculation. He has remarks on the date of *Romeo* (not later than 1594) and on the nature of Q1 and Q2. His theory (mentioned by Evans, p. 207, n. 1) that the Q1 reporter consulted Brooke's *Romeus* is without adequate foundation, resting on their agreement in a single word, 'enterprise'. His main concern is to show that Shakespeare contributed to a long-established practice the idea of doubling 'by function'.

[9] W. W. Greg, *The Shakespeare First Folio* (Clarendon Press, Oxford, 1955), p. 363; Williams, reviewing Walker's *Textual Problems* in *Shakespeare Quarterly*, 4 (1953), pronounced her argument from verb endings in *Othello* 'classic in its simplicity and force' (p. 482).

[10] Sanders's statement seems to echo Honigmann's criticism (*Stability*, pp. 109–10) of *another part* of Walker's textual theory.

the prompt-book) from which F also derived. The more agents responsible for transmitting Shakespeare's text to Q, the less likely that the precise Shakespearian mix of spellings would be preserved. Besides, Sanders believes that Q and F were based, at however many removes, on separate holographs; so, unlike Walton, he postulates no single archetype as source of the pattern detected by Walker. Walton's counter-hypothesis may nevertheless be right; or Walker's evidence may be susceptible of other explanations. But the matter needs to be fully thought through and Walker's data related to the habits of Folio Compositors B and E, who set *Othello*.[11]

Sanders ventures no stemma but lists three 'possible editorial paradigms'. The second – 'that F derives from a copy of Q1 wholly or partly corrected from a redaction of the same Shakespearean holograph' – is so ambiguous that the vastly different theories of Alice Walker and the Arden editor, M. R. Ridley (who doubted F's dependence on an exemplar of Q), are subsumed under the same head. His own belief is 'that Q1 and F are derived from two distinct manuscripts of equal authority, both of which have been variously corrupted in transmission, by scribes and compositors in Q1 and by editorial-intervention and compositors in F'. He has the 'strong impression... that what we are dealing with is Shakespeare's first version of the play (behind Q1) and his own transcription of it (behind F), during the process of making which he not only created additions for dramatic clarification or imaginative amplification but was also enticed into changes in words and phrases which appeared to him at the time as improvements on his first thoughts' (p. 206). This seems plausible, at least in its broad outlines.[12] What of the practical consequences? Sanders considers himself 'free to offer what he thinks to be a "best" version of the play in the full knowledge that in fact he is making a third version of it'. So in Sanders's edition Othello tells the Senate that he had described to Desdemona his redemption from slavery, 'And with it all my travels' history' (1.3.138). 'With it all' comes from Q. Sanders comments: 'F's "portance in" (= conduct during) is rather out of keeping

with the modesty Othello is trying to project in this self-defence'. Where, then, did F's variant originate? In making his choice on purely aesthetic grounds Sanders evades this question. Can anyone doubt that the F Latinism, which reappears in *Coriolanus*, is Shakespeare's? Nothing that Sanders says in his general textual analysis gives any reason to posit a non-Shakespearian agent in the transmission of F who is likely to have changed the vapid 'with it all' to the rare 'portance in', but the change from Q's to F's reading is exactly what we might expect from Shakespeare as he replaced a neutral phrase in the course of the revision that Sanders himself postulates. Alternatively, Q's variant could be the vulgarization of a scribe to whom F's was unintelligible. Perhaps Sanders believes that Q and F here present Shakespeare's first and second thoughts, but rejects the substitution as an artistic blunder. If so, he needs to mount a determined attack on the doctrine that – unless revision produces versions so disparate as to require separate editing – an author's 'final intentions' should prevail.[13] My own view is that if F contains Shakespeare's revisions, editors should adhere to it except where they believe that its readings are unauthoritative: this proviso allows plenty of scope for reinstatement of Q oaths, for use of Q to supplement F and correct its misreadings,

---

[11] The best evidence against F's dependence on Q copy is in Gary Taylor's paper, noted last year (p. 214).

[12] I doubt that a second holograph was ever prepared. Q seems to have been based on a private scribal transcript of the original foul papers, F (whether directly or indirectly) on the prompt-book, which, however complex its history, derived ultimately from the foul papers and included both unauthoritative deviations from them and Shakespeare's own expansions and changes. Common origin in a single holograph might explain the QF shared errors and spellings that would otherwise bear witness to F dependence on a corrected exemplar of Q.

[13] The most recent discussion of this topic is by James McLaverty, 'The Concept of Authorial Intention in Textual Criticism', *The Library*, 6 (1984), 121–38. But his argument that we must be at liberty to edit whichever authoritatively published version we choose to edit, whether or not it is the 'final' one, is not germane to the present issue. McLaverty does not countenance an eclectic mixing of an author's second thoughts and superseded first thoughts.

mechanical errors, and sophistications, for emendation of possible shared errors, and even for adoption of some of Q's supposedly 'indifferent' variants.[14]

In fact most of Sanders's decisions are compatible with such a policy, but it would, I think, discourage him from adopting Q's version of lines 1.3.273-4, where F's reallocations and adjustments seemed even to Greg the product of 'deliberate revision' (First Folio, p. 367). Sanders makes many sound choices, defending them well. He favours 'Indian' over 'Judean' (5.2.343). In that debate 'I do remain as neuter', but he seems to me wrong in preferring Q's 'balance' to Theobald's 'beam' for F's 'braine' at 1.3.319, 'enscarped' (Q 'enscerped') to F 'ensteep'd' at 2.1.70, and F's 'thou...hath' to Q's 'thou...hast' at 2.3.340. At 1.3.260 he emends QF 'defunct' to Theobald's 'distinct'. The passage is difficult, but the entreaty in the Book of Common Prayer Baptismal Service 'that all carnal affects may die in them' and St Paul's admonition of Timothy and the Romans to mortify the lusts of youth surely validate the QF collocation of 'young affects' and 'defunct' in the Christianized Othello's denial of a selfish sexual motive for his request.[15] Moreover, Sanders's theory that Q and F derive independently from separate holographs would imply that two different inscribings of 'distinct' were each misread as the difficilior lectio 'defunct'[16] – a train of events so improbable that either the theory should be modified or the emendation rejected.

The collation excludes 'simple expansions' (p. 52), and apparent inconsistencies in the handling of F's contractions are unexplained.[17] As far as 2.3.102 F 'th'' is expanded to 'the'; from 2.3.146 onwards it is reproduced. Most of F's contractions of 'it' as ''t' are preserved, but not those at 1.1.68, 3.4.164, 5.2.227. At 1.2.5 and 5.2.312 't'haue' becomes 'to have', though each time the elision improves the metre, and 'o'', normally retained, is printed as 'of' at 3.4.76. On the other hand, Sanders silently introduces some contractions: 'Who's' for F 'Who h'as' (Q 'who has') at 2.1.65, 'You've' for F 'You haue' (Q 'You ha') at 2.1.107, 'What's' for QF 'What is' at 2.3.232; and he adopts Q 'that's' rather than F 'that is' at 5.2.353. At 3.3.165 Alice Walker emended F 'whil'st 'tis' (Q 'whilst tis') to 'while

'tis' on grounds of euphony; Sanders follows her without recording the emendation. Sanders glosses troublesome phrases efficiently enough without emulating Ridley's flow of astute and stimulating comments. Some notes are curious. At 5.2.218 Emilia asserts that she 'will speak as liberal as the north' ('as the ayre' in Q). 'Some editors' have, according to Sanders, taken Emilia to mean that 'she will speak with the bluntness that characterises people from the north of England'. Can he possibly see any merit in this suggestion? If not, why clutter up his commentary with such obvious absurdities?

As the most likely period for the play's composition Sanders settles upon 'late 1603' or 'early 1604'. We know that Othello was performed at Whitehall on 1 November 1604. Stanley Wells has suggested that the earliest possible date for the play's completion is roughly a year earlier, in October 1603, since an epistle written 'the last of September, 1603' appears in Richard Knolles's History of the Turks, published later in that year, and reports of the number and movements of Turkish galleys in 1.3 of the play have been traced to Knolles's account of the Battle of Lepanto.[18] How, then, are we to explain borrowings from Othello in the Bad Quarto (Q1) of Hamlet, published by Nicholas Ling and John

---

14 There would be little point in editing Q and F separately. The case differs from that of King Lear, where substantial cuts are a feature of the alleged revision in F. Nobody denies that F Othello's additions improve the play, without significantly altering its design, and other putative second thoughts concern verbal details.

15 The point is made by Lawrence J. Ross in his Bobbs-Merrill edition of the play.

16 Unless one of the misreadings was Shakespeare's own as he transcribed his foul papers, but such authorial 'misreading', creating a word that most editors have accepted, would be tantamount to revision, and the improbable coincidence that the scribe behind Q also misread 'distinct' as 'defunct' would remain.

17 Cambridge modernization is generally less consistent than Oxford's, and when a speech is directed successively at several persons the Oxford volumes are more careful to indicate the switches by dashes or directions. The Cambridge practice of presenting source material in unmodernized form also seems inconsistent.

18 'Dating "Othello"', Times Literary Supplement, 20 July 1984, p. 811.

Trundle in 1603, following an entry to James Roberts in the Stationers' Register for 26 July 1602? Alfred Hart called attention to these.[19] He showed that the actor-reporters of the Shakespearian bad quartos, working from memory, sometimes confused a passage in the play they were attempting to reconstruct with a similar passage in some other play in their repertory, and thus imported into their version matter foreign to the original. *Hamlet* Q1 draws on many plays, mainly Shakespearian. Its debt to *Othello* seems clear. The graveyard scene, as represented in *Hamlet* Q1, contains two apparent borrowings from *Othello* within the space of twenty-three lines. The memorially reconstructed manuscript of *Hamlet* was not necessarily in existence when Roberts entered the play on the Stationers' Register: he was perhaps planning to publish the good text that he eventually printed for Nicholas Ling in 1604/5. And since the memorially corrupt Q1 (1603) claims that the play had been acted by 'his Highnesse seruants' its publication cannot have preceded 19 May, when the Chamberlain's men became the King's. But even if *Hamlet* Q1 was printed quite late in 1603, the reporter who concocted the text could hardly have achieved his familiarity with *Othello* had *Othello* not reached the stage by early 1603 at the latest, since London theatres appear to have been closed from about 19 March 1603 till 6 April 1604 – initially because of the Queen's illness and death and then because of a severe outbreak of plague. Sanders remarks that 'Hart's detection of echoes from *Hamlet*, if not particularly persuasive, at least does nothing to affect a post-1602 dating' (p. 2). This reveals a complete misunderstanding of Hart's argument.

From the mass of criticism devoted to *Othello* there emerges no 'consensus about the nature of its unique world or the ordering of its moral landscape'. However, 'its success as a work for the theatre' is undeniable. 'What must be faced in any future critical account is what the stage history makes quite clear: that completely satisfying performances can be given which have at their heart quite different readings of the central character' (p. 28). Sanders does not himself take up the challenge, though he describes a variety of stage Othellos. But under sub-sections on 'sources', 'Othello's race',

'the plot and its inconsistencies', 'the play and its critics', 'the language of the play', and 'stage history' he introduces readers to a wide range of critical opinion. 'Total erotic commitment is inextricably linked with that other centre of Othello's being out of which it grew and which it ultimately replaced: his pride in the exercise of his profession of arms' (p. 22). This is important, and Sanders educates the modern antimilitarist to accept it. The infection of Othello's speech by Iago's vocabulary has often been noted. Sanders makes the point in some vivid sentences leading up to an apt analogy: 'Iago's Scarfe-like view has become for Othello a nightmare of Hieronymus Bosch' (p. 34). He stigmatizes F. R. Leavis as 'incapable of appreciating drama', but fails to expose the fundamental error of Leavis's account of the play. Writing of Othello's 'insistence on making [Desdemona] the sole object of his full powers of romantic projection', Sanders quotes his speech on being reunited with her at Cyprus ('If it were now to die...', 2.1.181–5) and comments: 'Just how totally unsuitable a character for the burden of such idealisation Desdemona actually is finds expression in her horrified response to this' (p. 35), which is, 'The heavens forbid / But that our loves and comforts should increase, / Even as our days do grow' (2.1.185–7). Is this 'horrified'? Or should any actress sharing Sanders's conception of the lines be summarily dismissed from the cast?

The Oxford series continues with two sharply contrasted Roman tragedies. 'One of the stupidest and most uninspired plays ever written, a play in which it is incredible that Shakespeare had any hand at all' – T. S. Eliot's abuse capped a long tradition of hostility to *Titus Andronicus* and denial of Shakespeare's sole authorship. In the age of Artaud the play's reputation has revived. Yet Eugene M. Waith's interesting stage history reveals that the tragedy is most satisfying to audiences when little stress is laid on its kinship to 'theatre of cruelty' as popularly conceived. Gore and gristle are not enough. The best productions, while retaining elements of slaughterhouse realism, have been keyed

---

[19] 'The Date of "Othello"', *Times Literary Supplement*, 10 October 1935, p. 631; *Stolne and Surreptitious Copies* (Melbourne University Press, 1942), pp. 398–401.

to the ritualistic and symbolic. In the opening scene Titus offends against justice and mercy, and an ordered state quickly degenerates into a 'wilderness of tigers'. 'When will this fearful slumber have an end?', asks Titus in 3.1. As if in some absurdist nightmare, lopped limbs image a mutilated body politic.

'Again and again reviewers have been struck by the spectacular opening scene, by the expression of Titus' agony in the third act, and by Aaron's blend of the diabolical and the paternal' (p. 58). Waith's evaluation and interpretation of the play are attuned to the perceptions of theatre-goers. He summarizes the main findings of modern criticism, to which he has himself made notable contributions. One small point perhaps needs qualification. Though aware of the complexities of our response to Titus, Waith accuses him of 'blindness to the difference between Saturninus and Bassianus' (p. 63). But Titus' fatal mistake in picking Saturninus as Emperor is due less to imperception than to ingrained principle. Saturninus' claim to rule rests on primogeniture; Bassianus wants a free election on merit. The play is vague about constitutional matters, but Titus' conservative Roman piety makes his choice inevitable.

After surveying a range of opinions and arguments, Waith concludes that Titus Andronicus was written by Shakespeare alone within the period 1590–2, and revised by him for the first recorded performance of January 1594, when Henslowe marked the play as 'ne' (new). One powerful ally whom he fails to enlist is Marco Mincoff, whose subtle stylistic analysis in Shakespeare: The First Steps (Bulgarian Academy of Sciences, Sofia, 1976) distinguishes between Peele's verse and the opening act of Titus Andronicus, where, in his opinion, Peele was Shakespeare's chief model.

An edition of Titus Andronicus must be based on the Quarto of 1594, evidently set from foul papers. The Folio reprints the derivative Q3, but adds the 'fly scene' (3.2) and an apparently authentic line (1.1.398). Waith considers that Shakespeare interpolated 3.2 in the course of revision in late 1593. F also alters and augments stage directions, and in Waith's judgement the copy of Q3 used by the printer must have been annotated with sporadic

reference to a playhouse manuscript. The main textual challenge for any editor of Titus Andronicus is to deal effectively with the false starts and loose ends that Q is presumed to have inherited from Shakespeare's working draft. Some anomalies within act 1 have been referred to Shakespeare's insertion (whether in the course of initial composition or during later revision) of extra episodes – Titus' killing of Mutius and the sacrifice of Alarbus. Waith excises eight Q lines at 4.3.104–5, justifying his boldness in an appendix (pp. 211–12) which shows the context in facsimile, and follows other editors in omitting at 1.1.35–6 three and a half Q lines thought to belong to a stage of composition at which the sacrifice of Alarbus had not been envisaged. The lines occur within Marcus' long speech describing Titus' campaign against the Goths:

> Fiue times he hath returnd
> Bleeding to Rome, bearing his valiant sonnes,
> In Coffins from the field, [and at this day,
> To the Monument of that *Andronicy*
> Done sacrifice of expiation,
> And slaine the Noblest prisoner of the *Gothes*.]
> And now at last laden with honours spoiles,
> Returnes the good *Andronicus* to Rome,
> Renowned *Titus* flourishing in Armes.
>
> (Q 1594, A3^v; excision bracketed)

There are difficulties about the theory that these lines allude to an event that Shakespeare later decided to show on stage. As J. C. Maxwell remarked in his new Arden edition, 'The general account of Titus' return...reads very oddly after the more specific account...of what he has done on his return', and the prior shift from a review of what happened 'five times' to mention of an action performed 'this day' is strangely abrupt: the whole movement of the speech requires that the 'sacrifice of expiation' be described as habitual. Moreover, the expression 'at this day' is not elsewhere used by Shakespeare to mean 'on this day',[20] and it seems slightly unnatural to say that the sacrifice is done *to* the

---

[20] The phrase 'at this day' does occur in *Henry V*, 1.2.53, where it means 'nowadays', and in *2 Henry VI*, 4.2.149, where it means 'to this very day'. In the passage excised by Waith editors correct 'that' to 'the'.

monument. One solution is to assume that 'dore' was misread as 'daie' (but spelt 'day' by the compositor), Marcus' point being that Titus traditionally performs a sacrifice in front of the family vault.[21] The action heralded by the long stage direction at 1.1.69 thus follows Titus' normal pattern – the consignment of his dead sons to the tomb and the sacrifice of a noble Goth.

A welcome feature of Waith's edition is his ample provision of stage directions, some taken from F. These give much-needed guidance to movements on, off, and about the platform and upper area; and the several points of difficulty are helpfully discussed in the commentary. The text contains errors at 2.3.90 (where Q reads 'doth', Waith 'does') and 4.3.86 (Q 'not thou', Waith 'thou not'). At 4.2.152 Steevens's conjecture, 'Muley lives' is so superior to Q1's 'Muliteus' that it should surely be admitted into the text. (Maxwell's note on this line justly weighs up the pros and cons.) And minor adjustments might reasonably have been hazarded at 4.3.66 ('aimed'), 4.4.66 ('his'), and 5.1.65 ('treasons'). Like other editors reviewed here, Waith is reluctant to emend on metrical grounds: among emendations and conjectures worth adopting are those at 2.3.69 (omit 'thy'), 2.3.72 ('swart'), 2.3.85 ('note'), 2.3.115 (omit 'ye'), 2.3.126 (either 'she braves' or a monosyllabic substitute for 'painted'), 2.4.38 ('Philomel'), 4.2.136 ('are joined'), 4.4.61 ('Arm, arm'), 5.2.50 (omit 'thee'), 5.3.136 ('Come, Marcus, come'); and one might tentatively add 3.1.12 ('O tribunes'), 3.1.280 (omit 'And'), 5.1.94 (omit 'thou'), and 5.2.22 (omit 'witness'). Some of these alterations would sharpen rhetoric as well as metre. The cluster of likely corruptions in 2.3 suggests a fit of compositorial carelessness. In his collation note at 2.3.180 Waith, like Maxwell, gives Q1's reading as 'satisfiee (or satisfice)'; it is certainly 'satisfiee'.

Waith says nothing about the composition and press-work of Q1. F. E. Haggard's examination (in a Kansas dissertation of 1966) of the recurrence of damaged types convinced him that Q was set from a single case and therefore by a single compositor, but do/doe/doo variants differentiate sheets A–E from sheets F–K and there are some suggestive shifts

in the spelling of O/Oh. The Quarto remains a potential subject for bibliographical investigation.

Among the best-known documents related to the Elizabethan theatre is the puzzling Longleat drawing, which appears to conflate two episodes from *Titus Andronicus* and appends passages from 1.1 and 5.1 linked by two invented lines. Waith concludes that the young Henry Peacham, later famous for his emblem books, *Minerva Britanna* (1612) and *Emblemata Varia* (c. 1621), and for *The Complete Gentleman* (1622), was indeed the illustrator and transcriber, and that the enigmatic date below his putative signature on the Longleat leaf implies that drawing and script were penned in 1595/6, perhaps after Peacham had witnessed the performance of the play at Sir John Harington's country house on 1 January 1596. In his Folger facsimile of the 1594 Quarto, Joseph Quincy Adams argued that the Longleat MS text had been copied from the First Folio, and two agreements in error within the space of 38 lines (MS F 'sonnes', Q1–3 'sonne', and Q2–3 F 'Tut', Q1 'But') would not normally be dismissed as coincidental. With regard to the second of the shared errors (or perhaps conjectural emendations, since 'Tut' is attractive) Waith suggests that possibly 'both Peacham and the Q2 compositor misread the "B"', which is somewhat smudged in the one surviving copy of Q1' (p. 26). The 'B' is badly smudged as a catchword on I2, but in the text at the top of I2ᵛ it is perfectly legible.

Discussion of Shakespeare's treatment of his source material for this tragedy is plagued by uncertainty over the status of a brief prose history of Titus Andronicus preserved in a mid eighteenth-century chapbook held by the Folger library. A Titus ballad printed with the history also survives in several seventeenth-century broadsides. Both these

---

21 The emendation was proposed by Joseph S. G. Bolton in *Shakespeare Quarterly*, 23 (1972), 261–2. In the 1961 revision of Maxwell's edition, H. F. Brooks suggested that 'at this day' could mean 'on the day corresponding to this' – that is, always on the day of his return, with 'at last' implying 'for the last time'. Emendation to 'as this day' overcomes most of the difficulties, if the phrase is then taken to mean 'as he *proposes* to do'.

accounts of Titus' ordeals are reprinted by Waith in modern spelling as appendixes. He takes his text of the ballad from Richard Johnson's *Golden Garland* (1620), which he calls 'the earliest surviving version' (pp. 4, 204). This is not quite accurate. 'Titus Andronicus' Complaint' is preserved in manuscript among the Shirburn Ballads, edited by Andrew Clark in 1907, and it belongs to part of the collection thought to have been written out during the years 1600–3.[22] The traditional view, taken by Geoffrey Bullough in his *Narrative and Dramatic Sources of Shakespeare*, is that the Folger history reproduces what is, in substance, Shakespeare's main source, while the ballad-writer drew on both prose history and play. However, Marco Mincoff, supported by G. K. Hunter, has argued that the ballad, which displays points of exclusive contact with both other versions, is an intermediary between them, the ballad depending on the play and the history on the ballad. Mincoff's claim is that the ellipses proper to a ballad narrated by the hero on a *Mirror of Magistrates* pattern have misled the prose-writer into his major divergencies from the play. Waith rejects Mincoff's arguments and reaches the orthodox conclusion – wrongly, in my opinion.

Ballad and history use the same couplet for Lavinia's stump-written accusation: 'The lustful sons of the proud Empress / Are doers of this hateful wickedness'. It is much more likely that the story teller has borrowed a key couplet from the ballad than that on the one occasion on which he attempted rhyme he fortuitously produced verse that perfectly fits the ballad's pentameter stanza – a popular two-couplet quatrain designed to be sung to the tune of 'Fortune my Foe'. Further, the only character names in the ballad – Titus Andronicus, Lavinia, Marcus – are also the only personal names shared by history and play. This is unsurprising if the prose-writer relied on the ballad-maker, who had no use for most of the play's names and may have forgotten them. It is less easy to see why, if the history was written first and freely invented, it should, while naming Marcus and Lavinia, leave unnamed the counterparts to Aaron, Saturninus, Bassianus, Quintus, and Martius, and name the Queen of the Goths and her sons – as Attava,

Alaricus, and Abonus – only in its totally unparalleled opening sections, treating them as anonymous in those parts of the story which it shares with the ballad. The episode in 5.2 in which Titus is visited by Tamora, Demetrius, and Charon in disguise is briefly recorded in the ballad:

> The Empress then, thinking I was mad,
> Like furies she and both her sons were clad,
> She named Revenge, and Rape and Murder they,
> To undermine and know what I would say.

In the later seventeenth-century texts 'clad' is corrupted to 'glad' and 'She' to 'So', so that enigmatic terseness becomes total unintelligibility. The prose writer, baffled, omits the episode, but tortures sense out of the misprinted rhyme-word with the claim that Andronicus's apparent madness 'mainly *pleased* the Empress and her sons'.

Waith leaves Mincoff unanswered on these and similar points.[23] Some of Waith's defences of the traditional position ignore Mincoff's tenet that the prose-writer had no knowledge of the play (pp. 31–3).[24] In an appendix Waith imputes to Mincoff three misstatements (p. 210). The second is not a misstatement: Waith's comment does not contradict Mincoff's. Waith's third challenge is to Mincoff's assertion that nothing beyond what is contained in

---

[22] The Wood Collection in the Bodleian Library contains an early edition for 'the Assignes of Thomas Symcocke', an imprint which dates it 1618–29; and one edition in the Pepys Collection, 'printed for E. Wright', probably followed a Stationers' Register entry to Wright and others on 14 December 1624; Wright's is the only text to give the presumably correct 'bent' for 'felt' in stanza 3, line 1. Other extant editions date from about 1675 onwards.

[23] The last is an elaboration of one of Mincoff's. He did not note the significance of the history's echo of a ballad misprint. Mincoff's treatment of the ballad is in *Notes and Queries*, NS 18 (1971), 131–4.

[24] In evidence of a direct relationship between the chapbook and the play Stanley Wells privately cites a handful of minor verbal agreements (not noted by Waith) exclusive to these two accounts. But the parallels may be coincidental: on Mincoff's assumption that the ballad drastically compressed the play and the chapbook expanded the ballad, the chapbook's expansion could hardly have failed independently to reintroduce a few words and phrases (such as '*loss* of blood') originally present in the play.

the ballad clearly connects Shakespeare's play with the history. Waith offers as a link the fact that the pit into which the slain Bassianus is thrown is covered – 'with rude-growing briers' in the play, 'lightly with boughs' and a 'sprinkling [of] earth' in the history. The ballad lacks such a detail. But the prose-writer could hardly have failed to infer it, as the obvious means of explaining why Titus' sons fell into the hole. The first of Waith's points is more interesting. Mincoff had said that the ballad records no events that could not derive from the play. Waith counters that whereas Shakespeare's Lavinia 'marries the Emperor's brother [Bassianus] before Aaron's child is born', in the other two versions Lavinia 'marries a son of the Emperor after the Empress has had a child by the Moor'. Waith adds his own slight inaccuracy here, since both ballad and history speak of betrothal, not marriage. More significantly, as Mincoff pointed out, the ballad-maker merely recounts that the Empress bred a blackamoor 'in time', anticipating the illegitimate birth at the point appropriate to his purposes, without meaning to imply anything about the chronological sequence of events. The prose-writer has misunderstood. Most significantly of all, the variants concerning the relationship of Lavinia's husband or husband-to-be to the Emperor confirm Mincoff's conclusions. The ballad says that Lavinia was betrothed to 'Caesar's son'. In a context in which Shakespeare's Saturninus and Tamora are 'Emperor' and 'Empress' this is misleading, and the writer of the prose history embroiders his misconception by designating Lavinia's intended husband as 'the Emperor's only son by a former wife'. But the ballad-writer has picked up the phrase 'Caesar's son' from 1.1.10 of the play, where Bassianus applies it to himself, before his elder brother Saturninus is chosen Emperor. This echo has hitherto remained unnoticed. It furnishes a nice illustration of the process by which the ballad, enigmatically echoing the play, beguiles the prose-writer along a false trail.

Once the chapbook has been discounted as derivative, we are free to explore Shakespeare's debt to *The Spanish Tragedy* and *The Jew of Malta*, and to Ovid, Bandello, and the Roman historians.

No doubt Shakespeare's audiences were shocked,

and even at times moved, by his first Roman tragedy. By his second, according to Leonard Digges, writing in 1640, they were 'ravished', departing the theatre in 'wonder'. Reading *Julius Caesar* in A. R. Humphreys's splendid edition, which delights and instructs at every point, one shares their admiration. As commentator Humphreys is alert to the dialogue's nuances and adroit in conveying his perceptions. He has a talent also for culling the choicest remarks of other critics, and frequent citations from North's Plutarch illustrate his points about Shakespeare's transmutation of his source material. A note on the play's concluding speech is representative: 'Some productions make Octavius speak this arrogantly, stressing "*my* tent" (against the metre) and making a different exit from Antony's. But however ungenial his nature generally, to do so distorts the intention here, where a Roman magnanimity fitting the end of Brutus is common to all.' The introduction includes sections on *Julius Caesar*'s place in the canon, Shakespeare's shaping of his sources, his sense of Roman values, politics and morality, the style, and the play in performance. Humphreys's observations under these headings coalesce into a distinguished contribution to Shakespeare criticism – subtle, humane, and exact. Emotionally receptive and intellectually vigorous, Humphreys benefits also from an editor's intimacy with Shakespeare's great English histories. He encourages a due complexity of response to a play that has often been simplified, in and out of the theatre. His own involvement is complete, and his conclusion inspires: 'One remembers *Julius Caesar* not for diagrams of dictator, altruist, instigator, and demagogue, but for the depth of its insights into men and women in public and private life on whose behaviour great issues depend, and for its confirmation of the Aristotelian tenet that poetry is a higher and more philosophical thing than history' (p. 72).

Copy for the Folio text of *Julius Caesar* was evidently a clean scribal transcript of Shakespeare's autograph, and 'such compositorial slips as can be detected or suspected are infrequent and venial' (p. 73). Humphreys makes a dozen or so requisite corrections. Less straightforward is 'in strength of malice' at 3.1.174, where a phrase meaning 'without malice' would be natural. Humphreys rejects 'un-strengthened' as 'too odd for the play's lucid style'; perhaps, but it confers greater lucidity on the passage than his own tortuous explanation of F. He might also have supplied from Ben Jonson's *Timber* Metellus' protest, 'Caesar, thou dost me wrong', which provokes Caesar's notorious response (revised in F) at 3.1.47–8: without Metellus' outcry the lines lack point. Humphreys includes a judicious assessment of the theory, urged by Brents Stirling and Fredson Bowers, that the text bears signs of more extensive revision in 2.1. and 4.2. In the latter scene Portia's death is announced by Brutus to Cassius, and then by Messala to Brutus, who denies prior knowledge of it. The first revelation has been widely regarded as a substitute for the second, or as a late insertion meant to modify our response to Brutus' public show of stoicism. Apparent confirmation of textual disturbance in the manuscript copy for F was afforded by the concentration within the problematical area (and within a section of 2.1) of departures from the normal form of speech-prefix for Cassius. John Jowett has now neatly proved, through careful computation, that the atypical forms do not derive from copy but were set because of a printing-house shortage of *ssi* ligatures.[25] While Jowett's impressive article removes from the revision theory its bibliographical prop, Thomas Clayton attacks its very base.[26] As he notes, the BBC television film of *Julius Caesar* 'demonstrates the facility with which an apparent major anomaly, as witnessed in the study, the double account of Portia's death, may be assimilated into a performance where it...makes...evident dramatic sense and continuity' (p. 237). Re-examining 4.2 and finding it 'deeply revealing', he deduces that Shakespeare's intentions are fulfilled by F as it stands.

Julius Caesar is also the subject of J. K. Rogers's investigation, in which he refines on previous efforts to determine the Folio compositors' stints.[27] Most of the text was set by Compositor B, Compositor A having been responsible for the three pages kk2ᵛ–kk3ᵛ. Rogers collates previously offered data with his own measurement of the exact amount of spacing around certain punctuation marks. This qualitative spacing evidence is consistent with the other evidence, and it enables him to make out a good case for thinking that on pages ll1–ll2 and ll5ᵛ, the last four to be set, the two men worked simultaneously. Their putative shares in these pages fall into segments that are multiples of three lines – the number held in their composing sticks. To show that the alternation of contrasted preferences within pages is not fortuitous Rogers examines control pages agreed to have been set by a single compositor and divides them into three-line segments, which prove reassuringly homogeneous. The correlation that Rogers finds between spacing practices and the testimony of spelling, variant speech-prefixes, and damaged types might not persuade D. F. McKenzie. In a sequel to his brilliantly subversive 'Printers of the Mind', he questions the use of spacing evidence in compositor studies, pointing out that in Joseph Beaumont's *Psyche*, a folio in fours printed at the Cambridge University Press in 1701–2, seemingly significant patterns in the use and avoidance of spaced commas bear no relation to the compositorial stints recorded in surviving documents of unimpeachable authority.[28]

Thomas Clayton and Malcolm Pittock independently defend the Folio's 'to'th'Legitimate' (Q 'tooth'legitimate') in Edmund's soliloquy, *King Lear*, 1.2.21.[29] Pittock favours Sisson's gloss: 'The base shall turn into the legitimate, shall usurp legitimacy'. Clayton's interpretation is similar: 'Edmund the Bastard – as though "base", or "Base", were a formal titular epithet – shall inherit

---

[25] 'Ligature Shortage and Speech-Prefix Variation in *Julius Caesar*', *The Library*, 6 (1984), 244–53.

[26] '"Should Brutus Never Taste of Portia's Death but Once?": Text and Performance in *Julius Caesar*', *Studies in English Literature 1500–1900*, 23 (1983), 237–55.

[27] 'The Folio Compositors of *Julius Caesar*: A Quantitative Analysis', *Analytical and Enumerative Bibliography*, 6 (1982), 143–72.

[28] 'Stretching a Point: Or, The Case of the Spaced-out Comps', *Studies in Bibliography*, 37 (1984), 106–21.

[29] Clayton, 'Disemending *King Lear* in Favour of Shakespeare: "Edmund the base shall *to* th' legitimate " (I.ii.21)', *Notes and Queries*, NS 31 (1984), 207–8; Pittock, '"Top the Legitimate"?', pp. 208–10. The phrase 'the right note of triumph' was used by new Arden editor Kenneth Muir in justification of 'top'.

the eminence Edgar possesses now and the title he would legitimately succeed to in due course'. He believes that in performance this meaning could 'readily and forcefully be made clear by emphasis and gesture'. Perhaps there are actors who could achieve this feat. In the BBC *Lear* Michael Kitchen needs only the merest upward nod of the head to convey 'the right note of triumph' in 'top'. This emendation, adopted by most modern editors (who assume that Q has contaminated F), links punningly with 'base', which precedes, and 'grow', which follows. Clayton considers the misreading of 'top' as 'too' 'unlikely'; Greg thought that it might have occurred quite naturally if the tail of the 'p' were obscured (as it could have been by the long 's' of 'stand' in the line below). 'I have adopted the *Roman* sentiment, that it is more honourable to save a citizen, than to kill an enemy', said Samuel Johnson in his Shakespeare preface, exalting explication over emendation. But the problem is to distinguish between odder members of the home army and enemy infiltrators. Clayton is sure he is saving a citizen; I suspect his patient is a foe.

Another rescue attempt is made by Karl P. Wentersdorf.[30] When in *Twelfth Night* the injured Sir Toby inquires after Dick Surgeon, Feste tells him: 'O he's drunk sir *Toby* an houre agone: his eyes were set at eight i'th morning'. Sir Toby replies: 'Then he's a Rogue, and a passy measures panyn: I hate a drunken rogue' (5.1.198–201). Because *OED* defines 'passemeasure' as a slow dance of Italian origin (*passamezzo*) and calls it a variety of pavan, of which 'pauin' is a common Elizabethan-Jacobean spelling, editors have emended F 'panyn' to 'pavin'.[31] The assumption is that a befuddled Sir Toby connects the tardy Dick Surgeon with a slow dance composed of eight-bar 'strains' and so, like the surgeon's eyes, 'set at eight'. Some editors see allusions to 'a drunken gait' or 'a solemn coxcomb'. Wentersdorf points out that 'panyn' is a possible Elizabethan spelling of 'paynim' or 'pagan', and that 'the scene in which the crux occurs contains one of the best-known image-clusters in the Shakespearean canon, the *revolt–flood* cluster, and . . . one of the elements in this linkage is the motif of *pagan savagery*'. The complex, which crops up over thirty

times and includes seventeen components, is fully realized in *Twelfth Night*, 5.1, and 'panyn' virtually completes it. This may be fortuitous. If not, then it is fortuitous that F, with a simple minim correction, meaningfully juxtaposes two closely related dance terms. This seems the more difficult coincidence to swallow. Still, Wentersdorf's suggestion is attractive. Drunken abuse may rely less on sense than on sound, and the punning associations of 'passy measures panyn' seem as relevant as any dance: the surgeon is 'past measure' – one over the eight, a hopeless case, incurable, incorrigible, immoderate, and boundless in his villainy; as a merciless 'pagan' he is no doubt a butcher to boot.

Sidney Thomas reacts forcefully and unfavourably to Hoeniger's article on *Pericles*, reviewed last year.[32] The writing in acts 1 and 2 'is not archaic or formalized', Thomas retorts; 'it is simply incompetent, flat in diction, lifeless in rhythm, and unconvincing in content'. He will be relieved to hear that the computer has finally managed to distinguish between 1–2 and 3–5 of *Pericles*. The logical next steps are to determine whether computerized tests of frequencies, proportions, and collocations of common words can discriminate between *Pericles*, 1–2, and all other acts in the Shakespeare canon (as a simple analysis of rhymes decisively can), and, if so, whether the tests also discriminate between *Pericles* 1–2 and dramatic work by Shakespeare's contemporaries – except, perhaps, George Wilkins or

---

[30] 'The "Passy Measures Panyn" Crux in *Twelfth Night*: Is Emendation Necessary?', *Shakespeare Quarterly*, 35 (1984), 82–6. Different in spirit from the reasoned defences of Clayton, Pittock, and Wentersdorf is Thomas M. Greene's rhapsodic approval of a corrupt text, 'Antihermeneutics: The Case of Shakespeare's Sonnet 129', in *Poetic Traditions of the English Renaissance* (Yale University Press, New Haven, 1982), ed. Maynard Mack and George deForest Lord, pp. 143–61. Greene wants 'the actual mysterious artifact history has handed down to us with all its built in puzzlements and uncertainties' (p. 146).

[31] In fact the *OED* citations also connect passemeasure with galliard and cinquepace, alternative names for a quick and lively dance; the passemeasure pavan was less slow and solemn than the ordinary pavan.

[32] 'The Problem of *Pericles*', *Shakespeare Quarterly*, 34 (1983), 448–50.

John Day. In the meantime, M. W. A. Smith gives a cautious account of the application of Andrew Morton's techniques to authorship problems connected with Shakespeare and his fellows, and assesses alternative ways of handling the data.[33]

Through a meticulous examination of stage directions in the Folio text of *The Tempest* John Jowett establishes the likelihood that several, mainly the more elaborate, include non-theatrical rephrasings and expansions by Ralph Crane as he transcribed Shakespeare's foul papers.[34] Since the non-Shakespearian overlay, if a reality, cannot decisively be separated from the Shakespearian base, and since Crane was probably familiar with the play in performance, an editor should 'in general... retain the Folio directions, only modifying or rejecting them in specific instances' where they might mislead (p. 120).

Sailendra Kumar Sen is unnecessarily bothered by Orlando's question in *As You Like It*, 1.2.268–70[35] – unnecessarily, because there is no interaction between Orlando and the two women until Celia first addresses him at line 242, he does not listen to anything Rosalind and Celia say before that, and Rosalind's words in line 246 do not make a love-struck Orlando's questioning of Le Beau otiose. This is all perfectly obvious in the theatre. Judith Rosenheim examines the couplets in *Measure for Measure*, 2.1.37–40, and in particular the Folio's 'brakes of Ice'.[36] She contends that modernization of 'brakes' to 'breaks' renders the phrase 'coherent and applicable to the play'. In her efforts to prove this, she finds Isabella guilty of a failure 'in both chastity and charity'. Robert F. Fleissner argues that *Hamlet* Q2's 'dram of eale' contains an orthographic pun, apt in the context, on 'evil' and 'ale'.[37] Stanley Wells and John Kerrigan reply to Manfred Draudt's article on the 'Rosaline–Katherine tangle' in *Love's Labour's Lost*.[38]

S. K. Sen has made the surprising discovery that in his editorial notes Malone often misquoted Shakespeare, presumably because he trusted to memory.[39] Giorgio Melchiori argues that in line 16 of the Induction to *2 Henry IV* the Quarto (1600) punctuation, 'Blowne by surmizes, Iealousies coniectures', should be retained and the last two words

modernized as 'jealousy's conjectures', not 'jealousies, conjectures', which editors derived from F.[40] Gilian West evaluates interpretations and emendations for some difficult passages in *1 Henry IV*.[41] Her proposal to emend 'hest' at 2.3.62 to 'heft' is most attractive, and her succinctly presented case for 'thought's the slave of life' at 5.4.81 is cogent. Less convincing is her suggestion that Titan should 'keech' rather than 'kiss' a dish of butter in Hal's mockery of Falstaff at 2.4.120–3; melting kisses are the sun's speciality (compare 'common-kissing Titan' in *Cymbeline*, 3.4.163), and the nineteenth-century intransitive verb 'to keech', meaning to set hard, cannot reasonably be extended to mean in this context to melt (transitively) and allow to harden.

Some copies of *Hamlet* Q2 are dated 1604, others 1605 – which probably means that the book was printed in 1605, on modern reckoning, since James Roberts would not have thought it worthwhile to alter the date until after the legal year 1604/5 ended on 24 March. Willem Schrickx tacks this point on to an article dealing with the composition date of Dekker's *The Meeting of Gallants*.[42] His vision of

33 'Recent Experience and New Developments of Methods for the Determination of Authorship', *ALLC Bulletin*, 11 (1983), 73–81. Smith draws on his articles 'The Authorship of *Pericles*: An Initial Investigation', *The Bard*, 3 (1982), 143–76, and 'The Authorship of *Pericles*: Collocations Investigated Again', *The Bard*, 4 (1983), 15–21.

34 'New Created Creatures: Ralph Crane and the Stage Directions in "The Tempest"', *Shakespeare Survey 36* (Cambridge University Press, 1983), 107–20.

35 'Orlando's Question in Act I Scene 2 of *As You Like It*', *The Library*, 5 (1983), 392–5.

36 '*Measure for Measure*, II.i.37–40: Sounding "Breaks of Ice"', *Shakespeare Quarterly*, 35 (1984), 87–91.

37 'That "Dram of Eale" Again: Textplay in *Hamlet*', *American Notes and Queries*, 21 (1983), 98–9.

38 'The "Rosaline–Katherine Tangle": A Correspondence', *The Library*, 5 (1983), 399–404; Draudt also contributes.

39 'When Malone Nods', *Shakespeare Quarterly*, 34 (1983), 212–14.

40 'The Role of Jealousy: Restoring the Q Reading of *2 Henry IV*, Induction, 16', *Shakespeare Quarterly*, 34 (1983), 327–30.

41 '"Titan," "Onyers," and Other Difficulties in the Text of *1 Henry IV*', *Shakespeare Quarterly*, 34 (1983), 330–3.

42 'The Date of Dekker's *The Meeting of Gallants* and the Printing of *Hamlet*', *Hamlet Studies*, 5 (1983), 82–6.

'Shakespeare preparing his manuscript for the press' while Dekker was simultaneously writing his pamphlet early in 1605 is, of course, pure fantasy.

The Division of the Kingdoms, noticed last year, consolidated the case for supposing that differences between the Quarto and Folio texts of *King Lear* bespeak revision by Shakespeare. Reviewers have varied in their reactions, but even the most sceptical concede that *some* of F's readings are probably Shakespeare's second thoughts. This concession is itself a retreat from the position held by Greg, Duthie, Kirschbaum, Chambers, Walker, Kittredge, and others, who believed that all variation between Q and F *Lear* was due to corruption in one text or the other. But how much of the variation can be attributed to revision, and, most crucial of questions, was Shakespeare responsible for F's cuts, totalling some three hundred lines? Writing before the appearance of *Division* but in response to the published claims of Warren, Urkowitz, and Taylor, Kenneth Muir examines the effects of the cuts, which accelerate the play's progress in acts 3 and 4, and pronounces them 'dramatically disastrous', instigated by 'the first of the vandals, to be followed by Tate and a long line of actor-managers and directors'.[43] F's more than one hundred lines of additional dialogue, on the other hand, 'restore Q's accidental omissions'.

Muir makes some telling points, but his arguments do not all bear scrutiny. For instance, when Muir played Gloucester to Wilson Knight's Lear, he found, as in an earlier production he had directed, 'that after the blinding, and despite an interval between Acts III and IV, Gloucester had very little time between his exit in 3.7 and his reappearance in 4.1 to change his clothes or put on a cloak, and to have his eyes bandaged'. He has even less time, Muir points out, if we follow F in cutting nine lines at the end of 3.7 (though F adds three lines to Edgar's soliloquy at the beginning of 4.1): 'the dialogue between the servants is a theatrical necessity'. However, if Muir was scrambling to get ready for his entrance in 4.1, 'despite an interval between Acts III and IV', the King's Men must either have managed Gloucester's change of appearance much more expeditiously or themselves have relied on an act interval,[44] because even the conflated text, if played continuously, allows Gloucester less time offstage than the interval alone would have allowed Muir. Besides, the manuscript behind F is agreed to have served as a prompt-book and Muir has, perhaps unwittingly, been driven to postulate a theatre person who, while aiming to reduce *King Lear*'s overall playing time, rendered it at a key point unplayable. The prompt-book belonged to Shakespeare's company: is this likely behaviour from one of their members?

---

43 'The Texts of *King Lear*: An Interim Assessment of the Controversy', *Aligarh Journal of English Studies*, 9 (1984), 99–113.

44 It is possible that both answers are right – that in Q the half-minute dialogue between the servants helped give a quick-changing Gloucester enough time despite continuous action, and that in F, revised for the Blackfriars around 1609, an act break was used.

INDEX